NATO ASI Series

Advanced Science Institutes Series

A series presenting the results of activities sponsored by the NATO Science Committee, which aims at the dissemination of advanced scientific and technological knowledge, with a view to strengthening links between scientific communities.

The Series is published by an international board of publishers in conjunction with the NATO Scientific Affairs Division

A Life Sciences B Physics	Plenum Publishing Corporation London and New York
C Mathematical and Physical Sciences D Behavioural and Social Sciences E Applied Sciences	Kluwer Academic Publishers Dordrecht, Boston and London
F Computer and Systems Sciences G Ecological Sciences H Cell Biology I Global Environmental Change	Springer-Verlag Berlin Heidelberg New York London Paris Tokyo Hong Kong Barcelona Budapest

NATO-PCO DATABASE

The electronic index to the NATO ASI Series provides full bibliographical references (with keywords and/or abstracts) to more than 30000 contributions from international scientists published in all sections of the NATO ASI Series. Access to the NATO-PCO DATABASE compiled by the NATO Publication Coordination Office is possible in two ways:

- via online FILE 128 (NATO-PCO DATABASE) hosted by ESRIN, Via Galileo Galilei, I-00044 Frascati, Italy.

- via CD-ROM "NATO-PCO DATABASE" with user-friendly retrieval software in English, French and German (© WTV GmbH and DATAWARE Technologies Inc. 1989).

The CD-ROM can be ordered through any member of the Board of Publishers or through NATO-PCO, Overijse, Belgium.

Series F: Computer and Systems Sciences Vol. 92

The ASI Series Books Published as a Result of Activities of the Special Programme on ADVANCED EDUCATIONAL TECHNOLOGY

This book contains the proceedings of a NATO Advanced Research Workshop held within the activities of the NATO Special Programme on Advanced Educational Technology, running from 1988 to 1993 under the auspices of the NATO Science Committee.

The books published so far as a result of the activities of the Special Programme are:

Vol. F 67: Designing Hypermedia for Learning. Edited by D. H. Jonassen and H. Mandl. 1990.

Vol. F 76: Multimedia Interface Design in Education. Edited by A. D. N. Edwards and S. Holland. 1992.

Vol. F 78: Integrating Advanced Technology into Technology Education. Edited by M. Hacker, A. Gordon, and M. de Vries. 1991.

Vol. F 80: Intelligent Tutoring Systems for Foreign Language Learning. The Bridge to International Communication. Edited by M. L Swartz and M. Yazdani. 1992.

Vol. F 81: Cognitive Tools for Learning. Edited by P.A.M. Kommers, D.H. Jonassen, and J.T. Mayes. 1992.

Vol. F 84: Computer-Based Learning Environments and Problem Solving. Edited by E. De Corte, M. C. Linn, H. Mandl, and L. Verschaffel. 1992.

Vol. F 85: Adaptive Learning Environments. Foundations and Frontiers. Edited by M. Jones and P. H. Winne. 1992.

Vol. F 86: Intelligent Learning Environments and Knowledge Acquisition in Physics. Edited by A. Tiberghien and H. Mandl. 1992.

Vol. F 87: Cognitive Modelling and Interactive Environments in Language Learning. Edited by F. L. Engel, D. G. Bouwhuis, T. Bösser, and G. d'Ydewalle. 1992.

Vol. F 89: Mathematical Problem Solving and New Information Technologies. Edited by J. P. Ponte, J. F. Matos, J. M. Matos, and D. Fernandes. 1992.

Vol. F 90: Collaborative Learning Through Computer Conferencing. Edited by A. R. Kaye. 1992.

Vol. F 91: New Directions for Intelligent Tutoring Systems. Edited by E. Costa. 1992.

Vol. F 92: Hypermedia Courseware: Structures of Communication and Intelligent Help. Edited by A. Oliveira. 1992.

Hypermedia Courseware: Structures of Communication and Intelligent Help

Edited by

Armando Oliveira

Secção Autónoma de Didáctica e Tecnologia Educativa
Universidade de Aveiro
Campo Universitário de Santiago, P-3800 Aveiro, Portugal

Springer-Verlag
Berlin Heidelberg New York London Paris Tokyo
Hong Kong Barcelona Budapest
Published in cooperation with NATO Scientific Affairs Division

Proceedings of the NATO Advanced Research Workshop on Structures of Communication and Intelligent Help for Hypermedia Courseware, held at Espinho, Portugal, April 19–24, 1990

CR Subject Classification (1991): K.3.1, I.7.2, H.5, I.2

ISBN-13: 978-3-642-77704-2 e-ISBN-13: 978-3-642-77702-8
DOI: 10.1007/978-3-642-77702-8

Softcover reprint of the hardcover 1st edition 1992

Typesetting: Camera ready by authors
45/3140 - 5 4 3 2 1 0 - Printed on acid-free paper

Preface

This book is based on the NATO Advanced Research Workshop on Structures of Communication and Intelligent Help for Hypermedia Courseware, which was held at Espinho, Portugal, April 19–24, 1990.

The texts included here should not be regarded as untouched proceedings of this meeting, but as the result of the reflections which took place there and which led the authors to revise their texts in that light.

The Espinho ARW was itself to some extent the continuation of the ARW on Designing Hypermedia/Hypertext for Learning, held in Germany in 1989 (D. H. Jonassen, H. Mandl (eds.): Designing Hypermedia for Learning. NATO ASI Series F, Vol. 67. Springer 1990). At that meeting an essential conclusion became apparent: the importance and interest of hypermedia products as potential pedagogical tools.

It was then already predictable that the enormous evolution of hypermedia would lead to its association with multimedia technologies, namely for the production of courseware. Parallel to the improvement of the didactic potential and quality which results from this association, it nevertheless brought along a natural array of difficulties, some old, some new, in the conception and use of hypermedia products.

Today there is agreement that one of the most promising technological advances for education is represented by the use of text, sound and images based on nonlinear techniques of information handling and searching of hypermedia architectures.

The problem of hypermedia is fundamentally one of communication; this leads to an attempt at defining a language for hypermedia.

On the other hand, the problems associated with the hypermedia use of the screen image as a working space raise new questions which we consider it necessary to take into consideration. Multidisciplinary research work such as the iconographic study of the screen image together with the study of text comprehension are two of these concerns.

All these aspects contribute to our main goal, which consists of improving the use of interface ergonomy in order to increase transparency, ease of manipulation, and user autonomy, as well as ease of learning.

The pedagogical application of an intelligent help system for use may be an important help for the learner, thus allowing him/her not to lose his/her way and to follow all the pedagogically relevant paths.

We admit neither that there is a universal learning behavior nor that all individual behaviors are crucially different. From what we know from studies of learning we admit that there is a limited number of user models which cover the great majority of cases. (Would this be the same for courseware authoring?) In this sense we are interested in drafting the authoring and user structures that are implied by hypermedia, and consequently the most important question for us is what branches of psychopedagogical knowledge should be thoroughly studied in order to preserve goals for the optimization of the educational use of this new medium.

In terms of authoring, the structure cannot be based only on knowledge (both content and pedagogical knowledge) but must also aim at two objectives: (i) to suit the natural way of using it, and (ii) to support the learning of hypermedia use.

The Espinho ARW

Taking these arguments into consideration we planned the Espinho ARW along four main themes, which, although interrelated, allowed for a fairly specific treatment of ideas within each topic. The themes were hypermedia design, hypermedia language, intelligent help, and ergonomic aspects, and key concepts for each of them were suggested to the participants:

- *Hypermedia for learning:* hypermedia design, hypermedia structure, hypermedia construction, authoring tools, evaluation of tools, learning tools, instructional systems design, exploratory learning environments, browsing and learning facilities.

- *Hypermedia language:* hypermedia audio-visual media language/communication logical code, hypermedia grammar, iconographic aspects and structure of the screen image, shape and location of the working areas, interactive tools for learning, nodes, mixture of sound and text and pictures, moving sequences, animated icons and cursors.

- *Help tools for hypermedia and AI in hypermedia:* aids to learning in hypermedia, help for localizing, educational dialog help, cognitive aproach, cognitive model of the user, cognitive model of the learner, hypercard intelligent tutoring system, intelligent help for browsing and didactic modules.

- *Ergonomics for hypermedia:* user interface for learning, human-computer interaction, learner-machine interface, hypermedia supported cooperative learning, information model in hypermedia learning environments, knowledge representation and knowledge acquisition for educational hypermedia systems.

The ambition implied by the co-presence of such diverse but complementary themes, whose study seems to us indispensable for the evolution of hypermedia, led us to take as the main aim of the ARW the fostering of contacts and the stimulation of future cooperative work among experts who are exploring current developments and future trends of the new hypermedia technology applied to the field of education, and also experts in other research sectors who might contribute with important and eventually necessary knowledge for the making of adequate and optimized educational hypermedia and multimedia products.

The emphasis of the meeting was placed on the study of the contribution of research which takes advantage of advanced technology from the fields of AI and cognitive science. Its focus was also directed on the problems of the new structures.

Two main perspectives were apparent from the work developed in the workshop. One is of a more pragmatic nature, whose centre of interest is the attempt to improve existing hypermedia products, taken as instruments, particularly in the area of professional training in various fields. Essentially, this perspective tries to integrate knowledge from diverse areas so as to make specific hypermedia products more effective. This group of researchers aims at improving the technical and operational aspects of the educational hypermedia scenarios, and studies the solutions to be applied to hypermedia courseware with the aim of facilitating and perfecting techniques such as browsing, navigating, or help.

The other perspective, eventually of a more ambitous nature, considers hypermedia as a powerful aid for learning in general, and aims at studying the mechanisms of the hypermedia-aided learning process, and also the conditions and basic principles for its development. This group of researchers, who are more cautious and reserved about the immediate applicability of these means, insisted mainly on the need for research into the cognitive mechanisms involved in the interaction with hypermedia for an effective and correct exploitation of the educational potential of hypermedia in the future.

There was nevertheless consensus on the fact that research within these two perspectives should proceed in parallel and that there is the utmost interest in fostering and encouraging a greater and better interchange of obtained results.

We sincerely hope that this publication will contribute towards this goal.

The book has been organized more in formal terms than in any other. It was not therefore our concern to alter either the language or the ideas expressed by the authors.

Had it been possible this publication would have been in hypertext format: the richness of information and the various links from the more general papers to the more specific ones would have meant an enhanced access to the information contained in the book. Moreover, the several scientific affiliations of the authors and therefore the varied domains in which they wrote their papers would have profited from a hypertext-like presentation of the information contained here. However, constrained by the sequential format of printed paper, my sole concern has been to sequence the several papers in such a way as to ascribe them a thematically coherent readability.

The book is divided – in a somewhat unconstrained and interdisciplinary way – into four main parts. The papers in Part 1 deal with hypermedia, its tools, and their educational applications. The concern of the papers in Part 2 is at the interface between education, language, and hypermedia. The papers in Part 3 deal with the psychological processes involved in problem solving and the ergonomic aspects of hypermedia use. Finally, the contributions in Part 4 discuss AI methods and techniques for hypermedia products.

I would nevertheless like to make it clear that the transitions between the parts and between the papers – for the reasons stated above – are fuzzy, and an effort is necessary to find the points of contact between them.

Acknowledgements

The following people participated in the Espinho workshop:

Balestro, Paulo – Italy
Bastien, Claude – France
Bastien, Mireille – France
Blaye, Agnès – France
Carretero, Mario – Spain
Duchastel, Philippe – Canada
Duffy, Thomas – United States of America
Espéret, Eric – France
Figueiredo, António Dias – Portugal
Galaricha, Carlos – Portugal
Gomes, Álvaro – Portugal
Harland, Mike – United Kingdom
Jonassen, David – United States of America
Kolski, Christophe – France
León, J. A. – Spain
Lowyck, J. – Belgium
MacLeod, Miles – United Kingdom
Mandl, Heinz – Germany
McAleese, Ray – United Kingdom
Moreira, António – Portugal
Moreira, António – Portugal
Oliveira, Armando – Portugal
Pereira, Duarte Costa – Portugal
Rhéaume, Jacques – Canada
Romiszowski, Alexander – The Netherlands
Silva, Armando – Portugal
Späth, Preben – Denmark
Spiro, Rand J. – United States of America
Taveira, Maria do Céu – Portugal
Vasconcelas, Ana Isabel – Portugal

I would like to thank every participant in the workshop and all the authors represented in this book for their precious and enlightened contributions. Also, I thank everybody involved in the editorial work for this book, especially António Moreira and António Moreira, two *brothers* in names and in arms.

I dedicate this publication to Dias Figueiredo, a colleague and a dear friend, who with his incentive and encouragement led me to organize this ARW, and to my daughter Eve and my son Gil, who had to put up with my constant absence throughout the workshop and the many hours spent with the organization of the book.

University of Aveiro
April 1992

Armando Oliveira

Table of Contents

3 Help Tools for Hypermedia and AI in Hypermedia

4 Ergonomics for Hypermedia

1 Hypermedia for Learning

Hypermedia and Multimedia

Armando Oliveira

Universidade de Aveiro, Portugal

Taking into account the recent and spectacular advances in informatic instruments which permit their full use by non-specialists in informatics by way of a more transparent and more convivial access, and basing ourselves on the premise that these instruments were essentially based on concerns which were intuitive rather than experimentally tested on the user model, we believe that the effective improvement of their mediatic conception currently requires, above all, studies centered on the natural and effective ways of using them.

If it is true that today the first rule of mediatics is that it should be the systems which adapt to the behaviour of the user and not the user who modifies his habits in accordance with the requirements of the system, this attitude is still somewhat new and there do not yet exist, in our opinion, sufficient scientific studies which could guide or organize a more efficient way of reaching this objective.

The speed of the advances made in recent times by informatic technology in the clarity and conviviality of the systems has been such that serious parallel studies into user models were not permitted. It is felt that the point has been reached in which it is precisely these studies which must lead this evolution; otherwise, we shall run the risk of future systems being less adequate than those which actually exist. New technological solutions are currently being studied like the oral command and the evolution of intelligent processing, which will certainly contribute towards the desired ergonomy, but their incorporation will only be profitable if combined with an improved mediatic knowledge of the solutions already available.

The evolution of modern informatic management technologies is directly linked to the evolution of the ergonomy of the systems which support them. Respecting the totality of the user activities the ergonomy of the systems should consider interactivity here as one of its major concerns, a keyword in these new information and communication technologies, along with its convivial aspect.

The interface should become more and more convivial, allowing the user to go through the tasks in a way which is natural and easy to understand and execute, and interactive, attributing to the user rather than the author the choice of information to be dealt with and the order and depth of its processing.

Conviviality and interactivity are therefore important factors in judging the ergonomic value of an interface, directly related with its motivational value, i.e., the degree of psychological acceptance of the system.

As far as conviviality is concerned, a great step forward was achieved with the generalization of exploration systems, in which there exists a functional separation between the instrument which gives orders and the instrument which deals with data entry on account of the ease of use which this provides. This separation, supported in mediatic elements (such as windows, pop menus, icons, buttons, pictogrammes, visual branching, etc.) and in the evolution of the graphic interface, constitutes today the stated goal of all the DOS already existing or in preparation.

Communication, a key element in the teaching/learning process, has as its disposal today new means in the form of modern techniques for the management and search of information linearly or sequentially unstructured and transported through text, image and sound. These new means seem to us pedagogically promising.

The hypermedia documental architectures present us with a system of reading/writing which is non-linear, following the principle that natural human thought processes are not sequential but conexial, that is, by the association of ideas. This similarity to human information processing makes it legitimate to suppose that they will become in the near future one of the most privileged methods of computer-assisted teaching on account of their adequacy. The computer on account of the immateriality of the objects which it manipulates and visualizes, constitutes an ideal support for this kind of non-linear writing/reading which printed support material, for example, does not provide. This type of structure is still at the center of recent research into the video-disk, CD-ROM and the CD-X, which constitute fundamental elements of multimedia support to teaching, and whose capacities require new methods of information search based on power of association and intuition.

Hypermedia systems permit the conception, production and management of information in the form of screen images in which the interactivity that should exist between the user and the system takes place in this work space (the screen image), by way of operations of interactivity which are particularly, but not exclusively, the buttons. They permit the creation of information and service banks within which the users navigate in search of information. They permit then a navigation based upon the successive showing of screen images composed of text and graphics and accompanied occasionally by sound.

A hypertext document on the other hand, requires of the user only a minimal knowledge of the material contained in it, and the knowledge necessary for its exploitation is practically non-existent. We can say that the hypertexts are based on a specific form of storage and presentation of information in such a way as to allow the user to decid, at a moment's notice, upon the type and order of information he wishes to access. This characteristic originates from the fact that it is possible to create links between items allowing the user to navigate the hypertext by making use of these previously defined links. We understand this flexibility in the access to information supported by these applications to be a real advance with the advantage of generating an environment of autonomy in exploitation.

Based on the hypertext concept and taking advantage of the progress in graphic interfaces, various programmes have appeared recently (of which Hypercard was the first and most divulged) which we classify on the whole of hypermedia products which are in our opinion currently the most finished example of convivial and interactive systems. Moreover, they have the great advantage of constituting a new type of author language, making use of simple but powerful language, close to natural language as well as object-oriented languages. The hypermedia products are considered as sets of information units, which can be connected in the most varied manners by means of the electronic support provided by the computer. Their basic structural hypermedia problems are: to define the units of information (the so called information nodes), the structure of the links between these units and the presentation of that information. The contents of the nodes must be obtained by filtering-strategies (the selection of relevant information) and zoom-strategies (the choice at the level of detail), consistent with the objectives of the document. As for the structure, although all the links are theoretically possible, it is important that the mechanisms of predictable use be analysed in order to privilege the links which optimize that use. As far as presentation is concerned, many solutions exist, although two main types can be presented: the interface in which a combination of texts and graphics are presented to the user. This we shall call graphic interface, with "hot spots" generally buffers. The other extreme, in which the conceptual nodes are explicitly represented and the relationship between them properly characterized we shall call network interface. A choice will need to be made between a continuous presentation (scrolling) of text with images, or a discrete presentation in frames or cards. In the first case, the use of techniques of typographical highlight will be of first importance while in the second we will have to evolve in the direction of the definition of an audiovisual language for the screen image. The choices depend, among other things, on the type of information access activity, for besides search (find) – the most conventional activity which is applied when the intention is to find well defined information in the document (like in data bases) –, we find navigation and browsing. Navigation is a style of exploration of electronic documents which is based principally on graphic clues. For its part, browsing is a type of exploration characterized by the existence of an aim or objective which is not well defined. This type of exploration can naturally lead to a situation of guided discovery learning (McAleese) with all its recognized advantages in education, since it preserves maximum motivation and, by permitting a metacognitive control of learning, substantially preserves its efficiency (Ingwerson, 1986). However, two problems which are referred to in the literature and are related to the exploration of such documents arise with much relevance: one of them is the possibility of losing the objective of browsing (the phenomenon known as "getting-lost-in-hyperspace"); the other is the progressive lessening of the capacity to note contrasts. In order to minimize both problems tools commands known as browsing tools are necessary. Among these we have graphic or arborescent historials to help the user situate himself within the structure. Also considered fundamental are the simplification and adequation of the structure and the presentation of the document to its predictable use. This happens in such a way that, as regards simplification, all the existing relationships between the conceptual fields of any two information nodes should not be established but rather those presumed to be the most adequate for the metaphor in use. In this way, simple networks rather than out-of-proportion networks can be set up in which each link, instead of being connected to all the others, is connected only to those with which it has stronger associations. Hierarchic or pseudo-hierarchic structures are created, as far as possible, which are much simpler to follow since a summit can be distin-guished and the cognitive scaffolding of that structure set up. This is essential to its suitability to discovery learning.

At the same time combinatory explosion is avoided which is a problem in computer implementation, and the "getting-lost-in-hyper-space" phenomenon is minimized on account of the fact that scaffolding is fundamental to objective exploration. As to the form of presentation, if one hopes to maintain concentration on the objective it is preferable to adopt a graphic interface. If it is more important to keep constant track of the cognitive path followed and the perspectives of this path then a network interface will be preferable. In the first case the predominant exploration strategy is browsing; in the second it will be navigating.

It should be noted, however, that although it is important to know how users construct the road in the exploration of an hypermedia system, the most important factor is not the order which they choose, but the effect that such a choice (D. Charney, 1987) will have in the learning process.

When attempting to define situations in which hypermedia constitutes a privileged means of learning support, non-formal areas in which an environment of programmed learning is inadequate must be mentioned in the first place. Underlying implied knowledge and in order to develop critical capacity, conflicting explanations, historical perspectives, personal opinions, facts, etc., must coexist. It so happens, however, that other areas well structured by a strong paradigm when from a cognitive point of view conceptual modes are somewhat distant from the perceptual, and from an affective point of view it is important to develop attitudes of curiosity and research, hypermedia can serve as an excellent means of configuration in order to privilege a constructivist perspective of learning, guided by the structure imposed on the presentation of information.

Analogies between the real world of an hyperdocument and the real world or a scientific theory which is to be studied, facilitate for the users, as long as a good metaphor is chosen, the construction of a suitable mental model.

Computers, particularly as a support to the modern technologies of hypermedia exploration and multimedia strategies, are much more than a closed structure of organization and transmission of messages. Therefore, the role attributed to the computer as a privileged support of configurative communication can not be forgotten, particularly in the applications involving the use of interactive image, a privileged mechanism for access to the organization of the cognitive representation of the message. This new prosthesis of the complex process of communication lacks deep and innovative study into the interaction between man and computer which will have to be based on the study of a grammar of the interactive image and coherent with the results of research in cognitive science, particularly Cognitive Psychology and Artificial Intelligence.

Several types of educational hypermedia applications are beginning to appear in large quantities on the software market. But the majority not only fail to take full advantage of the potential of these means but often do so in a pedagogically disastrous way. We have no doubt about the interest which surrounds the exploitation of this potential in the creation of educational applications of quality. Likewise we have no doubt that in order to achieve this quality, it is necessary to intensify the current phase of research and improvement, both in the construction of these applications and in the effects of its uses. It is thought that the results obtainable from such research will constitute a precious aid, both in the improvement of technological hypermedia and its educational use, and in the clarification of the mechanisms of the learning/ teaching process.

To attempt to construct a cognitive model of the user, with reference to their activity in exploring hypermedia documents is an essential step if we intend to create programmes adapted to the user. The depth of hypermedia information exploration seems to be directly associated with the initial representation of task and the functional cognitive capacity for the utilization of the systems of existing relations and for the successful abstraction of general rules associated with their mental representations, two of the basic requirements in hypermedia exploration if the system of dislocation is to be controlled. At the same time, in order to make hypermedia educational documents more appropriate to the learners, it is of primary importance to discover what intellectual activities characterize their cognitive processes in the learning situation. Any system of education must base itself on what it considers to be the "model/pupil" "pupil/model". It is always on the basis of the diagnosis made of the pupil that the system determines what should be learnt and how to act in order for progress to be made. In hypermedia systems, rather than be able to determine the state of knowledge of the pupil, the diagnostic model should be able to describe and interpret the global strategy of the user during the process of knowledge acquisition: the items of knowledge which are activated, the representation of problems elaborated, the planning process used, the criteria used in the choice of courses of action, etc.

The elaboration and adequacy of new mediatic bases relies therefore on simultaneous, interlinked research in two specific scientific fields: that of informatic technology in the New Technologies of Information and that of the representation of human knowledge. These are specific, yet increasingly dependent fields since the scientific evolution in each of these requires knowledge from the other. The need to consider human cognitive processes was encountered in the development of Artificial Intelligence and Cognitive Engineering, as well as in the construction of "intelligent" informatic systems. It becomes indispensable however when we attempt to make the informatic systems (hardware and software) suitable to the users, since for this purpose it is of primary importance to discover the collection of intellectual activities which characterize cognitive functioning while actually using these means. On the other hand, the study of the representation of human knowledge cannot now be made without a powerful contribution from the computer which is wonderfully suited to this representation. The possibilities which the computer has of representing knowledge in a diversified and efficient way, are the basis of the cognitivist revolution (Carey, 1976). The recognized suitability of the computer for the representation of knowledge make it the best current model of study for this representation. In fact, computers can directly store states of activation as well as the connections between the activated entities in analogy to what happens in the central nervous system. On the other hand it can register symbols representing in this case mental states in units of knowledge, like rules, propositions, images and temporal series and the relationship between them.

In the first case we have the recent connectionnist systems most suitable for the emerging generation of parallel processing computers of which the most well known examples are the PDP models (McClelland and Runelhart, 1986). More neurologically plausible, they are limited in that they are applied only, or at leastcurrently, to very simple learning cases. In the second case, we have much more generalized symbolic systems in existing computers. Among these, it is common to distinguish between discrete systems in which representation is made as a collection of symbols, and holistic/analogous systems in which the symbols are inseparable from the relationships which connect them. These can be characterized in a number of ways ranging from topological or geometrical relationships materializable in images, to systems of differential equations with the more or less explicit intervention of spatial and temporal coordinates. Among the discrete systems, a distinction can be made between those based on propositions or declarativies (Kintsch and Van Dijck, 1975), those based on rules or procedures like SOAR (Laind, Newell & Rosenbloom, 1987), and those hybrids of declarative and procedural Knowledge like ACT* (Anderson, 1983). Of the holistic/analogous systems, the Theory of Mental Models (Johnson Laird, 1983) is particularly significant.

Any research in this field presupposes, then, a multidisciplinary approach and the differentiated collaboration of specialists (psychologists, informatics technicians, ergonomics experts, mediatic engineers, ...), but also a clear option as to type of approach chosen as well as a precise definition of the limits of the areas and situations to be investigated.

Our interest lies in particular in educational hypermedia and multimedia systems, which include specific problems, approaches and solutions. We intend to study and improve the suitability of these systems to the representation of knowledge, and also to the representation of the transformation of knowledge (as in the learning situation).

In reply to the demand for education which continues to grow and expand, in respect of the fields covered, of the levels and audiences implied and of the type of educational technology used, it has become necessary to begin the process of modernizing the offer of education. This process will concern itself, among other things, with the evolution of educational systems themselves, so that these may become better adapted to the motivations and requirements of individuals, whether based on a collective or an individual necessity. The offer of education should evolve, then, towards an ever increasing flexibility and constitute a valid and effective response to the undeniable right of the individual to education. It will also need to base itself on the new material and pedagogical possibilities which recent technological evolution has provided. Systems of teaching, based on the active and autonomous participation of the learner, and supported by new technologies (hypermedia exploration; multimedia strategy; artificial intelligence; simulation, etc...) are one of the most promising aspects of this modernization.

Although the computer, on account of its characteristics, is well adapted to individualized teaching, it appears unthinkable to study the ergonomics of any system on the basis of an "individual model" of a given user. Moreover there currently does not exist, and probably never will exist, a "universal model" able to represent the process implied in a learning situation, however well-defined (we do not include cases of simple conditioning as learning situations). What does exist are general theories about learning, which although fundamental to the framework guiding this study, are not sufficiently open to formalization to permit the construction of an operational model in the sense we intend; that is, a model capable of modelling learning in a situation of assisted teaching, clarifying the mediatic foundations of interaction between man and computer.

Even if we consider only the case of hypermedia teaching, there are multiple means of access to knowledge, although certainly not so many as there are individuals. For this reason the great challenge lies in detecting and understanding the bases of a limited (and therefore operational) number of models capable of covering the majority of the means of access which actually exist. Nevertheless, we are aware that this limited number of theoretical models will not, at least in an initial phase, be sufficiently formalisable to permit the creation of a set of rules which represent the learning activities involved in hypermedia exploration. This awareness constitutes two major advantages: on the one hand it obliges us to moderate the temptation to attempt the construction of intelligent tutorial systems which cover the totality of activities involved in hypermedia exploration; on the other hand the acceptance of the theoretical nature of the models forces us to center our attention on their more general and common characteristics, and so to study preferably the structure of aims inherent in the learning activity supported by hypermedia products.

The evolution of intelligent tutorial systems is currently facing an important dilemma: either it is to base itself on pupil models which are sufficiently simple and precise, yet, as they are only relevant to specific learning situations, are only locally operational; or, if we hope to use them in more general situations, the models either cease to be precise enough to be operational or they quickly become too complex and the systems lose a great deal of their efficiency.

Our proposal consists in attempting, in the light of the general theories of learning, to define as clearly as possible the afore-mentioned limited number of models of hypermedia learning so as to elaborate upon them mediatic concepts capable of effectively improving the ergonomy of hypermedia educational systems. As for intelligent aids to be introduced, we believe that they should be based on other instruments of artificial intelligence and not on these models.

Taking educational hypermedia exploration to be a problem-solving situation, we can have recourse to models of learning simulation based on Anderson's theoretic ACT model. According to this theory, at he start of learning in a new field and before being able to try and solve a problem, the pupil will have to have acquired certain knowledge in that field: instruction learning. This knowledge is codified in declarative form: schemes, semantic networks. On the other hand, the model presupposes that the pupil also possesses a set of very general knowledge (acquired before beginning the learning of the new field) with respect to problem solving: weak methods like retrospective analysis, the equipment of problems which have an analogous (surface) structure. This initial general knowledge is represented in the form of production rules. When the pupil is faced with a problem, production rules (representing his knowledge of the general methods of problem-solving) use the knowledge in the new field (coded in declarative form) to create a sequence of specific actions in the proposed problem situation. This is what Anderson calls "interpretation".

The production rules of the weak methods are expressed in an extremely general form: the items of these rules are all the variables which will be instantiated by declarative knowledge. The general nature of the rules gives them the advantage of being applicable to a fairly large group of fields, but with the disadvantage that their application requires an important mental investment in order to manage the aims and declarative knowledge which should be present in working memory. When production is applied several times to a specific situation, the process called "procedure" creates a production whose elements Condition and Action are instances of original production. When a sub-group of productions is activated several times in accordance with the same sequence (without necessarily dealing with the same particular situation), the process called composition produces a copy of that series of productions and combines them into a single production: these combined productions have the status of "macro operators" of the field. The procedure and composition constitute the two faces of the mechanism called "compilation". The knowledge acquired is the new productions created by the compilation mechanism, and they are more efficient (in speed, percentage of success) than the application of general production of weak methods. It is important to note that from a given group of productions a number of combined productions can theoretically be constructed. The process of composition should therefore not be automatic, but guided by the structure of aims which is inherent to the learning field. Thus, the production which represent an acquired knowledge can be more or less general, but necessarily less general than the weak methods from which they emerge.

The consequence of this view of knowledge acquisition in the form of production is two-fold:

1- There is intra-field transfer as long as the structure of aims of a new problem can be reached by the productions generated by the compilation mechanism during learning. That is, there is transfer between the problem situation which has the same structure of aims, whether they present or not the same surface structure. There will be no transfer between problem situations which have the same surface characteristics but which do not have the same structure of aims.

2- Inter-field transfer is, for Anderson, unlikely. We feel, however, that it is possible to consider, the structure of inter-field transfer aims without leaving Anderson's model on condition that it is adequately conceptualized.

In these new positions taken by Anderson on the mechanisms of acquisition and transfer of knowledge we emphasize, on account of our current interest, that the cognitive abilities in a given field are coded in the form of a series of production rules which are organized according to a structure of hierarchical aims. The key to the question which interest us lies therefore in defining through experimentation, the structure of the aims associated with it in order to establish, in accordance with this structure, a series of rules for the production of hypermedia documents which facilitate, by means of ergonomics, the mechanisms of compilation. The aim of the project is therefore to test the set(s) of production rules organized in a structure of hierarchical aims in such a way as to optimize the teaching/learning process which the new educational technologies permit, and to broaden the area of its transfer capacity. Our task, therefore, is to establish and improve the basic conditions which should be obeyed in the conception and use of hypermedia and multimedia software, so that the users can become experts in educational exploration/exploitation, whatever their field of teaching, with ease and rapidity.

Recent work has indicated two possible directions for such research: to work on the initial representations (structure the task better) and introduce the learning of efficient exploration strategies.

To this end, we suggest that, working from concrete problems, different formalizations are elabored and compared from the point of view of their heuristic value, bearing in mind the following: on the one hand the nature of the situation; on the other, the human cognitive process involved in their treatment.

Literature

1. Anderson J. R, The Architecture of Cognition, Lawrence Erlbaum Assoc., 1983
2. Beeman W. O. et al, Hypertext and Pluralism: From Lineal to to Non-lineal Thinking, Hypertext 87 Papers, 1987
3. Bunge, M., Racionalidad y Realismo, Madrid, Alianza, 1985
4. Carey, S., Cognitive Science and Education, American Psychologist, 41, 1123-1130, 1986
5. Habermas J., A Ideia da Universidade: Processos de Aprendizagem, Revista de Educação, 2, 1, 3-9, 1987
6. Johnson- Laird P. N., Mental Models, Cambridge University Press, Cambridge, UK, 1983
7. Johnson-Laird P. N., The Computer and the Mind, Harvard University Press, Cambridge Massachussets, 1988
8. Kintsch W. & Van Dijk T.A., Comment on se Rapelle et on Résume les Histoires, Langage, 40, 98-116, 1975
9. Ingwersen P., Cognitive analysis and the role of the intermediary in information retrieval. In Davies, R. (Ed.), Intelligent Information Systems; Progress and Prospects, Ellis Horwood, UK, 1986
10. Marx, G., Welcome to our non-linear Universe, Vézprem, Hungria, 1987
11. Mc Aleese, R, Concepts as hypertext nodes: the ability to learn while navigating through hypertext nets. In Jonassen, D. & Mandl, H., Designing Hypermedia for Learning, NATO ASI Series, Series F: Computer and Systems Sciences, Vol. 67, 97-115, 1989
12. McClelland, J. L., Rumelhart D. E. and the P.D.P. Research Group, Parallel Distributed Processing. Explorations in the Microstructure of Cognition, Vol. 2: Psychological and Biological Models, Bradford Books, MIT Press, Cambridge, Massachussets, 1986
13. Newell, A., Unified Theories of Cognition, in press, 1990
14. Oliveira, A. J., Costa Pereira D., Psychopedagogic Aspects of Hypermedia Courseware. In Jonassen, D. & Mandl, H., Designing Hypermedia for Learning, NATO ASI Series, Series F: Computer and Systems Sciences, Vol. 67, 251-262, 1990

The Acquisition and Representation of Domain Specific Knowledge Using NoteCards[1]

Ray McAleese[2]

University Teaching Centre, University of Aberdeen, Aberdeen AB9 2UB, Scotland

Abstract: This chapter reports on the general approach taken by recent intelligent tutoring work in Aberdeen. NoteCards was used as a hypertext system to capture domain specific knowledge. The theoretical stance for knowledge acquisition is constructivist.[3] Knowledge was distributed over the surface of a hypertext net using concept labels and typed relationships. Deep knowledge was embedded at nodes.

1. Introduction

NoteCards[4] has been used to to capture experts understandings of domain knowledge. As a hypertext system it facilitates the distribution of knowledge across a network of nodes. Further, graphical interfaces that portray the detail and the extent of the network, can be used to prompt user[5] to provide more information, concepts, etc.

As part of a collaborative project in the UK the University Teaching Centre[6] built and developed a system to represent expertise about several domains.[7] Early work with concept maps suggested a number of general concept types.

— Processes
— Products
— Agents
— Properties
— Procedures

These concept types are generic.[8] That is, there are many other concept types that can be subsumed under these categories. Similarly there are a number of Link types that taken with the Concept types gives the expert a Concept Tool Kit.[9]

— Being
— Showing
— Including
— Using
— Causing
— Similarity

2. Concept Tool Kit

It is possible using the idea of a tool kit to construct understandings. Figure 1 shows such a Tool Kit in schematic form.

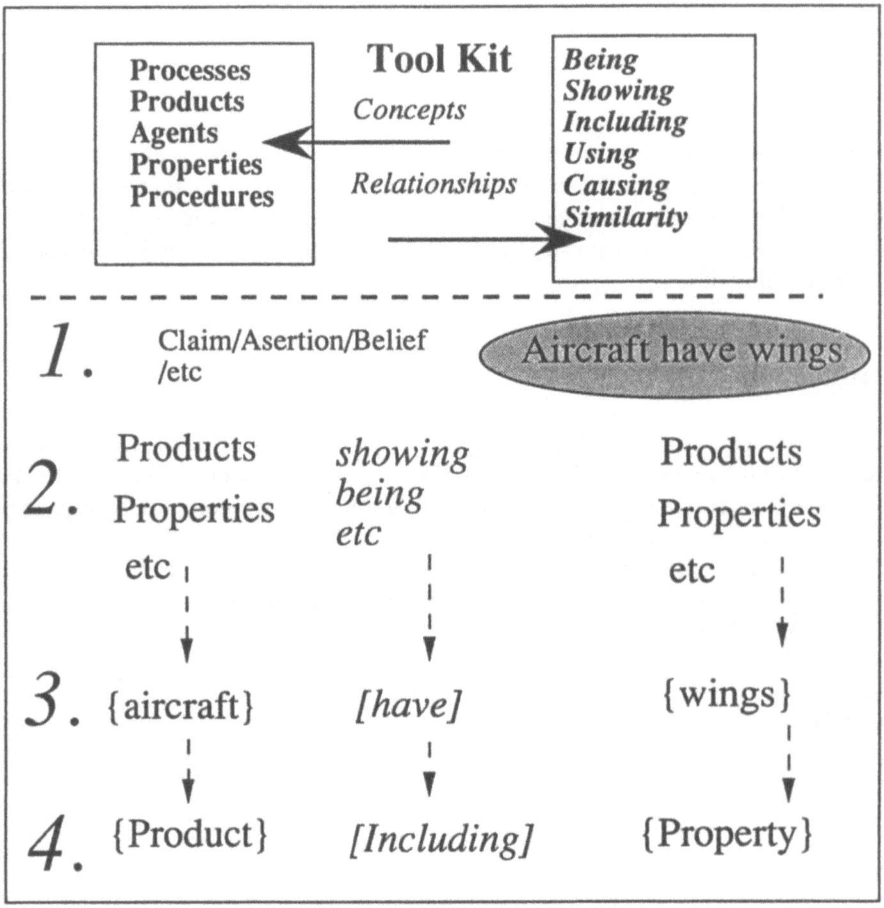

Fig. 1

With the Tool Kit the user can make an assertion, express a belief etc. (1.)[10] He/she chooses appropriate Concept Type(s) and Relationship/ Link Type(s) from the available card types (2.) from the generic concepts The concepts and relationships of the assertion are parsed into the Tool Kit elements (3. & 4.)[11]

Using a development of NoteCards called IDE[12] and work in Aberdeen called KIM it is possible to specialise the cards and the link types. Figure 2 shows a specialised card type {**Agent**} with an associated icon.[13]

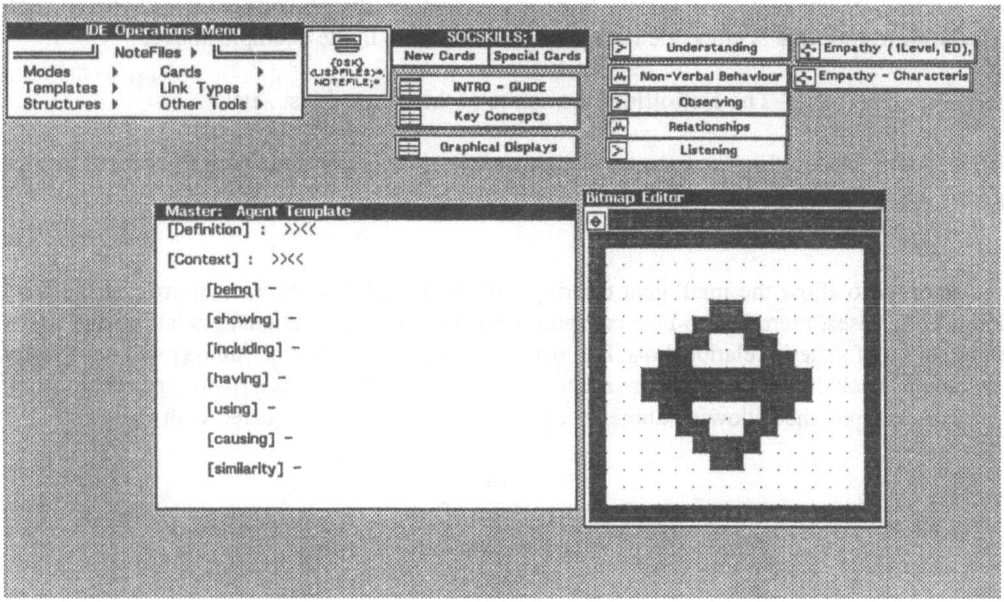

Fig. 2

This card type contains 9 active buttons that will generate other cards. The buttons, **Definition** and **Context** generate "Deep Knowledge" cards allowing the expert to define and put in context a concept, of concept type {**Agent**}. (For example, {**Air Traffic Controller**}) Apart from the two Deep Knowledge buttons there are seven link buttons that can be used to construct meaningful statements of the type:

Concept - link - **Concept**

The seven typed relationships are used, as explained, to construct understandings. Figure 3 shows an example of Deep Knowledge[14] with the concept {Relationships} showing (as a NoteCard) a Definition, a button that will link the card to a context card and two relationships filled out.

{Relationships} - [showing] - **{(SD) Relationships}**

and

{Relationships} - [causing] - **{Clients}**

It is important to remember that the Surface knowledge is distributed across the hypertext net. The Deep Knowledge is embedded at the nodes. Therefore in the example above:

" **The Definition:** the nature of the interactions... etc"

is **Deep Knowledge.** Figure 4 shows a simple view of eight concepts with their relationships giving a Surface representation.

In order to allow the intelligent tutoring part of the IIKS system to interrogate the KIM knowledge bases, there had to be a compromise between natural language relationships and a minimal set of generic relationships. For example the generic link type **[being]** will have many synonyms. Each of the synonyms are related to the generic link type as a **[is-a]** type relationship.

For example, the following abbreviated list of link types were equated with **[being]**:[15]

is-a
is a form of
is the same as
are kind of
can be
is a kind of
is on
...
etc

Figures 5 and 6 indicate the relationship between the generic concept types and the types of understandings that can be created. In Figure 5 the Procedure card {**Explaining- Social Skills**} has a **Definition Card**, a **Content Card** and a **Procedure Card** (NEXT STEP) associated.

The link type **[being]** is shown in summary as being constructed as follows;

The {**procedure**} card is linked with a **[being]** link to an {**Agent**} card. (In NoteCards the other values in the box at the top of the card indicate the way the system treats the location of the icons etc on the card.)

Figure 6 gives a good example of the Deep Knowledge at the node

{**Explaining- Social Skills**}

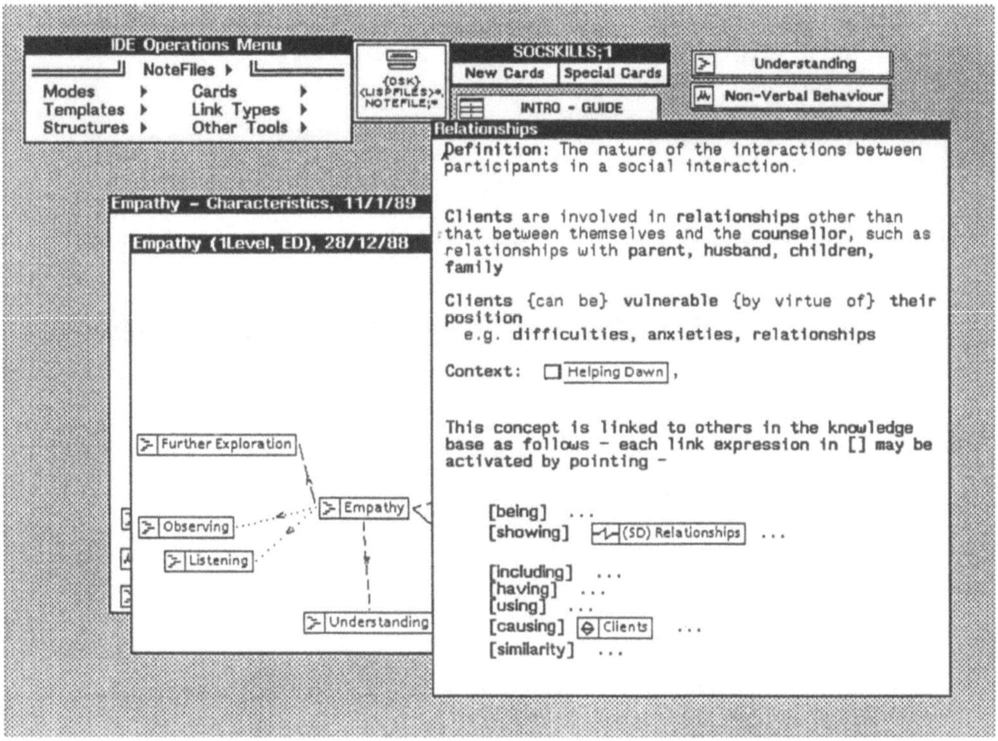
IDE Operations Menu
NoteFiles
Modes
Templates
Structures
Cards
Link Types
Other Tools
SOCSKILLS;1
New Cards
Special Cards
INTRO - GUIDE
Understanding
Non-Verbal Behaviour
Relationships
Definition: The nature of the interactions between participants in a social interaction.
Clients are involved in relationships other than that between themselves and the counsellor, such as relationships with parent, husband, children, family
Clients {can be} vulnerable {by virtue of} their position
e.g. difficulties, anxieties, relationships
Context: Helping Dawn,
This concept is linked to others in the knowledge base as follows - each link expression in [] may be activated by pointing -
[being] ...
[showing] (SD) Relationships ...
[including] ...
[having] ...
[using] ...
[causing] Clients ...
[similarity] ...
Empathy - Characteristics, 11/1/89
Empathy (1Level, ED), 28/12/88
Further Exploration
Empathy
Observing
Listening
Understanding

Fig. 3

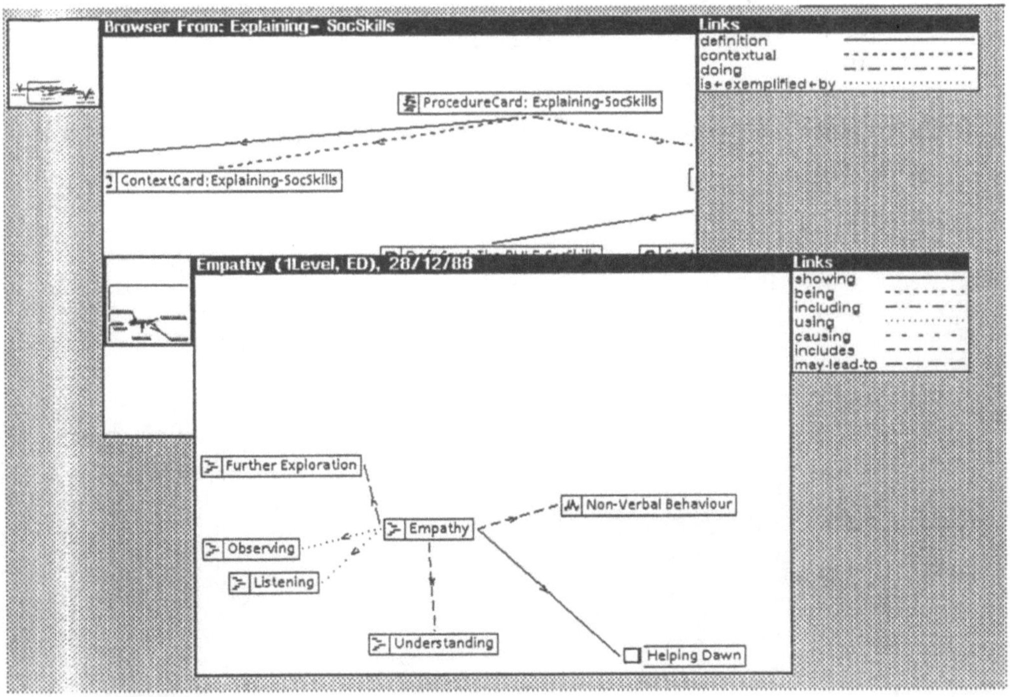
Browser From: Explaining- SocSkills
Links
definition
contextual
doing
is+exemplified+by
ProcedureCard: Explaining-SocSkills
ContextCard: Explaining-SocSkills
Empathy (1Level, ED), 28/12/88
Links
showing
being
including
using
causing
includes
may-lead-to
Further Exploration
Non-Verbal Behaviour
Empathy
Observing
Listening
Understanding
Helping Dawn

Fig. 4

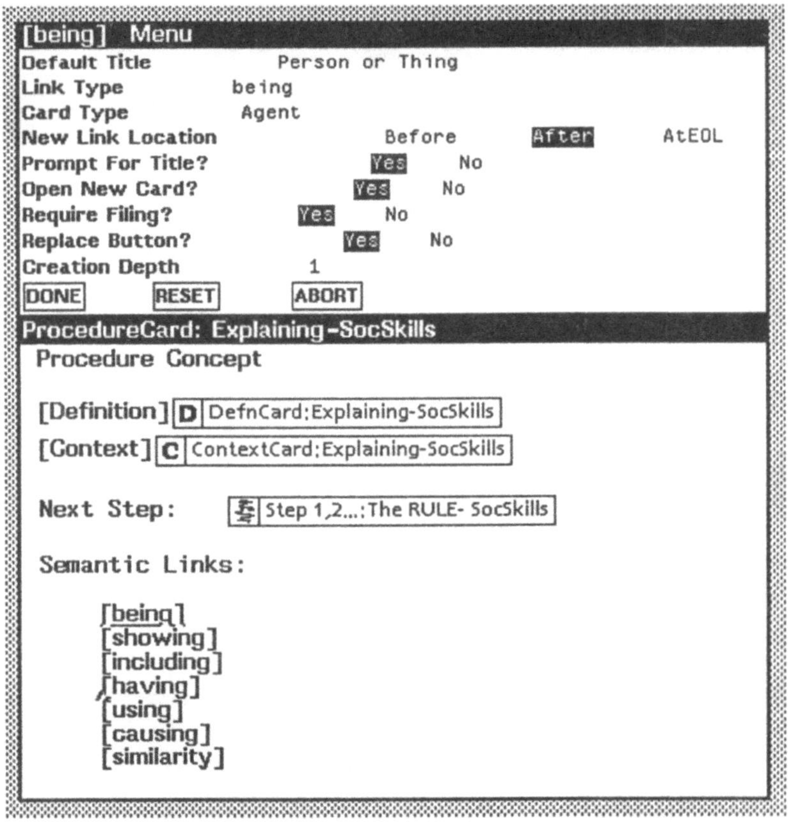
[being] Menu
Default Title Person or Thing
Link Type being
Card Type Agent
New Link Location Before After AtEOL
Prompt For Title? Yes No
Open New Card? Yes No
Require Filing? Yes No
Replace Button? Yes No
Creation Depth 1
DONE RESET ABORT
ProcedureCard: Explaining-SocSkills
Procedure Concept
[Definition] D DefnCard:Explaining-SocSkills
[Context] C ContextCard:Explaining-SocSkills
Next Step: Step 1,2...:The RULE- SocSkills
Semantic Links:
[being]
[showing]
[including]
[having]
[using]
[causing]
[similarity]

Fig. 5

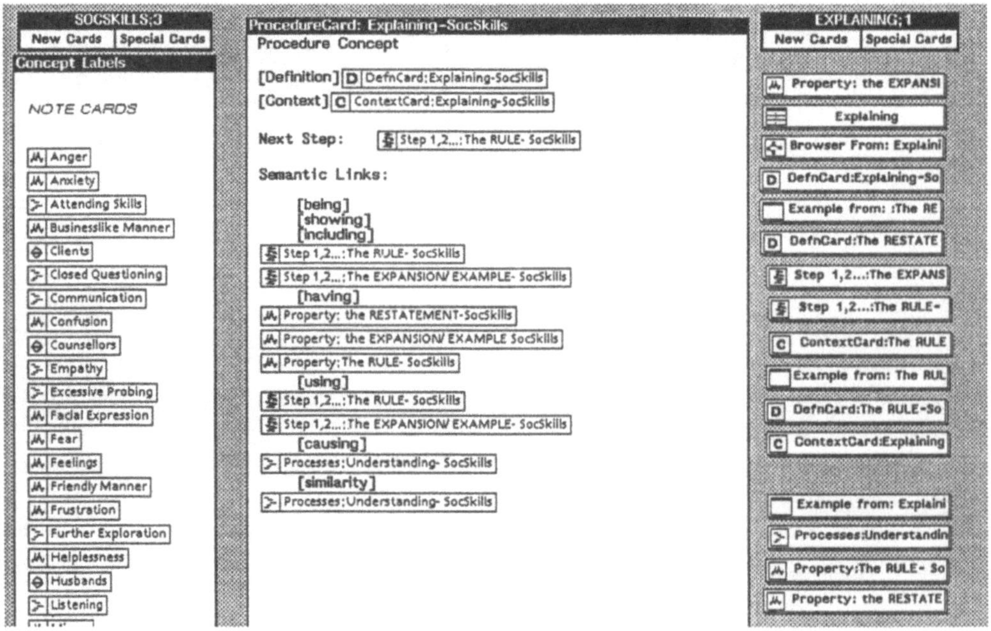
SOCSKILLS;3
New Cards
Special Cards
Concept Labels
NOTE CARDS
Anger
Anxiety
Attending Skills
Businesslike Manner
Clients
Closed Questioning
Communication
Confusion
Counsellors
Empathy
Excessive Probing
Facial Expression
Fear
Feelings
Friendly Manner
Frustration
Further Exploration
Helplessness
Husbands
Listening
ProcedureCard: Explaining-SocSkills
Procedure Concept
[Definition] DefnCard:Explaining-SocSkills
[Context] ContextCard:Explaining-SocSkills
Next Step: Step 1,2...:The RULE- SocSkills
Semantic Links:
[being]
[showing]
[including]
Step 1,2...:The RULE- SocSkills
Step 1,2...:The EXPANSION/ EXAMPLE- SocSkills
[having]
Property: the RESTATEMENT-SocSkills
Property: the EXPANSION/ EXAMPLE SocSkills
Property: The RULE- SocSkills
[using]
Step 1,2...:The RULE- SocSkills
Step 1,2...:The EXPANSION/ EXAMPLE- SocSkills
[causing]
Processes:Understanding- SocSkills
[similarity]
Processes:Understanding- SocSkills
EXPLAINING;1
New Cards
Special Cards
Property: the EXPANSI
Explaining
Browser From: Explaini
DefnCard:Explaining-So
Example from: :The RE
DefnCard:The RESTATE
Step 1,2...:The EXPANS
Step 1,2...:The RULE-
ContextCard:The RULE
Example from: The RUL
DefnCard:The RULE-So
ContextCard:Explaining
Example from: Explaini
Processes:Understandin
Property:The RULE- So
Property: the RESTATE

Fig. 6

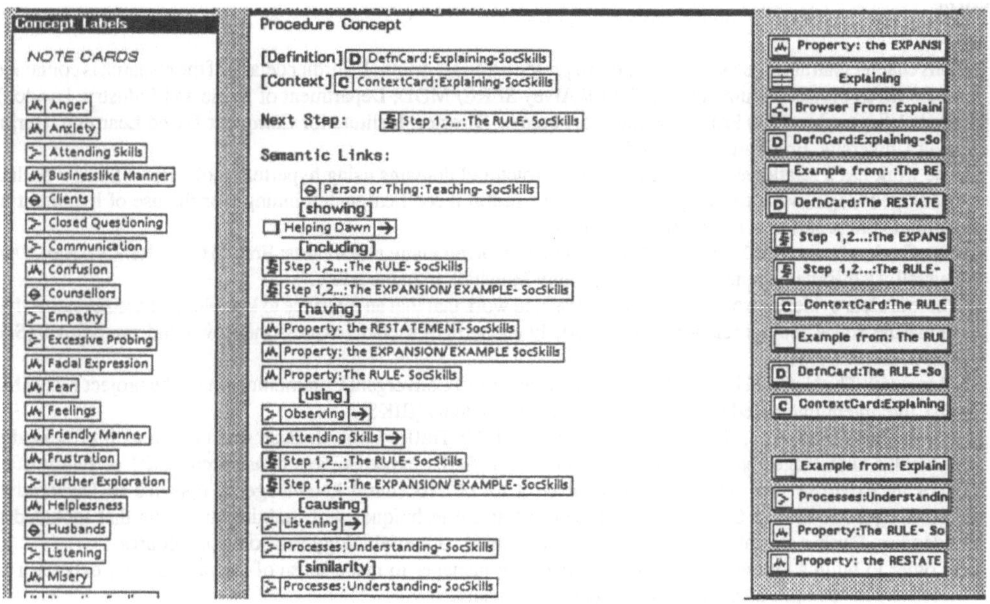

Figure 7 shows a fuller representation of knowledge around the same node.

3. Conclusion

The outcome of this work was to establish the way an extensible hypertext system can be tailored to give knowledge acquisition capabilities. Hypertext system were not designed to provide interfaces for knowledge acquisition; they support this work when the underlying data model for hypertext is free enough to permit the grain size of the nodes to vary from unity [16] to large chunks of text.

Notes

1. This chapter is an abridged version of the oral presentation at Espinhol. Further details of the research is contained in the IIIKS project documents (MMI 110/ Alvey SERC/ MOD; Department of Trade and Industry, London)
2. From 1 September 1990 Professor Ray McAleese is Director, Institute for Computer Based Learning, Heriot Watt University, Edinburgh, Scotland.
3. The work has a relationship to research on ill-structured domains using hypertext tools. Rand Spiro who has developed Cognitive Flexibility Theory presents useful theoretical underpinnings for the use of hypertext to facilitate the acquisition of ill-structured areas.
4. NoteCards was a major Xerox PARC project that involved many researchers: Frank Halaz, Randy Trigg, Dan Russell, Dan Jordan, Anne-Marie Jensen, Cathy Marshall, to name a few.
5. There is clear evidence from this project and related work that that an interface to knowledge based systems that shows the nodes and the relationships pictorially encourages users to express their own understandings. (See McAleese, R (1990))
6. Along with The National Physical Laboratory, Logica and Convergent Communications. The project was MMI 110, Intelligent Integrated Interfaces to Knowledge Systems (IIIKS).
7. The domains used were, Social Skills, Cooking and Air Traffic Control. Each was chosen as it presented a particular knowledge representation problem. Social Skills expertise was considered "soft" or relativistic. Cooking expertise was choosen as it involved a lot of Procedural knowledge as opposed to Declarative knowledge. Air Traffic Control was choosen to test the techniques with training materials that included a videodisc. Further air traffic control has some aspects of soft terminology and some procedures.
8. In order to build a system that permitted a dialogue manager to make sense of utterances from experts it is necessary to "compromise" with agreed generic concepts.
9. The Concept Tool Kit was the main deliverable from the Alvey research. The idea of a tool kit makes it easy for an untrained expert to represent understandings using the concept map formalism.
10. An assertion or belief is something understood or felt to be understood by the domain expert. There is no "truth" value or certainty check. It would be possible to indicate the certainty value of an assertion using a form of fuzzy reasoning or simply attaching a probability value to all assertions.
11. There were two stages in the work. During the first stage the expert was able to use free language to express the concepts and the relationships. In the second phase the freedom was constrained by a) applying the Tool Kit rigidly; b) using the parsing facility to assign the generic link type to the free expression of the expert.
12. • IDE is Instructional Design Environment developed by Dan Russell, Dan Jordan and others at Xerox PARC. IDE is a tool kit used by Xerox instructional designers to analyse and construct training materials.
    • KIM is an acronym used in the University of Aberdeen by Ray McAleese to descriptive a general research theme called Knowledge and Information mapping. KIM goes back to 1984 with work Ray McAleese undertook in Concordia University. The original KIM interface was an Apple II computer.
13. It is important to note that the graphical interface is very important in such work. The domain expert uses the interface to prompt utterances. Each concept type is given an icon to distinguish concept types from each other in the NoteCard Browsers.
14. The term "Deep Knowledge" is not entirely satisfactory. It has come about in practice in Aberdeen to distinguish the information that is embedded IN cards at nodes to be distinguished from the distributed knowledge that consists of the totality of the node and the relationships. There is no inference of "tacit" or other connotations to the use of the term here.
15. The computation of the generic link types from the free language links provided by experts was a non-trivial task. A set of procedures were applied to the NoteCard files to parse out the links between cards and to replace the expert values with a generic value assigned by a database. This work was undertaken in LISP as an extension to NoteCards.
16. See Chapter (6 by Ray McAleese, in Jonassen, D H and Mandl, H (Eds) (1990), Designing Hypermedia For Learning, NATO ASI Series F, Vol. 67 , Springer-Verlag.

Tools for Monitoring and Analysing the Use of Hypermedia Courseware

Miles MacLeod

Hatfield Polytechnic, College Lane, Hatfield, Herts AL10 9AB, UK.
Tel: +44 (0)707 279000 Ext 2321. Fax: +44 (0)707 279670. Email: commm@hatfield.ac.uk

Abstract: Hypermedia systems for learning have potential for placing control of presentation of information firmly in the hands of the learner. Ideally, concepts and their inter-relationships can be explored at the learner's chosen pace. However, if aspects of the system are ineffectively designed, the learner all too often becomes lost, or simply fails to find relevant information. Ease of use depends upon more than the organisation of the underlying structures of links and nodes. Of central importance are the manner in which these structures and substructures are represented to the user; the signalling of jump opportunities; and the actions, commands and feedback by which navigation is accomplished. Monitoring the use of such systems - at an appropriate grain of analysis and in controlled circumstances - can yield useful objective evaluative data about these factors, especially where multiple navigation structures and command options coexist.
AutoMonitor [7], is a software device for monitoring hypermedia systems, created in HyperCard™. It captures a timed record of interaction between user and system, at the level of actions upon discrete interface objects (such as buttons, fields and menu-items), together with a navigation trace, in a format suitable for feeding directly into a spreadsheet for semi-automated analysis. In this paper, AutoMonitor's design and rationale are outlined. Its application is discussed, with particular reference to a specific example of hypermedia courseware, and the subsequent analysis of data via a spreadsheet is described, illustrating the kinds of analysis of interaction and navigation which monitoring can facilitate. The relationship between the structure of systems and appropriate evaluation methods is considered.

1. Introduction

The design of hypermedia systems can be studied and analysed from several theoretical and pragmatic viewpoints; in this paper, the field is viewed from the perspective of Human-Computer Interaction (HCI) and cognitive ergonomics. Of primary concern here are those factors which influence the ease of use of a system. Hypermedia systems are at heart interactive: they store information in the form of nodes and links which connect nodes, and must present these in such a way that people can use the system effectively, efficiently and with satisfaction. The underlying structure, while central to the system, is not intrinsically visible to the user. Hypermedia systems must be designed to inform the user adequately about their content and structure, and must provide the user with the means for exploration, navigation and control; means which do not exceed the capabilities of that user.

HCI draws on a substantive body of existing theoretical and empirical work, and can offer a number of techniques which may be exploited to evaluate hypermedia systems at various stages of their development, from early design ideas through to fully implemented systems. Once a working prototype has been created, it becomes possible to capture and analyse data about its use, which can subsequently be fed back into the development process. Monitoring the use of interactive software, and creating a time-stamped record of interaction, can provide objective data for the evaluation of that software unobtainable by other evaluation techniques. However, the choice of precisely what is to be recorded is crucial. It is all too easy to generate vast quantities of redundant or uninterpretable low-level data. It is also possible (but less common) to record events in insufficient detail. Choosing the correct grain of analysis for the interaction record is therefore of central importance. Macleod [8] argues that, for direct manipulation systems, an appropriate grain is found at the level of discrete actions upon what the user perceives as objects; this enables analysis at a level which in a layered model would be described as the task or semantic level.

For evaluating the use of hypermedia systems, it is desirable to monitor two separate classes of event:

- navigation or browsing - the sequence of nodes visited, and links traversed
- the specific means by which the user achieves that navigation or browsing

In combination, such data provide an objective record of what the user has explored, and how. A hypermedia system may present the user with alternative structures and methods for navigation, and also with alternative means of performing navigation actions. Monitoring the interaction enables the statistical analysis of which nodes were visited, and of the chosen methods and means. It also enables study of the individual choices made in specific situations. Monitoring is best used in combination with other evaluation techniques: the context and circumstances in which the system was used are highly relevant, as are the user's subjective opinions, and - where a system is designed for tuition or learning - assessments of the learner's knowledge.

2. Structures in hypermedia systems, and their relation to navigation and browsing behaviour

Typically, a hypermedia system is formed of a network of links and nodes, within which it may be possible to identify substructures of various degrees of complexity. The overall structure is influenced both by the intrinsic organisation of associative links within the body of information, and by the style of the hypermedia authoring environment. Wright and Lickorish [18] identify a number of different categories of hypermedia structure. Beyond text with a strong linear discourse structure (perhaps with footnotes), such structures may be loops; modules; hierarchies; matrices; or networks. A distinction between structure and presentation, in the senses which Wright [16] identifies in conventional technical texts, is less clear in hypermedia systems, where the presentation to the user of links is fundamental to the structure of the system.

An authoring environment which offers scrolling text and expandable headings, for example Guide™, encourages largely hierarchical structures, with dense textual nodes. In such systems, the headings and sub-headings can play the role of a contents list, displaying to the user relatively high-level information about the organisation of the system, with an adjustable level of detail (much in the manner of an outliner). The formation by the user of a global view of the embedded links - which reach out from the depths of the text - is a more difficult task. A user survey by Nielsen and Lyngbæk [14] of a hypertext version of a technical document implemented in Guide, found less user satisfaction with the hypertext jump facilities than with the pop-up notes and text expansion, and that a majority of the respondents agreed with the statement *when reading the report, I was often confused about 'where I was'*. A widely recognised further difficulty, for the users of many systems, lies in discovering what is there to be explored. One quote elicited by Nielsen and Lyngbæk ('I soon realised that if I did not read something when I stumbled across it, then I would not be able to find it later') indicates the further problem of a user being unable to re-find information which had been encountered once already.

Card-based systems tend to encourage smaller nodes, and richer sets of links. HyperCard™, since its release in 1987, has arguably been the single greatest promoter of interest in hypermedia, and despite its limitations can be used to implement complex and relatively sophisticated systems. But it is also responsible for a tendency to dilute the popular concept of hypermedia. HyperCard is widely used for the development of quasi-hypermedia systems: graphically interfaced databases with an underlying matrical structure. In such systems, a simple search along two or more dimensions (such as year and subject) locates a unique node.

Hypertexts generated in HyperCard have an additional facility for creating transient user-defined links, via use of the 'find' command. This kind of unstructured link - where the destination is simply an instance of a text string, and hence not necessarily semantically linked - can produce unpredictable results, and has potential for causing user disorientation. However, it is argued by some authorities (e.g. [12]) that a certain amount of 'getting lost' may be beneficial, if it enforces exploration, and hence facilitates discovery-learning. While there is undoubtedly merit in this argument, the view taken here is that a principal goal in designing a hypermedia system should be to give the user a high degree of control in their exploration and navigation, by providing the user with multiple means of locating relevant information.

2.1 Giving the learner control, and enabling the formation of clear conceptual models

Presentation of information in book form, via printed text and graphics, employs many devices to assist the reader in locating information, and in forming a conceptual model of its organisation. The physical nature of the medium provides constant cues to current position, gives opportunities to mark and annotate, and allows search by flicking through pages. Authors may organise the information by chunking into labelled chapters, sections and paragraphs, with an overview in the form of a contents list. An index informs about location of specific items. Within the text, links are signalled to references, footnotes, diagrams, appendices and panels. (Wright [16] provides a research review). However, text is essentially a linear sequential medium. Information in a book is presented in a fixed order, which is available for the learner to follow. This has transparent advantages in tuition, for leading the learner through well-constructed arguments, and presenting information in an order the author feels appropriate for understanding. It has disadvantages when the learner is already familiar with some of the content, or is unfamiliar with necessary concepts presented elsewhere in the text.

Hypermedia systems - particularly those designed with discrete nodes at the level of concepts, and a rich set of links - can enable the learner to explore concepts as required. To be effective, such systems must provide access, guidance and overview facilities at least on par with a book. A lost learner has lost control. A second problem, often overlooked, is how to suggest a suitable order in which to explore information, for those learners who may prefer to be guided. Monitoring the use of prototype systems designed to address these problems - such as [9], outlined in Section 3 - can provide useful evaluative data, difficult to obtain by other means.

Conveying to the user a clear conceptual model of some navigational structures found in computer-based systems, such as matrices, is relatively straightforward. A more taxing question is how to represent a complex network structure in such a way that the user can gain a useful mental representation of the organisation of its nodes and links, and thus identify relevant nodes to visit. Graphical representation in the form of an overview diagram - a map or browser - is one relatively direct means of providing the user with the basis of a clear system model. Browsers are generated automatically in some systems, e.g. NoteCards [4]. In others, such as HyperCard, browsers must be generated manually. The broader questions of how spatial representations of hypertext structures relate to learners' knowledge structures are not considered here; Jonassen [5] and Mayes et al [12] provide thoughtful reviews.

While commercial authoring environments encourage certain styles of representation at the expense of others, researchers have explored a variety of means of presenting, and conveying, structure to users. Simpson and McKnight [15] demonstrate that a hierarchical contents list may be more effective than an alphabetical list, in assisting the formation of an accurate mental map of hierarchically structured systems, and that a current position indicator can aid efficiency. Wright and Lickorish [17] compare the use of links embedded in the text *versus* use of an index card listing available nodes, and find their relative merits task-specific, and dependent upon the information structure of the hypertext.

A further important question is the degree to which such representation of structure may help the successful *navigation* to relevant nodes. **Global** guides to structure and content, such as browsers, contents lists and indexes not only convey a model of what a system contains, but also may serve as access mechanisms. Relevant **local** factors influencing navigation and browsing behaviour include: the manner of locally representing individual opportunities to jump to a link destination; the means available for performing navigation actions; the type of visual feedback received on jumping; the degree of confidence in being able to return easily to the starting point of a jump. Nicol [13] provides an introduction to some of these user interface issues relevant to hypermedia design in HyperCard. Evensen and Rheinfrank [1] propose a basis for developing an extendable standard for local cues.

Hammond and Allinson [2,3] categorise maps, indexes and tours as guidance and access tools, and report some effects on learning of the provision, or not, of these supportive structures. The guided tours reported by Hammond and Allinson are of a design which for the duration of the tour removes a degree of control from the user: navigation choice is limited to selecting when to move on to the next frame in the pre-determined sequence, although the user is free to leave (and later rejoin) a guided tour. Marshall and Irish [11] describe the use of Guided Tours in NoteCards as a means of organising hypertext for presentation. They identify a need for hypertext authors to provide large amounts of meta-information, explaining what the author is doing, and why. Their approach appears to embed the original hypertext network in a cocoon of explanatory, supportive and guiding material; the effects of such a high degree of guidance on the balance of control between learner and tutor is unclear. One aim of [9] is to suggest to the learner, but not to impose, sequences for exploration.

The design of hypermedia tuition systems presents a further complication. Rather than simply allowing access to individual relevant nodes as desired, from any given starting point, it is important that all nodes are visited which are necessary for conveying the information content of the system. Some means must be provided of informing the user of unintentionally unvisited nodes. Overview maps and indexes partially perform this function; an index of unvisited nodes is more specific. In practice, with systems implemented in HyperCard, many users resort to stepping through the individual cards sequentially, to discover those which they have missed.

2.2 User actions

Movement from one node to another may be achieved by various user actions, such as button clicks, menu choices, or keypresses. In HyperCard, users principally jump to a node by clicking on a text or graphical button linked to that node. This action conflicts with the standard user actions required in the Macintosh Desktop User Interface, where a single click on an object selects that object (signalled by reverse video highlighting), and a double-click is required in order to 'open' (or go to) the object.

Evaluative data gained from monitoring interaction at this low level can be useful in establishing a design standard which enable the easy use of a system. An example is provided by pop-up fields and windows, here considered as loop structures. These may be displayed when the user points at a screen button and depresses the mouse (mouseDown), and displayed only while the mouse is held down. Superficially, this would not be consistent with either the single or double click standard. Alternatively, they may be toggled; that is, displayed on mouseUp, and hidden on a subsequent mouseUp on the same screen button; and/or they may be hidden by clicking on the field or window itself.

HyperCard provides basic built-in navigation facilities: menu choices and command keypress combinations which allow travel to adjacent cards in the current sorted order, and to first and last cards; and backward stepping through the sequence of recently visited cards. Hypermedia authors may choose to disable the direct use of some of these, in order to constrain semantically irrelevant jumps. Where these are not disabled, a record of the occurrences and context of people resorting to the use of these facilities can be captured, and may help in identifying shortcomings in the intended navigation facilities provided by the hypermedia author.

3. An example of hypermedia courseware

This section outlines a simple example of hypermedia courseware, in order to provide a concrete basis for describing the kinds of information which can be captured by monitoring the use of such systems. 'HyperCard Basic Concepts' [9] is an example of hypermedia courseware designed to give the user an ample set of supportive structures, incorporated fully into a hypermedia system based on small nodes and numerous links. Employing small nodes enables concepts to be presented individually - yet embedded in, and linked to, their context - and via a low density of text, thus avoiding the disadvantages of forcing learners to extract information from dense screen displays of text.

An omnipresent question in the design of hypermedia courseware is how to resolve the conflict between the desire to introduce students to new concepts only when they are ready for them, and the freedom which hypermedia systems provide for browsing rapidly into distant and inappropriate domains. 'Basic Concepts' reflects one approach to resolving this conflict, and also to overcoming some of the navigation problems outlined above: specifically the difficulties of forming a global image of what the system contains, and of discovering its as yet unexplored corners. It employs what may be termed 'conducive redundancy': the coexistance of multiple navigation structures within a single hypermedia system. These structures are designed to allow the user to explore the system in different ways at different stages of learning, and to have multiple means of recovering from getting lost. An aim is to provide sufficient cues to allow the user to form complementary conceptual models of the system itself.

Rather than providing explicit guided tours, a principal design goal is to allow sequential structures (and sub-sequences) to coexist with the network of hypermedia links; sequential structures from which the learner is at any time free to branch out. Kornbrot and Macleod [6] report the evaluation of user behaviour within such a system, by means of the monitoring and analysis of which structures learners freely *choose* to use as learning progresses.

'Basic Concepts' aims to combine gracefully several different structures, and various aids to the conceptualisation of structures:

- A **linear sequence**, intended to lead students, gently. This sequence comprises those cards which present the major concepts, arranged in what is considered a pedagogically appropriate order, and numbered. It does not include cards which illustrate or exemplify subordinate points; the user can of course go to these illustrative cards, via links from within the main sequence, but they are located beyond the last card of that sequence. The user can step through the sequence using standard arrow screen buttons, or the arrow keys. Users are at no time forced to follow this sequence.
- A **network** of hypermedia links, for exploring individual concepts and their connections. The network is designed to provide easy access to related ideas at all points. It has been found necessary to **qualify some of the links**, early in the linear sequence, with a dialog box outlining the knowledge needed to understand what lies at the end of the link. This gives the student the opportunity to make an informed decision about whether or not to traverse that link.
- A graphical **'active map'**, or browser, (Figure 1) is accessible from any location. This provides a spatial representation of the nodes, a simplified view of their links, a current position indicator, and an indication of cards already visited. It also serves as a readily-available access mechanism, giving the user an immediate means of going to any card (point and click), as well as depicting semantic relationships. The map selectively emphasises a **hierarchical structure** within the network, by highlighting the relevant links. This shows the relationships between objects in HyperCard. Alternative hierarchical structures could have been depicted, for example highlighting the relationships between properties. A more sophisticated system might make alternative maps available.
- **Sub-sequences** of logically related cards within the network. These reflect an element of **modularity**. They are indicated on the map by overlapping the images of those cards; and on the cards themselves by arrows at the lower edge of the text field, indicating adjacent related cards.
- Local **loops**. These take the form of pop-up text fields, providing local explanation without risking navigational disorientation; and self-contained simulations and exercises, not offering further links.

4. Monitoring Interaction

To be effective and convenient for use in the process of evaluating a system, a monitor should:

- record events and actions at an appropriate grain of analysis. The generation of copious quantities of low level information (e.g. cursor coordinates and pixel values [10]) may give the appearance of capturing a comprehensive record of interaction, but that information is not useful if it cannot be analysed and interpreted.
- be unobtrusive, both in its physical presence, and its effects upon interaction (e.g. it should not noticeably slow down system response).

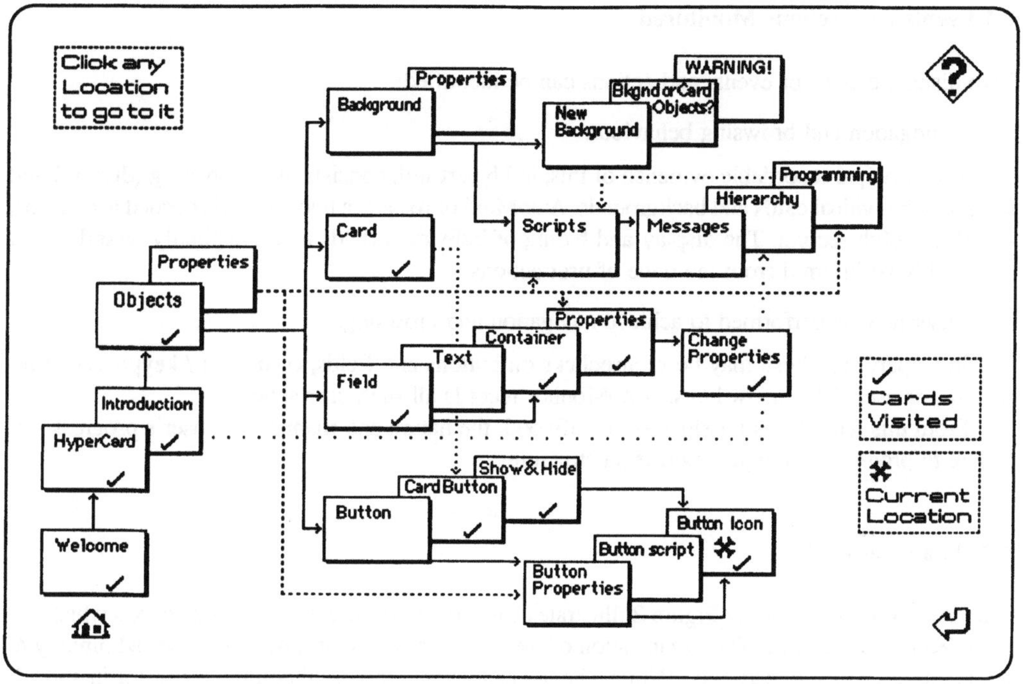

Figure 1. The 'HyperCard Basic Concepts' browser

- present its output in a convenient form, suitable for analysis.
- be easy to operate.

AutoMonitor [7] is a tool for monitoring the use of HyperCard software, which meets the above criteria. It comprises a set of modifications to the stack to be monitored. The HyperTalk script of the stack, and of its component objects (buttons and fields), is rewritten in such a way that a monitor record will be created by the objects themselves during interaction. This record is built up in a global variable, so that its creation does not interfere noticeably with the speed of system response; it is transferred to a text field at regular intervals 'on idle' (when the system is not busy).

All the modifications necessary to create an AutoMonitor are performed automatically by an installer stack, StackMonitor, which can be used to convert almost any HyperCard stack. A user interface for the monitor is created, which provides facilities for inspecting the record; recording a user name; deleting the record; writing the record to an external text file; and opening that file in a Macintosh application. An XFCN resource is added to the stack to extend HyperCard's rather limited file-handling capabilities.

AutoMonitor has been further developed since the version described in [8], to allow the direct transfer of the interaction record to a spreadsheet or database for analysis, and to provide extra facilities. Some choice of which actions are to be monitored is now also made available, at the time of conversion.

4.1 Events and Actions Monitored

Two distinct classes of events and actions can be identified:

• navigation and browsing behaviour.

The principal recordable evidence of this, in HyperCard, consists of the opening (display) and closing of individual cards and backgrounds. AutoMonitor records a trace of cards opened and closed, timed to 1/60th second. The display and hiding of individual fields is not explicitly recorded, but can readily be inferred from the trace of user actions.

• user actions performed to achieve navigation and browsing.

In HyperCard, these may be mouseclicks on buttons and fields, command / keypress combinations, or use of the arrow keys. AutoMonitor records all such user actions.

From this record it is possible to identify both the nature and manner of a user's progress - or failure to progress - though hypermedia structures.

4.2 Data generated

The brief example shown in Figure 2 illustrates some of the different events and actions which are recorded by the monitor. The organisation of the record is such that it may be exported directly to a text editor or to a spreadsheet. [Note: The tab character is the usual column separator in spreadsheets; but, inconveniently, HyperCard will not store tabs in its text fields. AutoMonitor solves this problem in the following way: it stores and displays its records in a text field, using the umlaut character as a column separator. Global substitution of tab for umlaut must therefore be performed before opening AutoMonitor output files in a spreadsheet. This substitution will be performed automatically by AutoMonitor, if the shiftkey is held down while clicking on the File Monitor Text button.]

Together, these events and actions provide the essential information for retrospective analysis both of navigation and of the user actions by which it is achieved. In the example shown in Figure 2, the mouse action recorded is the release of the mouse button (mouseUp). This is the user action by which most events are triggered. MouseDown is sometimes also used, for example for the display of pop-up fields and pop-up menus. MouseDown can also be recorded by AutoMonitor, if required.

Other user actions are recorded as discrete events: the choosing of menu items from pull-down menus; the choosing of menu items by command / keyPress short-cuts; navigation by means of the arrow keys. In Figure 2, the use is shown of each of these three means to invoke the 'go to last card' command.

4.3 Identifying the Component Objects in a Stack

StackMonitor provides a facility ('List Objects...') for listing the names of every background, card, field and button in a stack. This can facilitate the both the tailoring of object names within a stack, and the subsequent interpretation of actions upon those objects. The format of the object list is compatible with the interaction record format. It may be used:

• for inspecting existing object names

• to check for missing or duplicated names

A Small Sample of an AutoMonitor Interaction Record

Sample Record:

>>>>>>> User name entered as "Miles Macleod"<<<<<<<
>>>>>>> 4:49:49 pm,Tue, Jan 16, 1990 <<<<<<<

218361	^	mouseUp	card button "next"			
218375				opened	basic_unit	bg 2
219411	^	mouseUp	card button "showAboutBrowsing"			
220042	^	mouseUp	card field "aboutBrowsing"			
220207	^	mouseUp	bkgnd button "MAP"			
220219				opened	map	bg mapBg
220698	^	mouseUp	card button "map.field_demo"			
220707				opened	field_demo	bg 2
221998	^	mouseUp	card button "Change the field..."			
221999	*	(do)menu	tool 3			
222022	*	(do)menu	menu item Field Info...			
222150	*	(do)menu	tool 1			
223398	^	mouseUp	bkgnd button "MAP"			
223412				opened	map	bg mapBg
224688	A<	kPress	left Arrow			
224703				opened	about_bgs	bg 2
225981	©	cmd/kPress	menu item Next			

Organization of columns:

[Note: In this figure, column 1 is overlapped with columns 2 to 5]

Experimental details..
1____

Time.... *User Actions*.. *System Actions*..............................
2_______ 3__ 4________ 5______________________________ 6______ 7_________ 8_______

Key to columns:

Column 1 is reserved for subject, date and stack details
Column 2 records time in units of 1/60th second. Elapsed time from the start, and the duration of each event, can be calculated very easily within a spreadsheet
Column 3 shows symbols representing different user actions. These are for ease of visual inspection of the record, and for search
Column 4 identifies the user action
Column 5 names the object acted upon
Column 6 lists system actions (opening and / or closing of cards)
Column 7 names the card
Column 8 names its background

Figure 2. The 'go to last card' command

• in the creation of an index of objects in a given stack, for use in the semi-automated analysis of interaction records from that stack.

5. Approaches to the analysis of interaction data

The chosen grain of the interaction record - at the level of actions upon discrete objects - allows even non-automated analysis of the data to yield useful insights into the use of a hypermedia system. A typical twenty minute session of studying 'HyperCard Basic Concepts' (when the subject has been given a learning task, in a normal educational computer laboratory setting, with the prospect of subsequently being tested on knowledge acquired) generates between 150 and 300 lines of record.

The format of the interaction record has been designed for a dual purpose:

• to be comprehensible via visual inspection;

• to be analysable via a spreadsheet.

Visual inspection gives a general picture of a subject's total activity, indicated by the length of the record. Chosen actions can be easily identified by the action symbols recorded in column 3 of the record. More detailed inspection enables the identification of which navigation structures and guidance facilities have been used as the interaction progresses, both from the sequence of cards visited and from the buttons clicked. In this instance, linear navigation employs the 'Next' and 'Prev' buttons (or arrow keys or menu choices); use of the map employs the 'MAP' button; access to local loop structures is via specifically named buttons; exploration of the network of links employs differently named embedded text buttons.

It is important to note that such analyses can be greatly helped or hindered by the underlying **method** for naming stack objects. For example, in 'Basic Concepts', buttons which provide an opportunity for a non-linear to jump to another card are given the prefix "go_"; those which display a field are prefixed "show_". These names are not displayed to the user. They are employed simply for the purpose of assisting the retrospective identification of different navigation actions.

5.1 Analysis via a spreadsheet and statistics package

Semi-automated analysis of interaction records can yield statistical data about the behaviour of learners in terms of user actions and navigation actions; it also enables the study of learner behaviour in terms of the specific **categories of information content** explored, and of specific behaviour within different content areas. It is possible to extract information about individual learners, and about groups of learners, concerning use of the alternative means of achieving navigation; relative use of different navigation structures; times between jumps; total times, number of visits, and nature of activities within different information content areas, and for each card; degree of backtracking; and how these factors may change as an interaction session progresses. Not to be overlooked is the identification of cards NOT visited, and buttons not clicked upon: this requires comparison between the interaction record and the stack object list.

A set of EXCEL™ templates and macros for analysing AutoMonitor output has been developed by Dr Diana Kornbrot, of Hatfield Polytechnic. At present these are tailored for the analysis of monitor output from 'HyperCard Basic Concepts'. Their use is reported by Kornbrot and Macleod [6]. Such templates have development potential for more general use.

This approach to analysis requires the substitution of numerical codes, which are easily manipulated within a spreadsheet, for the alphanumeric names of objects, object classes, and system and user actions, which enable the human interpretation of the interaction record. Its development comprised the following steps:

A. At a conceptual level:

A.1 Identification of classes of

- user actions

- here, the classes used were those recorded by StackMonitor (e.g. clicks on screen buttons; menu choices; key-presses).

- navigation actions

- identifiable via the classes of navigation object acted upon (e.g. screen buttons 'Next' and 'Prev', menu item 'Go Next' and 'Go Prev', and keyboard arrowkeys Left and Right, are all associated with linear navigation).

- information content of cards

- derived from a content analysis of the hypermedia learning system being monitored.

A.2 Allocation of a code number to each of these classes.

A.3 Definition of 'events', within which identifiable actions may occur. In the example analysis, the principal event is a 'card visit', defined as the period for which an individual card is displayed to the user. More complex event definitions are possible. Events have features whose values can be used as independent variables (e.g. card i.d.; card information content category i.d.) or as dependent variables (e.g. elapsed time; actions on objects during the event).

B. Implementation:

B.1 Construction of spreadsheet templates to manipulate the coded information.

B.2 Importing into the first template a comprehensive listing of component objects (backgrounds, cards, buttons and fields) of the HyperCard system being studied. Such listings are generated by StackMonitor.

B.3 Manual assignment, in the first template, of the appropriate code number to each action and object in the list.

C. The use of the templates in the analysis of experimental data:

C.1 The interaction record for an individual subject's learning session, automatically captured and formatted by the monitor, is copied into the first template.

C.2 Formulae in the template assign the appropriate codes for the specific instances of navigation actions, grouped by card-visit events. Figure 3 shows part of the first template at this stage of data analysis.

C.3 The coded output from the first template is then transferred to subsequent templates which enable statistical analysis and graphical presentation of results both for individual subjects and for groups of subjects.

An example graphical representation of frequency of actions upon different navigation objects, performed by subjects in the study reported by Kornbrot and MacLeod [6], is shown in Figure 4. The analysis employed in that study differed in some respects from the theoretical description of navigation structures given in Sections 2 and 3 (above). Specifically, a major element of the analysis was concerned with identifying navigation in terms of the content areas explored (those results are not illustrated here); secondly, it concentrated on the use of the different classes of screen button - which constituted the bulk of navigation and browsing actions employed by subjects in the study -

Coded Data							Raw Data							
sub	time	act	obj	sfo	card	bgnd	>>>>>>>> User name entered as "haik"<<<<<<<<							
							>>>>>>>> 5:54:10 pm, Tue, Jan 16, 1990 <<<<<<<<							
6	0.00				0	0		68660	^	mouseUp	card button "Monitor"			
6	5.82	1	5		0	0		69009	^	mouseUp	card button "Next"			
6	5.88			1	33	3		69013				closed	Welcome	bg IntroBG
6	6.37			2	7	1		69042				opened	basic_unit	bg Background 2
6	8.93	1	4		7	1		69196	^	mouseUp	bkgnd button "MAP"			
6	9.02			1	7	1		69201				closed	basic_unit	bg Background 2
6	17.28	1	8		7	1		69697	^	mouseUp	card button "go_programming"			
6	17.68			1	23	4		69721				closed	map	bg mapBg
6	18.22			2	6	1		69753				opened	about_object_hierarchy	bg Background 2
6	28.57	1	4		6	1		70374	^	mouseUp	bkgnd button "MAP"			
6	28.63			1	6	1		70378				closed	about_object_hierarchy	bg Background 2
6	44.02	1	8		6	1		71301	^	mouseUp	card button "go_how_works"			
6	44.07			1	23	4		71304				closed	map	bg mapBg
6	44.55			2	19	1		71333				opened	how_does_it_work?	bg Background 2
6	49.55	1	4		19	1		71633	^	mouseUp	bkgnd button "MAP"			
6	49.63			1	19	1		71638				closed	how_does_it_work?	bg Background 2
6	53.18	1	8		19	1		71851	^	mouseUp	card button "go_card_buttons"			
6	53.22			1	23	4		71853				closed	map	bg mapBg
6	53.87			2	3	1		71892				opened	about_card_buttons	bg Background 2
6	71.10	1	9		3	1		72926	^	mouseUp	card button "about"			
6	86.28	1	9		3	1		73837	^	mouseUp	card button "about"			
6	96.83	1	9		3	1		74470	^	mouseUp	card button "show_card_props"			
6	97.43	2	13		3	1		74506	*	(do)menu	menu item Card Info...			
6	112.32	1	0		3	1		75399	^	mouseUp	bkgnd field "BgField"			
6	116.65	1	9		3	1		75659	^	mouseUp	card button "about"			

Stage 1 of Data Analysis

	Codes from StackMonitor object list					
	type	action	object index	clo/op	card name	background
1	1	mouseUp	bkgnd button "Go Home"	closed	about_buttons	bg Background 2
2	2	(do)menu	bkgnd button "goRecent"	opened	about_cards	bg Bg2
3	3	command/keypress	bkgnd button "Go_Basic_Concepts"		about_card_buttons	bg IntroBG
4	4	keyPress	bkgnd button "Map"		about_fields	bg mapBg
5	5		bkgnd button "Next"		about_messages	bg bkgnd id 7827
6	6		bkgnd button "Prev"		about_object_hierarchy	
7	7		bkgnd button "Return"		basic_unit	
8			bkgnd field "BgField"		bg_intro	
9			bkgnd field "dateField"		bg_properties	
10			bkgnd field "map coords"		button_info1 simln	
11			bkgnd field "numberfield"		button_info2 simln	
12			bkgnd field id 10		button_script simln	
13			bkgnd field id 20		by_script_only	
14			bkgnd field id 3		card_or_bg?	
15	9		card button "about"		create_new_fields	
16	11		card button "Change the field..."		field_as_container	
17	12		card button "Clear Monitor Field..."		field_demo	
18			card button "cover"		field_text	
19	11		card button "currentloc"		how_does_it_work?	
20	12		card button "File Monitor Text..."		HyperCard_objects	
21	8		card button "Go Home"		icon_choice simln	
22	8		card button "goRecent"		icon_choice2 simln	
23	8		card button "gotoIcon"		map	
24	8		card button "go_about_buttons"		new_bg!	
25	8		card button "go_about_cards"		not_contiguous	

Stage 1 of Data Analysis [continued]

Figure 3. First template of data analysis

and no differentiation was made between the use of the various menu and keyboard navigation commands provided generically by HyperCard. Sub-sequences were not explicitly identified (these correlate closely to the information content categories); and no attempt was made to relate navigation behaviour to the hierarchical structures represented to the user. However, the study does clearly illustrate the kind of information which can be extracted using the monitoring and analysis tools described in this paper.

5.2 A contextual caveat

Statistical data may by its nature convey an impression of scientific rigour, but it must always be considered with circumspection. In investigating the use of hypermedia systems for learning, the context in which learning takes place, and the subjective views of the learner, are ignored at the investigator's peril. Data derived from monitoring is not a substitute for the subjective views and comments of the user [although it is worth noting that data about objects NOT interacted with may identify aspects of the system about which the user remains unintentionally ignorant]. However, when studied together with a verbal protocol, the analysis of an interaction record of task performance - and its relationship to knowledge acquisition in a specific learning context - can provide a revealing picture of the use of a hypermedia system, unobtainable by other means.

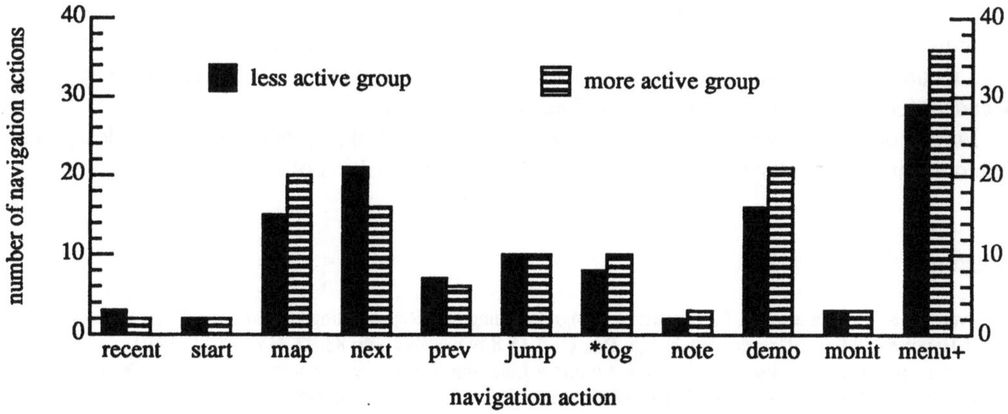

Mean number of different kinds of navigation action for "less" and "more" active students

Key :

Mouseclicks on screen buttons, related to use of

(1) Navigational structures: *next* = forward along linear sequence; *prev* = backward linear; *jump* = hypermedia network; **tog* = local loop;

(2) Guidance and support facilities: *map* = navigation via browser; *recent* = backtracking;

(3) General interaction features: *demo* = interaction with learning material within nodes; *start* = start button; *monit* = monitor user interface.

Navigation actions other than mouseclicks: -

menu+ = navigation via generic HyperCard facilities: menu choices, command/keypress, arrowkeys, use of HyperCard 'Recent' screen (nature of navigation here not categorised).

Figure 4. Frequency of actions upon different navigation objects

6. WhiteBoard: a facility for recording written comments

In addition to the recording of verbal protocols, it can also be helpful in evaluating a hypermedia system to have constantly available - as an integral part of that system - some convenient long-term means of recording and collating users' written comments about aspects of its design and usability; and, importantly, of being able to locate those comments easily for future reference. WhiteBoard is a facility, implemented in HyperCard, for storing, displaying, searching, and making hard copy of written comments, and also for appending comments from other WhiteBoards. It provides online help, a direct manipulation author index, and quick and easy direct manipulation search facilities, which can locate all instances of any word clicked upon.

WhiteBoard can be installed (independently of AutoMonitor) in any HyperCard stack, by the StackMonitor utility. When it is installed, a 'comment' button is added to each background of the target stack. This takes the user to the WhiteBoard card, and invites a comment. Comments are visible to all users, but may be deleted only with a password, and cannot be retrospectively modified, thus preserving intact a history of comments made by multiple users of a given stack.

7. Potential for extension of AutoMonitor

AutoMonitor is implemented mainly in HyperTalk, in HyperCard 1.2. This means that it is a relatively simple matter for any HyperCard programmer to tailor the interaction record generated, to suit individual experimental requirements. This may involve either trimming down the classes of event recorded; or extending the record to include actions where HyperCard itself may have been extended, for example the use of non-standard pop-up menus.

Further development of the system is proposed in HyperCard 2.0, together with the design and development of generalisable sets of EXCEL templates for analysis of AutoMonitor output.

Literature

1. Evensen, S. and Rheinfrank, J.: Towards a Design Language for Representing Hypermedia Cues; in Proceedings of Hypertext '89 Conference, Pittsburgh, PA, USA (5-8 November), pp 83-92, NY, ACM, 1989.
2. Hammond, N. and Allinson, L.: Travels Around a Learning Support Environment: Rambling, Orienteering or Touring? in Proceedings of CHI '88 Conference, pp 269-273, NY, ACM, 1988.
3. Hammond, N. and Allinson, L.: Extending Hypertext for Learning: An Investigation of Access and Guidance Tools; in Sutcliffe, A. and Macaulay, L. (Eds) People and Computers V (Proceedings of HCI'89 Conf, Nottingham, 5-8 September), pp 293-304 , Cambridge, CUP, 1989.
4. Halasz, F., Moran, T.P. and Trigg, R.H.: Notecards in a Nutshell; in Proceedings of CHI+GI Conference, pp 45-52, NY, ACM, 1987.
5. Jonassen , D.H.: Semantic Network Elicitation: Tools for Structuring Hypertext. In Hypertext: State of the Art, R. McAleese and C. Green (Eds), pp 142-153, Oxford, UK, Intellect, 1990.
6. Kornbrot, D.E. and Macleod, M.: Monitoring and Analysis of Hypermedia Navigation. to be published in the Proceedings of INTERACT '90, The Third IFIP Conference on HCI (Cambridge, UK, 27-31 August), Amsterdam, Elsevier (North-Holland), 1990.
7. Macleod, M.: AutoMonitor and StackMonitor (Macintosh HyperCard software tools). Distribution by HISC, Instructional Technology Division, University of Colorado at Denver, Colorado 80204, USA, 1990
8. Macleod, M.: Direct Manipulation Prototype User Interface Monitoring; in Sutcliffe, A. and Macaulay, L. (Eds) People and Computers V (Proc HCI'89 Conf, Nottingham, 5-8 September), pp 395-408, Cambridge, CUP, 1989.
9. Macleod, M.: HyperCard Basic Concepts (Macintosh HyperCard software). Distribution by HISC, Instructional Technology Division, University of Colorado at Denver, Colorado 80204, USA, 1990.

10. Maguire, M. and Sweeney, M.: System Monitoring: Garbage Generator or Basis for a Comprehensive Evaluation System?; in Sutcliffe, A. and Macaulay, L. (Eds) People and Computers V (Proceedings of HCI'89 Conf, Nottingham, 5-8 September), pp 375-394, Cambridge, CUP, 1989.
11. Marshall, C.C. and Irish, P.M.: Guided Tours and On-Line Presentations: How Authors Make Existing Hypertext Intelligible for Readers; in Proceedings of Hypertext '89 Conference, Pittsburgh, PA, USA 5-8 November, pp 15-26, NY, ACM, 1989.
12. Mayes, T., Kibby, M.R. and Anderson, A.: Signposts for Conceptual Orientation: Some Requirements for Learning from Hypertext. In Hypertext: State of the Art, R. McAleese and C. Green (Eds), pp 121-129 Oxford, UK, Intellect, 1990.
13. Nicol, A.: Interface Design for Hyperdata: Models, Maps and Cues. In Proceedings of the Human Factors Society - 32nd annual meeting, pp 308-312, 1988.
14. Nielsen, J. and Lyngbæk,U.: Two Field Studies of Hypertext Usability; in Proceedings of Hypertext II Conference, York, UK, 28-30 June, 1989.
15. Simpson, A. and McKnight, C.: Navigation in Hypertext: Structural Cues and Mental Maps; in Proceedings of Hypertext II Conference, York, UK, 28-30 June, 1989.
16. Wright, P.: Issues of Content and Presentation in Document Design; in Helander, M. (Ed.) Handbook of Human-Computer Interaction, pp 629-653, Amsterdam, Elsevier (North-Holland), 1988.
17. Wright, P. and Lickorish, A.: An Empirical Comparison of Two Navigation Systems for Two Hypertexts. In Proceedings of Hypertext II Conference, York, UK, 28-30 June, 1989.
18. Wright, P. and Lickorish, A.: The Influence of Discourse Structure on Display and Navigation in Hypertexts; in Holt, P. and Williamson, N. (Eds), Computers and Writing, pp 90-124, Norwood, NJ, Ablex, 1989.

Hypermedia and Pre-service Teacher Education: Some Possibilities in Analogy with Didactics

António Moreira

Universidade de Aveiro, Portugal

Abstract: Being a novelty, especially in the field of teacher-training, hypermedia appears to be a promising tool for bringing together the several fields of knowledge any foreign language teacher needs to manipulate in order to make didactic decisions. In the Portuguese context, where opportunities for facing real teaching situations are confined to the teacher-training year, hypermedia products would seem to be of great value. This paper will introduce this topic of teacher-training through hypermedia and suggest areas in which such databases could be put to good use.

1. Introduction

I would like to introduce this paper by making it clear that I am not a hypermedia expert. Being in the field of foreign language didactics, namely the didactics of the English language, and being interested in teacher supervision, hypermedia products first came to my attention as a mere computer curiosity. Their potential only became apparent, both for learning and for research on learning, at least within the scope of my most immediate interests, when I became involved, together with two other university colleagues, in the development of a very simple Hypercard programme for the teaching of two English didactics concepts — the concept of *realia* and the concept of *authentic material*, into which I am not going to go at the moment —, and to which we gave the name of AMREPS — Authentic Material, Realia and "Escola Paralela" — (Alarcão, Moreira & Oliveira, 1989).

This came about because of the recurring verification that pre-teacher students at pre-service teacher education courses at the University of Aveiro consistently confused both concepts, as we explain elsewhere (Alarcão & Moreira, 1989). This application, to which StackMonitor (Macleod, 1989) was coupled is still being improved and will be applied during the course of this academic year. Pilot trial runs of the programme have so far been extremely interesting and promising.

2. Pre-service teacher education and didactics

Pre-service teacher education as an established educational practice in teacher-training colleges and universities has been, to a great extent and particularly in Portugal, either what Stones (1984) called *sitting with Nellie* or a hotch-potch of different approaches and attitudes, usually as numerous as the number of people actually involved in accompanying or supervising the novice teacher in his/her first attempt at getting an official qualification as a fully fledged teacher. I nevertheless acknowledge that there have been, and still are, a great deal of truly concerned supervisors who, by means of their constructivist attitudes towards teacher-supervision have tried to change this state of affairs, namely by approaching the teaching of didactics in a more serious and scientific way (Silva, 1981; Cachapuz, 1985; Thomaz, 1986).

In previous years — the 1960s and 1970s, especially — it was still commonplace to talk of didactics as of an art or even a collection of recipes. This gave rise to a certain amount of confusion which identified didactics with other disciplines, the so called applied sciences, and which devoted themselves to offering a few general hints about teaching procedures to the prospective teaching professional. The Anglo-Saxon tradition — which has survived up until now and, in a few cases, has even been adopted among us — gives didactics a pejorative colouring, giving preference to the designation of teaching methodology or methods of teaching. In fact the designation of didactics is practically non existent in the jargon of teacher-trainers in England.

This state of affairs is owed to the traditional and even somewhat desired dependence of didactics *vis à vis* some sciences which do not seem to want to let go of a branch which is crying out for emancipation. It is also owed to a certain image of "patchwork of knowledge" which, up until very recently, didactics gave the impression of advocating. It is even owed to the fact that no one seems to want to attribute to didactics the status of a discipline with its own epistemological autonomy, which it now struggles to make prevail, especially in relation to technological sciences. Among the few very honorable exceptions (although not overtly stated) to this state of affairs we count cognitive psychology — especially in its focus on artificial intelligence — and the new technologies of information from which artificial intelligence cannot be separated.

The will to impose itself as a science, together with the studies which were undertaken, especially after the 1970s, within the field of didactics, has given it the scope of independence which was begun at that time. This can be seen echoed abroad by the independence which didactics is conquering, and also by those who advocated this emancipation, of whom Besse (1987) and Galisson (1986) are just two of the most recent. This can also be seen in Portugal where a few authors (Alarcão, 1989; Andrade & Sá, 1989) have highlighted the autonomy of the field of didactics.

3. Didactics and hypermedia — the analogy

Didactics as a field of study, which was criticised for not being well-strucutured and thus non-scientific, imposes itself for being different. Didactics is a young science and as such adapted to its time: it bases itself on ecleticism, flexibility, non-structuredness and reflexive thinking.

Evolution towards autonomy has thus happened naturally. It might be because of the existence of a non-saturated academic area; it might be because of the interest which didactics congregates in the issues it studies. One thing is for sure though: in spite of the disdain of some, didactics has conquered the status of a curricular area with a firm foundation in teacher-training, and particularly in Portugal.

But what makes didactics interesting? Basically the duality of its focus. On the one hand, its interdisciplinary and holistic character; on the other hand, its stratified and selective dynamics. It is in these two aspects that the analogy of didactics with hypermedia finds its foundation, and also why I think hypermedia may be of crucial value for its even more definite affirmation. Generally speaking hypermedia consists of any structure of information storage which allows for its use in a non-sequential, i.e, non-oriented/pre-set way. Thus a specific set of electronically related contents could be presented (although I would prefer the term consulted) as a composition of several media (sound, text, pictures). The advantage of these models of information processing lies in the premise that they do not impose a learning model due to their lack of pre-packaged linearity. Furthermore they allow for the co-presence of different information presentation formats in the same information system. This facilitates the individualised association of ideas at different levels of analysis, taking at the same time advantage of the intuitive freedom of the user.

We could thus say, maintaining the analogy, that didactics is a hyperscience. And it is such because it is encyclopaedic — it gets its information from a whole array of different sciences without pretending to master them in all their complexity and specificity. It is also a non-sequential/"non-structured" science because it does not follow pre-determined paths in its methodology. It is, as a consequence of this, a selective science: it selects the information to be treated; it selects the order in which this information is to be treated; it selects the depth/level at which this treatment is to be set. It is, to use Spiro's terminology (Spiro, 1987), an ill-structured domain.

The analogy which I have been trying to establish should not nevertheless be completely devoid of a few cautionary words. As in hypermedia the didactician can easily get himself lost in the hyperspace of the information which surrounds him. You can be in a library, a number of books surrounding you, good books at that — one on linguistics, another on psychology, still another on teaching techniques and one on error analysis; still a few cassettes, some flash-cards, a dictionary, etc. Any one exemplar of these media is, considered in isolation (or even in bulk), discrete in the information it conveys. Nothing connects one item to the other except for the man-made abstraction which ascribes it the characteristic of being possibly useful in a teaching situation, either via reference or direct application. All of them are inequivocally information "databases". Their didactic use has nevertheless to be filtered by the teacher — and thus use him/her as a didactical interface — who Carrilho Ribeiro defines as someone whose role

> "consists in choosing from an enormous variety of alternatives, the assumptions about values, scientific principles and technical procedures, and in being apt to justify his decisions, according to the actual circumstances of teaching at the when and where in which he practises his teaching duties.
>
> If that is so, the professional mission of the teacher can be interpreted as the creation of a way of thinking, of analysing and of dealing with the teaching/learning process which is flexible and differentiated." (Carrilho Ribeiro,1989: 82-3) - [my translation].

4. Chain and choice as didactical principles for hypermedia

This filtering of information to which I have referred above will thus function along two different vectors: one which is predominantly horizontal (the chain vector), and another which is predominantly differential (the choice vector). The first one has to do with the educational/contextual dimension of the didactic treatment of a pedagogical issue, and here we find the "multi-level-knowledge-database" dimension of hypermedia for learning; the second one has to do with the depth of this same treatment, only this time context gives way to content, and here we find the interpenetration of didactic treatment and hypermedia flexibility.

A tentative representation of this type of didactic filtering activity would be graphically displayed as something like this:

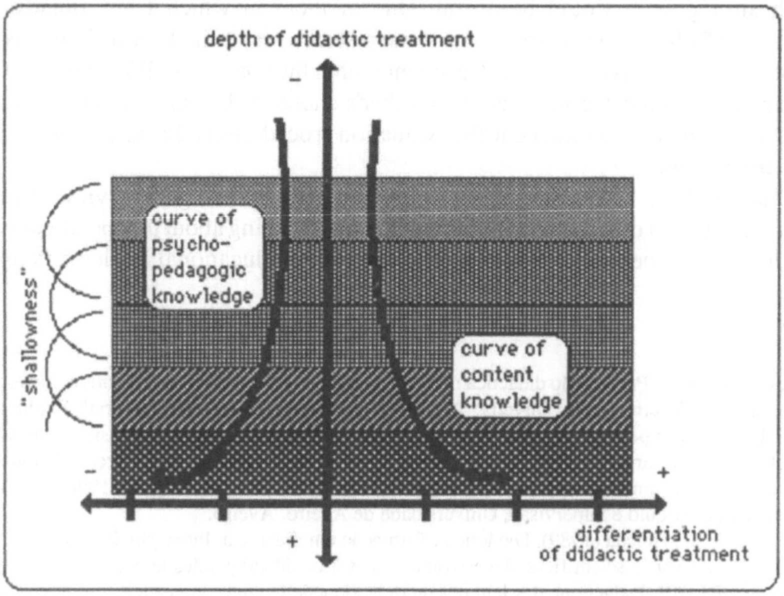

Relationship between depth and differentiation of information treatment from the perspective of didactics

This tries to illustrate or rather clarify the aspects under which didactic treatment of specific information which – although containing in itself the possibility of an infinite variety of paths and links within the subsidiary knowledge environments – should always be what we would like to call *shallow*, not in the sense of being superficial, but rather in the sense of being manageable, that is, within an educationally safe "breathing" range. For this purpose, and according to the depth at which you are working, you can either wear a "snorkel" or a complete "aqualung" device. The issue is that what is absolutely necessary is to avoid less useful associations, the so called junk-links. In this perspective, the higher the age of the target group, the more important the full grasp of content will become. Conversely, the lower the age level of the target group, the more important psychopedagogical knowledge will be.

5. Concluding remarks

This interaction of vectors is extremely simplified if monitored by hypermedia. Where acquaintance with subtly different aspects of teaching/learning interaction situations can be almost simultaneously illustrated, confronted, diagnosed and differentiated – which is something we can only gain with years and years of experience – a teacher-to-be will possibly be much better prepared to face his/

her pupils in the teacher-training year if this experience were to be antecipated by means of specially prepared hypermedia courseware.

To conclude this presentation I would like to suggest that there are important areas in teaching where such an approach would be useful. One of them in which I am already personally committed, and of which I expect to present some research results in the near future, is concerned with error identification, diagnosis and treatment within the context of EFL teaching. Other areas might include the relationship between the teacher's choice of language and its adequacy to the particular classroom event; another one the evaluation procedures and aims versus the test formats for its implementation.

I hope this paper will start a discussion which will permit a less general view of the parallel I tried to convey between didactics and hypermedia, thus bringing about the specification of details which might give this perspective a sound foundation for educational implementation.

Literature

1. Alarcão, Isabel (1989). Preparação didáctica num enquadramento formativo-investigativo. Inovação, 2, 31-36.
2. Alarcão, Isabel, Moreira, A., & Oliveira, A. (1989). AMREPS - Authentic Material, Realia and "Escola Paralela", Programa Hypercard para ensino de conceitos de Didáctica do Inglês, Universidade de Aveiro, Aveiro.
3. Alarcão, Isabel & Moreira, A. (1989). A construção do conhecimento a partir da interacção aluno/texto didáctico ~ desenvolvimento de um programa de computador. In Tavares J. & Moreira, A. (eds) (1990), Desenvolvimento, Aprendizagem, Currículo e Supervisão, Universidade de Aveiro, Aveiro.
4. Andrade, Ana & Sá, Helena (1989). Didáctica e formação em didáctica. Inovação, 2, 133-143.
5. Besse, H., (1987). Sur la scientificité des savoirs relatifs à la didactique des langues secondes et étrangères, Colloque du CREDIF: Didactique des langues ou didactiquede langue? Transversalités et spécificités, Paris, June, (typed document).
6. Cachapuz, A. F. (1985). Modelos de formação inicial de professores (Licenciaturas do Ramo Educacional e em Ensino): Natureza e funcionamento, O Jornal da Educação, 87, Nov./Dec., 26-28.
7. Carrilho Ribeiro, A. (1989). Formar Professores, Texto Editora.
8. Galisson, R. et al. (1982). D'autres voies pour la didactique des langues étrangères. Paris, Hatier/CREDIF.
9. Galisson, R. (1986). Éloge de la didactologie/didactique des langues et des cultures (maternelles et étrangères), D/DLC, Études de Linguistique Appliqué, 64, 39-54.
10. MacLeod, M. (1989). StackMonitor, Macintosh Hypercard Software. School of Information Sciences, Hatfield Polytechnic, Hatfield, UK.
11. Silva, Isabel (1981). Psychopedagogy and foreign language teacher education: an investigation into the application of a psychosocial skill model of learning. Ph. D. Thesis. University of Liverpool, UK.
12. Spiro, R. J. et al. (1987). Knowledge acquisition for application: cognitive flexibility and transfer in complex content domains. Technical Report 409. Center for the Study of Reading. University of Illinois at Urbana-Champaign.
13. Stones, E. (1984). Supervision in Teacher Education, a Counselling and Pedagogical Approach, Methuen, London.
14. Thomaz, Marília (1986). Towards a constructivist model for science teacher education. Ph. D. Thesis. University of Surrey, UK.
15. Wallin, Erik (1988). Notes on didactics as a field of research. Scandinavian Journal of Educational Research, 32, 1.

Design Considerations in Hypermedia Tutorials

Preben Späth

Orfeus, Graham Bellsvej 1A, DK-8200 Aarhus N, Denmark

Abstract: In this paper the main interest is to look at some new pedagogical possibilities in the hypertext/hypermedia environment. My background is several years of teaching without the computer, and 3 years with this new instrument in language instruction. Practice of different CAL-software systems forms the basis of the following questions and suggestions related to utilizing hypertext/hypermedia specifically in foreign language instruction at the secondary level. The aim is to discuss design considerations to be considered in the making of hypermedia tutorials.

Keywords: CAL, hypertext, hypermedia, pedagogy and software, design considerations, hypermedia tutorials.

1. Hypermedia as Instructional Tools

1.1 Hypermedia and Pedagogy

If we see hypermedia as tools for education we have to consider what they can bring to pedagogy that would not otherwise be there. In other words we should ask the famous question 'What can only computers do?'

Some characteristics specific to the computer as a hypermedia tool are:

— immense storage of information,
— quick access to the information,
— different kinds of information, including information residing on various media.

What normal pedagogical instruments can be implemented with hypermedia?

— books (storage of information),
— transparencies and videos (display of information),
— music and speech (storage and display of sounds),
— teachers (storage and linkages of information, tasks etc),
— paper and pencil (expressing ideas, questions etc).

(Doland [3] gives interesting hints on hypermedia as instructional tools and discusses the many possibilities with these new media.) As a consequence of these new media we will have to reconsider *pedagogical issues in the new environment:*

The *questions* to be asked are:
— What are the pedagogical effects of the new approach?
— What are the effects on education as we know it today?

The outlines of a revised pedagogical theory might look like this:

Objective: The student acquires competence with respect to knowledge and attitude and some potential of communication. If the act of communication is meant to lead to recognition of some kind and to knowledge, it must necessarily depend on the *initiative of the student.*

The ultimate goal is therefore the acquisition of knowledge - including overview of the domain, the ability of selecting relevant bits of information etc. - but also the joy of accumulating knowledge which in itself is what we all want to promote in our students. Furthermore an important goal is to make the student understand the importance of the context of any kind of information.

Contents: As teachers/designers we must reconsider the domains to be presented to the student and their nature/structure as well as how to present these domains. When the objects of a domain are presented in a hypermedia system, it has the effect that the student understands that all phenomena are "existing objects" that have come to existence and that they may be regulated, changed, influenced etc by the individual. For example the student will experience that he/she can call "new" objects on to the screen by clicking the mouse - and on the other hand he/she will be able to make objects disappear. It is very important that the student realizes that the objects (i.e. the bits of information) have - normally - been put there by another human being. A very promising project is going on at the University Teaching Centre, Aberdeen, concerning how to structure domains/knowledge bases [4].

Methodology: The domain should be presented in such a way that the student recognizes that every object is part of one or more connections involving cause and effect, analogy, association, explanation etc.

The designer therefore has to consider the relationship between the domain and the prerequisites of the student. In other words the designer has to make sure that the student does in fact recognize the different kinds of connections (links). This might be acquired by labelling the connections individually so that the student shall know at any given point which kinds of connections are available and naturally where they lead to.

Psychologically speaking we may present the individual objects in such a way that the student working with the hypermedia experiences challenge, confrontation, association, specification, explanation, exploration etc. You could put this another way by asserting that concepts like surprise and mystery should be as natural ingredients of hypermedia as they are in normal education.

What is hypermedia all about, one might ask. A precise definition will not be given here, but from a pedagogical point of view you could say that what makes a student working with hypermedia special compared to traditional instruction is among other things that *the teacher is not there.* This can lead to the conclusion that we should look for qualities in the teacher which are positive and possible to transfer to this new medium. What pedagogical properties do we want to transfer to the computer?

Of course the ability of the teacher to be a "database" of information is easily transferred to the computer. But more specifically you could argue that the ability of the teacher to ask questions and even more important to give advice are properties which are crucial if we imagine the student working alone in a hypermedia environment. A possible conclusion here can be that the hypermedia system must be able to give advice but on the other hand probably not take total control of the student.

This issue has to do with the question whether we need a student model in hypermedia, i.e. a model that is able to guide the student in hyperspace or perhaps only a model that can give advice and nothing else, so that the student not only feels but actually is in control of things. We are here approaching the bridge between hypermedia and Intelligent Tutoring Systems - and why not cross that bridge? The discussion of the structure of the domain knowledge in ITS is equally crucial in a hypermedia environment - and certainly the concept of the student model is very important in both kinds of systems. A survey of connections between Artificial Intelligence, Psychology, Information Science, and Education is found in [2].

Another conclusion could be that the student - as when normal instruction takes place - should always have the opportunity of writing down notes and ideas while the instruction is in progress.

1.2 Advantages

As teachers we should approach this new medium with a critical mind.

This means we will have to find out the advantages which the hypermedia environment offers, but on the other hand we must be aware of the problems to be taken into consideration and hopefully solved in order to make hypertext/hypermedia a well suited instructional tool:

1) The student has *access to an immense collection of information* (text and/or graphics) that are structured hierarchically or non hierarchically, sequentially or non sequentially. The stress is here on the word 'immense' because one of the most interesting aspects of hypermedia/hypertext is that the contents of many normal books are available within the click of the mouse. Secondly there may be a big advantage in having access to a lot of informations structured in a non hierarchical and/or non sequential manner. One pedagogical advantage is the fact that it is for the student to decide which information should be displayed next - not for the author of the traditional text book. Consequently the student is in control and the "database of informations" is structured in accordance with the individual needs of the student.
2) *Different kinds of information on different media*: the informations may be text, images, questions to be answered, sound, animation etc. In normal instruction we have no access to this unique characteristic of hypermedia.
3) Individually the student decides which links to follow, i.e. *the student is in control* - not a passive object under the influence of a teacher. At least the student will hardly realize that he/she is being manipulated (cf. the previously mentioned student model discussion).
4) The student decides, so his/her *motivation* will determine what happens next. This is a crucial point in utilizing hypermedia as instructional tools, and this issue is also decisive in outlining the principles of a student model. The question is how much initiative will be left over for the student - and is building a student model actually cheating the student?
5) *Individualization:* Another consequence of the student being in control is that the hypermedia system so to speak adapts to his/her level. Every student will surely find his/her own way through hyperspace.
6) *Different views of the same concept*: This calls for critical reading in the sense that the hypermedia must allow for looking at different explanations of all or at least most of the concepts. For instance, in History the events may have conflicting explanations dependent on the view of the historian.

7) *The integration of several tools* in traditional instruction is another possibility. Theoretically one might look at a hypertext/hypermedia system as a means of manipulating and/or investigating an information database. But additional possibilities do exist: The student gets advice to visit the encyclopedia, later the student might want to check the meaning of some words in the dictionary or he/she is invited to look at a video sequence, listen to a speech or a piece of music etc. Furthermore the interactive aspect will allow the student of e.g. a foreign language to work through certain drills/lessons adapted to the level and needs of the individual student. Last - but not least - the student should always have access to writing his/her own notes or comments while working with the system.

1.3 Problems

However there are problems, not only with the money for the software and hardware which is not the issue of this paper although it certainly is an important aspect.

1) "*Getting lost in hyperspace*" is naturally a danger as the universe of information grows. Getting lost means:
   - not knowing where to go in order to find the information you are looking for,
   - not knowing which kind of information you are actually looking for. This may often be the case when the number of links to information becomes overwhelming.

2) *Lack of overview.* If the student does not know what information is available he/she cannot decide where to go next. The design problems in this respect are:

   - if too few link buttons are displayed the student does not have the many choices that constitute a hypertext document,
   - if too many link buttons are displayed the student might get confused.

3) *Active versus passive.* This aspect is concerned with the nature of the actual hypermedia/ hypertext system, in that some systems only allow the user to make choices with the mouse which guide the user around the hyperspace, while the structure of the hyperspace does not change itself. In that case the user is merely looking into a world of information without the possibility of changing it in any way. Other systems are able to adapt to the user so that the links are changed depending on the actual choices.

2. Hypermedia systems for IBM computers

In Denmark schools are equipped mainly with two kinds of computers none of which is MacIntosh. Most secondary schools and a growing number of primary schools have IBMs (PC and PS) or compatibles. In the other schools the computers are of a Danish brand called the Piccoline which uses the CCPM operating system, but it can be changed to run with MS-DOS. So in Denmark we will not - within the next couple of years at least - have access to MacIntosh in the schools although the Macs are spreading, too. For this reason we have at present to work with DOS programs, and in the hypertext/hypermedia world this means that we are working with two systems, GUIDE (which also runs on the MacIntosh) and LINKWAY (which has many features in common with Hypercard). Frkonja [6] compares the three hypermedia systems HyperCard, Guide, and Linkway.

3. Design features

Halasz [7] has identified some interface and design issues from existing research. The following features are concentrated on the pedagogical aspects.

3.1 Standard link buttons

It might be helpful for designers of hypermedia to cooperate with psychologists on investigating the number and characteristics of link buttons that can be displayed on a screen. This has to do with the optimum number of buttons to be present at one time without the student getting lost. The point is that one or two buttons will normally be too few if we want to exploit the advantages of hypermedia mentioned above. On the other hand too many will not be good either, so the question remains: Which number of buttons will be best?

Another aspect of this issue is concerned with the visualization of the link buttons. Together with psychologists we might be able to find out if some icons (metaphors) are better than others. Having found the best suitable icons we could stick to them so that the students will always know that a link button with specific characteristics will establish a certain type of linkage. Fairchild [5] deals with the exciting perspectives of automated icons.

3.2 Universal icons

Though some hypertext authors will protest I propose - for consideration at least - the idea of establishing a collection of universal icons. This does not mean that every author would have to use exactly and exclusively those icons. But if psychologists could point out the icons that are best suited to indicate certain links why shouldn't we listen to them? The traffic signs work all right in most countries.

The problem of common icons should of course be solved in two stages because on one hand we will surely find that several icons will depend on the local subculture whereas others will be universal.

3.3 Types of linkages

Although it does not seem appropriate to make a list of linkages to be used in all hyperdocuments it could be interesting to investigate the ideas of McAleese [9] about a limited number of linkages, including being, showing, having, including, using, causing and similarity. In this field we might consider the concept of universal icons that correspond to these types of linkages.

3.4 Overview (browsing)

Concerning overview it is very important from a pedagogical point of view that the student all the time knows:

where he or she is in the hyperspace,
what is waiting behind the buttons,
what will happen if he or she chooses to go backwards.

An idea to make sure that the student has an overview might be as follows:

1) to establish a certain number of fixed icons on the same spot of the screen where the student can get help, know how to get on, know how to get an overview of the whole hyperspace etc.
2) on the other hand the designer can - among the permanent buttons - offer a button which allows the student to see from the point where he or she is at the moment, all the links and nodes in the hyperdocument. As we all know there is always a centre, i.e. the link where the student is at the moment - and from this point one might give a kind of "surface knowledge" about the hierarchy of the links and nodes.

An interesting report on experiments with different navigation systems is found in Wright and Lickorish [12].

3.5 Metaphors

An important part of the interface are the metaphors that are used. A famous metaphor is the desktop - initiated by Apple. But there are many others, and as designers of hypertexts we should be well aware of the fact that from a psychological point of view it will make the work with hypertexts easier if the users - the students - can recognize metaphors or environments from real life (See Carroll et al. [1]). Naturally one important goal in making hypertexts is that working with them must be as easy as possible - so we have to seriously consider which metaphors to use. I deliberately use the plural form because nobody says there can be only one metaphor. Several metaphors will normally be combined - e.g. desktop, window, book etc. (Cf. Weyer and Borning [11]).

Good examples of metaphors are besides the desktop the expert tour guide, the room metaphor - different rooms for different tasks: if you want a grammar lesson you go into room X, if you want translations of the words in a text you go to room Y, carrying with you the words you do not know - thereby implying yet another metaphor. Examples with the travel metaphor are presented in Hammond and Allinson [8]. Smith [10] discusses the tensions between the metaphorical model and 'magic' aspects.

4. An example

Perhaps it will be easier to make some of my points clear with illustrations like the following screen dumps of a hypertext course used in teaching German as a foreign language. For this particular course I have been using Guide, version 2.0, and the aim is to show some of the ideas discussed in this paper.

One of the very interesting things about Guide (which goes for some other hypertext systems, too) is that the mouse cursor changes as it passes over areas on the screen with special characteristics. For example Figure 1 shows the initial screen when the student has started the Guide lesson.

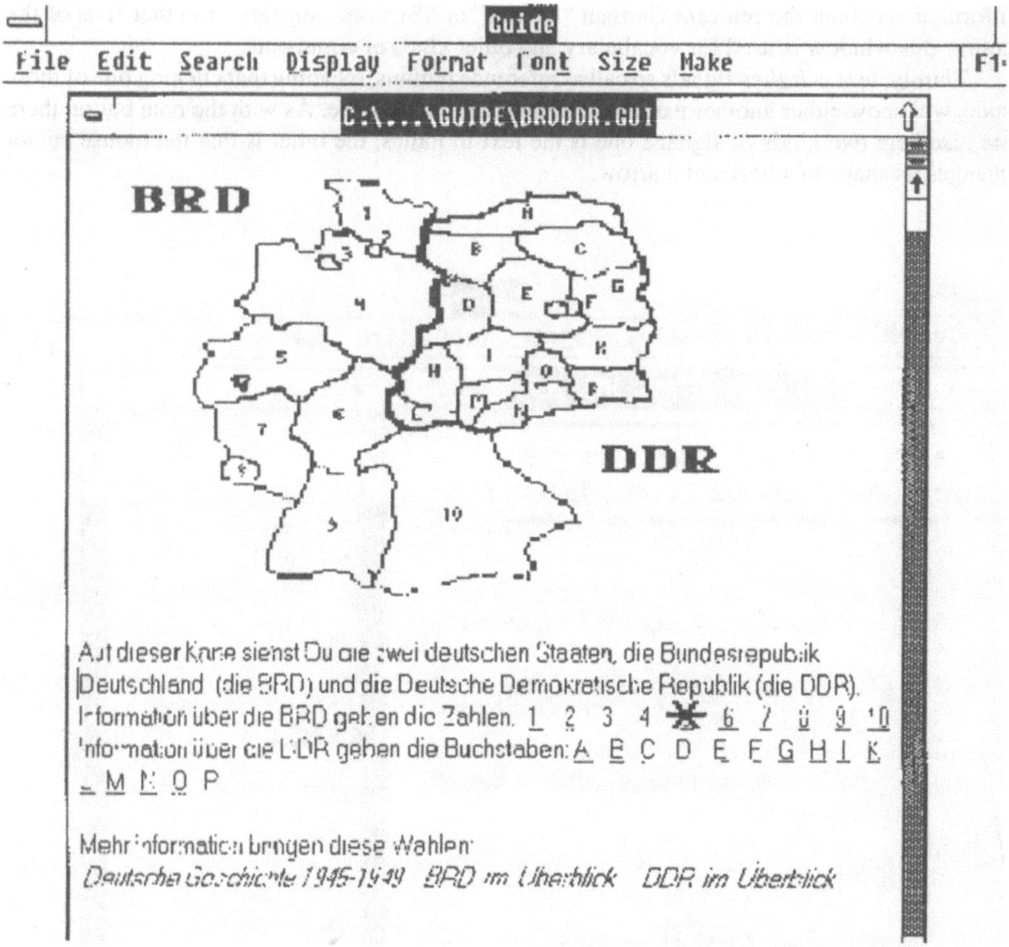

Fig. 1 - Initial screen of a Guide lesson for German

Several characteristics are obvious:

— the permanent menu bar at the top always gives the student an opportunity to stop when he/she wants to, to have the text displayed larger or smaller, to search for specific text strings, to get back to the start of the hyperstack etc.
— one should also notice that graphics can be easily integrated into the hyperstack
— even more interesting is the fact that the text is displayed in three ways (on this screen at least)

Firstly, normal text — i.e. text not "active" in the hyper sense — is simply displayed with normal typography.

Secondly, the underlined bits of text signal that something is hiding behind these pieces of text. This fact is signalled in two ways, for the change of the mouse cursor shape to an asterisk has the same meaning. If the student clicks on one of these hot spots - and keeps the mouse button down - a note will appear in a small window on the top right of the screen. In this example informations about the relevant German "Länder" or "Bezirke" appears - in other files of the course this window is used for vocabulary and other kinds of comments.

Thirdly, text in *italics* signals so called reference buttons, meaning that clicking one of these spots will show either another part of the active file or a new file. As with the note button there are also here two kinds of signals: one is the text in italics, the other is that the mouse cursor changes its shape to a horizontal arrow.

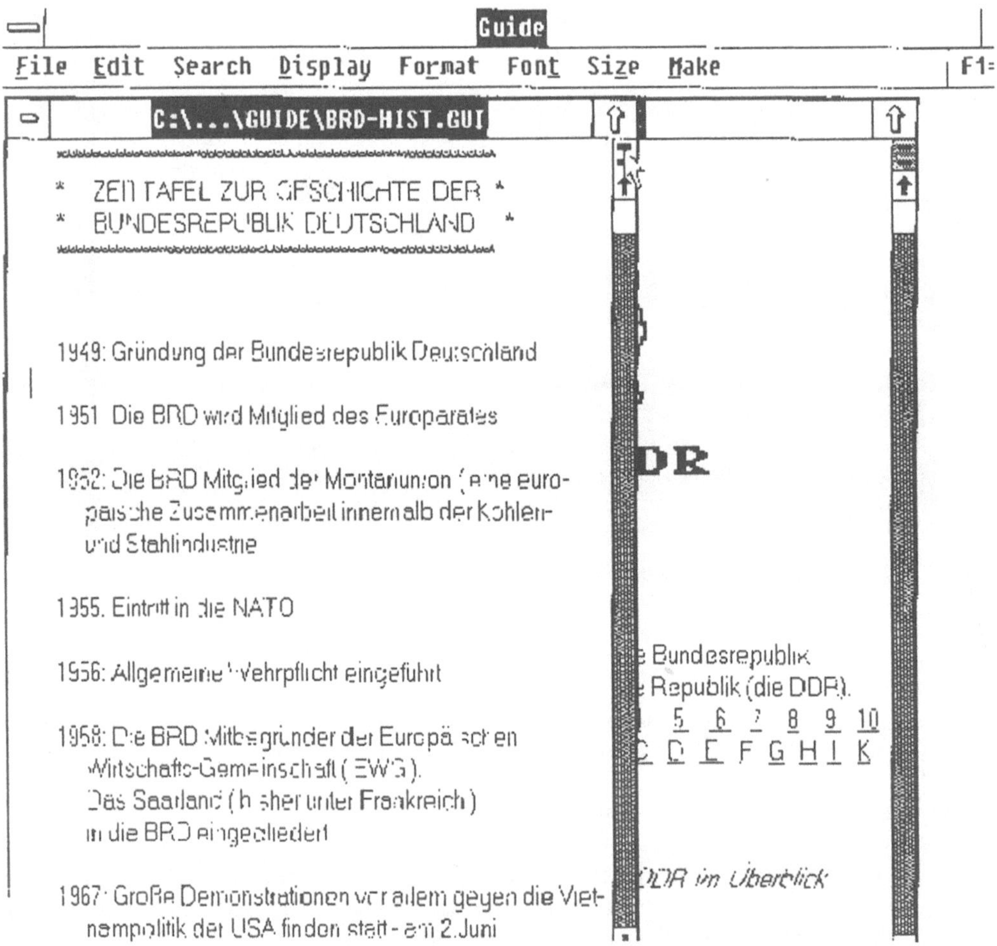

Fig. 2 - The student has clicked on the button "BRD im Überblick"

Figure 2 illustrates the screen as it looks after the student has clicked on the text "BRD im Überblick" on Figure 1. The student can scroll through the text to get an overview of the history. At some places in this file bits of text are labelled as note buttons and reference buttons, which again lead to other files etc. To get back from a reference the student must click the upper right corner of the window which is also shown on Figure 2.

Figure 3 illustrates the screen that is displayed if the student clicks on "Deutsche Geschichte 1945-1949" (in italics) on the initial screen. Again the underlined words are note buttons (displaying historical information). Four spots are characterized as reference buttons.

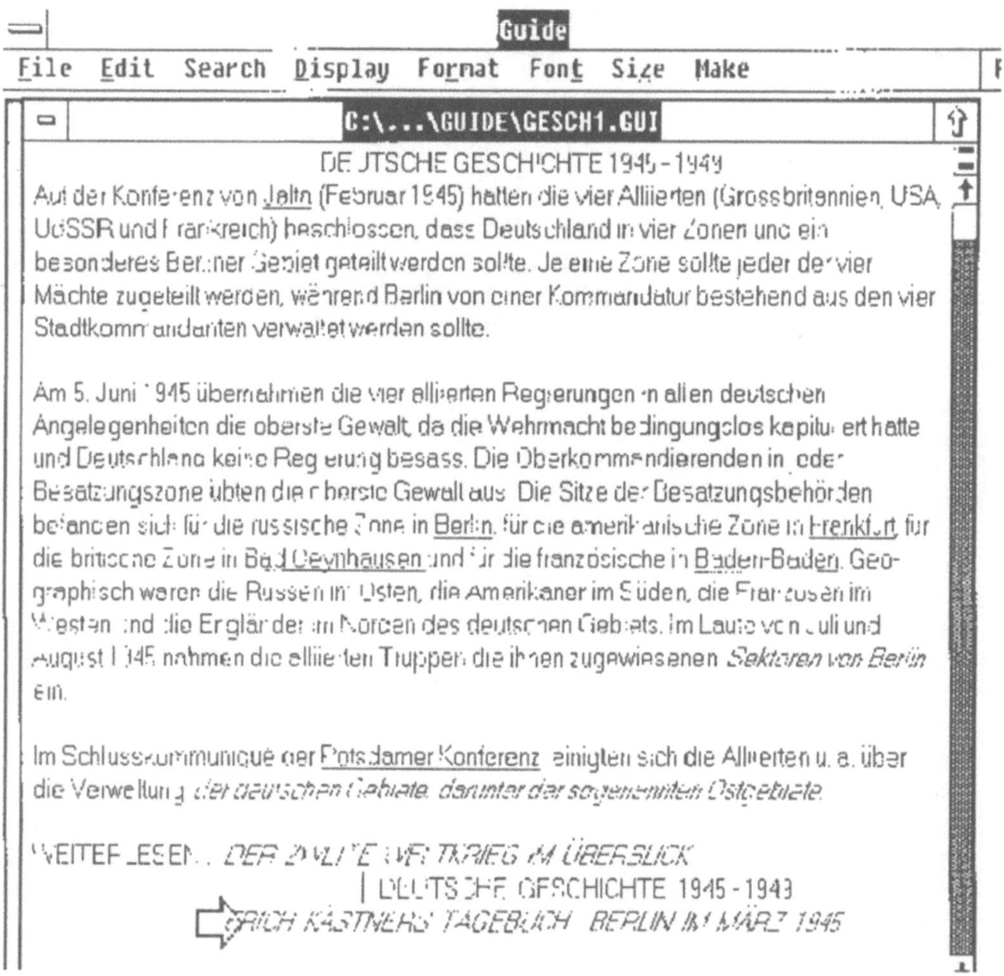

Fig. 3 - Guide-screen with different types of linkages

The first one ("Sektoren von Berlin") will show a map of Berlin where the four sectors are new buttons leading to informations about why the city of Berlin was divided.

The second reference button ("der deutschen Gebiete, darunter der sogenannten Ostgebiete") activates a file with a map of Germany before the Second World War. The point is to show the Eastern territories, and when the student clicks one of these the situation of today is displayed on top of the old map.

The third reference button ("DER ZWEITE WELTKRIEG IM ÜBERBLICK") will activate a text file describing the main events of the Second World War including the conferences of the allies which have to do with the Eastern territories. Some of the words in this file are then reference buttons leading to the map of Germany before the War (previously mentioned).

The fourth reference button ("ERICH KÄSTNERS TAGEBUCH: BERLIN IM MÄRZ 1945") links to a file containing an extract of Kästner's diary. The text in this file is rather difficult for Danish students so many words are underlined. As the student knows that this means 'vocabulary' there is always the possibility to click a word and hold the button down while the Danish translation is displayed in the upper right corner. The title of the text - shown at the beginning of the file - is in itself a reference button linking to a file with informations on Erich Kästner.

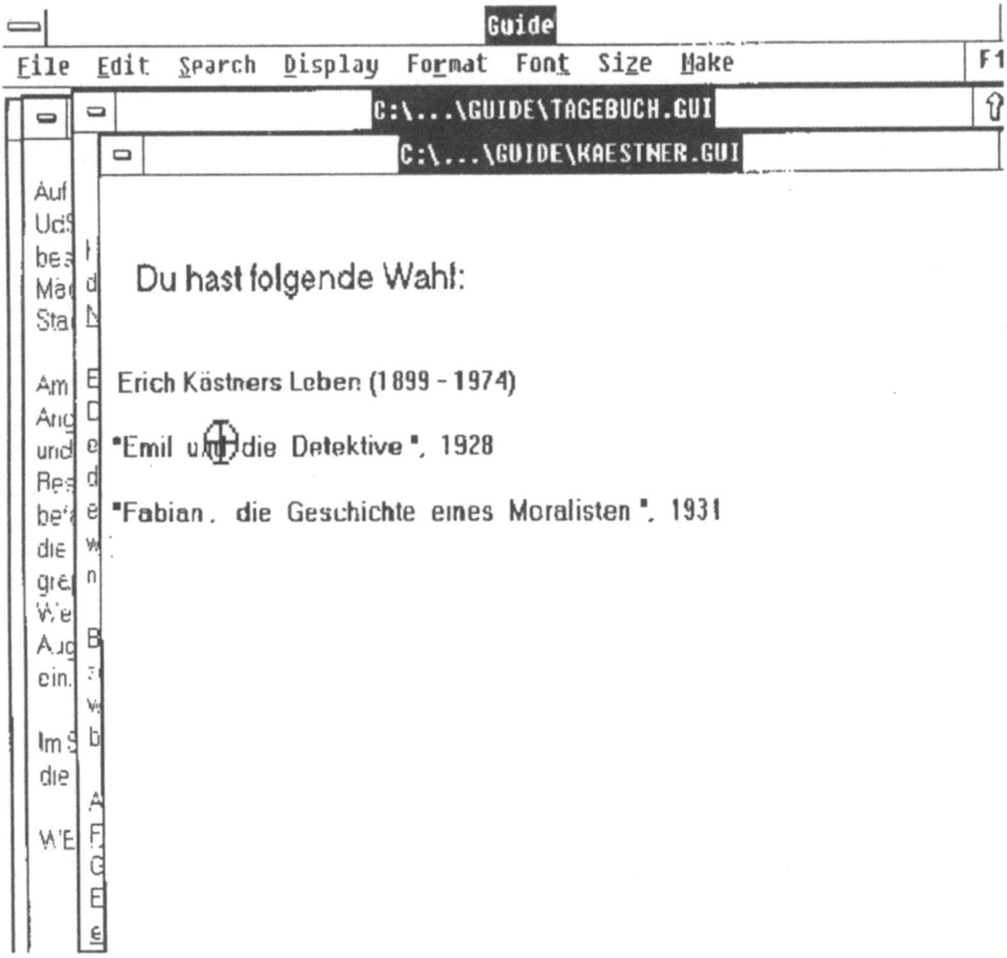

Fig. 4 - Example screen with replacement buttons

The last figure (4) is a screen dump of the beginning of the Kästner file. It shows the third - and last - type of button to be used in Guide: the replacement button. As with the other types of linkages this type is signalled in two ways, one is showing the text in bold types, the other way becomes visible when the mouse moves over this kind of text. As can be seen on Figure 4 the mouse cursor has a cross-hair shape. In this situation, when the mouse button is pressed, the bold text is replaced by something else - in this case the first text will be replaced by a picture of Erich Kästner along with an overview of his life.

The second and third buttons will be replaced by summaries of the two mentioned works of Erich Kästner. It should perhaps be pointed out that all the time the student can go back - either one step by clicking the upper right corner of the active window - or by picking the Display menu which contains the option of going back to the start of the stack.

As previously pointed out these figures are shown only to give an impression of how we might design the different linkages so that the student will always know how to get on. Whether these symbols are the best is not the issue here - it is only an example. Another point is the fact that while working with the hyperstack the student can always get back to the start or step backwards as many steps he/she wants. Of course there are things to criticize in this system, too, but at least this is an example of a hyperstack that has actually been used in practice - and I might add - it is in fact an easy job for the teacher to create hyperstacks with this tool.

5. Conclusion

The interface is - if not all - then at least very important in designing hypermedia for instruction. A guideline for this approach should be that working with the hypertext should be as easy as possible. For example it is necessary that the navigation and the browsing must under no circumstance be a problem.

Future research should be concerned with investigating icons, i.e. not only experimenting with the goal of finding the optimum number to be displayed simultaneously, but also with the physical characteristics of universal and culture dependent icons. Another issue might be trying to work out a collection of metaphors that have proved suitable in educational environments.

The key to designing hypermedia tutorials in a way that suits the pedagogical trends lies in investigating the interface. This involves among other things the concepts of icons and metaphors. On the other hand we must define the pedagogical strategies and methodologies which are a consequence of using hypermedia as instructional tools.

Literature

1. Carroll, J.M., Mack, R.L., Kellogg, W.A.: Interface metaphors and user interface design, In: Handbook of human-computer interaction (M. Helander, ed.), Amsterdam: North-Holland, 1988
2. Churcher, P.R.: A common notation for knowledge representation cognitive models, learning and hypertext, In: Hypermedia, Vol. 1, 3, (235-254), London: Taylor Graham, 1989.
3. Doland, Virginia M.: Hypermedia as an interpretive act, In: Hypermedia, Vol.1, 1, (6-19), London: Taylor Graham, 1989.
4. Duncan, Elizabeth B.: Structuring knowledge bases for designers of learning materials, In: Hypermedia, Vol.1, 1, (20-33), London: Taylor Graham, 1989.

5. Fairchild, K.M., Meredith, G., Wexelblat, A.: The tourist artificial reality, In: Proceedings of CHI' 89, New York: ACM, 1989
6. Frkonja, Jeff: Hypertext Options for the Educational Software Developer, In: Computers in Life and Education, Vol. 6, (65-72), Seattle: NRCLE, 1989.
7. Halasz, F.G.: Reflections on Notecards: Seven issues for the next generation of hypermedia systems, In: Communications of the ACM, 31, (836-852), 1988
8. Hammond, N., Allinson, L.: The travel metaphor as design principle and training aid for navigating around complex systems, In: People and Computers III (Diaper & Winder, ed.), Cambridge University Press, 1987.
9. McAleese, Ray: Navigation and browsing in hypertext, In: Hypertext: Theory into Practice (McAleese, ed.), Oxford: Blackwell Scientific Publications, 1989.
10. Smith, R.B.: Experiences with alternative reality kit: an example of the tension between literalism and magic, In: IEEE Computer Graphics and Applications, 7, (42-50), 1987.
11. Weyer, S.A., Borning, J.A.: A prototype electronic encyclopedia, In: ACM Transactions on Office Information Systems, 3, (63-88), 1985.
12. Wright, P., Lickorish, A.: An empirical comparison of two navigation systems for two hypertexts, In: Proceedings of Hypertext 2, University of York (UK), 1989.
13. Wright, P.: Interface alternatives for Hypertext, In: Hypermedia, Vol.1, 2, (146-166), London: Taylor Graham, 1989.

Hyperconstruction: a New Way to Develop, to Teach, and to Learn

Jacques Rhéaume

Université Laval, Québec, Canada

We have recently begun a project to write, design, develop, and implement an interactive television course for undergraduate education. In these early stages of analysis, our thoughts are "browsing" between the new technology of the Videoway media, the hypermedia technology, the content, and the instructional approach.

In this paper we want to look at the link between those technologies and the task of authoring a course supported with these media. What theory should be elaborated or evoked?

Videoway is the trade name of a so-called interactive video system developed by Videotron, a television cable company, based in Montreal. Our challenge is to write a course that gains benefits from the features of this system. The technical description of this kind of interactive video is easy to give but the question of the pedagogical usefulness of such a system has not been addressed yet. And we still less know how to write such a course. One thing is sure, the actual use of the system is neither impressing nor inspiring but we cannot say that the potential is not there. This interactive video system is essentially four synchronized television channels from which the user can choose at any time through a remote control. A 256k RAM is also available to keep record of answers, to digitalize pictures or to automatically switch to the best suited channel at a given time.

At the outset, our project is technologically oriented. On the other hand we also know that a media in itself does not foster learning nor facilitate teaching (Clark, 1988). Therefore we cannot begin the design of this new course merely with the technology in mind, we need a writing help and a mind tool that takes care of the technical aspects and that does not violate the principles of good instructional design. Our project becomes a little more pedagogically oriented if we consider Videoway as a subset of hypermedia. Hypertext/hypermedia is not *per se* pedagogical but at least it begins to be documented.

Hypermedia have been used for three years by our students in instructional technology but if we consider their hyperwares, we see different kinds of tutorials or games; at times, we see "browsers" and trouble shooting tutorials linked to videodiscs. They enjoy using this kind of software but they rarely think of themselves as end-users. In the same way, the literature and the conferences that deal with the problems of hypermedia in education are learner-oriented. But it is not necessarily so. Hypermedia is a new tool, a creative tool, "a software erector set" (Atkinson), a media for thinking and communication (Conklin, 1987). The uses of hypermedia have not all been explored yet. We propose here to consider hypermedia as a new way to develop, to teach, and to learn.

It is possible to think of hypermedia as creative tools, mind tools, construction tools. As tools, hypertext/hypermedia raises a new set of questions for education. Indeed, the dream of creating information-rich instructional environments is becoming a reality. If these tools are to be used by an author-designer, we do not think that "the richness of non-linear representation carries a risk of potential intellectual indigestion, loss of goals-directness, and cognitive entropy" (Dede, 1988). Hypermedia provide good displays of ideas and give a way to influence the organization of our ideas (Conklin, 87). Since there is a close relationship between the process of thinking and the process of writing, hypermedia can become the best tools for a writer, at least for a writer-designer of interactive materials.

For us, the learner is but implicitly present and our hypermedia are not primarily built to be used by a learner. The author-writer is the first and may be the only reader-learner in our project. This iterative process is well known whether we are in a teacher-learner environment or not. Every creation produced is the threshold of a recreation by the learner or by the writer-reader. The real reader rewrites for herself what the author has first written (Barthes, 1970). The real author rereads for herself what she has first written. Hypermedia is a construction where new meanings, probably not new goals, can be discovered afterwards. More than a regular text, hypermedia emulates a semiotic nosing: where there is a fact, we discover a meaning, where there is a sign, we discover a message (Barthes, 1985). Hypercard for instance has made affordable this idea of Barthes and we can say: where there is a button, we discover a link, a meaning, a message. And by the same token we have begun to write interactive materials.

It is too early to develop a new theory that can be immediately transformed into practice but we can at least state concepts and strategies that we abstract from former theoretical frameworks. The first concept is very old, it is the concept of naming. If you read the first pages of the Bible, you meet Adam and Eve wandering in the Garden where they give names to things and animals. This means that they know something about them; they make relations between the names and the reality that they perceive. The world does begin to become meaningful. And this is nowadays the beginning of science. All that we know is classified somewhere in kinds, parts, or lists. This is the concept of taxonomy (Foucault, 1966, 1970).

But persons, things, events, facts are not isolated. We make relations and with these facts, we make boards or landscapes that represent the environment or the vision where these facts take place. With these visions, the world becomes meaningful. Everybody builds for himself his own vision of the world where he places his experiences and his knowledge (Wittgenstein, 1961).

We also believe in design theories, namely the component display theory or the newer component design theory. The kind of zoom in, zoom out between successive elaborations of an item and the whole picture makes explicit the intuition of Wittgenstein (Reigeluth, 1983).

At last, as is repeated everywhere, hypermedia could also be viewed as a concretization of the schema theory and the semantic networks. The organization of our ideas is seen here as semantic memory schemata. A set of attributes, of concepts arranged in a network of interrelated concepts, is known as a semantic network. The schemata in our semantic network are linked together by way of various associations to combine ideas, infer, extrapolate or otherwise reason from them (Jonassen, 1988).

In practice, hypertext is chosen as a tool to write a Videoway course because it allows non lineal writing as well as multi linking. With our media in mind, writing is not only the matter of selecting and sequencing informations in a script, writing is rather the matter of organizing chunks of information with provisions for meaningful links. As a hypertext author, our task could best be described in 4 steps: 1- "I", the human agent, the author with a general aim or plan, with specific competence and resources, with specific mental models, I am the main part of the process; 2-I collect and edit information. I make portions with selected items and foresee meaningful links, I build the network or the database. Unlike ordinary databases, all the information here is relevant and useful, chosen on purpose. These informations become more meaningful by links to more information, illustration, and interpretation or subjective viewpoints; 3-I edit and design the presentation. "To edit" has two meanings: first, to prepare and select text for publication, the accent is on the content, second, to select footage movement, illustration, screen, the accent is on the impact. The design means the pedagogical design; 4-I write the course, I read it and so far the process is iterative.

Our adventure is quite too young to foresee the results of the end product but hypermedia are shown to be useful to deliver the script of an interactive course. Indeed, hypertext is an integral part of our text because it is the only way to write and read a multi-layered text. Hypermedia is also seen as a good way to simulate an interactive video course. For instance when we ask collaborators, unfamiliar to hypermedia, to develop a specific part of the content, they do not experience difficulties in using hypertext and they immediately see where their contribution is to be inserted. Of course, our project is to be continued.

Literature

1. Barthes, R. (1970), S/Z, Seuil, Paris.
2. Barthes, R. (1985), L'aventure sémiologique, Seuil, Paris.
3. Clark, R. (1988), "The contributions of Cognitive Psychology to Educational Technology ", Technologie et communication éducatives, CIPTE, Montréal.
4. Conklin, J. (1987) Hypertext: An Introduction and Survey. IEEE Computer, 20(9).
5. Dede, C. (1988) The role of hypertext in transforming information into knowledge. NECC, Dallas, TX, June 1988.
6. Foucault, M. (1966) Les mots et les choses, Gallimard, Paris.
7. Foucault, M. (1970) L'archéologie du savoir, Gallimard, Paris.
8. Jonassen D. H.(1988) Designing Structured Hypertext and Structuring Access to Hypertext, Educational Technology, June 1988.
9. Reigeluth, C. and Stein, F. (1983) The Elaboration Theory of Instruction. In C. Reigeluth (Ed) Instructional-design theories and models: An overview of their current states. Englewood, NJ: Lawrence Erlbaum and Assoc.
10. Wittgenstein, L. (1922/1961) Tractatus logico-philosophicus, Routledge and Kegan Paul, London/Gallimard, Paris.

Hypermedia and Science Education - The Case of Chemistry

Duarte Costa Pereira

University of Porto, Portugal

1. Introduction

Hypertext is recommended in the educational literature for support of subject matters where different opinions and interpretations may exist (Costa Pereira et al., 1990d). Apparently the robustness of the science paradigm excludes the scientific subjects from this type of support. This is anyway only apparent because the existence of an overwhelming paradigm doesn't mean that the scientific discourse is unified. Apart from the universal pedagogic existence of the division theme/rheme (Gomes & Costa Pereira, 1991), theme referring to the topic itself and rheme to its explanation, it is important to understand that science has not even a unified thematic discourse but, on the contrary, has different discourses where not only the referents, but also the rules change dramatically. This comes not only from the occasional use of models (analogical and sometimes even pictorial representations (Costa Pereira, 1989 and 1990c)), from the use of specific sign systems (as the symbols and equations in chemistry (Gomes et al., 1989)) but also, and above all, because the epistemologic foundations of most established sciences are, in fact, hybrid. For instance, physics (Harré, 1984) adopts in part the Aristotelian views of substance and also the more modern view of action at a distance and the notion of field which are difficult to make compatible. On the other hand, since the eighteenth century all sciences have evolved, thanks to their reductionism and mechanicism, but nowadays, with the advent of chaos theory (Gleick,1989) through non-linearity, it is necessary to live also with these ideas. This has important consequences, as for instance, the geometry implied by the latter is very different from the conventional euclidean geometry as it is based on the notions of self-similarity and recursion (fractal geometry). Also, within the conventional scientific paradigm (kuhn, 1970), equilibrium was always emphasized, but, nowadays, for the study of complex systems, everybody knows that it does not usually stand (Prigogine, 1986), nor even does a periodic attractor state apply, for many times the attractor is fractal (strange attractors).

It is possible to say that, in general there are, within each conventional science, and according with the same generally accepted scientific paradigm (period of normal science) more than one declarative or descriptional (theme) discourse, and of course even more explanatory (rheme) discourses. This is essentially due first to the use, in each science, of more than one level of epistemologic objects, the rule being that there should be at least one macroscopic and one microscopic level of description. In each of these levels we may distinguish propositional and analogical representations, the first corresponding to the theories and the second to the also very important scientific models. With all this complexity, if we refuse extreme views of pragmatism and instrumentalism, Science can only survive with certain key concepts, as the one of energy, that being common to all levels, allow the transfer from one level to another and from a descriptional mode to an exploratory mode or from analogic representations to propositional ones. Of course hypertext or even better hypermedia with all their versatility are ideal supports for such complicated systems.

Apart from that, hypertext can lead to guided discovery learning situations (McAleese, 1989), with all the accepted advantages in science education, once it preserves motivation and favours the control of learning conditions (Gagné, 1965). Hypertext also allows learner metacognitive control of the learning phenomenon, enhancing it (Ingwersen, 1986) which makes it all the more important for science education particularly in sciences like physics and chemistry where problem solving is considered increasingly important. These last facts give hypertext/ hypermedia in science education an exploratory dimension that should be considered apart from the already mentioned explanatory function. This is all the more important since at hypertext level, perhaps for the first time, emission and communication grammars might communicate between them (Gomes & Costa Pereira, 1991), producing a very much desirable equilibrium between the declarative and procedural aspects of science education. In fact the last ones have clearly been emphasized in recent times by the current paradigms in science education (discovery learning, adequacy to the cognitive development and even the most recent based on alternative conceptions).

2. Architectural problems

There are two questions that are frequently mentioned in the general literature of hypertext (Costa Pereira, 1990a, 1990d): one is the possibility to loose the searching goal; the other one is the increasing difficulty of distinguishing the details. These are particularly important in scientific hypertexts and in order to minimize these two problems it is necessary to implement search techniques - the browsing tools. Examples of these tools are the graphical path structure. These aids should be complemented with searching techniques as well as with the so-called key-words corresponding to the key concepts, as for instance the already mentioned concept of energy. It is important to associate scanning (covering large areas without depth) and exploring (finding out for the extent of the information given) techniques to this search.

It is always necessary to match the document's structure and presentation to the different kinds of expected utilizations. For instance, as far as structure is concerned, one cannot use all the existent associations between the conceptual fields of two information nodes, but should emphasize the most appropriate relations concerning the used metaphor. In order to achieve this it is necessary to construct a simplified network, in which each node must be linked to not more than three or four nodes, instead of being linked to all the others. Therefore the user can follow this pseudo hierarchic structure in an easier way. In this structure a top node can be visualized and the user is also provided with what may be called a "cognitive scaffolding". This last feature is essential to a guided discovery learning strategy. The "combinatory explosion" (a problem for the computer implementation) can then be avoided, and the phenomenon of "getting lost in hyperspace", frequently mentioned in the literature, is also minimized, once "scaffolding" is essential to support the search (to search with a defined goal).

Apart from all these design problems for scientific hypertext, it is important to say that these products might be used in the future as one module of a true multimedia system (Costa Pereira, 1990b), the others being (1) a real time interface for acquisition of data and experimental control, (2) modelling packages and (3) intelligent tutoring systems, capable of tracing the learning profile and suggesting the most efficient learning strategies (Oliveira & Costa Pereira, 1990).

3. The case of chemistry

The case of chemistry is especially complex (Costa Pereira, 1979, 1990a) as its historical and epistemologic roots are very diversified. Although in most philosophy of science literature we see that the essential features of chemistry derive from a corpuscular system (Harré, 1984) it is also thought (Bent, 1965) that as chemistry is the science of huge sets of many atoms it must rely on the science of atoms (quantum mechanics) and also on the science of "huge" sets (statistical mechanics). As it tries to interpret through the behavior of the microscopic parts of matter the macroscopic manifestations it is of course subsidiary to thermodynamics (statistical thermodynamics).

3.1 Descriptive discourses

Trying to be as simple as possible in these complicated matters it is possible to distinguish at least three distinct chemical descriptive (thematic) discourses, apart from many more explanatory (rhematic) discourses. This is disregarding interpretations like the ones of Dagognet (1969) that refer to languages of chemistry symbols (this last interpretation is certainly wrong as these systems are no more than sign systems without the properties of a language).

The three levels of description that we propose are:

1) The structural or quantum/electronic level
2) The reactional or statistical/molecular level
3) The macroscopic or classic thermodynamic level

Let us, very briefly consider each one of them.

3.1.1 The structural or quantum/electronic level

First of all we have to admit a structural level where both atomic and pluriatomic (through the chemical bond concept) structures are considered. Essentially the theoretical discourse is one of quantum mechanics and the epistemologic objects are the electrons with emphasis to the more energetic ones (the valence electrons). The basis for this discourse are indeed the postulates of quantum mechanics (propositional rigorous representation), and their immediate consequences (as the uncertainty principle and the Pauli exclusion principle) but there are also a lot of rules of thumb (propositional, non-rigorous) as the octet rule, the electron pair repulsion "theory", the ligand field theory, etc. together with analogic representations (models of the atom, of the ionic crystals, of the metallic crystals, etc.). It is possible to say that the state of affairs at this level of chemical description is confused, and this is due particularly to the existence of two approaches, many times confused with the problem of chemical bond: the valence bond theory and the molecular orbital theory. There are concepts such as hybridization or delocalization that having been "born" in one of the theories are not completely transposable to the other. This gives outsiders an idea that chemistry is a very conceptually poor science (as for instance René Tom (1985) recently stated) but in fact what exists is a great deal of discourse confusion at this level.

This confusion does not avoid that, for the essential problems of structural chemistry, it remains relatively simple for us to avoid the dynamic problems (the models for all sciences since the eighteenth century) and base the entire structure of chemical systems essentially in the steady state solutions of the Schrödinger equation. This is a good enough approximation since the spacing between electronic levels is sufficiently high for, at the temperatures common at the Earth's surface, we only have the fundamental electronic levels filled (Bent, 1965). In fact, apart from the explanatory discourse between levels 1 and 2 (the structural or quantum/electronic level and the reactional or statistical/molecular level), particularly for the description of transition states, photochemical reactions, the ground quantum level will be sufficient for the more intricate thematic descriptions.

3.1.2 The reactional or statistical/molecular level

There are at least two levels within this description: one that is only concerned with the tendency of the systems and the other that specifically accounts for the functional dependency of the chemical quantities with time.

The first one gives rise to the attractor perspectives of the chemical systems be they the point attractors leading to the conventional chemical equilibrium, the circular attractors leading to oscillating reactions or even the strange attractors leading to chaos! As it is well known most of the chemical descriptions are equilibrium ones, the periodic and chaotic situations, although very common in biological systems, being ill-investigated for the time being!

The second one deals exactly with the temporal dependencies of the concentrations of the species relying on their characteristics that may, in certain cases as the ones of self-catalysis of biochemical reactions conduce to, intricate paths with a certain periodicity and that may even be conducive to chaotic situations.

Subjacent to all these concepts there is a theory of aleatory propagation of a certain property which is called energy. Entropy is only a way of accounting in a summative (not multiplicative way) the probabilities of the states reached!

Either by considering the tendencies or the exact temporal rates the important question is that energy distributions, shock probabilities and other statistical concepts are essential to this level of chemical reasoning, and although there are different theories like the collision theory and the transition state theory underlying all these reasonings, the fact is that it is a stochastic paradigm that rules essentially identical to the one that came into being in the late nineteenth century with statistical mechanics, which in a way overturned the all-powerful (since Newton's time!) deterministic, differential equation paradigm! It may even be said that the field of chemical kinetics is a true compromise between the two ruling tendencies (the deterministic and the stochastic) of the science paradigm.

3.1.3 The macroscopic or classic thermodynamic level

One of the most amazing discoveries of mankind is the one of synergistic, that is responsible for the whole of thermodynamics. It is indeed extremely interesting to understand that billions of billions of particles are perfectly well described by some independent parameters like temperature, pressure and volume which are themselves linked by a state equation. The most interesting of all that is that all these descriptions can be linked to the other levels through appropriate discourses, particularly the one of statistical thermodynamics.

It is indeed interesting to see that there is a perfect compatibility of the macroscopic definitions of pressure, temperature and even entropy, with the microscopic ones, as may be seen at an extremely elementary level, using a model as the Einstein solid for accounting for the distribution of energy (Costa Pereira, 1990e).

3.2 The explanatory discourses

It has been said that chemistry itself relies on explanatory concepts loosely defined as valence and chemical bond (Tom, 1985). In fact, as was previously stated the most difficult aspects of chemistry are the explanatory (rhematic) discourses that try to map one level into another. This is done in many and efficient ways, but essentially using models of the particular instances. As chemistry is a "huge" science it has been developing in separate branches and the concepts used as well as the strategic explanations are very different from one field to another. The explanations most frequently use the already observed coherences within the discourses but they do vary from the electronic explanations of the mechanisms in organic chemistry to the static idea of energy of activation or to the all-powerful idea of free energy of a system in statistical thermodynamics.

The solidly built organic chemistry mechanisms used the contemporary (in the 1920s) notion of electronic duplet and the ideas of nucleophilicity and electrophilicity, among others. A completely different arrangement of concepts comes out of the more recently developed inorganic reaction mechanisms, where the electronic situation is usually more complicated, and concepts like ligand field theory, Lewis acidity, hardness, etc. appear.

There are nevertheless regularities in chemical description and explanation, one of them being that the extensive variable is, contrary to the use in physics, not mass but amount of substance (which is in fact coherent with the dominance of a corpuscular epistemology in the field).

Also much is to be expected in the generalized use of computers as representation tools in chemistry, in particular the true advent of a new chemical semiotics (Costa Pereira, 1990a), not based as it has been on the all-powerful, although rough, concept of electronic duplet, but on more sound notions as electron densities, bond order, bond polarizabilities, etc., easily calculated and represented by the computer in a hypermedia environment.

3.3 The exploratory discourses

This last aspect is a strategic one and derives from the attempt of combining the positive aspects, relative to science education, of some informatic products into a single flexible package called for convenience hypermedia, as it is a multimedia product controlled by a hypertext basis.

This basis cannot use all the possible associations that exist, but should emphasize the most appropriated relations, that is link the various thematic discourses through the most adequate rhematic (explanatory) discourse, so it is necessary to construct a simplified network, in which each hypertext node must be linked only to a few nodes and find a top node from which the user is provided with a "cognitive scaffolding" system. This last feature is essential to a guided discovery learning strategy.

Apart from this hypertext basis the hypermedia system would consist of a series of modules being in fact a true multimedia system (Costa Pereira, 1990b). The emphasis is put on flexibility, non-linearity, exploratory behavior and true interactivity. Although different implementations may occur, the following modules would generally be present:

(1) a real-time interface for acquisition of data and experimental control easily accessible from the hypertext basis through external commands,
(2) modelling packages (Costa Pereira, 1989), capable of reflecting either through variable modelling or through object modelling, stochastically or determistically, the dynamic behavior of systems, particularly in chaotic circumstances,
(3) intelligent tutoring systems, capable of tracing the learning profile and suggesting the most efficient learning strategies (Oliveira & Costa Pereira, 1990).

In conclusion, the use of hypertext with an intelligent help system for chemical descriptions, with the possibilities of paradigmatic and syntagmatic associations (Gomes A., Costa Pereira, 1989) and above all having the possibility of being connected to real-time interfaces and modelling devices (Costa Pereira, 1990b), apart from being of enormous help in chemical education, will certainly improve the uniformity of chemical explanation and, with it, its coherence and rationality, so comments as the ones of René Tom (1985) would no longer be valid!

Literature

1. Bent, H. A., The Second Law of Thermodynamics, Oxford University Press, 1965
2. Costa Pereira, D., Structure of Communication and the Learning of Chemistry, PhD dissertation, UEA, 1979
3. Costa Pereira, D., Da Problemática da Representação aos Modelos em Ciência, Revista Portuguesa de Educação, Vol.II, nº3, 75-96, 1989.
4. Costa Pereira, D., Hipermedia no Ensino da Química, Actas do Encontro Computadores no Ensino da Física e da Química, Coimbra, 1990a
5. Costa Pereira, D., Hypermedia in Science Education, Proceedings of the East West Invitational Seminar on New Technologies and Education, Leningrad, USSR, 1990b
6. Costa Pereira, D., Lencastre, Leonor, A Compreensão de Textos como Construção de Modelos Mentais, Análise Psicológica, 1, VIII, 61-70, 1990c
7. Costa Pereira, D., Lencastre, Leonor, Guedes Vaz, J. C., Educational Aspects in the Use and Design of Hypertext Documents, Proceedings of EURIT The European Conference on Technology and Education, Herning, Denmark, 1990d
8. Costa Pereira, D., Consequências da Distribuição Aleatória da Energia, Boletim da SPQ, 39, (Série II) 31-35, 1990e
9. Dagognet, F., Tableaux et Languages de la Chimie, Éditions du Seuil, Paris, 1969
10. Gagné, R., The Conditions of Learning, New York: Holt Rinehart and Winston, 1965
11. Gleick J., Chaos: Making a New Science, New York, 1989
12. Gomes A., Oliveira A., Costa Pereira, D., O Hypercard e o Ensino Assistido por Computador, Personal Computer World, 29, 3, 86-92, 1989
13. Harré, R., The Philosophies of Science, Oxford University Press, 1984
14. Ingwersen, P., Cognitive analysis and the role of the intermediary in information retrieval, in Davies, R. (Ed), Intelligent Information Systems; Progress and Prospects, Chichester, UK: Ellis Horwood, 1986
15. Kuhn, T. S., The Structure of Scientific Revolutions, Chicago: University of Chicago Press, 1970

16. McAleese, Hypertexte: Theory into pratice, Aberdeen, 1989
17. Oliveira, A., Costa Pereira, D., Psychopedagogic Aspects of Hypermedia Courseware, in Jonassen, D., Mandl, H., Designing Hypertext for Learning, Ch. 14, 251-262, NATO ASI series; Series F: Computer and Systems Sciences, vol. 67, Springer-Verlag, New Iorque, 1990
18. Prigogine, I., Stengers, I., La Nouvelle Alliance, Paris, 1986
19. Tom, R., Parabole e Catatrofi, Il Saggiatore, Milano, 1985

Designing Hypermedia for Computer Assisted Career Guidance

Maria do Céu Taveira[1], Bártolo P. Campos[1], Duarte C. Pereira[2] and José C. Vaz[2]

[1]Institute of Psychological Intervention, Education and Development. Faculty of Psychology and Education. Porto State University, Portugal. [2]Minerva Project. Porto State University, Portugal.

1. Career Guidance

Computer career guidance (CACG) systems have become one of the most commom comprehensive guidance resources, both in educational and employment settings (Association of Computer Based Systems for Career Information, 1990; Chapman & Katz, 1982; Sampson, Shahnarasian, & Reardon, 1987, 1988). The first systems were developed in U.S.A. and in Canada, in the mid 1960s, but from the early 1970s, a number of systems have been developed in Europe, too, with inspiration from North America (Plant, 1989; Taveira & Campos, 1989; Watts & Ballantine, 1981).

Until recently, most career guidance software was designed to promote essentially linear thinking. In general, they are conceived as self-help materials, assume software versions on IBM or IBM compatible microcomputers, and use sequential methods for searching information with text format. Moreover, the majority are based on compensatory approaches to information, characterized by an intra-alternative exhaustive search. Typically, the more sophisticated systems provide some combination of (a) self-assessment of interests, abilities, values and other personal characteristics of the students, provided on-line or via the completation of guide-book exercises and counseling, prior to the computer; (b) the dissemination of educational and occupational information, for example, by listing occupations with similar educational requirements, aptitudes, interests, and earning; (c) the generation of vocational alternatives; (d) the instruction and/or modeling in career decision-making process, and (e) strategies for implementating career plans (Sampson, Peterson and Reardon, 1990, p.144). A few experiments have been made with interactive video, giving access to information on educational and occupational alternatives (Plant, 1989).

2. Hypermedia and Computer Assisted Career Guidance

The development of CAGSs depends, among other things, on the evolution of new information techniques. Hypermedia offer advantages for the development of career guidance software. First, they facilitate the use of informatics by non-informatics interested in those instruments and processes, like career counseling professionals. For example, simplicity and power of HyperTalk programming gives career counselors opportunity to write their own programs and to assume full responsibility for directing this powerful technological resource and, consequently, to eliminate the inappropriate use of computer technology in this area, by the absence of leadership (Sampson, 1986).

Second, taking into account that (a) the processing of personnal, educational and occupational information is a central element of career exploration and planning processes, and that (b) the way individuals explore the world of education and of work may reveal the strategies they use to make their decisions (Gati, 1986), then, we consider hypermedia features may provide new facilities to users to developp better ways to make career projects. In fact, research on the strategies for collection and processing of occupational information in making career decisions sugest that most individuals are very parsimonious in exploring information - they consider aspects that are clearly nonindependent and, in most cases, they use a strategy of following only some of the options rather then all of them; they also search more information in some alternatives than on others, (because of real-life constraints no one explores all options in depth), and, moreover, the larger the number of potential alternatives considered, the lower the percentage explored (subjects tend to eliminate some alternatives according to certain criteria) (Gati, 1986). Also, the individual potential to explore career information seems to be directly related to the availability of choices (Philips, 1982).

Thus, sequential and exhaustive models of information searching and processing do not necessarily describe the way people process the information and make their decisions. Conversely, nonlinear and nonsequential relations between bodies of information seem to be more adequate to develop guidance software because it offers an enviroment that attempts to simulate on-line human processes of exploration.

Because when using hypersystems we do not require the user to follow pre-determined structures or access routes through bodies of information (like in traditional CAGS), data within the system can be endlessly cross-referenced, routes can be determined by the user and, if the system has been organized aproppriately, then, multiple meanings can be created according to the disposition or needs of the user. Crosswalks between data elements can allow users to relate those data elements for decision-making, which is relevant since in most models of carrer guidance a vital function is helping individuals to assess themselves in relation to properties of occupations. HyperCard, for example, provide the users the possibility to create semantically meaningful relationships between diferent information and ideas, and promotes connectivity - the ability to show that any single concept, problem or idea must be understood from a variety of perspectives (Beeman et al., 1987; Donaldson, 1988).

One recent goal of career counseling is to promote aquisistion of personal flexibility, as an ideal mode for coping with continuous change and complexity in society, specially in the occupational world (Taveira & Campos, 1989). The hope is that personal flexibility will help individuals not only to acquire knowledge about themselves in career situations but also to learn new ways of thinking, and to generate and coordinate flexible and sucessful responses to the environment in order to improve their career development. Hypermedia tools can help to facilitate these tasks. To a large context, it is possible leaving control of the process of exploration in the hands of the users: they can be more than observers and learn to engage actively in the exploration process, in an environment that allows to manipulate information and concepts, the use of graphic imagery and visual modes of thinking and also multiple pathways through bodies of information, again, facilities not offered by conventional CAGS. In other words, with tools such as HyperCard, we can represent internal geography, via external medium, and we can offer opportunities to the user to approach the same landmarks from diferent directions, like in other real life experiences. Control is provided by the fact that links are to certain topics and not to others, but the intuitiveness of the system makes the screen appear more like an invitation than a control. Another advantage is the possibility of storing huge collections of information in a variety of media, in extremely compact form, and with easy and quick access - diverse materials can be assembled and delivered to students and can be linked both explicitly and implicity.

In short, the use of hypermedia environments into CAGSs makes it possible to pursue and to facilitate, with the computer, some of the present values of career counseling for human development such as personal flexibility, autonomy and self-proficiency in planning a career. Also, we can therefore examine students exploration styles and patterns, providing cues regarding the type of strategy he/she uses in processing the information along the interaction with the program. These type of structure adapts itself to the needs and disposition of specific students, with diferent backgrounds and motivations, allowing an individualization of intervention.

2.1 PROJECTOS: a computer-assisted career guidance system for secondary education

After some years of practice, research and training supervision in the field of career counseling and guidance, and taking into account the analysis of current practices and student needs, as well as the recently opportunities offered by new information technologies in this field, a research project designed to develop, implement and evaluate the design of a prototype of an adaptative CAGS is being developed in the Institute of Psychological Intervention, Education, and Development, at the Faculty of Psychology and Education of Porto State University. This Portuguese CAGS, designated PROJECTOS, is designed to help secondary students further in their career planning. PROJECTOS uses hypermedia and is being developed in HyperCard system.

The aims, scope and assumptions underlying the development of this guidance software package as well as some characteristics related to its structure, content and procedures will be briefly described.

2.2 Aims, assumptions and scope of PROJECTOS

PROJECTOS is designed to help adolescents and young adults further in their career planning. It aims to facilitate the expression and the skills of career exploration, the process of career commitment and to teach suitable pathways of planning specific decisions. In this system, the user interacts with the computer in such a way as to examine and explore his/her own interests, to obtain and use relevant career information and to formulate career projects. Tentative career preferences can be modified along the interaction with PROJECTOS as the student gains new insights and additional information. The options involve educational, occupational and employment alternatives - the emphasis, however is not merely the content but also the processes of career exploration and commitment - conceived as psychological processes of the relationship between individuals and the world. More specifically, career exploration is assumed as a life-long process of relationships between individuals and particular environments within which different levels of career commitment may occur. The immediate physical, social and psychological context within which those relationships are constructed - the situation in which exploration takes place - as well as how the developing person constructs or makes meaning of that situation, are important dimensions of the process. The relationship between the indi-vidual and the world should be the focus of intervention activities. When activities focus on the individual component (i.e., assessment of vocational interests), we are working with the individual construction of the world, that's to say, the world of educational, occupational and employment; but also, when intervention activities focus on the exploration of educational and occupational alternatives, one must keep in mind that we are working with changes in the individual self-concept related to those realities. Further, we assume that exploration of available alternatives promotes the process of self-evaluation, influencing the cognitive representation of personal atributes and the configuration or pre-shaping of career projects.

PROJECTOS can be a self-help career material but will only have fully impact if used as an integrated part of a systematic career counseling program. the system will be used in the typical settings for the delivery of career counseling and guidance services (i.e., secondary schools, youth and career counseling and guidance centers settled down in the community, and private offices). It is being designed for use in individual career counseling, although it can be modified to be used in group counseling and with other populations.

PROJECTOS uses hypermedia and is being developed in SuperCard system. It is a standalone system, runs in Apple Macintosh IIcx, and requires an AppleColor High-Resolution RGB Monitor (screen size 640 by 480) and an Image Writer or a Laser Writer.

2.3 System design configuration and features

PROJECTOS is a system of separated but interrelated sections. Although specific pathways through PROJECTOS are suggested, users are allowed to explore through the system in different ways depending on the exploration needs and level of commitment they consider at the beginning or along the experience.There's ability of users to enter the system at their points of interest, and to retain a record of their interactions as well as print outs of feed-backs and sumaries. Figure 1 presents a schema of PROJECTOS general structure.

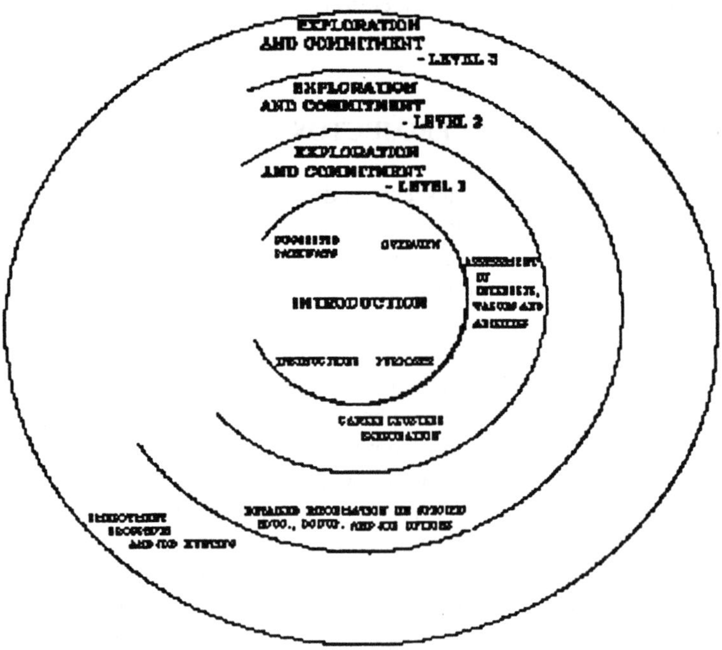

Fig. 1 - Schematic structure proposed of PROJECTOS

Introduction presents the general purposes and an overview of the system, as well as recommended pathways to explore its different components and the few simple computer keys needed to use it. Suggested pathways through the system may vary according to the following situations: (a) user interacts with PROJECTOS as a self-help material (self-service information facility) or (b) user interacts with PROJECTOS after individual or group counseling. Suggestions about the suitabilitily of exploration pathways can also vary according to the user's career decision (i.e., choosing a field of study or an occupation, selecting a job) and career problem (i.e., lack of information regarding himself/herself or the educational or occupational alternatives or both, the absence of a framework for combining the information, indecision).

Users can proceed the interaction with PROJECTOS by exploring, in different ways, career alternatives. For example, they may proceed by exploring personal vocational interests related to occupational fields and levels, and then searching for more detailed information on career alternatives.

Interests assessment helps the users to explore their "likes" through assessment of interests in an on-line inventory which provides job activity interest scores related to the following occupational clusters: science, technology, consumer economics, outdoor, business, clerical, communication, arts, and service. Occupations are classified into major groups and levels within each group (i.e., science-professional and science-skilled). A self-interpretation profile is offered which point to relevant personal interests clusters. The administration, scoring and interpretation of the inventory results can be a starting point to guide conselees in the exploration process of available alternatives.

Each cluster is keyed to curriculum choice, occupation and job information. For each cluster, users can obtain information on related educational fields and courses, related occupations and job contexts, skills and abilities needed in the jobs, and suggested activities to get experience. At this level of exploration, assessment of values or of abilities can be also conceived, taking into consideration the mentioned career clusters classification.

Users begin with some rough classification of alternatives into a few clusters and can continue with more refined distinctions along the other sections with interactive structured search of and/or direct access to information about educational, occupational and job opportunities.

Exploration of specific information about Education, Work and Employment Worlds helps the students to identify available and possible educational and occupational scenarios, and to relate education to work.

For *educational planning*, they may obtain information about (a) vocational interests field/ level of education (b) courses designation (c) duration (d) degrees offered (e) institution type (f) school type (g) geographic location (h) entrance requirements (i) academic programs (j) admission requirements to other levels of education (l) where to find more information.

For *identifying occupational and job alternatives*, they may obtain information about: (a) vocational interests fields (b) job titles (c) work tasks/activities (d) work setting (e) necessary tools and equipment (f) personal qualities required/other requirements (g) personal values (h) special conditions (i) average income (j) promotion opportunities (l) related educational programs/specific occupational training (m) related military occupations (n) related job prospects (o) job hunting skills needed (p) where to find more information.

Decision and action plan aids can be included in all levels of exploration, helping the users to evaluate their plans in terms of satisfaction, realism and commitment, and also to formulate action plans and take steps to achieve their goals.

In PROJECTOS, related information on the counselee and on educational, occupational and employment worlds can be carried out almost simultaneously, along the interaction with the computer (data on educational and occupational options is also organized in terms of the mentioned psychological vocational interests classification). For this purpose, the screen presents sensible working-areas which can be activated by the mouse and, in consequence, actions are produced (Gomes, Oliveira & Costa Pereira, 1989; Costa Pereira & Oliveira, 1990). For example, the screen areas under study for the Exploration of Education, Work and Employment Worlds components are: an Help Navigation Area, an Interactivity Action Area, and an Information Area (Fig. 2).

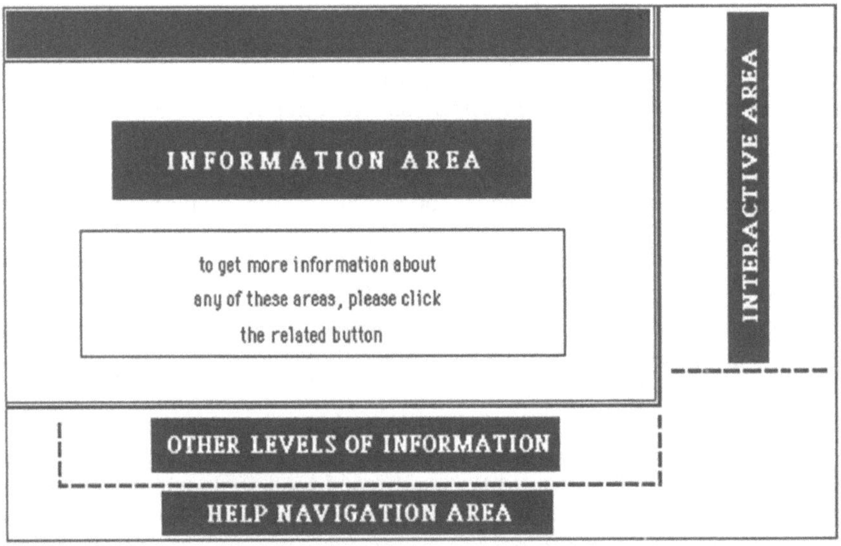

Fig. 2 - Screen structure of "PROJECTOS"

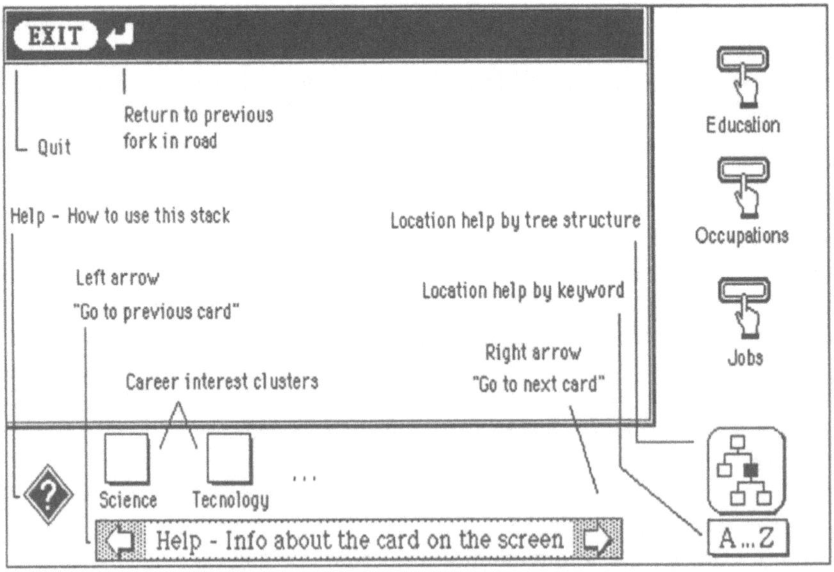

Fig. 3 - Buttons of the help navigation area

Help Navigation Area includes layers of organizational structure that relieve some of the negative effects of hyperspace such as desorientation and distraction. These navigational aids can be (a) buttons that allow the access to visual schemata of the system where the topic on which the user is exploring can be outlined - a hierarchical tree; (b) buttons that link the content of the card in the screen with other topics-a key word index; (c) areas of information about the card on the screen; (d) buttons that link the user to instructions about recommendable pathways through the system; (e) buttons of return and of arrow (Fig. 3).

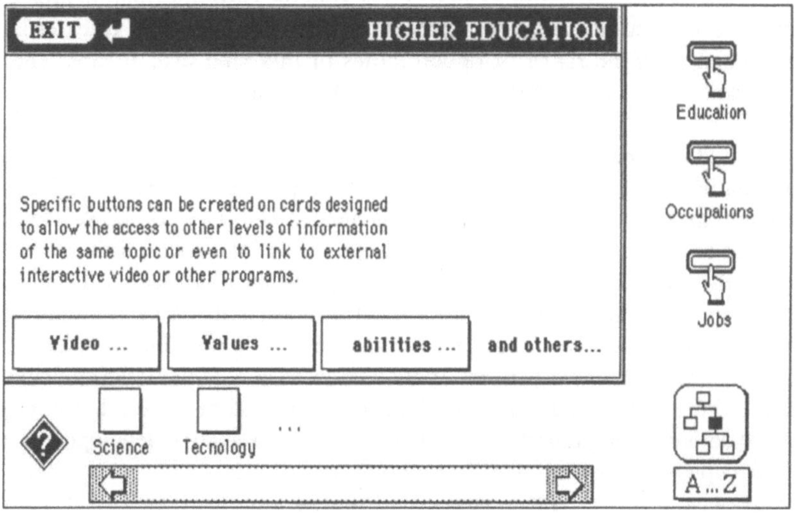

Fig. 4 - Example of specific buttons

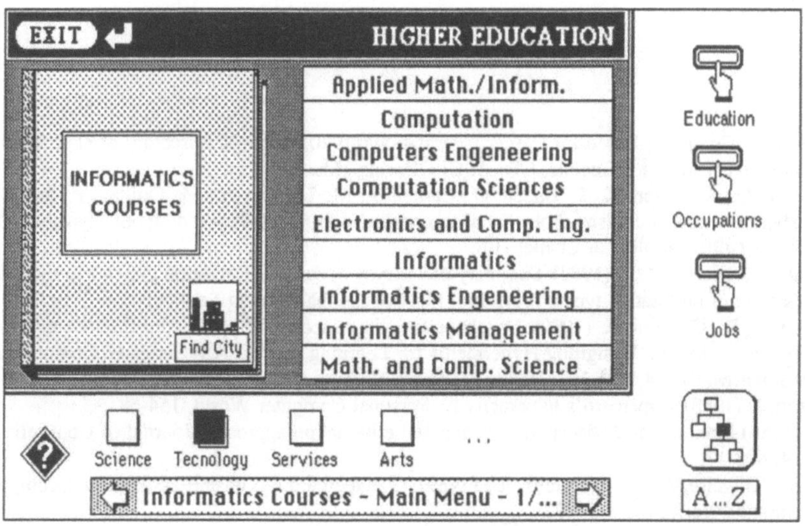

Fig. 5 - Example of "PROJECTOS" screen

Interactivity Area can provide access to different levels and types of information by the manipulation of buttons always present in the screen. These buttons can be clicked in different ways and at different moments of the exploration process. In PROJECTOS, there are interactivity buttons related with Educational, Occupational and Employment realities.

For example, students can search information on courses related to their main interests fields and, if during this exploration activity decisions are made in terms of commitment with some alternatives, he/she can query the system in other directions, pressing "Occupations" button and search for information about the characteristics of occupations in that field of vocational interests.

Information Area specific buttons can be created in the card information area to allow the access to other levels and activities of exploration and to link the user to external programs and devices, broadening the range of opportunities of this kind of software. The scope and depth of exploration can vary accordingly to the different needs and dispositions of the users (Figs. 4, 5).

For example, the users may crosswalk through different interest domains and look for available alternatives in terms of education or work in a non-sequential way, just clicking on the prefered item associated to a button which generates an option window. Moreover, users may also choose to browse through educational options, using specific criteria.

PROJECTOS will help the counselee to develop his/her unique path of exploration: he/she can search for all available information regarding alternatives or can explore for more information on some alternatives and for less on others. It is possible to offer a context (an interactivity environment) where two important characteristics of exploration namely, amount and direction of information search, can be varied. The system fosters the development of exploration and commitment processes, enhancing preferences and the development of cognitive educational, occupational and job worlds structure.

In conclusion, the move with hypermedia towards a more flexible and open access to information in CAGSs is consistent with the shift towards a more open professional model in career guidance where the individual is the focus of intervention.

Literature

1. Association of Computer-Based for Career Information. (1990). 1989-90 Directory of state-based career information delivery systems. Eugene, OR: ASCI Clearing-House.
2. Beeman, W. O., Anderson, K. T., Baden, G., Larken, J., Mc Lard, P. A., Mc Quillan, P., and Schields, M. (1987). Hypertext and pluralism: from lineal to non-lineal thinking. Proceedings of Hypertext' 87.(67-78). University of North Carolina at Chapel Hill.
3. Chapman, W., & Katz, M. R. (1982). Summary of a survey of career information systems in secondary schools and assessment of alternative types. Princeton. NJ: Educational Testing Service.
4. Costa Pereira, D., Oliveira, A. (1990). Psychopedagogic Aspects of Hypermedia Courseware. In D. Jonanssen and H. Mandl. Designing Hypermedia for Learning. NATO ASI Series F: Computer and Systems Sciences, 67, 14, 251-262. Berlim: Springer-Verlag.
5. Donaldson, J. (1988) Hypercard's hyperactivity. Personal Computer World, 154-58.
6. Gati, I. (1986) Making career decisions-a sequential elimination approach. Journal of Counseling Psychology, 33, 4, 408-17.
7. Gomes, A., Oliveira, A., Costa Pereira, D. (1989). O Hypercard e o ensino assistido por computador. Personal Computer World, 29, 3, 86-92.
8. Katz, M. (1988). Une nouvelle technologie dans la guidance: l'ordinateur interactif. L'orientation scolaire et professionnelle, 17, 2, 109-123.

9. Mc Aleese, R. (1989). Navigation and Browsing. In R. Mc Aleese (ed.) Hypertext: theory into pratice. London: Blackwell.
10. Nielsen, J. (1990). Survey of hipertext usability. In J. Nielsen. Hypertext and Hypermedia. Boston: Academic Press.
11. Philips, S. D. (1982). The development of career choices: the relationship between patterns of commitment and career outcome in adulthood. Journal of Vocational Behavior, 20, 141-152.
12. Plant, P. (1989). Technology is the answer: what is the question? On computers in careers Guidance in Western Europe. Paper presented at the Second European Conference on Computers in Careers Guidance. Cambridge, UK.
13. Sampson, J. P., Jr.. (1986). Computer apllications in testing and assessment (Special issue). Measurement and Evaluation in Couseling and Development, 14, 567-583.
14. Sampson, James P., Reardon, Robert C., Lenz, Janet G. (1991) Journal of Career Development, 17,3,185-192.
15. Sampson, J. P., Jr., Shahnasarian, M., Reardon, R. C. (1987). Computer assisted career guidance: A national perspective on the use of DISCOVER and SIGI. Journal of Counseling and Development, 65, 416-419.
16. Sampson, J. P., Jr., Shahnasarian, M., Reardon, R. C. (1988). Factors influencing the use of DISCOVER and SIGI. Journal of Career Development, 15, 75-86.
17. Sampson, J. P., Peterson, G.W., Reardon, R.C. (1990). Counselor intervention strategies for computer assisted career guidance: an information processing approach. Journal of Career Development, 16, 2, 139-154.
18. Taveira, M. C: Campos, B. P. (1989). Novas Tecnologias de Informação na Orientação Vocacional. Cadernos de Consulta Psicológica, 5, 81-94.
19. Taveira, M. C., Campos, B. P. (1990). Hypermedia and career counseling for personal flexibility. Proceedings of the AIOSP XIV World Congress Montréal, Canada.
20. Watts, A. G. , Ballantine, M. (1981). Computers in careers guidance: an overview. Careers Journal, 1-3.
21. Williams, G. (1987). Hypercard. Byte, 109-117.

Knowledge Acquisition with Texts by Means of Flexible Computer-Assisted Information Access

Heinz Mandl, Wolfgang Schnotz, Emmanuel Picard, and Michael Henninger

Abstract: In this empirical study, it was tested how far learning results differ in presenting learning material by means of hypertext versus simultaneous graphical text presentation and how far these differences are dependent on specific learning objectives and on the readers' specific learning prerequisites. According to the aptitude-treatment approach, it was evidenced that, on the one hand, subjects with higher general learning prerequisites generated higher learning results in combination with hypertext presentation. On the other hand, subjects with lower general learning prerequisites generated higher learning results in combination with simultaneous text presentation on paper.

1. Introduction

To date, research on learning with texts has mostly referred to the processing of sequentially organized verbal information presented in written discourse. The structure of such linear organized texts determines - provided the text is read from top to bottom - in which sequence the reader constructs the corresponding mental representation. According to the way text is organized, different mental representations can result although the content of the text is the same. This is due to the fact that certain cognitive processes are facilitated and certain others are hindered by certain types of text organization.

Frequently in textbooks, different topics, theses, and so forth, are described according to different points of view and opposed to each other. One possibility to accomplish this is, first, to describe one topic as a whole and then to do the same with the other topic. Such type of presentation can be designated as object-oriented text organisation. Another possibility is that the topics are dealt with under a certain aspect, and subsequently under the next aspect, and so forth. This type of representation can be designated as aspect-oriented text organisation. Both types of sequencing offer certain advantages and have specific disadvantages. Schnotz (1982, 1984) found that a text organized in object-oriented manner focuses the attention onto how the several pieces of information about one specific topic are intertwined. In opposition, an aspect-oriented text organization rather puts the commonalities and differences between several topics to the fore. Furthermore, it was evidenced that an object-oriented text organization allows for a more effective learning in learners with lower prior knowledge than an aspect-oriented text, since these learners experience more difficulty in the afforded mental switching from one topic to the other. In reverse, an aspect-oriented text structure seems to allow for more effective learning in learners with higher prior knowledge, since, on the one hand, the mental switching from one topic to the other seems to be less difficult for them and, on the other hand, the comparing between topics is facilitated. Accordingly, different text versions should be developed for learners with differing learning prerequisites which is, of course, hardly feasible.

2. Graphical Display versus Hypertext

As a possible solution to the problem described above, Waller and Whalley (1984) suggested a form of presentation wherein all text sections are presented simultaneously on an accordingly large sheet of paper. In their study, they found that this so-called graphical display - in combination with the corresponding instruction - led to a more intensive comparative processing than the aspect-oriented or object-oriented text versions. Obviously this type of presentation offers very propitious preconditions for both the understanding of single topics and the comparison between them, since, in the graphical-display condition, the learner has the opportunity to relate pieces of information without having to turn pages and to perform difficult search processes. Of course, such type of flexible access structure can only be implemented with texts of limited length.

A less restricted possibility to realize such a flexible information access, wherein the learner can proceed according to his or her individual learning prerequisites, is offered in the framework of computer-assisted learning, especially with so-called hypertexts (Nelson, 1967). A hypertext is an electronic document, the individual sections of which could be represented as nodes within a network, wherein the learner can freely browse. Such a hypertext offers to the learner, such as the simultaneous graphical presentation, freedom of accessing the individual text sections according to his or her learning prerequisites and information needs. In the case of hypertext, flexible access is not limited to a restricted number of text sections fitting on one sheet of paper. Flexible access to a much larger number of text sections is possible. Every text section can, for example, be represented by its heading in a menu. If the heading is activated, the text subsumed under the heading appears immediately.

The present study aimed at answering the question of how learning with texts containing the feature of flexible-access structure presented by means of simultaneous text presentation differs from learning the same content presented by means of hypertext. In that context detailed insights about knowledge acquisition with hypertexts were to be gained.

However, processes of knowledge acquisition ensue in different ways according to the learner's objective and his or her individual learning prerequisites (cf. Gagné, 1962; Mandl & Spada, 1988; Weinert, Helmke & Schneider, 1989). In a text of the type described above, the learner can pursue different objectives. He or she may, for example, want to understand the topics separately and try to construct a coherent mental representation of each: such a strategy can be defined as object-oriented processing. He or she may endeavour to understand each of the topics individually, but may additionally want to compare the topics according to several aspects: such a strategy can be defined as aspect-oriented processing. In object-oriented processing versus aspect-oriented processing, the learner adopts different perspectives: In object-oriented processing, the analysis of the semantic relation within topics is on the fore. In aspect-oriented processing, a perspective is suggested wherein the analysis of the semantic relations between topics is focussed.

Learners differ according to their individual learning prerequisites such as prior knowledge and intelligence. Since in understanding texts the presented information is structured by means of one's own prior knowledge and since numerous cognitive processes are to be activated, one can expect that learners react differently to certain types of text presentation in combination with certain processing orientations. On that background, the following issues arise:

— Do learning processes and learning results differ in presenting a content by means of hypertext versus a simultaneous graphical text presentation?

— Are these effects of the type of text presentation on learning processes and learning results different according to specific processing orientations?
— Are these effects on learning processes and learning results different for learners with differing learning prerequisites?

3. Method

3.1 Subjects

Subjects were 64 students. The mean age was 25.7 years (s = 3.8). The participants (28 women, 36 men) were randomly distributed into four groups. Before the onset of the main phase, a pretest was performed. In that pretest, a part of an intelligence test of Horn (1983) was administered, in order to assess general cognitive abilities. Furthermore, a prior-knowledge test was administered in form of testing knowledge about relevant terms whereby the relevant terms were mingled with distractor-terms. The subjects had to illustrate these terms in written form. No remarkable differences appeared between the groups with regard to the score of prior knowledge and intelligence.

3.2 Learning Material

The experimental text used by Schnotz (1982, 1984) served as learning material. The experimental text contains the description of two types of psychotherapy: psychoanalysis and behaviour therapy. Each type of therapy had five sections. The length of the text was 1079 words. Additionally, each of the 10 sections had a corresponding subheading. The experimental text was presented in different ways: as hypertext or as simultaneous graphical presentation.

In the hypertext presentation, the texts were read at the computer. A menu containing ten screenbuttons was presented. Five buttons ordered in a column lead to themes of psychoanalysis, five other buttons in another column to themes of behaviour therapy. If one of the ten buttons was clicked, the text announced by the button appeared. After reading the text, one had to click on a button which returned to the menu. Starting anew from the menu, one could select another section, etc. In the simultaneous graphical text presentation on paper, all texts were presented with corresponding subheadings on a sheet of paper (size DIN A 3). The order of the sections was the same as in the hypertext-presentation.

3.3 Procedure

The four groups of subjects were administered different treatments according to a 2x2-factorial design (*type of presentation x instruction*). They obtained the text either as hypertext or as simultaneous text presentation; and they received either the instruction to read the text with the objective in mind to later present the topics separately in written form (i.e., object-oriented instruction) or the instruction to read the text on the background of the task, to later present the topics in written form and to compare them with each other (i.e., aspect-oriented instruction). The subjects could read the text without time limitation.

After the learning phase, the subjects worked on a computer based comprehension test consisting of 57 items. They had to react to a series of statements: There were two keys at their disposal: green for "Yes, the statement is true" and red for "No, the statement is false". In the so-called non-comparison items (N=42), the focus was only on relations within the objects; in the comparison items (N=15), comparisons between both types of therapy were made. The instruction was worded with the intention for the subjects to work thoroughly and fast. After the comprehension test, the subjects had to either present the two topics separately in written form (i.e., object-oriented instruction), or to describe and compare the topics with each other in written form (i.e., aspect-oriented instruction). For this performance there was half an hour available.

In assessing the comprehension test, the following data per subject were obtained: number of non-comparison items with correct solutions, number of comparison items with correct solutions, number of solved non-comparison items per minute, and number of solved comparison items per minute. In assessing the written protocols, the following data per subject were obtained: number of text propositions literally reproducing the topic or reproducing the gist of it, number of transitions within the two topics (i.e., how many transitions occurred from one subtopic to another within the very same type of therapy), and number of transitions between the two topics (i.e., how many transitions occurred from one subtopic of one therapy to a subtopic of another therapy).

The group of 64 subjects was median-splitted according to prior knowledge and intelligence. Thus, on the part of the learning prerequisites, two additional factors were to be taken into account: prior knowledge (higher/lower) and intelligence (higher/lower). For the different dependent variables, a 3-way analysis of variance was calculated with the factors *type of presentation x type of instruction x prior knowledge* and another 3-way analysis of variance with the factors *type of presentation x type of instruction x intelligence.*

4. Results

In the following the effects of hypertext versus simultaneous text presentation, aspect-oriented instruction versus object-oriented instruction as well as intelligence and prior knowledge on the learning results will be described. The analysis refers to the subjects' performance in the text reproduction and the comprehension test.

4.1 Text Reproduction

First, the effects of the following factors were assessed: type of presentation, instruction, and prior knowledge. Concerning the two types of presentation, no clear differences appeared. Only prior knowledge (in the variable *number of propositions*: $p < .05$, $F_{(1,55)} = 6.1$) and instruction (in the variable *number of transitions within topics*: $p < .05$, $F_{(1,55)} = 10.6$, and in the variable *number of transitions between topics*: $p < .01$, $F_{(1,55)} = 37.6$) showed significant main effects. Persons with higher prior knowledge produced a greater number of propositions and transitions than persons with lower prior knowledge. In aspect-oriented instruction, a higher number of transitions between topics was produced than in object-oriented instruction. In reverse, learning with object-oriented instruction led to a higher number of transitions within a topic.

In the analysis of variance with the factors *type of presentation*, *instruction*, and *intelligence*, the main effect of intelligence was significant (in the variable *number of propositions*: $p < .10$, $F_{(1,55)} = 3.4$ and in the variable *number of transitions within topics*: $p < .05$, $F_{(1,55)} = 4.0$). Subjects with higher intelligence produced more propositions and transitions. The factor *instruction* also revealed a significant effect. In object-oriented instruction a greater number of transitions within topics was produced than with aspect-oriented instruction ($p < .01$; $F_{(1,55)} = 8.9$). In the variable *number of transitions between topics* a higher number of transitions resulted with aspect-oriented instruction than with object-oriented instruction ($p < 0.01$; $F_{(1,55)} = 46.5$). The interaction *intelligence x type of presentation* in the variable *number of transitions between topics* ($p < .05$, $F_{(1,55)} = 4.3$) showed that in subjects with higher intelligence learning with hypertext led to a higher number of transitions than learning with simultaneous graphical text presentation. However, subjects with lower intelligence had a higher number of transitions in learning with simultaneous graphical text presentation than with hypertext. However, that effect appeared only in aspect-oriented instruction. The subjects who received an object-oriented instruction hardly reached differing results in the respective factor combinations (*type of presentation x instruction x intelligence*: $p < .05$, $F_{(1,55)} = 7.1$).

Summing up the results on retention performance we can say that the use of hypertext did not result in an improved retention of the learning material. If one takes the subjects' learning prerequisites into consideration, differences between the types of presentation appeared. In learning with hypertext, subjects with higher learning prerequisites (higher prior knowledge, higher intelligence) reached a higher number of proposition and a higher number of transitions than in learning with the simultaneous graphical text presentation. However, subjects with lower learning prerequisites reached higher scores in learning with the simultaneous graphical text presentation than with hypertext.

4.2 Text Comprehension

Among the three factors *type of presentation*, *instruction*, and *prior knowledge* only prior knowledge resulted in significant main effects. In the variables *non-comparison items* ($p < .01$, $F_{(1,55)} = 10.0$), *non-comparison items per minute* ($p < .01$, $F_{(1,55)} = 7.4$), and the *comparison items per minute* ($p < .10$, $F_{(1,55)} = 3.2$), persons with higher prior knowledge produced higher scores. The three way interaction in the variable *comparison items per minute* ($p < .10$, $F_{(1,55)} = 3.0$) was especially interesting. It was shown that in learning with the simultaneous text presentation subjects with higher prior knowledge and aspect-oriented instruction obtained higher performance scores than subjects with lower prior knowledge. However, in simultaneous graphical text presentation subjects with lower prior knowledge and with object-oriented instruction produced more correct answers than learners with higher prior knowledge. In learning with hypertext subjects with higher prior knowledge attained higher comprehension scores than subjects with lower prior knowledge in both instructional conditions.

In the analysis of variance with the factors *type of presentation*, *instruction*, and *intelligence* no main effect was significant. However, the interaction *type of presentation x intelligence* was significant in the variable *non-comparison items* ($p < .10$, $F_{(1,55)} = 2.9$) and in the variable *comparison items* ($p < .10$, $F_{(1,55)} = 2.8$). There were similar effects in both interactions: Subjects with higher intelligence attained higher scores in learning with hypertext than in learning with simultaneous graphical text presentation. In reverse, subjects with lower intelligence attained higher scores in learning with simultaneous graphical text presentation than in learning with hypertext. Furthermore, the interaction *intelligence x instruction* was significant in the variable *comparison items* ($p < .10$, $F_{(1,55)} = 3.1$). It was found that subjects with higher intelligence attained higher scores in the comprehension test with aspect-oriented instruction than with object-oriented instruction. Subjects with lower intelligence scored better in the comprehension test with object-oriented instruction than with aspect-oriented instruction.

Summing up the results in the comprehension variables, no main effects were found, whereas the interactions were clear-cut. Subjects with higher learning prerequisites performed better in learning with hypertext than in learning with simultaneous graphical text presentation. However, subjects with lower learning prerequisites performed better in learning with simultaneous graphical text presentation than in learning with hypertext.

5. Discussion

The results of this study show that learning with hypertext is not necessarily more advantageous than learning with simultaneous graphical text presentation. The data reveal the necessity to analyse the problem more deeply. The assumption expressed at the beginning of this chapter, i.e. that the type of presentation and the individual learning prerequisites interact, is ascertained by the presented data. Learning with hypertext seems to foster higher performance in subjects with higher learning prerequisites. In simultaneous graphical text presentation of learning material, these subjects show up lower performance than subjects with lower learning prerequisites. This effect might possibly be caused by motivational effects of hypertext due to its novelty. Subjects could have worked on that form of text presentation with more interest. If this was the case, however, the effect should be valid for all subjects. Since subjects with lower learning prerequisites frequently scored worse in learning with hypertext than in learning with simultaneous graphical text presentation, that explanation obviously does not cover the facts. One could assume that learning with hypertext affords a higher cognitive effort which implies more difficulty for subjects with lower learning prerequisites than for subjects with higher learning prerequisites. However, this still doesn't explain the drop in performance in subjects with higher learning prerequisites when learning with simultaneous graphical text presentation. Assuming that the simultaneous graphical text presentation affords less cognitive demands, one might want to explain that drop in performance in subjects with higher learning prerequisites while learning with simultaneous graphical text presentation with the assumption, that cognitive difficulty might trigger a higher cognitive effort in subjects with higher learning prerequisites. The possibility of such an interpretation is enhanced by the effects of the factor *instruction* in subjects with higher learning prerequisites, where the more difficult aspect-oriented instruction lead to higher performance. This finding corresponds to the assumption resulting of the aptitude-treatment-interaction approach (ATI, Snow & Salomon, 1975), that instructional treatments interact specifically with individual learning prerequisites.

According to the supplantation approach of Salomon (1970, 1979), an improvement of learning performance might be expected with hypertexts, since specific cognition related operations are required for text processing. This expectation could not be confirmed in this study. Only subjects with higher learning prerequisites seemed to be able to profit from the explicit elicitation of such operations and to obtain higher learning performance.

In sum, these results show that no significant general differences appear in learning between the different types of text presentations. Thus, a more detailed analysis of the relation between learning prerequisites and text presentation seems to be necessary. Such an analysis is also necessary in the issue of whether the type of text presentation interacts with the orientation of processing. In this case, effects only appeared, if the factor *learning prerequisites* was taken into account. More detailed investigations of processing during learning with these different types of text presentation in combination with learning prerequisites and orientation of processing will be necessary in the future.

Literature

1. Gagné, R.M. (1962). The acquisition of knowledge. Psychological Review, 69, 335-365.
2. Horn, W. (1983). Leistungsprüfsystem L-P-S. Handanweisung. Göttingen: Verlag für Psychologie.
3. Mandl, H., & Spada, H. (Eds.). (1988). Wissenspsychologie [Knowledge Psychology]. Munich, Weinheim: Psychologie Verlags Union.
4. Nelson, T.H. (1967). Getting it out of our system. In Information Retrieval: A Critical Review. In G. Schechter (Ed.) (pp.191-210). Washington, D.C.: Thompson Books.
5. Salomon, G. (1970). What does it do to Johnny? Viewpoints. Bulletin of the School of Education, Indiana University, 5, 33-62
6. Salomon, G. (1979). Interaction of media, cognition, and learning. San Francisco: Jossey-Bass.
7. Schnotz, W. (1982). How do different readers learn with different text organisations? In A. Flammer & W. Kintsch (Eds.), Discourse Processing (pp. 81-98). Amsterdam: North-Holland.
8. Schnotz, W. (1984). Comparative instructional text organization. In H. Mandl, N.L. Stein & T. Trabasso (Eds.), Learning and comprehension of text (pp. 53-81). Hillsdale, NJ: Lawrence Erlbaum.
9. Snow, R.E., & Salomon, G. (1975). Lerner-Merkmale und Unterrichtsmedien [Learner features and instructional media]. In H. Dichanz & G. Kolb (Eds.), Quellentexte zur Unterrichtstechnologie II (pp. 122-139). Stuttgart: Klett.
10. Waller, R., & Whalley, P. (1984). Graphically organised prose. In E. De Corte, H. Lodewijks, R. Parmentier, & P. Span (Eds.), Learning and instruction. European research in an international context: Volume 1 (pp. 369-381). Oxford/Leuven: Leuven University Press and Pergamon Press.
11. Weinert, F.E., Helmke, A., & Schneider, W. (1989). Individual differences in learning performance and in school achievement: Plausible parallels and unexplained discrepancies. In H. Mandl, E. De Corte, N. Bennett & H.F. Friedrich (Eds.), Learning and instruction. European research in an international context: Volume 2.1 (pp. 461-479). Oxford: Pergamon Press.

2 Hypermedia Language

Learning Through Browsing : Observations on the Production of Self-directed Learning Systems for Language Students

Mike Harland

Department of Hispanic Studies, University of Glasgow, Scotland

Abstract: The paper outlines experience gained in the production of a language learning system which incorporates some of the elements of hypermedia, including text, sound and graphics. Issues such as navigation, user help and orientation, iconographic and screen design problems, and multidimensional structuring are discussed, as well as the need for basic guide-lines to promote browsing as a *Learning* method. Emphasis is placed on interactive forms of hypermedia which aid this learning process, rather than those that just provide answers, as in the case of general reference systems. The need to design "semi-intelligent" forms of user prompting and help facilities is emphasized. It is argued that linear learning methods are less "intuitive" than we think and a turning point has been reached in our approach to learning and, consequently, to teaching.

1. Hypertext, HyperMedia, MultiMedia: where is the learning?

As a linguist and full-time lecturer, who has spent a large amount of time attempting to create a hypermedia system for language learning, I should like to raise certain issues for discussion, both from the practical angle as well as from a theoretical and hypothetical viewpoint, since I believe research in HyperMedia has so far not faced the issue of learning, as opposed to referencing and information gathering. I shall first question the terminology itself.

HyperThingummyIsm

'HyperText' is an increasingly "fuzzy" term: Ted Nelson apparently invented the term as a way of describing 'non-sequential writing'; Roy Rada [11] defines HyperText in more technical terms as 'text database + semantic net + interface'; while Janet Fiderio [4] has proposed four distinct functional types - (i) on-line browser, (ii) problem resolver, (iii) library or literary exchange system, (iv) multi-purpose hybrid. As the technology developed, 'HyperMedia' has gradually taken over in this "fuzzy" terminology, and next we shall have 'MultiMedia' to contend with!

In the face of all this blurring of concepts, therefore, I should like to discuss certain features which I believe have led to these ambiguities and then try to propose some important distinctions that will have to be made, not only in terminology but also in the methods by which hypermedia systems are constructed.

Although HyperText may be used as a "buzz word" in many new computer applications to mean all kinds of relational interlinking mechanisms, I follow the line that we should apply the word HyperText solely to text. This means that the term only concerns the inter-relating of individual words, 'chunks', or files of text. To apply the term to any system that incorporates both words and graphics is, I believe, a misnomer and can lead to grave misunderstandings as to how to promote a stable interaction between the learner/referencer and the medium.

Text is essentially a two-dimensional form of communication and the kind of cognition involved is linked to this plane. Once one tries to combine any two of the three media (text, graphics or sound) the interactions involved change cognitively and this should properly be referred to as HyperMedia. Unfortunately, a lot of people seem to confuse MultiMedia with HyperMedia and overlay the words with contemporary connotations of 'communications Media', so that what lies at the back of their minds are the parallel ideas of 'magazine journalism'=text, 'CD/Hi-Fi'=sound, 'TV/Cinema'=graphics. Even so, whatever the superimposed concepts that produce so much "razzamatazz" in MultiMedia demonstrations, where multiple screens and multiple technologies abound, I should like to stress the main, overriding distinction between Text on the one hand, and Graphics/Sound on the other: for the latter have a three-dimensional quality which is sometimes overlooked when people try to apply them to small VDU screens, never mind to overhead projections; they force the user/student into a much more relational environment and a proportionately more alien one to navigate, especially in the mind, so interfering with their 'cognitive mapping' and their methods of interaction. Indeed, the cognitive processes involved are in many ways still unexplored, specifically in relation to **learning** (as opposed, that is, to the task of **referencing**).

The preoccupation with user orientation and navigation has led to a lot of research into screen layout, graphical presentation and visual aids such as icons, menus and dialog boxes to improve ergonomics. Icons especially have been seen as a more immediate way of relaying key concepts to the user (but not without some problems as we shall see later). However, much of these preoccupations will perhaps disappear in true learning systems, because these will most likely require familiarization and over the longer term the student will grow to understand the interface more. Iconic and graphical cues can be a positive navigational aid - that is not in contention (sound itself can often be a far more intuitive or natural form of discourse cue and has great potential); but if the designer of any 'HyperMedium' fails to remember for even one moment that he/she has left the two-dimensional plane of the printed text for the three-dimensional universe of words, pictures and sounds, where far more individually subjective perspectives are possible, then the design will be unstable and the result will be unpredictable, like Alice's Wonderland.

Through the WIMP looking glass

One can see this immediately occurring in basic Hypertexts themselves, through the graphical 'accidents' of the WIMP interface: once the text is 'animated' through the device of a scrolling field, or placed in 'perspective' by 'framing' it in several, or even just one, popup window, then as far as the user is concerned the text has been transposed into a more relative 'HyperMedium' and from then on his/her interactions and depth of comprehension will be subject to far different effects than those of the simple printed page: reading a scrolling text, for example, requires a motor skill which momentarily 'distracts' the mind from comprehension, much as turning the page of the traditional book can produce a mental hiatus; windowed text will cause a focussing of attention, so that multiple windows will inevitably lead to confusion over priorities and the relevance of textual content. *Context* has always been the determining factor in the semantics of communication through language and WIMP interfaces inevitably manipulate notions of context and meaning.

Returning, however, to the central notion of Learner Browsing, HyperText research has so far concentrated mainly on the physical nature of linkage and browsing ergonomics; that is to say, the user's skill (or lack of it) in mastering the browsing technique and solving the navigational problems.

Browsing, it seems, has been approached mainly as a means to **referencing**: - compare this approach with a driver who masters the controls of a car, learns the correct iconic messages (i.e. traffic signs), and manages to navigate from A to B picking up the shopping and dropping off the children. Rarely does he/she have time to fully take in the landscape and admire it, to work out the reasons for traffic filters, or placing of junctions, and certainly not learn about the social life of pedestrians, fellow drivers, etc. Browsing has been looked at more from a data retrieval angle and tends at times to give the learning and comprehension aims a secondary role.

A different perspective was at least opened up through using HyperTexts in reverse to give them a constructive function, through the concept of 'intertextuality' introduced by Havholm & Stewart [7]. Here group activity, interacting in real-time, produces links and semantic structures to produce a form of active learning: the relational nature of Hypertext thus becomes a tool for the reference process to be involved in increasing the knowledge base and adding to the data available, something that mere reference browsing does not produce in any guaranteed fashion. This focus on the learning process and the discovery of the **meaning** of a text is what HyperText and consequently HyperMedia should really be about, not just providing 'information' for the browser and 'entertaining' him/her with the 'fascination' of the medium.

Text and Context

As with language learning, therefore, the essential factor is Context. The type of HyperText or HyperMedia system one aims to design should primarily take into account the context of its subject matter. Different disciplines will require correspondingly varied functions from Hypertexts: the Sciences will look for animation and simulation as well as textual explanation and guidance. The Humanities will be more text based, but linguists at least will require simulation and animation of certain concepts, especially syntax and phonetics. Visual functions therefore play key roles, but the need for graphic, colour or sound elements should be decided on their contributory value, i.e. if they contribute to the learning or understanding process then they should be allowed and correctly applied for given effects; otherwise they are a distraction, a digression, or quite often an element of confusion [6].

Language (and by implication the process of language learning), for example, has its own particular as well as shared contexts: speech and text have an underlying rhythm or style; they have a structure giving emphases, pauses, progression and cohesion; they have rhetorical devices, idiomatic expressions and metaphorical levels producing images and symbols. HyperMedia design should therefore be aware of this 'grammar', 'syntax' and 'metacoding' and use its own elements to emulate these 'semantic structures' within language, as suggested by Marshall and Irish [8]: "The ultimate linearity resulting from link traversal brings with it a need to create coherence, manage transitions and supply context as in traditional written forms". In fact graphics, when visually linked to text, probably represent the most powerful means of promoting learning, including the animation of the text itself and the capacity now available to us for indicating the transfer and process of meaning through those same animation effects: for example, a zooming title window and a sound track at the start of a session can go some way towards mimicking the idea of that magic moment when one opens the covers of a book to start reading and exploring the text; the collocation of windows can give a sense of relationship and hence metaphor; just as graphics can confer a sense of imagery and symbol. Navigational techniques in HyperMedia should similarly reflect the mental processes of discovery, try to guide the reader, and not just show him or her the equivalent of a page number or position in the book.

The power of graphics and all the other empowering facilities of hypermedia now provide us with a means of suggesting, hinting, coaxing and guiding the student; they thus give us the opportunity to 'mediate' and 'negotiate' more fully with the learner in the learning process, without dictatorial control. There is a large 'vocabulary' still to be compiled which in many ways has probably already been discovered by the directors of theatre and cinema, but remains undocumented in any rigourous fashion. The implication is that good hypermedia design will of necessity need the skills of graphic artists and 'continuity' specialists, as suggested again by Marshall and Irish [8] in their Hypertext '89 paper: "Problems associated with screen layout require the skills and conventions of graphic design";"hypertext traversal has certain dynamic qualities suggesting the characteristics and associated difficulties of film-making or animation".

Conceal or Reveal?

One very important difference between referential and learner browsing comes with the dilemma of Concealment or Revelation: many of the facilities available under programmable hypertexts and OOP-based systems use the object properties of 'hidden' or 'visible' and their use can give rise to many stunning screen effects; judicious use of such facilities will also need to be encouraged and guide-lines found. But the more general idea of concealing or revealing different kinds of information will have to be fully researched - experienced teachers often intuitively know when or when not to give further information to a student as they keep in mind the pace or level at which the student is presently working. Any forms of interactive HyperMedia for learning will have to take cognizance of this issue: a reference browser may not wish to see where the computer has gone to get its information, but a student while learning quite often may need to be shown the process of data retrieval or processing, since he/she may need to understand that very process, especially when it is mimicking human cognitive processes. Tutorial and demonstration software already use this mode, but any expert forms of HyperMedia will constantly have to decide on the levels of transparency to adopt.

Context has already been linked to meaning and the measure of context is Relevance. No learning can take place without an awareness of context: it is an awareness of the relative importance of the different items that go to make up that context that provides them with their relevance; and the relative weight of their importance (i.e. their individual relevance) decides the overall meaning. A student, in deciding the relevance of any item, will arrive at an individual meaning, obtain a different learning experience. HyperMedia, because of its relativistic nature, is thus faced with a dilemma of responsibility: how far to dictate context and meaning (and so the form of learning) and how far to leave the 'weighting' of the links it makes open to free browsing. The task therefore of HyperMedia is to lead to understanding and produce meaning in a relative context: the task is divided between the need for **active guidance** and **passive help** facilities - a varying degree of both will always be required and the just 'balance' must be found.

2. Some recent experiences in a language learning HyperSystem

Let us now turn to a slightly more practical view of these preoccupations. A project between members of Glasgow and Oporto Universities has set out to explore the possibilities of bilingual dictionaries on computer which go beyond the bounds of the normal printed dictionary and seek to reunite it with the other tools of language acquisition such as vocabulary, grammar, syntax, and idiom books as well as technical, commercial and scientific termbanks. In addition to hypertext linking between the above, all can be further linked in modular fashion to any texts, linguistic or literary, and a whole series of interactive tutorial or exercise teaching modules. The present prototype is being developed under HyperCard and its scripting language HyperTalk, which because of its inherent modular nature enables it to produce a form of "inter-application communication": e.g. database, text, sound and graphic information can be interrelated, processed or transmitted over the constituent stacks independently of their particular functions - i.e. drill and exercise stacks can obtain information from database stacks, paste it into word processor files or match it against parsed input - thus any part of the 'modular network' can use the facilities of any other part.

2 and 3-dimensional shifts

Through the course of development the differences between referential and learning needs have only arisen gradually, so that many of the lessons learned have not yet been put into practice. Many of the structural and navigational guide-lines suggested by Hardman and Sharratt [5,6] have been discovered to be well founded, although these are meant for hypertexts rather than hypermedia. Differences come to light, for example, when mention is made by Hardman of a preference towards *wide* and *shallow* hierarchies for browsing: these terms are still mainly 2-dimensional and would not apply for instance in graphic browsing where one is 'zooming' *into* or *out of* pictures such as maps or of objects and their constituent parts - in the **relative** space of graphics 'shallow' or 'wide' descriptors for structures don't exactly apply (even if the general tenet would still seem to hold true, because the practice of repeated 'zooming' into a graphic simply turns the the user interface through 90 degrees and 'deeper' vertical browsing replaces 'wider' horizontal browsing). Once one starts to design large global systems, the emphasis I think would be better placed on *central* landmarks in navigation and the forcing of browser action along *radial* highways. Certainly, the intuitive linking of our dictionary to its own constituent satellites in this radial manner, and their later linking with other modules points to this. Besides which, HyperMedia must of necessity deal much more in terms of semantic networks and not just the cross-referred tree-structure hierarchies of HyperText.

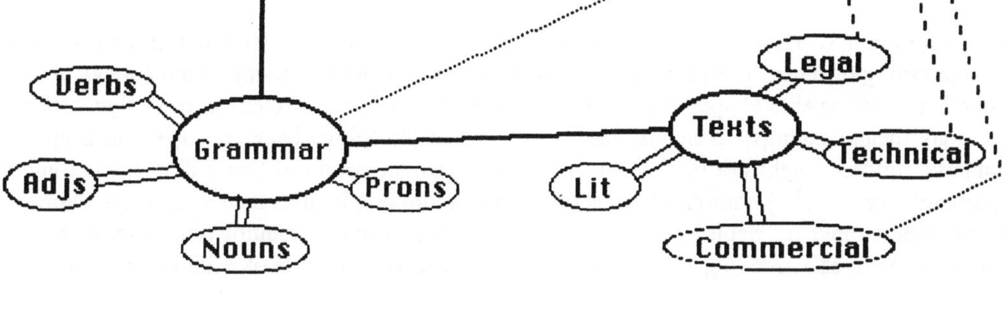

Any infringements of the 'traffic rules' should as far as possible be kept hidden from the user, or else browsing confined to a 'two-way return ticket' (dotted lines in diagram).

HELP!

The availability of **active** on-line help was a constant aim and the hope is that the application of AI techniques can deliver **context-sensitive** help (inference engines are already being developed for HyperCard). The problem with most active forms of help is that they produce a general surfeit of metainformation and what Marshall and Irish[8] describe as "aboutness". The importance of distinguishing between help for reference browsing and exploratory learning is best emphasized by Schank and Farrell[12]: "We propose that learning in schools should be experiential, learning by doing ... We attempt to replace the view of the computer as an electronic textbook for handing down answers with the view of the computer as a powerful medium for exploring ideas"; "Schools should teach children the questions, not answers". Similarly Jakob Nielsen's survey of hypertext usability [10] points to the need for loose forms of passive guidance to promote learning:"Users who were exploring the hypertext structure to try to learn about the subject it covered made heavy use of a guided tour facility and not very much use of the index, while users who were trying to answer specific questions behaved in the opposite way". In our case, passive guidance is subliminally present through the navigational 'corridors' that are allowed or disallowed by the system, but it is now imperative that ideas such as 'tours' within HyperMedia should be further built upon through the use of AI advice systems.

One example of such a use for passive guidance in our system would be to advise the user as to how he/she should best traverse the modules to carry out certain dictionary functions. Browsers could be queried on their exact needs and aims and advised accordingly as to their best 'route', e.g.:

1) they would be sent directly to the main keyword module as a straight lookup facility for immediate translation needs;
2) they would be directed towards the contextual usage modules if their needs involved any semantic or syntactic information;
3) the sound module would be accessed whenever practical instruction on pronunciation and phonetics were required;
4) the picture/graphics module would give information on visual or conceptual meanings for more technically specific or abstract meanings.

A Sign in Time:

Only programmable Hypertexts will be capable of such cognitive paths and icon design will aid the signposting of these. The problem with icons is that they are not always international, cross-cultural or even capable of spanning the many levels of user age and intelligence (a sign such as  may mean "savings" in Spain, but is nothing like the 'piggy-bank' metaphor in English. Similarly children might not readily understand the abstract notion of "return" in the common Hypercard icon 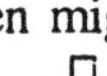). Animated icons offer much more possibilities than static ones - arrows that physically move or 'ripple' in different directions rather than just pointing or having 90° bends will be far more effective (a good example of a browsing icon is the book with turning pages). I see more mileage to be gained from icons than from symbols, and I would shrink from the notion suggested by Evenson, Rheinfrank and Wulff [3] of a new Hypermedia graphic sign-set (design guidelines for authors, yes ... but a whole design language for user cues, please no!).

Sound advice:

From an early stage the facility of HyperMacinTalk for mimicking native and foreign speech in the main dictionary was employed to give a rough pronunciation capability, but since then the MacRecorder with 8x compression of digitized sound has been applied. The uses for sound, however, were found to be far more extensive in HyperMedia than for more speech reproduction: sound can be yet another aid to hyperlinking. It can be a very economical navigation aid and is less intrusive in browser interaction and cognition than some visual effects or prompts. (Consider again the car driver: it is potentially dangerous to have one eye on the portable mini-television or one hand on the cell-phone, but we can all safely listen to the radio or talk to a passenger). Thus sound cues have been implemented for prompting the browser to interact or simply to click to return to a previous module. They have also been included in button scripts to help 'extend' the spatial constraints of screen size: e.g. a limited button name may not be meaningful to some browsers, but if an explanatory phrase is pronounced whenever the mouse is stationed over the button then the browser may gather its meaning. Sound thus has immense potential in navigational and cognitive situations.

The importance of "programmability":
selection control and variable response – linking on-the-fly

The basic idea of HyperText is that of providing a relational, non-linear function to user interaction. It often doesn't go much beyond controlled cross-referencing, fixed interlinking, or fixed annotation and replacement, however.

Using HyperCard, on the other hand, it was soon discovered that far more sophisticated responses to user interactions with the screen were possible. Thanks to an early "sticky button" technique in HyperTalk and now the fuller enhancements of the language in Version 1.2, it is possible to select any part of a text anywhere on screen without the need for pre-fixed buttoning. Linked with the programmable Find command and any of the "chunking" and text processing functions of HyperTalk, it becomes a powerful means of "variable linking" or what I would term "linking-on-the-fly".

This therefore goes far beyond the limited, *non-programmable and fixed* button text/graphic responses provided by hypertext applications such as GUIDE: it provides amongst other things the facility for producing **a form of intelligent response** to the user's direct input or selection of text from the screen, and can be controlled by keyboard, button or inbuilt script variable combinations, as well as being determined by such things as the order or time of selection.

A simple example of this is a hypermedia module in which any item of text (or an object graphic), can be selected without buttoning and interlinked or processed in whatever way the teacher wishes: i.e. matched to its foreign name or translation with pronunciation, linked forward to another related exercise, filtered through a termbank for all matches to be displayed in a popup window, searched for in a Verb Tables module and its function given, etc, etc. A more **interactive** version can be produced by programming it **in reverse**: random questions or tasks are presented and the student points to or selects items from the screen.

A simple vocabulary learning module was produced exploiting this reversible function, incorporating hyperlinking between text, graphics, and sound. It leaves the student free to interact according to his/her level of learning and understanding or need for stimulus. The context of a word is thus also linked to its meaning in several different ways and the process of what I would term "cognitive accumulation" introduced: the process of learning is made faster by a greater number of relational 'hooks' which can trigger the processes of recall; vision and sound are very strong 'hooks' on which to base this learning method.

Hypercard is also capable of sensing the location of the mouse pointer, so that even interactive navigation over the map of a room or town can be developed in response to directions given in the foreign language.

Another more complicated example of programmed interaction would be an exercise in which jumbled words are selected on the screen and dragged into position to form a sentence, their order is checked, translations of each word are requested, their spelling checked, better alternatives suggested (with a <why?> facility available, as in expert systems), and the whole process logged to a file for later analysis by the teacher. Elements of this idea have been used separately in a whole series of loggable exercises: gap-filling with error-matched input, contextual translation, split-sentence and word definition matching, as well as word order manipulation.

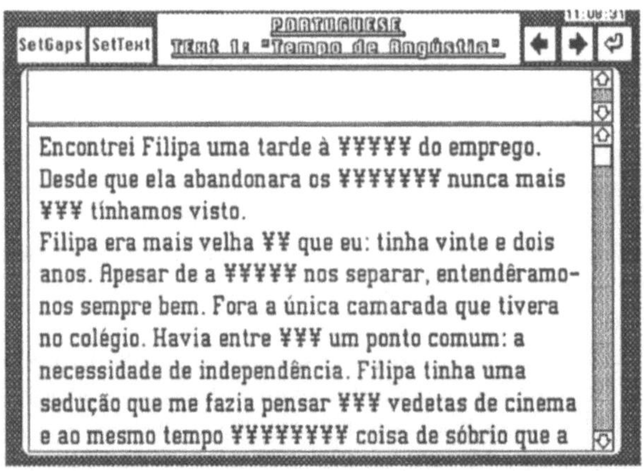

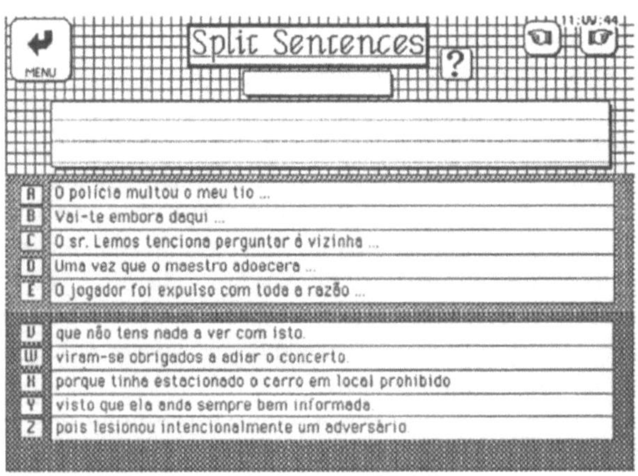

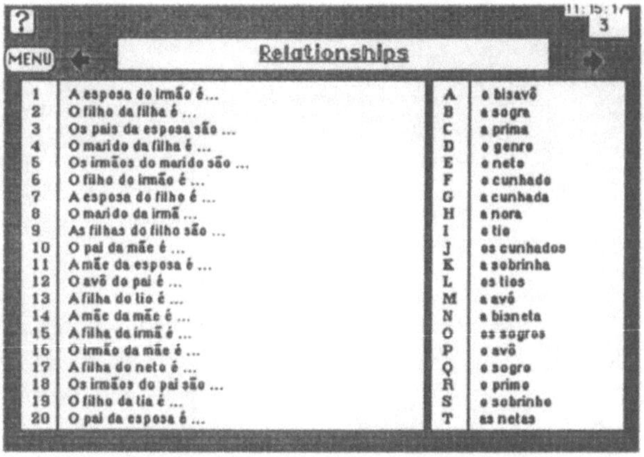

Facing up to the Interface: WYSIWID & WYDIWYS or 'What You See Is What You Do' and 'What You Don't Is What You Seek'!

Several facets of the project have so far been brought into discussion regarding their effect on learning. But the overall experience brings us back time and time again to the question of what the learner sees on the screen and really understands.

The main dictionary module has gone through several transformations: the conceptual layout of the printed bilingual dictionary was originally mapped directly onto the screen and only some of the traditional functions relegated to the 'satellite' modules, such as exemplary phrases, synonym/antonyms, and graphic representations. The result was a very 'busy' and very disorientating screen. The crucial ability to hide or reveal objects under HyperTalk then came into play: secondary text fields and buttons can be hidden until summoned; foreign versions of the native language can similarly be 'toggled' from language to language; menu controls and navigational choices can be relegated to popup menus or dialog boxes. The result is a much more compact, powerful, yet comprehensible interface to the user, where any doubts can be resolved through general on-line help facilities.

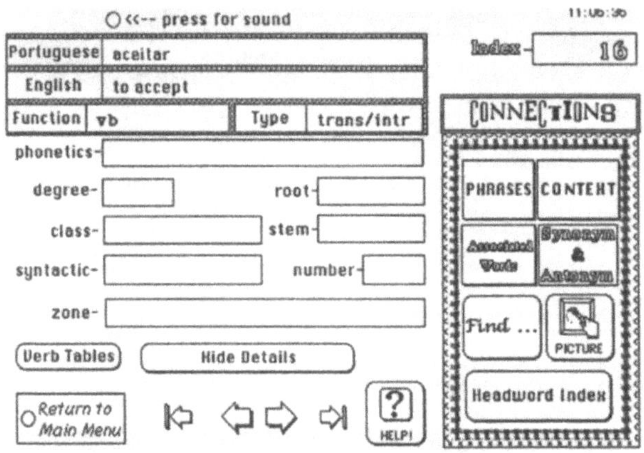

<<-- press for sound
Portuguese
aceitar
English
to accept
Function
vb
Type
trans/intr
phonetics-
degree-
root-
class-
stem-
syntactic-
number-
zone-
Verb Tables
Hide Details
Return to Main Menu
HELP!
Index
16
CONNECTIONS
PHRASES
CONTENT
Synonym & Antonym
Find ...
PICTURE
Headword Index

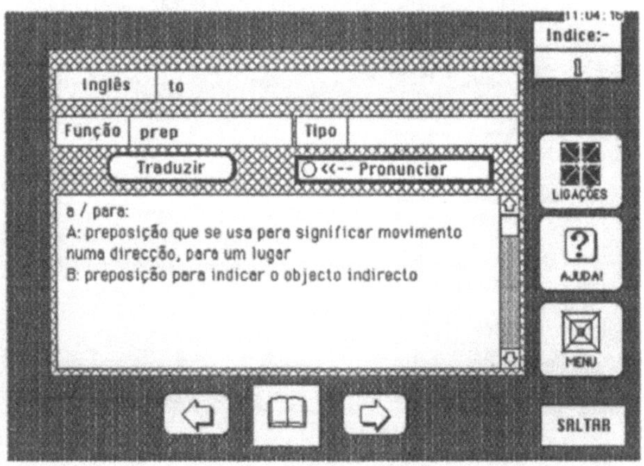

Indice:-
1
Inglês
to
Função
prep
Tipo
Traduzir
<<-- Pronunciar
a / para:
A: preposição que se usa para significar movimento numa direcção, para um lugar
B: preposição para indicar o objecto indirecto
LIGAÇÕES
AJUDA!
MENU
SALTAR

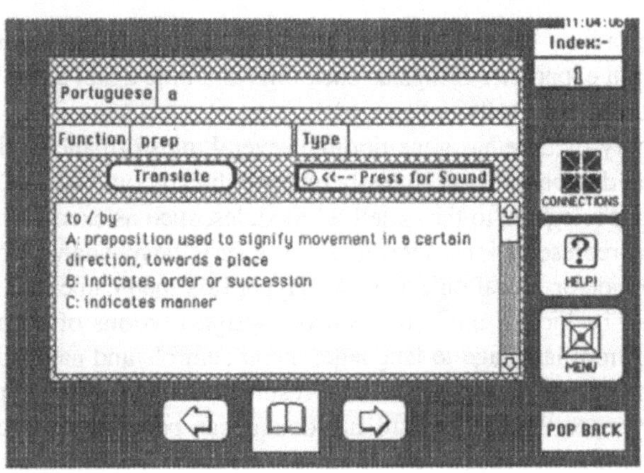

Index:-
1
Portuguese
a
Function
prep
Type
Translate
<<-- Press for Sound
to / by
A: preposition used to signify movement in a certain direction, towards a place
B: indicates order or succession
C: indicates manner
CONNECTIONS
HELP!
MENU
POP BACK

Other modules have gone through similar transformations and general user reaction suggests that overall simplicity and directness enhances comprehension and navigation. HyperCard's inbuilt visual effects for zooming, scrolling, wiping and dissolving are to my mind yet another of its major benefits. Hardman has already given excellent guide-lines for their usage and combination of effects give added possibilities for producing navigational metaphors. Above all, they add weight to navigational icons themselves by giving them visible credence - I am worried by IBM's present MSDOS version of LinkWay in which the screen temporarily blacks out at times, almost literally leaving the browser in the dark.

The main point here is that if the learner can **see the context, view what is relevant** and be stimulated into **seeking what is unknown or unseen**, then the cognitive process of relational browsing and the discovery of the 'relative relevance' between facts and objects will lead to a form of **non-linear** understanding akin to lateral thinking and intuition. This, personally, is seen as a higher, far better aim than the more linear processes that even basic fixed-link hypertexts produce, because they are built on **procedural, pre-programmed, personalized** structures.

Linear text and books versus HyperMedia learner-browsing

I should like to finish off by explaining further what is meant by 'intuitive', 'non-linear' learning, compared with the 'linearly' stored text of all reading matter, which for some reason is still viewed by many as more 'intuitive'.

For a couple of millenia man has instructed his young by sending them to school, providing them with an annotated view of experience and a technology based on linear text - the book. Before that, he learnt through an eclectic process of interactive experience and experiment with his world and his sensory ability to relate one object or action to another. The book does not prevent this process, since there are many and man still relates one piece of reading to his experience of another. But it still encourages a rigourously logical pattern of linear progression, pre-ordered information, often biassed according to its author's experience and thus devoid of any true debate with the reader, apart from in the mind itself or through the intervention of another biassed agent - the teacher.

A very Western, scientific view of learning has thus evolved, which does not accord with the natural cognitive processes or even the more traditional oral transmission of information through interactive dialogue and demonstration. One might even argue that the technology of the printed book has really only influenced the learning of the majority of people for barely 100, if not 500, years. Much of the utility of the linear book is in fact the mere **referencing** of non-relational knowledge, not **learning** *per se*.

HyperMedia technology, I therefore suggest, now offers us the possibility of returning to a much freer, non-linear and relativistic mode of learning, such as described by Beeman et al. [1]. Charney [2] worries about the lack of discourse cues in hypertexts. I would suggest that this is easily surmountable as long as we avoid presenting hypertext merely as text and use more intuitive metaphors for visual or graphical forms of navigation. Mayes, Kibby and Watson [9] in their lucid article on StrathTutor are especially encouraging with regard to learning-by-browsing and what they term "guided discovery learning".

HyperMedia, when all said and done, is initially an aid to role play and simulation; it later provides a means of discovery; and should, if well designed, lead to meaningful understanding and true learning. This may sound idealistic, evangelical or just pie-in-the-sky, but it is the nearest thing to the concept of 'growing up' that I have yet encountered in the whole of CAL-based teaching.

Literature

1. Beeman, W. et al.: "Hypertext and pluralism: from lineal to non-lineal thinking". Proc. Hypertext '87 Conference, 67-88
2. Charney, D.: "Comprehending non-linear text: the role of discourse cues and reading strategies". Proc. Hypertext '87 Conference, 109-118
3. Evenson, S., Rheinfrank and W., Wulff: "Towards a design language for representing Hypermedia cues". In: Hypertext '89 Proceedings, 83-92, ACM, November 1989
4. Fiderio, J.: "A grand vision". In: Byte, 237-246, October 1988
5. Hardman, L.: "Hypertext tips: experiences in developing a Hypertext tutorial". In: People and Computers IV, (D.M.Jones and R. Winder eds.), 437-451. Cambridge University Press, 1988
6. Hardman, L. and B., Sharratt: "User-centred Hypertext design: the application of HCI design principles and guidelines". Proc. Hypertext II Conference, York: 1989
   (For a discussion of the problems of losing oneself in a hypertext see also: Edwards, D.M., and L. Hardman: " 'Lost in Hyperspace': cognitive mapping and navigation in a Hypertext environment". In: Hypertext: theory into practice (R.McAleese ed.), 105-125. Oxford: Blackwell 1990)
7. Havholm, P. and L., Stewart: "Hypertext and 'Intertextuality' at the College of Wooster". In: Wheels for the Mind-Focus, Vol.4: N°2, 17-21
8. Marshall, C.C. and P., M. Irish: "Guided tours and on-line presentations: how authors make existing Hypertext intelligible for readers". In: Hypertext '89 Proceedings, 15-26, ACM, November 1989.
9. Mayes, T., M., Kibby and H., Watson: "StrathTutor®: the development and evaluation of a learning-by-browsing system on the Macintosh". In: Comput. Educ. Vol 12, N° 1, 21-229 (1988)
10. Nielsen, J: "The matters that really matter for Hypertext usability". In: Hypertext '89 Proceedings, 239-248, ACM, November 1989
11. Rada, R.: "Writing and reading Hypertext: an overview". In: Journal of the American Soc. of Information Scientists, March 1989
12. Schank, R.C. and R., Farrell: "Creativity in education: a standard for computer-based teaching". In: Machine-Mediated Learning, Vol 2, 175-194

Towards a Hypertext Semiotics

Álvaro Gomes[1] and Duarte Costa Pereira[2]

[1]University of Minho, Portugal. [2]University of Porto, Portugal

1. The ways of semiotics

Before considering Hypertext as a semiotic object we need to consider some rational previous aspects. First, we would like this brief contribution to be considered as a starting point for someone who has just arrived on the Hypertext Planet and not at all as the end point of the research already developed in this domain. Second, we would like to take it as a provocation: this is because on a former occasion (Gomes et al., 1989; Gomes & Costa Pereira, 1990), we rejected the term Hypertext, and proposed another, Holotext, for reasons explained then. It is usual to forgive newcomers a certain boldness even if it is too much as in this case.

In order to locate the problem we shall glimpse through the first efforts for building semiotics as a science, from the pioneers to the founders.We shall then attempt to clarify some aspects of the conceptual "geography" of the field: the opposition between the lexemes semiology and semiotics and on the other hand the various ways followed by different schools.We will finally discuss the central question and on reflecting over some aspects of the (hyper)text semiotics we will be contributing to initiate what could well be the launching of a hypertext grammar.

1.1 From the pioneers to the founders

If, with Jakobson (1988), we look at Antiquity, the Middle Ages and especially the Renaissance, we will be surprised with the interest already placed in the study of linguistic signs. Nevertheless it was only towards the end of the seventeen century that John Locke (1694), in the final chapter of his *Essay Concerning Human Understanding*, dedicated to the division of sciences, put forward the term "semeosis" or "the doctrine of signs the most usual whereof being words", considering it as the last of the "three great provinces of the intellectual world". When, almost a century later, Jean Henri Lambert (1764) designates the third part of his *Neues Organon* as "Semiotik oder Lehre von der Bezeichnung der Gedanken und Dinge" he recognizes his debt towards Locke over the term "semiotics". In the beginning of the nineteen century two important people stood: the Polish Joseph Marie Hoene-Wronski (Brown, 1969) and the Czech Bernard Bolzano, dedicating long studies to the problems of semiotics; towards the end of the century the most important contribution was that of Edmund Husserl (1890), who wrote *Zur Logik der Zeichen (Semiotik)*, although this document remained unpublished up to 1970!

A special reference is due to C. S. Peirce. We may truly say that he dedicated all his life to the semiotics. Indeed in a letter to Lady Welby on the 23rd December 1908 (note 1908!) he wrote that he considered semiotics as the basis of all sciences.

While Peirce lived already in a semiotic ocean, Saussure (1983) only faced semiology as a long term science. His contribution to this domain was much less than the one from Peirce but nevertheless its echo was incomparably greater! For Saussure " language is a system of signs that expresses ideas, and it is comparable to writing, to the deaf alphabet, to symbolic rhythms, to courtesy formulas, to military signs, etc. It is indeed the most important of all these systems. It is then possible to conceive a science studying the behavior of the signs in social life. Such a science would be part of social psychology and therefore of general psychology. We shall call it semiology (from the Greek "semeiôn", sign). It will tell us what are the signs and what are the rules that govern them. As this science does not exist as yet, it is hard to say what it will be, but it certainly has a right to exist and its place is previously determined. Linguistics is only a part of this general science. The laws revealed by semiology would be applicable to linguistics and so linguistics will be linked to a well defined domain in the set of human facts" (Saussure,1983). It is interesting to note that this text of Saussure corresponds to 1908/09, exactly the same year of the letter from Peirce to Lady Welby. The difference is that Saussure started 14 years before (1894) and Peirce 45 years before (1863)!

We were then towards the end of the nineteen century and communications were then making their first steps even (and overall) from a theoretical point of view!

Reading the most well known work of Saussure one may note that semiology is only referred very scarcely. Why is this that Peirce who contributed to the semiologic studies with one of the most complete and complex theorizations that ever were put forward, has been practically ignored as compared to the master from Geneva who only dedicates to this subject some (few) lines? Perhaps the explanation for this comes with the complexity of Peirce's works that were anyway known only some decades after. In his attempts to elaborate a taxonomy of the semiotic phenomenon, Peirce finally proposed 66 divisions and subdivisions (Jakobson, 1988), attempting to integrate all the species of signs. Peirce is not only concerned with the relation signifier-signified but also considers the iconic and indicative relations. The famous triple vision of Peirce in the theorization of semiotics is not a handy instrument, because of its complexity. This is the big problem! It was this fact that contributed for the role of Peirce in the theorization of the field to be overtaken by other not so important contributions. It is also surprising that it has been Saussure the great mentor of semiologic studies, due to the fact that both Peirce and Husserl were conscious of their own contribution to the birth of semiotics as a science, although Saussure only referred to it as a coming science, a science for the future!

1.2 Problems of conceptual "geography"

If Saussure presents us a sociological version of semiology, it is apparent that Peirce was more concerned with the logical dimension while Roland Barthes (1953;1964) many years after would follow a psychological view. Various were then the ways followed by the researchers, causing a kind of Semiologic War: on one hand the followers of the communication semiology (with names like Buyssens, Prieto, Mounin); on the other hand the adepts of a meaning semiology (where we should situate names as Roland Barthes and his followers: Kristeva, José Augusto Seabra, etc.) and finally those who attempted a synthesis by means of what was called a cultural semiotics (Umberto Eco (1984), etc.). Although this is not the proper place for this discussion, it is advisable to be aware of the many discrepancies found in the research of these domains.

Semiotics or semiology? The answer to this question is not at all easy. Historically, as we saw it is clear that semiotics came first (Locke, seventeen century) than semiology (Saussure, twentie century). If in this century's continental Europe Saussure's ideas are extremely influential, we cannot forget that in the Anglo-Saxon word the word semiotic was already coined long before this. In Europe there was only talk of semiology, until the works of Peirce and also of Charles Morris, started circulating; it is then that the lexeme semiotics is adopted. First the two lexemes semiology/ semiotics coexisted and competed for the same conceptual ground. Then, on a second phase, gradually, a subtle difference was established: semiology was the general subject where various semiotics were included (the highway code semiotics, the literary text semiotics, etc.); on a third phase the international committee, having met in Paris in 1969, established the International Association of Semiotica, accepting the term semiotica as equivalent to the term semiology, the two terms being faced as synonyms. As Thomas Sebeock recalls (Morris,1985), semiotics was created by analogy to pragmatics, syntactics, semantics. This association chose the name of its own international review adopting a compromise Latin term semiotica, leaving the primacy problem unsolved.

There are also other terms used in the literature apart from semiotica/semiotics /semiology. Although the complete treatment of this last problem is outside the scope of this work we would just like to refer some of these terms and their meanings: semiology is a medical science consisting on the study of the symptoms, in order to detect their causes. Semantics is the study of meaning of the linguistic signs. Semaseology is the study of the relation of the signs with their referents starting from the signifier to the signified and onomasiology is the study of signs starting from the signified to the signifier.

After these considerations let us consider the semiotic universe of text.

2. From a text semiotics to a hypertext semiotics

The development of the study of text as a semiotic entity has, in recent years, been very substantial; there is even a new discipline, called *textual linguistics*. It is important therefore that the concept of text be clarified. Often researchers proceed towards this concept similarly to the way Roland Barthes proceeded towards literature. "What is literature?" he asked. "It is whatever is taught under this name," he answered. We enter then a vicious circle and this is unfortunately very frequent. Let us put aside the classical definitions of Lazaro Carreter (Diccionario de Términos Filológicos), of the J. Dubois team (Dictionaire de Linguistique), Lewandowski (1982) and even of L. Hjelmslev (for whom text designated any statement, spoken or written, long or short, old or modern). Enríquez Bernárdez (1982) considering eleven definitions (presented by several investigators like Hartmann, Schmidt, Dressler, Gal´perin, Satkov, Agricola, Isenberg, Viehweger, Hausenblas, Fonseca/Fonseca, Kosevnikova and Revzin) presents a synthesis of the criteria more often used:

1 - the text as a communication unit,

2 - as (the product of one) activity,

3 - as a sequence of sentences,

4 - as a linguistic sign,

5 - other criteria (closure, internal relations, etc.).

Bernárdez's cumulative "definition" is better interpreted as the putting forward of a set of characteristics allowing the scientific community to work with this term.

This definition reveals itself as very imperfect, as it situates text on an eminently linguistic perspective. Aguiar e Silva (1983) transfers the concept to the semiotic level and therefore to a translinguistic level, as he says that "text is a permanent set of ordered elements, whose co-presences, interaction and functions are considered by a codifier and/or a decodifier as ruled by a certain sign system." We therefore see that a text is characterized by a certain number of formal properties, independently from the signs that constitute them, that may be indicium icons, conventional signs, etc. These properties of expressivity, delimitation and structurallity, deserve from us a deep reflection, particularly when we "jump" to the hypertextual level in the specific sense of this lexeme on an informatic context. Hypertext would correspond here to a kind of "macrotext" of entirely new characteristics. Also if we take text as a semiotic entity we might speak as Aguiar e Silva says of a filmic text, pictoric text, choreographic text, etc.

When we jump to the hypertextual domain the problems have to be considered at another level. A first question that we may debate is: to produce or to operate on a hypertext will be either an artistic, scientific or technical activity? In the Middle Ages we know that grammar was considered the art par excellence. The question is not as innocent as it appears because the methodology to use won't be exactly the same if the answer is be one or the other.

Guiraud (1983), inspired in Saussure, structures his semiologic investigation in three domains: the structure of the communication systems through non-linguistic signs; the study of social communication forms as rites, ceremonies, courtesy formulas, etc. (social codes); the study of art and literature (aesthetic codes) as being communication processes depending on the use of signs which are based on a general theory of sign (relevant aspects like zoo-semiotics, cybernetics and bionics are unfortunately not referred by him). One question might be formulated here: in a semiotic perception of hypertext, how should it be framed? At the level of arts or else at the level of sciences? Or should we consider it more as one technique? Guiraud, stating that by nature all arts are in debt towards the means of iconic and analogic meaning, opposed antithetically the logical signs and the expressive signs, defining the first as conventional, arbitrary, homologic, objective, rational, abstract, general, transitive and selective, while the second would be natural, motivated, analogic, subjective, affective, concrete, singular, immanent and total. This implies really two means of expression: the sciences and the arts, that is knowledge and feeling, intelligence and emotion, and in the limit the objective and the subjective. Between these extreme poles we might define more or less complicated scales. Peirce, as we saw, insisted on a triadic categorization (icons, indiciums, and symbols); Abraham Moles (1981) pointed towards thirteen degrees of iconicity or of abstraction (which comes to the same).

Rigorously, in hypertext we are not at the level of a sentence grammar, in the sense that recent studies contextual linguistics refer. We face, possibly for the first time in textual history, a grammar of really new characteristics and demanding new answers. Such a grammar is as indispensable a task as it is complex. We might say that we would be able to function at three grammatical levels of inclusive character: a first level (the sentence grammar); a second level (the text grammar); and a third level (the hypertext grammar). We have anyway a unique opportunity, if we except the cases of artificial languages: *perhaps this is the first time (at hypertext level) that emission and communication grammars might communicate with each other.* If the other grammars have been up to now obtained through successive inferences, the hypertext grammar would possibly take in account the moment of departure.

Before we seek for this hypertext grammar and attempt to identify what truly distinguishes it from the two previous levels, some questions related to the operational instruments of the two levels must previously be discussed in order for us to know if they are applicable in this third level (and with what degree). So, for example:

1 — The opposition paradigm/syntagm (from Saussurean linguistics) would not be or appeared to be overtaken, at the hypertextual level, being that at this level this opposition gains a new amplitude? Would we be facing what we dare to call holoparadigms (or hyperparadigms) and holosyntagms (or hypersyntagms), (Guiraud, 1983)?
Perhaps we would be in the presence of macro-categories or macro-classes. In effect we must bear in mind that hypertext is neither a sum nor a juxtaposition of textual fragments available on file, or on stacks or cards; the syntagmatic path followed by the operator isn't linear, in the sense the syntagm expression has been assuming in linguistics; it thus functions as clusters of morpho-syntactic and semantic-paradigmatic units, this is what we may call a textual poliphony (in the classic sense of the term and not in the sense Bakhtine and Oswald Ducrot adopt). It is as if the reading system for hypertext was not limited to the Western linear organization (left to right and top to bottom), and we were in a "navigation" situation (that is reading) where reverse paths were also possible (a hyper version of the Arab, Japanese or Indian reading processes) or even a "bustrofédon" system or similar. What reality is this before which we already are?

2 — At the declarative level, the concepts of sentence, statement, discourse, won't they also have a new dimension? In effect at the level that we can call "hyperphenotextual" we face a situation where the production of discourse is done by going through (not creating) already made statements. The "hypergenotext" would be, in principle, situated at the level of the programmer and not at the level of the operator. Would this mean that the opposition between the ethic and emic levels? The ethic text (a kind of kat'ergon) coincides, in the limit, with the emic text, once the individual free "runway" of the operator is controlled and limited (the programmer might tell the operator: "you'll be free to the extent I'll let you be free".

3 — What correspondence at the hypertextual level is there of anaphor and cataphor? How does "deixis" function at this level?

4 — What is the sense for the opposition theme/rheme at the present stage of hypertext program elaboration? As hypertext is a kind of tridimensional puzzle (Gomes, 1987), that puzzle may only keep its interest through a high degree of complexity and elaboration. Information theory easily demonstrates that if the information degree is equal or close to zero the interest of a game rapidly vanishes (Gomes & Costa Pereira, 1990). Knowing all the information we will not face an indispensable element: the rheme (comment). It seems to be possible to face text, all of it, as theme (topic). A very important aspect is, on the other hand, to know if hypertext is itself a mean (a channel) or a message. Perhaps McLuhan's well known statement – "The medium is the message" – would then become a prophecy. It might also be that hypertext hypostasises that leme. In this case if the programmer would not be inspired, rapidly the slogan "The medium is the message" would become "The medium is the massage." This is a risk but it certainly is also a challenge.

5 — Is it possible to assume hypertext as "architext"?

6 — What are the roles for "subtext" and "pre-text"?

7 — Does the trilogy "hypotext/intertext/hypertext" make sense at the hypertextual level?

8 — What implications at hypertext level has the opposition "co-text/context"?

9 — How does hypertext deal with the problem of cohesion and coherence (or, if we prefer, the problem of texture)?

10 — Finally, how may we analyze hypertext under the Saussurean linearity and arbitrariness principles?

These are only a few of the questions we might put forward. We hope they will be enough to make us conscious of the magnitude of the problem of hypertext semiotics, in order for us not to fall in the temptation of rushing into "easy" semiotic interpretations. Some will say that tomorrow will be too late for this project. Others would think that it is too soon. Who is right?

Literature

1. Aguiar e Silva, V. M., Teoria da Literatura, Livraria Almedina, Coimbra, 1983
2. Barthes, R., Le Degré Zéro de l'Écriture suivi de Éléments de Sémiologie,Ed. du Seuil, Paris, 1953 and 1964
3. Bernárdez, E., Introducción a la Teoría del Texto, Espasa-Calpe, Madrid, 1982
4. Brown, J. V., Aperçu de la Philosophie de Wronsky, Roma Tip. P.U.G., 1969
5. Eco, U., Semiotics and the Philosophy of Language, John Benjamins, Amsterdam, 1984
6. Gomes, A., Erro Ortográfico: Entropia, Morfogénese ou Homeorese, Universidade do Minho, Braga, 1987
7. Gomes A., Oliveira A., Costa Pereira D., "O Hypercard e o Ensino Assistido por Computador", Personal Computer World, 29, 3, 86-92, 1989
8. Gomes, A., Costa Pereira D., "Textíssimo, o Texto no Superlativo (Do Hipertexto ao Holotexto)", in FORMA, 2, 21-23, 1990.
9. Guiraud, P., A Semiologia, Ed. Presença, Lisboa, 1983
10. Husserl, E., Zur Logik der Zichen (Semiotik), 1890
11. Jakobson, R., Obras Selectas I, Ed. Gredos, Madrid, 1988
12. Lambert, J. H., Neues Organon,oder Gedanken uber die Erforschung und Bezeichnung des Wahren und dessen Unterscheidung von Irrthum und Schein I, II, Leipzig, Johann Wendler, 1764
13. Lewandowski, T., Diccionario de Linguistica, Ed. Cátedra, Madrid, 1982
14. Locke, J., An Essay Concerning Human Understanding, London, 1694
15. Moles, A., L'Image Communication Fonctionelle, Casterman, 1981
16. Morris, C., Fundamentos de la Teoría de los Signos, Paidós Ibérica, Barcelona, 1985
17. Peirce, C., Collected Papers, I-VIII, Cambridge Massachussets, Harvard University Press, 1931-1958
18. Peirce, C., Obra Lógico- Semiótica, Taurus Ediciones, Madrid, 1987
19. Saussure, F., Curso de Linguística General, Edición Crítica de Tullio de Mauro, Aianza Editorial, Madrid, 1983

Signal Effects on the Recall and Understanding of Expository Texts in Expert and Novice Readers

José A. León & Mario Carretero

Autonoma University of Madrid, Spain

Abstract: A primary goal of reading is to understand the writer's message correctly. To accomplish this goal, a reader must identify the information in the text that is most relevant to the author's message. A writer can facilitate the reader's task by using a variety of devices to signal relevant information. In the present study, we investigated the effects of signals on text comprehension and recall in different groups. Subjects were 48 Experts (post-graduate students) and 96 Novices (48 good readers and 48 poor readers, junior high school students). All subjects read two expository texts at different levels of difficulty. There were two versions for each text: with signals and without signals. Two recall tests were run: immediate free recall and delayed free recall. The results demonstrated that signals directed attention to the macrostructure they marked and led to a better encoding of the organization of target information in all groups. This effect increased with the difficulty of the text and the skill of the reader.

1. Introduction

One of the main objectives of reading is to understand the writer's message exactly. To achieve this aim, the reader should identify and assimilate the relevant information of the text. This task may be made easier for the reader by the text itself. The writer may use a variety of resources with the objective of "indicating" this important information to the reader. One of most frequent and mostly analysed aids in various studies has been the denominative "signals" [4-6,18].

A signal is a syntactical mark defined by a word or sentence from the text which, although it does not add any new information to the content of the text, it underlines the dominant logical relationships and the ideas which determine the macrostructure of the passage. This allows the reader to clearly identify the principal aspects of the text. Following Meyer [18], at least four kinds of signals can be established:

a) Those which give previous introduction to the content, summarised in a sentence in which the key information which will be more profoundly treated later on is expressed, using sentences like "The main causes of the discovery of America were..." or "The most important ideas of this article are...". Sentences like there help the reader to discover the relevant ideas of the passage.

b) Those which, also summarised, are given at the end of the text, in the form of a conclusion.

c) Signals, called ordinal or numeral by some authors [14,15], are usually employed when a plot of various points of view or several parts is introduced. In this case, each one is preceded by a number, letter or word (e.g. "firstly" or "finally").

d) Words expressing the author's point of view, like "Unfortunately" or "Suffice to say...".

A large part of the investigations carried out by specialists on the subject have been aimed at evaluating the effect these aids have on remembering and understanding and includes processes of selection and reconstruction of information [1,11,24]. Although a large number and great many kinds of signals have been studied, the results, however, have been different. While some authors have not found significant differences in memory between the use of signalled and unsignalled texts [2,9,18], others, however, have come to the conclusion that signaling makes it easier to remember the information it marks, although this, in some cases, inhibits the memory of the information which is not signalled. The selective effect of the information remembered has been shown as much in the use of isolated signaling, numerical signaling [14,15] or logical connectives [10], as in the combination of various signaling, such as titles, introductory sentences, across- chapter signals and other resources [7,8,13,16,20,22,23].

For this investigation we chose a combination of these signals: besides the title, introductory sentences in the form of summary and numerical signalings were used. We choose such markers for a number of reasons. Firstly, we were interested in those aids which gave general indications to the reader so as to facilitate the activation of the basic organizational schemes whereby the subjects organises the fundamental information of the passage. Thus, the title and the introductory sentences which contain relevant summarised information were chosen. As before, numerical signalings may affect the reader and the memory, but this time more specifically than before. In this case, ordinal numbers or words are explicit markers of the organisation of the information contained in the text on the diverse aspects or points of view wich are treated. Together they give a wider and clearer panorama of the macrostructure of the written material.

The purpose of this investigation has been to analyse experimentally how these signals affect the memory of subjects with different levels of reading competence and previous levels of knowledge in expository texts of different understanding difficulty. The hypotheses of the study were stated with regard to how these signals could affect the memory of different kinds of readers and in several passages of different understanding difficulty. They were as following:

1) How would signaling affect recall of texts which differed in lexical and semantic complexity, thus making their understanding more difficulty?

As we have already seen, there are some works which have not found any significant differences in the recall of subjects in signalled or non-signalled texts [2,18]. It might be the case that the absence of this significant is due to the fact that the actual simplicity of the text or the reader's ability render those signals irrelevant in order to understand, retain and recollect the essential information of the passage.

However, the signalled version puts up with an additional burden in reading, as it normally has a greater number of words which demand an additional effort from the reader as he/she has to read a larger number of words, which in form can reduce the effect of signals on memory. However, if we increase the understanding difficulty of the text, through lexical and semantic means, it is possible that with such increased difficulty, the signalled aid acquires meaning. This involves checking to see if there is some direct relationship between complexity and the effect of signaling on memory. And if this is the case, the signalled version will be more successful in recall than the non-signalled one.

2) A second objective concerns the type of reader. How does the reader take advantage of these aids? Are these aids used in the same way by readers with different levels of knowledge and reading skills? The results obtained in previous works indicate that good readers omits the complementary and redundant information in the memory task. For example, Meyer [20] said that "expert" readers in free memory tasks show a better retention of the logical relationships which were signalled than those which were not, something which is not found in inexperienced readers.

   Our aim was to confirm that the behavior of the more expert readers with a greater level of previous knowledge was more selective that of the inexperienced subjects, who were divided into two groups of different reading levels, poor and good readers.

3) Another aim was to prove experimentally that the signalled information was more resistant to the passing of time than the non-signalled information. If this the case, the information which represents the macrostructure of the text may therefore be recollected with greater probability than the non-signalled information in both free recall tasks, especially in the delayed task (seven days). There is empirical evidence concerning this hypothesis [18,20].

4) Finally and related to the aforementioned point: Do the signals aid to organise the remembered information of the text following the original plan of the structure of the text? In this last objective we tried to check empirically if the signals helped the reader to elaborate more coherently the organisational representation of the text. If the reader uses these signals to organise his/her representation of the text, he/she should be able to use each signal as a guide in the process of recall. If this is so, the result should be more organised and more complete when the signalled version is presented to the subject. Empirical evidence confirming this hypothesis is also available [12,15,23].

2. Method

2.1 Subjects

144 students participated in this study. Of these subjects, 48 were "expert" readers, graduates in History and Geography from the Autonoma University of Madrid, and 96 were "novice" readers with different levels of reading comprehension: 48 good comprehension readers (GC) and 48 poor comprehension readers (PC). They were all first year high school students at "Rey Pastor" school in Madrid.

As we were interested in choosing inexperienced subjects with a clear level of competence from 1st year High School, a thorough selection process wich fulfilled three criteria was carried out: A standard reading comprehension (A. Lázaro) test, a questionnaire which contrasted the opinions of Mathematics, Language, Natural Sciences and especially History teachers, due to the contents of the chosen texts. In this questionnaire the academic ability and performance of the studens were judged on a scale of 5 points (Very good, good, average, low, very low). And lastly a summarised task. Here all subjects read a short text; after reading it and with the text in front of them, they had to summarise it in a maximun of 10 sentences. Through this task, the presence and absence of the important ideas in the text and its overall comprehension was evaluated.

2.2 Materials

We chose two expository texts whose content was totally different so as to be clearly differentiated: "Supertankers" and "The origins of the discovery of America". The structure of the texts was analyzed using Meyer's method [18,21], and in fact the first text was a Spanish adaptation of the one used by this and others authors in diferent investigations [17,20,23]. The second passage was adapted for the experiment from a text by Cespedes del Castillo [3]. The extracts differed in their main rhetorical relation: "Supertankers" was an example of the problem-solution structure, and the "discovery" text of causation: cause-consequence. Another difference between them was the lexical and semantic level - the second text was more complex and specialized.

There were two versions of each text: one signalled and another unsignalled. Signaling consisted of stressing the text's central statements by summarizing text segments, or preceding text sentences with prior information, and using pointer words, numerical signaling, as well as mentioning explicity the relationships contained in the text. The length of the text on the "supertankers" text was 452 words in the signalled version and 401 words in the non-signalled version, with a total of 204 idea units. The second text, "Origins of the Discovery of America", contained 436 words in the signalled version and 366 words in the non-signalled version with a total of 199 idea units.

Other modifications which were carried out on the written material remained constant. All the texts and versions establised 10 hierarchical levels, the first five corresponding to the macropropositional level and the others to the micro-propositional level. The use of space (only one sheet, on one side) and of paragraphs wich could have underlined the logical structure of the text, was also equally applied in all written material.

2.3 Procedure

The study took place in two sessions. In the first one, the students received the text and a blank sheet on which they noted down their details and the code number of the text. The school children had 12 minutes to read the text and the experts 4. We made it clear that the text should be carefully read so as to complete a task after finishing, without, however, specifying what type of task it would be or how long they should spend on the reading. When the time was up, the passages were collected and the subjects were asked to remember as much of the text they had just read as possible. The maximum they were allowed for this phase was 15 minutes. In the pilot study, all the times taken were considered valid. When this task was completed, the students were given a short break and then the same procedure was followed with the second text.

In a second session, exactly a week later, and without warning, the subjects were asked again to try to remember as much as they could of the texts they had read the previous week. For this task, they were told to recall the passages respecting the order of reading. They were given the same maximum time as the previous week: 15 minutes.

2.4 Scoring

To measure the recall of each reader, we followed the analysis of the structure of the text prepared by Meyer [18,21]. The final score for each subject was related to four quantitative indexes and one qualitative index. They were the following:

Quantitative Indexes

- The number of idea units of the content remembered corresponding to the highest levels (1-5) which represent the macrostructure of the text (Scoring A).
- The number of idea units of the content remembered corresponding to the lowest levels (6-10) which represent the microstructure of the text (Scoring B).
- The number of basic rhetorical relationships present in the subjects' recall (Scoring R). Those which were considered to be basic rhetorical relationships were those within the first five levels of the content structure of each text.
- Finally, the total number of idea units remembered (Scoring G). This is the sum of the three previous scores.

Qualitative Index

Through this scoring the degree of compliance of the subjects' recall with the actual organization of the text, is evaluated. In other words, this index shows whether the plan followed by the writer when organizing his/her ideas to be expressed in the text is followed by the reader when trying to order the ideas expressed in his/her answers. On the basis of this criterion, three levels are established:

When showing what he/she has remembered the reader follows the high rhetorical structure level of the text and the principal elements immediately underneath (problem-solution, causation...) (5 points). When the reader, although he/she follows the rethorical organization on the text, he/her recall does not appear explicity it, but shows some of the basic elements of this organization (3 points), or when the recall does not express, neither centrally nor incidentally, the fundamental rhetorical elements (1 points). Such is the case of incoherent recall, where a few isolated facts which try to tie some details together are expressed.

The protocols were assessed by two evaluators, who in general, coincided in the analysis of the propositions by 93%, the protocols of the experts being the most difficult to judge for their richness in remembrance and the large number of inferences carried out. In this case, the degree of agreement fell to 87%, but normally coming to an agreement after the discussion of the differences which were found.

2.5 Design

The statistical analysis is formed by a mixed factorial design of 3*2*2, one for each text, with two intersubject factors, the group and the version, and one intrasubject one, the kind of recall task, making a total of 8 ANOVAs, four for each text and four for each one of the scores calculated: A, B, R and G.

3. Results: Analysis and Discussion

In the following tables the values obtained from the analysis of variance are presented. Tables 1 and 2 contain the retention performance results.

Table 1: ANOVAs corresponding to the SUPERTANKERS text, with two intersubject factors, reading groups (Gr) and Signal (S) and one intrasubject, recall task (Re), for each one of scores measured, A, B, R and G.

	A		B		R		G	
	F	P	F	P	F	P	F	P
SIGNAL	0.003	0.9538	0.941	0.3338	0.723	0.3965	0.405	0.5255
GROUP	17.772	0.0000	9.384	0.0001	35.912	0.0000	17.262	0.0000
S*Gr	0.824	0.4449	0.168	0.8470	0.539	0.5873	0.294	0.7478
Re	127.131	0.0000	221.795	0.0000	113.913	0.0000	273.056	0.0000
S*Re	0.214	0.6442	0.097	0.7559	0.117	0.7331	0.053	0.8186
Gr*Re	0.311	0.7354	5.386	0.0056	11.674	0.0000	5.806	0.0038
S*Gr*Re	1.537	0.2170	0.368	0.6948	0.075	0.9279	0.465	0.6317

Table 2: ANOVAs corresponding to the ORIGINS OF THE DISCOVERY OF AMERICA text, with two intersubject factors, reading groups (Gr) and Signal (S) and one intrasubject, recall task (Re), for each one of scores measured, A, B, R and G.

	A		B		R		G	
	F	P	F	P	F	P	F	P
SIGNAL	11.870	0.0008	0.439	0.5088	17.206	0.0001	6.084	0.0148
GROUP	28.935	0.0000	25.108	0.0000	51.628	0.0000	41.011	0.0000
S*Gr	1.642	0.1960	2.229	0.1107	2.364	0.9712	1.328	0.2663
Re	57.930	0.0000	236.203	0.0000	20.110	0.0000	246.551	0.0000
S*Re	7.033	0.0089	0.832	0.3633	0.180	0.6717	0.942	0.3336
Gr*Re	2.713	0.0694	0.895	0.4152	1.334	0.2650	2.786	0.0647
S*Gr*Re	1.985	0.1402	0.291	0.7497	1.246	0.2887	0.926	0.4028

3.1 Effects of signalling on the comprehension difficulty of the text

As can be seen in Figure 1, in the results obtained for Meyer's text (the simpler one) there are no significant differences between the signalled and unsignalled version in any of the features measured. These data are similar to those obtained in other studies by Meyer et al., where they have used this same text and others of comparable complexity and content [2,18-20]. In all these studies, a slight, but not statistically significant, improvement was found in the signalled version. One of the reasons for this lack of significance seems to be that the increase in length of the signalled texts puts an additional burden on memory since more time is used in reading and so greater effort is put into processing the information being read. These results seem to suggest, too, that for a text which is lexically and semantically simple, it is unnecessary to signal its macrostructure. In this case, the relevant information is similarly understood when signalling is not used. However, the opposite result was obtained for the second, more difficult text. Signalling the important information makes it better recalled in the treated version than

SUPERTANKERS TEXT

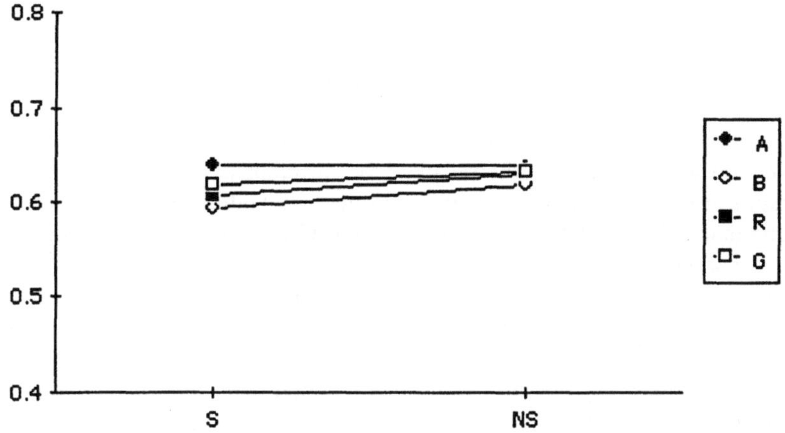

THE ORIGINS OF THE DISCOVERY OF AMERICA TEXT

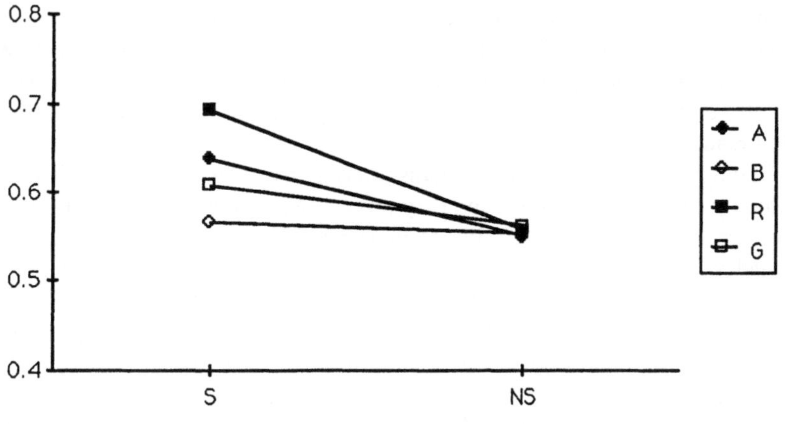

Fig. 1 - Variations produced in the subjects recall of different idea units (A, B, R and G) correctly remembered in each text ("Supertankers", and "The Origins of the Discovery of America") and in each version (signalled and non-signalled version).

in the unsignalled one as measured by the scores A and R ($p< 0.001$). In this case, our interpretation is that when the difficulty of the comprehension of the text increases, whether this is due to the use of more abstract concepts or because of terminology, signalling has a positive effect, in spite of the increase in the number of words (436 words as against 366 words), and in general comprehension and recall of the material read improves. As can be seen in this text, the improvement is only significant in the A and R scores, which means that only selected information is remembered. This confirms the idea that the aid to the text becomes more important as difficulty increases.

3.2 Effects of signalling on the different groups of subjects

A not less important question which we looked at in the second hypothesis referred to how the signalled version would influence the recall of the different groups of readers.

The results are different again depending on the text studied. So, if we look at the results for the "Supertankers" text, there are no significant differences among groups of readers in the signalled and non signalled versions.

On the contrary, if we look at the results for the "The Origins of the Discovery of America" text in Figure 3, we see that all the groups benefited by the signals, but not to the same extent. The GC group are most affected by this kind of aid. It is these better novice readers who lose or gain significantly with respect to information retained from signalled or unsignalled texts. Scores for A and R, which represent the macrostructure of the text, are affected significantly ($p<0.05$). This effect on recall is closely connected to the complexity of the passage. When faced with a text which is above their reading level, the signals aids students understanding and recall of relevant information. It is thus clear that these aids are extremely important for these adolescent readers.

With regard to the PC group, the poor younger readers, these aids produced a slight improvement in recall of the macrostructrue of the text. Nevertheless, our results show the tremendous difficulty this type of reader has to retain rhetorical information - the relations which define the structural hierarchy in written material. In general, these readers do not seem to use the signals efficiently to represent the signalled information in an organized structure, as the more skilled readers do.

The behaviour of the expert readers stems not only from their greater reading skill but also from the amount of previous knowledge they possess about the subject of the passage. In this case the content of the text was familiar to them and caused less difficulty than to the other groups of readers. This explains the fact that although recall of the signalled version improved, this did not reach a level of significance. It seems, therefore, that the reading skill of the subjects is a key factor in the way they benefit from the aids in the text, especially in the perception and assimilation of the main logical relations in the text structure.

Considering the scores of the subjects with regard to recall tasks obtained in the text on the discovery, a pattern of different recall is observed in the experts with regard to the secondary school readers (see figure 3), especially in the non-signalled version. While the level of recall in expert subjects tends to be stable, and even improves in the second recall task in scores A and R, the pattern of recall in junior high school students, on the contrary, has a more pronounced decrease in the delayed recall task. This effect supports the idea that the previous knowledge which the subject possesses on a related content with the material read is better remembered, among other factors, because it permits the new information to be situated within the organizational schemes in the mind of the subject, better resisting the passing of time. These readers do not find difficulty in the understanding and retention of this written material. On the contrary, when we refer to high school good readers, these technical and almost unknown written material for they, they shows obviously more difficult to lear and to retain the main information.

SUPERTANKERS TEXT

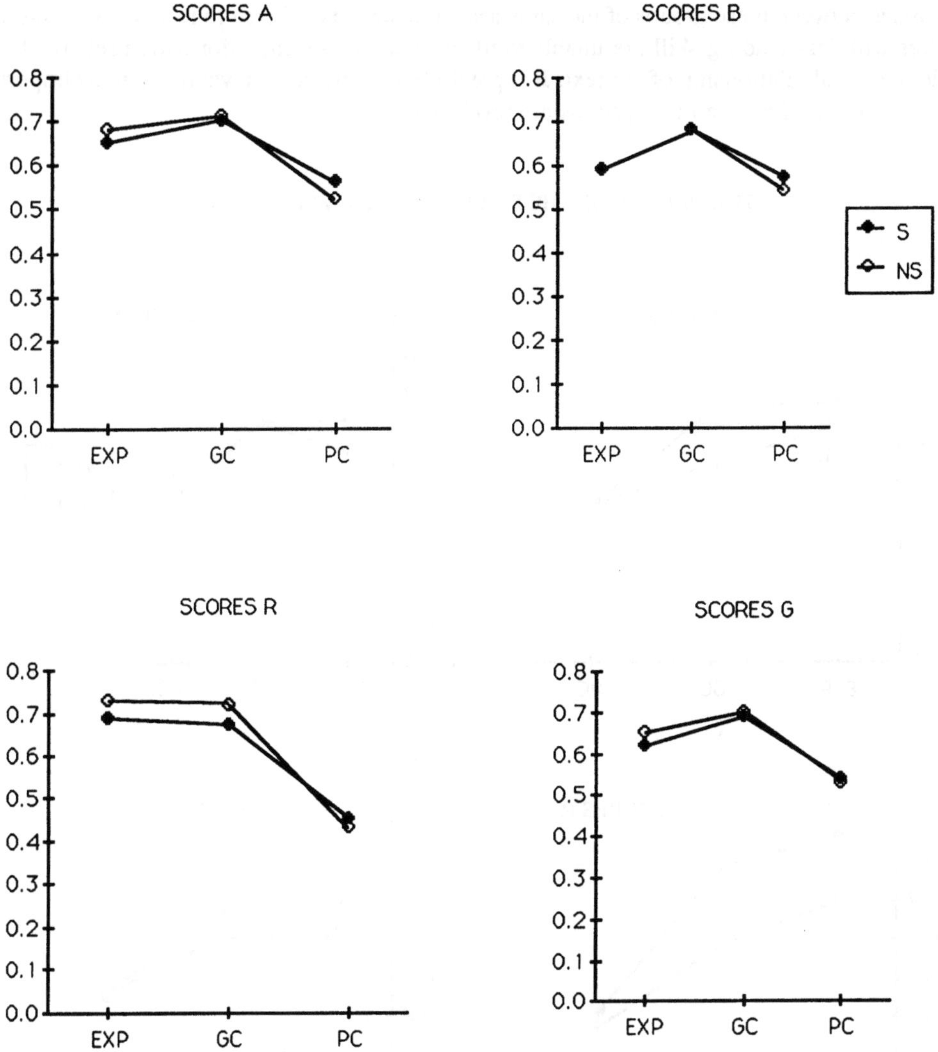

Fig. 2 - Variations produced in the different groups recall of different idea units (A, B, R and G) correctly remembered in 'Supertankers' text in each version (signalled and non-signalled version).

Another observation coming out of these data is the quality of recall. The expert subjects are more selective when remembering the most relevant information, the rethorical relationships represented by scoring in R and the macrostructure of the text symbolized by score A. The complementary information, identified by score B, is usually tackled less by this group, becoming, in some cases equal to that obtained by GC readers. The adolescent readers, on the contrary, do not show any kind of preference for the relevant information, but try to retain all possible information, be what it may. The abilities of the more competent readers allow them to obtain a greater quantity of information than their less able companions. An important difference between these groups of the same academic level is referred to in score R. Therefore, readers with less reading skill are unable to identify and retain the information relative to the basic rhetorical relationship of the text. It is precisely in these scores where the most important differences regarding the other groups are produced.

THE ORIGINS OF THE DISCOVERY OF AMERICA TEXT

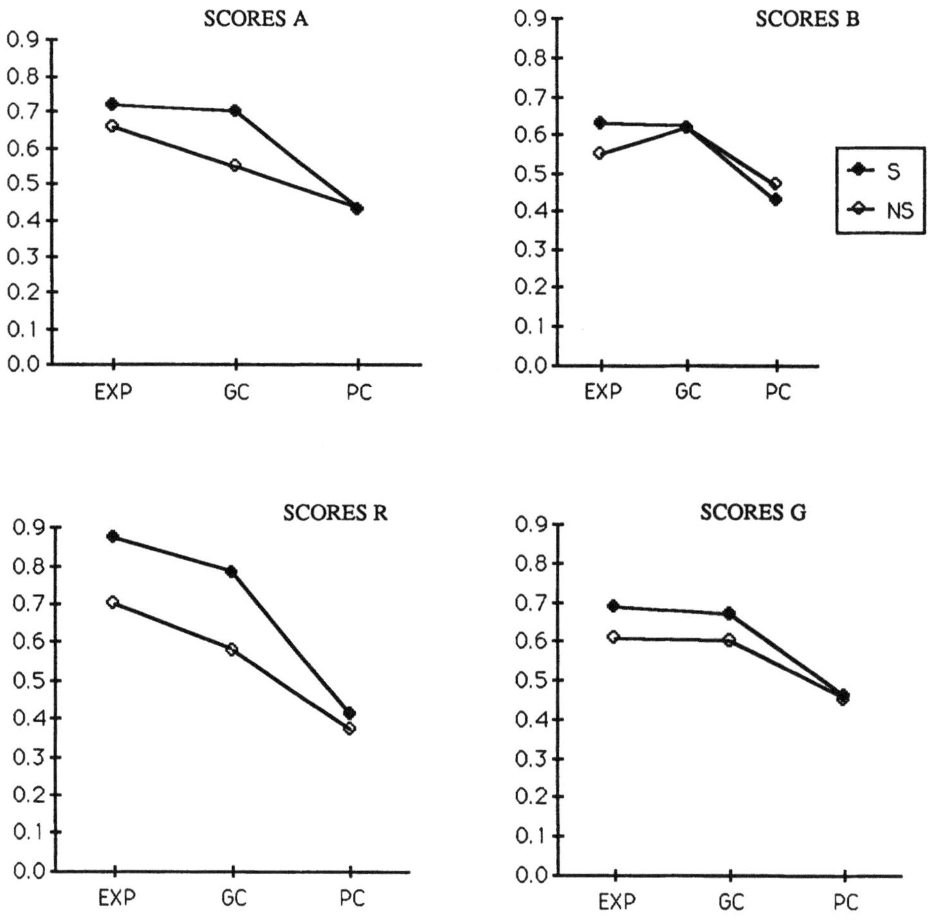

Fig. 3 - Variations produced in the different groups recall of different idea units (A, B, R and G) correctly remembered in The Origins of the Discovery of America'text in each version (signalled and non-signalled version).

THE ORIGINS OF THE DISCOVERY OF AMERICA TEXT

Immediate free recall task

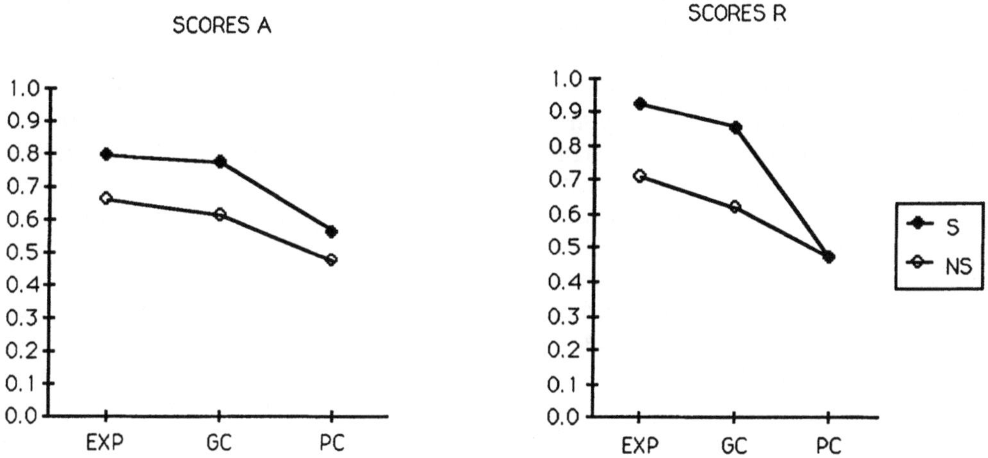

Delayed free recall task

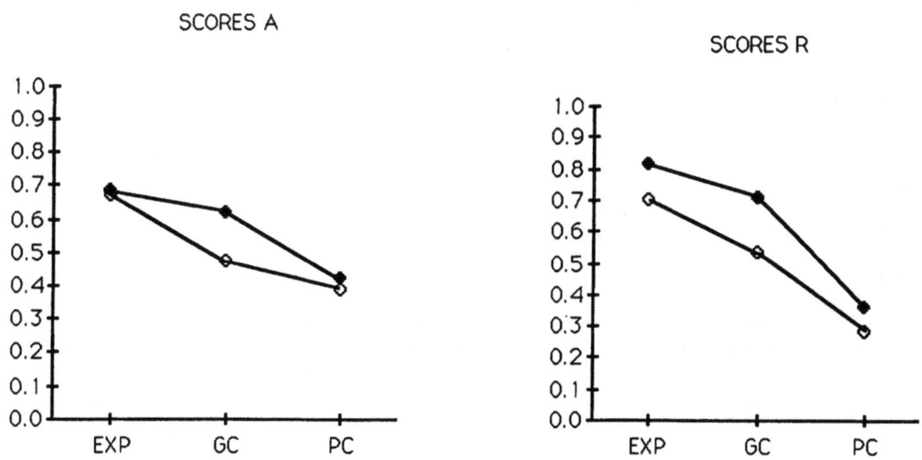

Fig. 4 - Variations produced in the different group readers in each recall task (immediate and delayed) and in each version (signalled and non-signalled version) of different idea units (A, B, R and G) correctly remembered in the text "The Origins of the Discovery of America".

3.3 Effects of signalling in the two free recall tasks

The scores of the subjects in the two recall tasks are, as expected, lower in the second ($p<0.001$). These differences are found in the two versions and in the two texts analysed, which confirms the third hypothesis. However in score A of the text on the discovery, a significant interaction between the signal and recall factors is produced ($p<0.05$) (see figure 4). In this case and in the immediate free recall task, the signalled version is totally superior in its recall ($p<0.001$), a difference which, although decreasing in the non-signalled version, continues to be significant at the same level. This interaction seems to arise from the tendency to stabilise its level of recall in the non -signalled version by the expert subjects and less so, by the GC subjects. A tendency which does not arise in the signalled version. This could be logical if we take into account that recall is greater in the signalled version (there is a greater number of words), and also in the greater in the effort that the reader apply when he/she try rememembered the information a week later. Another reason which may explain this effect is the use of the scheme by the expert. When the expert reads the signalled version, he uses rhetorical markers which make the information which he has read coherent, with hardly any effort on his part. When he reads a non-signalled text, this same reader makes a greater effort which forces him/her to use him/her own resources to establish the appropiate scheme and to situate the information wich he/she has read. As a result of this greater implication in reading, the information read is better understood and in later recollection it maintains its level of recall. This behavior is also observed in score R.

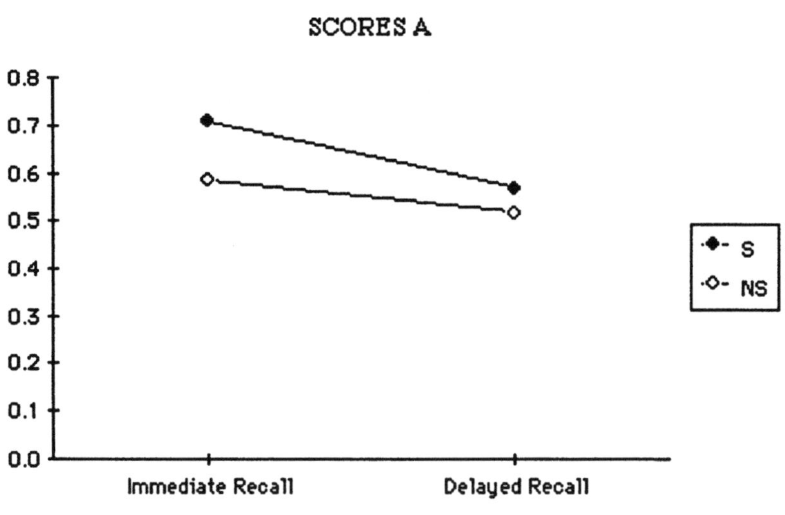

Fig. 5 - Interaction between Signal and Recall factores in scores A corresponding to "The Origins of the Discovery of America" text.

3.4 Effects of signalling on the organization of the information recalled

The influence of signalling clearly affected the organization of the information recalled in all the groups studied (see Table 3). For example, the group of experts has a higher score in the signalled version than the unsignalled, reaching 95.8% as compared to 75% in Meyer's text, and 100% as against 62.5% in the text about the discovery of America. This degree of difference was also found in the second recall task. These differences are even greater for the GC group in the second, more difficult text, in which 91.6% as compared to 37.5% was scored in the immediate recall task and 79.1% as compared to 33.3% in the delayed task. These differences, though now somewhat reduced, are found in the group of less skilled readers (PC). Thus we can conclude that signalling guides the readers in the organization of what they remember according to the plan followed in the text.

Table 3: Scores "O" obtained by the different groups of readers in each text, version and recall task. The data is expressed by frequence and the value wich is shown in brackets corresponds to the percentage. Text 1= Super oil tankers, texto 2 = Origins of the discovery; S = Signalled Version, NS = Non-signalled Version.

		IMMEDIATED FREE RECALL TASK				DELAYED FREE RECALL TASK			
		TEXT 1		TEXT 2		TEXT 1		TEXT 2	
Group	Punt.	S	NS	S	NS	S	NS	S	NS
EXPERT	V	10 (41.6)	5 (20.8)	16 (66.6)	3 (12.5)	6 (25.0)	6 (25.0)	12 (50.0)	6 (25)
	III	13 (54.2)	13 (54.2)	8 (33.3)	12 (50.0)	13 (54.2)	10 (41.6)	11 (45.8)	12 (50)
	I	1 (4.2)	6 (25.0)	0 (00.0)	9 (37.5)	5 (20.8)	8 (33.3)	1 (4.2)	6 (25)
GC	V	3 (12.5)	0 (00)	12 (50.0)	0 (00.0)	1 (4.2)	0 (00.0)	8 (33.3)	0 (00.0)
	III	19 (79.2)	18 (75)	10 (41.6)	9 (37.5)	13 (54.2)	11 (45.8)	11 (45.8)	8 (33.3)
	I	2 (8.3)	6 (25)	2 (8.3)	15 (62.5)	10 (41.6)	13 (54.2)	5 (20.8)	16 (66.6)
PC	V	2 (8.3)	0 (00.0)	1 (4.2)	0 (00.0)	2 (8.3)	0 (00.0)	0 (00.0)	0 (00)
	III	12 (50.0)	5 (20.8)	5 (20.8)	2 (8.3)	6 (25.0)	3 (12.5)	3 (12.5)	0 (00)
	I	10 (41.6)	19 (79.2)	18 (75.0)	22 (91.7)	16 (66.6)	21 (87.5)	21 (87.5)	24 (100)

In addition, we found that the greater differences between both versions, the signalled and the unsignalled, occur in the "Discovery" text. This confirms the idea that the effectiveness of this type of aid increases with the difficulty of the text.

4. Conclusions

The main conclusions of the experiment can be summarized as follows:

1 — Signalling only seems to have a purpose when the text is fairly hard to understand. We could conclude, though tentatively, that the more difficult - because of lexical and semantic complexity - the text is to understand, the greater the effect of signalling certain information.

2 — The effectiveness of signalling seems to be selective as regards the kind of information recalled. This, at least, is what is suggested by the results of the A and R scores which correspond to the macrostructure and the main logical relations in the text.

3 — Signalling seems to help all the readers, but especially those who are more competent, whose reading skills are more developed. The poor readers (PC) are often incapable of perceiving and remembering the main logical relations which control the structure of the passage. These readers do not seem to possess the strategies necessary for them to pick out the information signalled in the text - the most highly relevant information - with any ease. Against this picture we find that skill in reading and previous knowledge of the content are two factors directly affecting the quality and stability of recall, which does not fade when tested at a later date.

4 — Signalling helps to organize what is remembered by readers following the plan used by the author of the passage. Helped in this way, the relevant ideas are used to produce a more coherent and consistent representation.

These results show that signalling influences the recall of more skilled readers in three different ways. First, they point the reader towards the signalled information. Second, they influence the way the information read will be represented in the memory of the subject, and, finally, they influence the process of retrieval of information by the reader, as can be seen in the high rate of agreement between the organizational plan of the material remembered and that of the text. A last point to mention is that the immediate free recall task produced, as expected, higher scores than the delayed task.

Literature

1. Anderson, R.C. & Pichert, J. W.: Recall of previously unrecallable information following a shift in perspective. Journal of Verbal Learning and Verbal Behavior, 17, 1-12 (1978).
2. Britton, B.K., Glynn, S.M., Meyer, B.J.F. & Penland, M.J.: Effects of text structure on use of cognitive capacity during reading. Journal of Educational Psychology, 74, 51-61 (1982).
3. Cespedes del Castillo, G.: América hispánica (1.492- 1.898). In: Historia de España (M. Tuñon de Lara, ed.),Vol VI. Barcelona: Labor 1983.
4. van Dijk, T.A.: Relevance assignment in discourse comprehension. Discourse Processes, 2, 113-126, 1979.
5. van Dijk, T.A.: Macrostructures. Hillsdale, New Jersey: Erlbaum, 1980.
6. van Dijk, T.A. & Kintsch, W.: Strategies of discourse comprehension. New York: Academic Press, 1983.
7. Glover, J. A., Dinnel, D. L., Halpain, D. R., McKee, T. K., Corkill, A. J. & Wise, S. L.: Effects of Across-Chapter Signals on Recall of Text. Journal of Educational Psychology, 80, 1, 3-15 (1988).
8. Hron, A., Kurbjuhn, I., Mandl, H., and Schnotz, W.: Structural inferences in reading and listening. In: Inferences in text processing (G. Rickheit and H. Strohner, ed.). North-Holland: Elsevier Science Publishers, 1985.
9. Irwin, J.W.: The effects of coherence explicitness on college readers prose comprehension. Journal of Reading Behavior, 14, 275-284 (1982).
10. Irwin, J.W. & Pulver, C.J.: Effects of explicitness, clause order, and reversibility on children's comprehension of causal relationship. Journal of Educational Psychology, 76, 399-407 (1984).
11. Kintsch, W. & van Dijk, T.A.: Toward a model of text comprehension and production. Psychological Review, 85,363-394 (1978).
12. Kozminsky, E.: Altering comprehension: The effect on biasing titles on text comprehension. Memory & Cognition, 5, 482-490 (1977).
13. Loman, N.C. & Mayer, R.: Signaling Techniques that increase the understability of expository prose. Journal of Educational Psychology, 75, 402-412 (1983).
14. Lorch, R.F.Jr.: Effects on recall of signals to text organization. Bulletin of the Psychonomic Society, 23,374-376 (1985).

15. Lorch, R.F.Jr. & Chen, A.M.: Effects of Number Signals on Reading and Recall. Journal of Educational Psychology, 78, 4, 263-270 (1986).
16. Mayer, R.E., Cook, L.K., & Dyck, J.L.: Techniques that help readers build mental models from scientifictext: Definitions pretraining and signaling. Journal of Educational Psychology, 76, 1089-1105 (1984).
17. Mayer, R.E.: Structural analysis of Science prose: can we increase problem-solving perfomance? In: Understanding expository text (B.K. Britton & J. B. Black, eds.). Hillsdale, New Jersey: Erlbaum, 1985.
18. Meyer, B.J.F.: The organization of prose and its effects in memory. Amsterdam: North-Holland, 1975.
19. Meyer, B.J.F.: What is remembered from prose: A function of passage structure. In: Discourse Production and Comprehension of Text (R.O. Freedle, ed.). Hillsdale, New Jersey: Erlbaum, 1977.
20. Meyer, B.J.F.: Text dimensions and cognitive processing. In: Learning and comprehension of text (H. Mandl,N.L. Stein, & T. Trabasso, eds.). Hillsdale, New Jersey: Erlbaum, 1984.
21. Meyer, B.J.F.: Prose analysis: Purposes, procedures and problems. In: Understanding Expository Text (B.K.Britton & J.B. Black, eds.). Hillsdale, New Jersey: Erlbaum, 1985.
22. Meyer, B.J.F., Brandt, D.M. & Bluth, G.J.: Use of top-level structure in text: Key for reading comprehension of ninth-grade students. Reading Research Quarterly, 16, 72-102 (1980).
23. Meyer, B.J.F. & Rice, G.E.: The interaction of reader strategies and the organization of text. Text, 2, 155-192 (1982).
24. Spiro, R.J.: Accommodative reconstruction in prose recall. Journal of Verbal Learning and Verbal Behavior,19, 84-95 (1980).

Hypertext Processing: Can We Forget Textual Psycholinguistics?

Eric Espéret

Laboratoire de Psychologie du Langage
URA CNRS 666, University of Poitiers, France

1. Introduction

In this paper I would like to present some reflections about the psycholinguistic processing of hypermedia, and to illustrate them with empirical data produced in our laboratory. Only the restricted instance of *hypertexts* (a word we should only apply to texts, accordingly with Harland, 1990), among the various types of hypermedia, will be considered in my presentation, with a focus on comprehension processes (read-only use).

Moreover, my paper will aim at stressing the need for further studies devoted to fine-grained analyses of understanding from classical reading of textual information, before (or meanwhile?) these studies were considering these same processes when implied in handling complex situations, like hypertexts. Thus, I would propose a more psycholinguistic approach of hypertexts, which are also textual, though non-linear, materials.

As for some important ergonomic aspects, such as the use of differently coloured cards (Wright & Lickorish, 1988), or the effects of single or multiple-window displays (Tombaugh et al., 1987), they will not be taken into account in this paper.

2. Text and HyperText: specificities and issues

According to many researchers (Conklin, 1987; Rada, 1989, for instance), a hypertext should exhibit three main components:

— a database of text, made up of many text units (called pages, cards, notes, etc.)

— a net of computer-supported semantic links, which connects the different text units

— an interface for browsing and modifying this complex set of texts and links.

If genuine characteristics of either text or hypertext are not confounded with specific constraints implied by a task (search for information, for example), or with presentation type (paper versus screen), they can be sketchilly described as in Table 1.

COMPONENTS	TEXT	HYPERTEXT
Author's mind	non-linear semantic representation (hierarchized?)	
Production		
Product	Non-autonomous units Linearity Discourse cues marking links	Autonomous units Non-linearity Independant set of potential links
Reading	Sequential accessing to all elements according author's order	Free accessing to any element through browsing
Reader's Mind	non-linear semantic representation (hierarchized?)	

Table 1. Specificities of text and hypertext

Thus, the main differences between the two types of media are: a whole coherent semantic structure vs. a set of independent non-ordered semantic units; information on global organization available through index or content table vs. available through mainly links , and sometimes index; presence vs. absence of discourse cues providing the reader with directions to process on-line semantic information (cues indicating the level of importance, new elements, author's intents, links between arguments, etc.). The order in which information is introduced is one of those cues, which makes use of the regular linear reading of a text.

On the other hand, text and hypertext share the same input and output, from a psycholinguistic point of view: a non-linear semantic representation, perhaps hierarchized, in both author's and reader's minds.

Differences between text and hypertext lie in both having access to information and processing it; so, beginners in hypertext using, however expert in usual reading they may be, often face difficulties when handling this new medium. Foss (1989a and b) proposed a good description of hypertext browsing problems, based on their possible cognitive origins: first, the *disorientation problems*, due to unfamiliarity with the conceptual structure of the network (absent or insufficient cognitive representation, because of a lack of previous information); second, the *task management problems*, raised by a general cognitive overload in users, because of the multiple-decision monitoring demanded; and finally the *discourse processing problems* (here, my own words), stemming from the lack of discourse cues to help readers to construct a hierarchized semantic representation of the hypertext content.

Most of hypertext studies have been devoted to the first issue and have suggested various means to facilitate efficient navigating through hypertexts and information retrieval. The importance of this specific problem must not prevent us from considering a more classic aspect encountered by a reader when processing a hypertext; indeed, linguistic material is brought to bear in each of the three components previously referred to: common paragraphs giving information about a specific knowledge-domain; highlighted words or phrases, or menus, that indicate a possible path to another related chunk of information; finally, a command language for acting on the system.

All this material has to be processed by the hypertext user; and we can reasonably guess that it is processed in the same way as other linguistic material, at least in the first two cases (command languages are not natural languages), but with specific difficulties described as pertaining to the third type of problems. Studies undertaken in the field of textual psycholinguistics are likely to shed light on this aspect; it would be time waste to design new studies on language processing in hypertexts without exploiting the data and methods provided by this field.

3. Textual psycholinguistics and hypertext processing

Textual psycholinguistics has proposed many more or less local models of text comprehension for two decades. I have not enough space here to detail them, even if several have become famous in the literature (cf., for example, Van Dijk and Kintsch, 1983). Generally speaking (cf. figure 1), such models assume that comprehension consists of the construction of an unlinearalized and hierarchical semantic representation from sequential information brought by the text read.

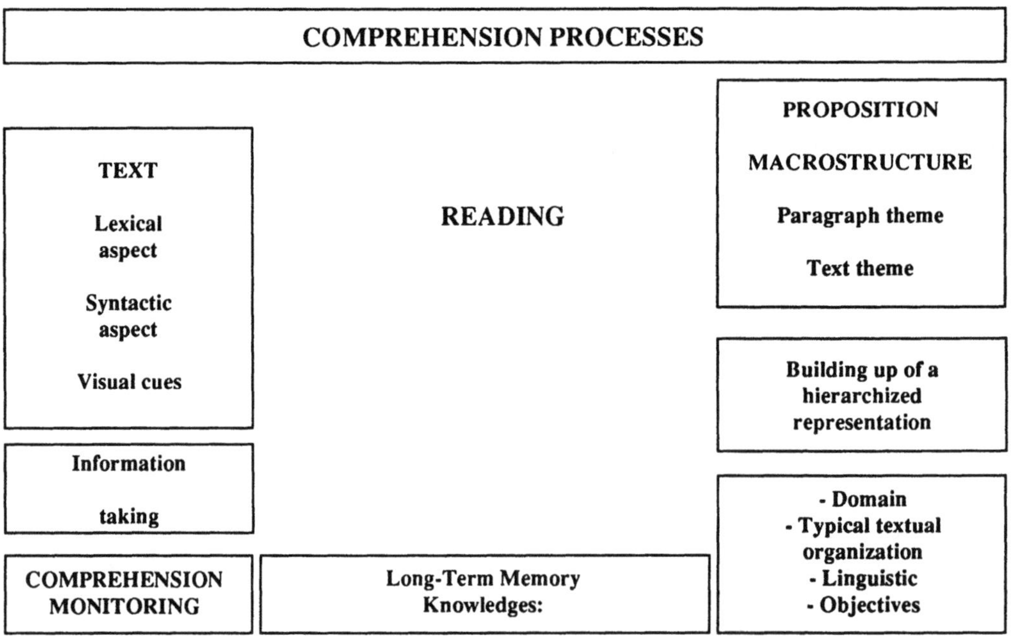

Fig. 1 - Cognitive processes and representations in comprehension reading

This construction brings two types of components into play: cognitive processes (goal-oriented sequences of operations (cognitive and linguistic ones), like macro-operations in Kintsch's sense), and various cognitive representations or knowledge. In these representations, three categories can partially control the ongoing processing of textual information: a) the representations the reader builds up about the task objectives; let us assume that they are constant for the most classical hypertext situations (search for information); b) domain-knowledge already acquired; c) psycholinguistic knowledge, concerning, for example, general textual coherence devices, or textual organizations (typical superstructures are the best known examples). These representations are effective in controlling information processing when they are activated, by specific cues, in readers' minds; the cues can be linguistic surface marks (a word, a title), or physical aspects of a text (new paragraph). Such "prompts" belong to the discourse cues evoked by Foss.

Thus, the results from usual textual psycholinguistics have to be taken into account to explain the strategies observed in beginners or experts, when they handle a hypertext system; in this way, Lachman (1989) showed the positive effect of providing users with on-line information, of macrostructural nature, when reading a technical text.

Furthermore, such hypertext situations could prove to be very interesting opportunities for analysing new functionings in regular language processing.

Now I would like to illustrate my reflections by what seems to be two main categories of phenomena to be analysed from a psycholinguistic point of view: first, how does a reader identify and process the semantic links displayed by each text unit; to recognize and correctly process each of these links is necessary for navigating through the database; second, how does the reader use certain visual cues in a text unit when building up a cognitive representation structured with the help of the information so extracted; this issue is important for segmenting texts and for conceiving of the screens, with their multiple-element information (like fields, buttons, icons).

4. Processing of the semantic net of links

Through browsing, people try to find information related to their initial question. Paths from a textual unit to another one are signalled on the screen by relational terms or phrases (sometimes called "buttons"), that can be chosen by the readers. A major consequence caused by this kind of "navigation" through a hypertext (multiple successive choices and digressions) is a disorientation of the subjects. Here, Foss (1989a) speaks of the "embedded digression problem" and the "art museum phenomenon". Given the state of knowledge on this point in psycholinguistics, my thoughts will only focus on the relational cues in *one* text unit: to take advantage of the non-linear structure of hypertext, a reader must process these relational statements in each text unit presented, according to his searching objective. To study the psycholinguistic processing of these elements, as it is brought to bear by a subject, I think we still need a simplified situation. J-F. Rouet (1988, 1990a, 1990b), in our Laboratory proposed this kind of approach in a series of experiments.

The general design of these studies was as follows: micro text databases were built-up in four different knowledge domains (for example: ozone generation); each database consisted of 6 paragraphs, each one corresponding to a particular topic in the knowledge domain considered. The four expository texts could be presented on the screen, either in a conventional (linear) form or with some limited hypertext features. In the latter case, variations of procedure could exist according to the experiments: for example, at the end of the reading of one paragraph, the relation to one of the other five remaining paragraphs was explicitly stated; this relational statement was replaced by a summary statement in the conventional form. Or the reader was imposed a linear reading situation, vs. an interactive reading situation (a path choice had to be made in a menu after each paragraph), with an added instruction to read the whole text, or just the parts they chose to display; or last, the reader had to use restricted menus, in which just a link with either one or two other paragraphs was specified. In all the studies, subjects were instructed to complete precise questions by seeking information in the texts proposed.

With this general design, a control was possible on certain cognitive operations requested by different sub-tasks involved in reading a hypertext. Different analyses aimed at comparing the searching and comprehension strategies used by young (11-year-old) and older readers (15-year), according to the experimental conditions, or their initial level of domain-knowledge.

Several results, issued from different studies in the series, are important for our current topic:

1. Subjects with a larger initial domain-knowledge, and/or a higher age, make selections of the displayed paragraphs in a more effective way (less useless selections, for example); moreover, they obtain higher comprehension scores. These results join those obtained by Elkerton & Williges (1984), about the role played by expertise in information retrieval strategies.

2. Training sessions with the interactive reading situation ("hypertext-like" situation) benefit only older subjects. Nevertheless, a longer training time seems also increase the use of these links by younger pupils (Rouet, 1990c).

3. Both young and older subjects process the relational statements at the end of a paragraph, but only the older ones give these statements the status of a transition between the current topic and the possible next one; for them, the processing of such statements improve their selection strategy.

Generally speaking, it appears from more qualitative analyses that only older readers have got a representation of what is an expository text, and what the linking statements are useful for. This kind of representation cannot be triggered by the only hypertext situation and has to be learnt. Other hypertext features have been shown to be learnt: multiple-window displays (Tombaugh & al., 1987), embedded menus and role of buttons (Foss, 1989), for instance.

5. Processing of the physical cues in a text

The physical aspect of a text, as it is viewed by a reader on a page or screen, proves to be a second important factor intervening in language processing. Reading times, taken as indicators of cognitive comprehension processes, seem particularly influenced by the physical organization, punctuation marks or underlining, for example.

These effects can't be studied through the usual techniques that don't display the whole text at the same time (self-paced device, or even moving window). So, D. Gaonach and J-M. Passerault (1988) Ballaire, Gaonac'h and Passerault (1989) designed another software package, called

ADFM *(Auto Décryptage par Fenêtre Mobile)*, that allowed the reader to use different categories of physical cues in processing texts, as if he was reading it normally. In this procedure, the entire text was displayed on the screen from the session beginning, but in a "cryptical" form: each letter was replaced by another one, randomly determined (cf. figure 2). When a subject depressed the space bar (or another key), the first text segment (phrase, sentence, or paragraph) was decrypted and could be normally read; another key depression decrypted the next segment, and so on. Different options could be chosen by the experimenter: for example, to maintain physical cues, like upper case letters, punctuation marks, paragraph markings, or not; or to change a text segment again into its crypted form, when the subject went on to the next one, or to leave it in a readable form.

```
.. .......... .......... .. ....., ... .. .. ..........
.... .'... .. .. ..., .. .. ..... .'... ... ...... .........,
.... .. .... ..... .le meilleur profit possible ktay dgp
spihsmdxcwod, dyok lseej grvj eni fatncddnhctergk.
Tnsaye bhkfelsevep op rfn tty hocojbbhnb, xk k'qbfpvfoj
mxtona ie gkmp ls ixxbafptyf gewfcn, pef hdflt j cn qnfhglsh
pjarescgjrs: tsfn mf sidnosuexdl enthm a cvpp.
```

Fig. 2 - Example of a screen presenting a ADFM text

This way of presenting text on a screen leads to an improvement of reading speed, in comparison with classical moving window presentation. This result seems to be due to the processing of physical cues that the reader is provided with by this technique.

Several experiments have been carried out with ADFM technique, to check the role played by different types of physical cues. In all studies, encrypted texts, with or without physical cues available, are compared using reading times or comprehension scores. The prominent results can be summarized as follows (Passerault & Gaonac'h, 1989):

1. When physical properties of the displayed text are available, like lengths of the lines and/or text, upper case letters and punctuation marks, subjects tend globally to read at a higher speed. Nevertheless, slow readers take advantage of this kind of information in a weaker manner. These cues seem to play such a role by facilitating the advance segmentation of the semantic content of the following sentences into propositions (as semantic units to be processed).
2. Underlining, used to draw the reader's attention towards important information in a target sentence, tends to increase the reading time of this sentence, but causes the previous sentence, and, with a somewhat weaker effect, the following one, to be read more quickly; this modification of reading times would correspond to an activation of representations about the specific organization of certain types of text (here, the use of analogy in an expository text). Such high-level representations would control time allocation (Gaonac'h & Passerault, 1990).
3. Time allocation in reading tasks is also partially monitored by the paragraphe marking: if marking of a new paragraph is replaced by a comma (after sentence n), subjects spend less time reading sentence n-1 and sentence n+1, and more time reading sentence n-2; converse effects are observed when the paragraph marking is maintained. Content and segmentation are the same in both cases; but paragraph marking triggers a specific reading strategy.

6. Conclusion

The two trends of research I have just presented here are illustrations of some issues we are necessarily facing when we try to analyse hypertext processing. Indeed, hypertext is a complex technical tool, with many different properties in interaction. As for the most efficient approach which could be taken, I would claim we still need to study elementary operations implemented at each step of its processing; and a good way to do that is to simulate (or more exactly, to emulate) partial elements (precise processes, components of the entire procedure), even if the results thus obtained have to be subsequently validated in a more ecological use of hypertexts. A more global approach could indeed prevent us from identifying the genuine difficulties encountered by hypertext users, as they could be concealed by many other minor problems encountered during the ongoing search for information.

To study such processes, we need use on-line protocols, with time-stamped events recorded, and whose results are likely to be easily interpreted. The ADFM software previously evoked is one instance of this approach (on compatible PC). MacLeod's Automonitor (1990), for Hypercard softwares, provides another very interesting tool to achieve the objective proposed here.

Literature

1. Ballaire, M-F., Gaonac'h, D. & Passerault (1989). Un logiciel d'expérimentation pour l'étude en temps réel de l'activité de compréhension. Roneoted text. Poitiers, Laboratoire de Psychologie du Langage.
2. Conklin, J. (1987). Hypertext: an introduction and survey. Computer, 20, 17 - 41.
3. Van Dijk, T.A. & Kintsch, W. (1983). Strategies of discourse comprehension. New York, Academic Press.
4. Elkerton, J. & Williges, R.C. (1984). Information retrieval strategies in a file-search environment. Human Factors, 26, 171-184.
5. Foss, C.L. (1989a). Tools for reading and browsing hypertext. Information processing and management, 25 (4), 407-418.
6. Foss, C.L. (1989b). Detecting lost users: empirical studies on browsing Hypertext. Roneoted paper, INRIA, Sophia Antipolis.
7. Gaonac'h, D. & Passerault, J-M. (1988). Le traitement des ruptures textuelles dans la gestion de l'activité de lecture. Colloque de la Société Française de Psychologie, Dijon.
8. Gaonac'h, D. & Passerault, J-M. (1990). Marquage de l'importance et traitement des éléments dans un texte: effets immédiat et différé. European Journal of Psychology of education, 5, 59-68.
9. Harland, M. (1990). Learning through browsing: observations on the production of self-directed learning systems for language students. In this volume.
10. Lachman, R. (1989). Comprehension aids for on-line reading of expository text. Human Factors, 31(1), 1-15.
11. MacLeod, M. (1990). Tools for monitoring and analysing the use of hypermedia courseware. In this volume.
12. Passerault, J-M. & Gaonac'h, D. (1989). The use of visual cues when reading a text on a computer display. Third European Conference for Research on Learning and Instruction. Madrid.
13. Rada, R. (1989). Writing and reading hypertext: an overview. Journal of the American Society for Information Science, 40(3), 164-171.
14. Rouet, J-F. (1988). Sélection et traitement d'informations thématiquement reliées en situation d'interaction sujet-ordinateur. 1er Congrès Européen "Intelligence artificielle et formation". Lille.
15. Rouet, J-F. (1990a). Processing relational statements in expository texts: a comparison of linear and interactive reading situations. paper proposed to Cognitiva (Spain).
16. Rouet, J-F. (1990b). Statégies différentielles de sélection d'informations dans la manipulation d'un logiciel de lecture interactive. In R. Martin (Ed.) Informatique et différences individuelles. Lyon, Presses universitaires de Lyon.
17. Rouet, J-F. (1990c) Interactive text processing by inexperienced (hyper-) readers. ECHT'90. Paris, Novembre.

18. Tombaugh, J., Lickorish, A. & Wright, P. (1987). Multiple-window displays for readers of lengthy texts. International Journal of Man-Machine Studies, 26, 597-615.
19. Wright, P. & Lickorish, A. (1988). Colour cues as location aids in lengthy texts on screen and paper. Behaviour and Information Technology, 7(1), 11-30.

Cognitive Ergonomics in a Language Learning Task

Mireille Bastien

1. Introduction

A problem: the use of determiners in language acquisition

A well-known difficulty in language acquisition by children is the mastery of determiners, and more especially, the use of articles.

As Fig. 1 shows, there are, in French, six articles to express quantifying and gender-marking functions.

		DEFINITE	INDEFINITE
SING.	masculine	le (the)	un (a)
	feminine	la (the)	une (a)
PLUR.	masculine	les (the)	des (some)
	feminine	les (the)	des (some)

Fig. 1 - The six French articles

I conducted an experiment, five years ago, with deaf children who where from 7 to 9 years old. I presented to them, on a computer screen, an utterance corresponding to a picture they saw just before (Toniazzo, 1985). The results clearly showed that the subjects had strong difficulty to take into account the relevance of the use of the articles. For example, if I showed utterances without articles or with a wrong one (as "le pomme" instead of "la pomme") the subjects quite always declared that the utterance was correct.

This problem is the same with younger hearing children. Karmiloff-Smith, for example, in her paper of 1986, reported a specific difficulty when young children use articles: children can correctly use the indefinite article "a" ("un", in French, for example "a handkerchief", "un mouchoir") but add a partitive when implying the numeral function of the indefinite article ("un de mouchoir" for "one handkerchief"). Note that French does not distinguish between "a" and "one" and use the same word "un".

The problem that young children have to correctly use the articles is nevertheless not a linguistic one. Indeed, they all know the six lexical elements "le, la, un, une, les, des". The difficulty they encounter is, probably, a logical one. More especially, they don't confuse singular and plural, but confuse definite and indefinite articles, that is to say between "a" ("un, une") and "the" ("le, la"), because it involves the mastery of the relationship between the whole and the part, as Fig. 2 shows.

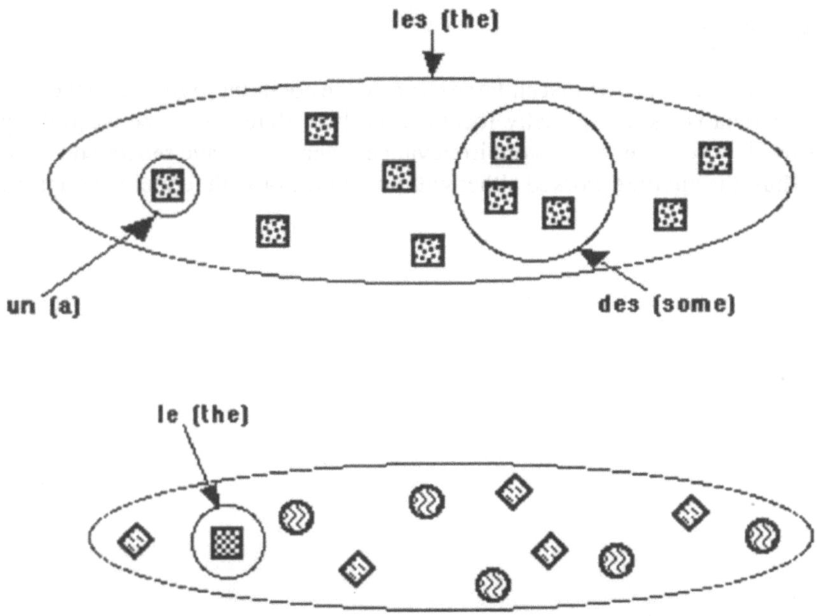

Fig. 2 - A logical representation of the French articles

Let us consider the logical ideas that are implied by the articles. For example, if I take "a square" ("un carré"), that means that I have a set of other same objects and that I take one among them. If I take "the square" ("le carré") that means that I have a set of different objects among which there is only one square. That is to say I must select a subclass composed of only one element. If I take "some squares" ("des carrés") that means that I have a set of n squares and that I must take a number of objects included between 2 and n-1 ($2 < x < n-1$). If I take "the squares" ("les carrés") that means that I have a set of at least two elements and that I must pick out all the elements which make it up.

To illustrate my talk, I would like to present a computer program that we have called Patricia.

2. Patricia: an Intelligent Tutoring System for the acquisition of articles.

In the theoretical viewpoint of "learning by doing" (Anzaï & Simon, 1979, George, 1983), C. Bastien and myself worked out a tutorial system to help children to learn the use of the articles. Its main goal is to provide a concrete representation of articles. The system was implemented on a Macintosh Plus Hypercard application which allowed us to use together text, pictures and animation. It includes three phases. The first concerns the acquisition of printed nouns of objects. The second is a phase of familiarization with the objects and the situations. The third is the central core of the system, the learning phase in itself.

2.1 Learning vocabulary

The goal of this phase is to ensure that children can read the nouns they will see on the screen. The objective of Patricia is more especially focussed on the differentiation between definite and indefinitive articles. So, in order to avoid irrelevant elements, we have separated the gender of the objects. Thus, the children worked either with masculine or with feminine nouns, as shown in Fig. 3.

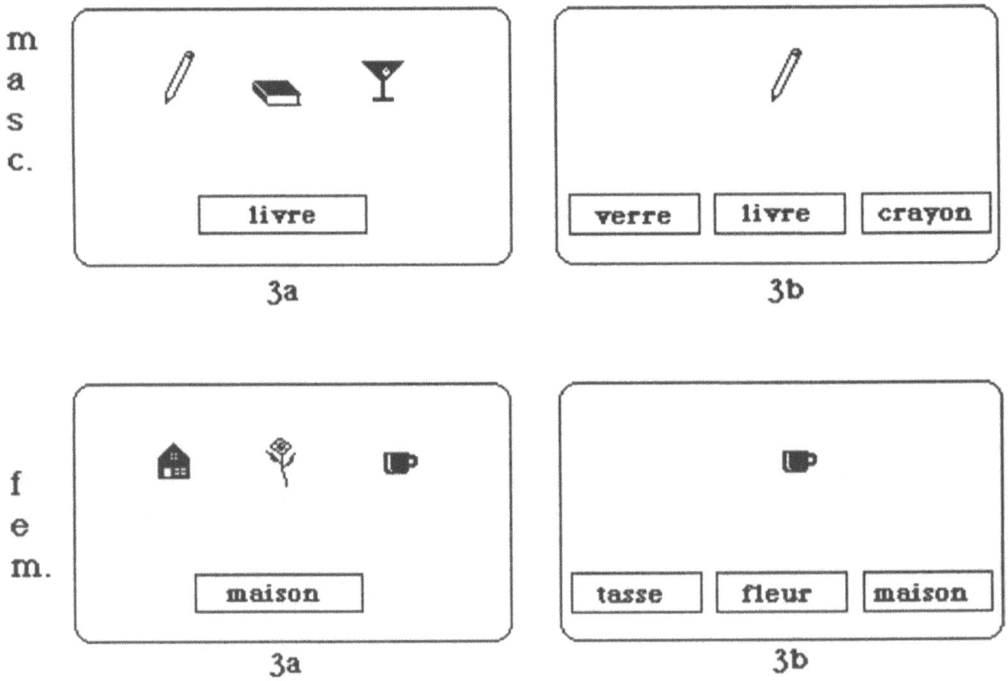

Fig. 3 - An illustration of the first phase: learning masculine or feminine vocabulary

In each case, the child sees on the screen a type 3a or 3b card. When a 3a type card appears, he must clik on the drawing representing the noun. When a 3b card appears, he must click on the corresponding noun. If he succeeds, he sees a message meaning "OK" and hears a nice sound, then a new card which is choosen at random, appears. If he fails, he sees a signal "no" and hears an unpleasant sound and he sees the same card again.

Note that kind of learning is purely associative.

2.2 Phase of familiarization

On the upper part of the screen, are randomly printed the three feminine or masculine nouns the child has just learned and the four corresponding articles. On the lower part is printed, in a window, "Patricia takes ...." ("Patricia prend ...."), as shown in Fig. 4.

The child is told that a little girl, named Patricia will take in her basket the objects he will order her to pick out. He can choose among the words of the lexicon to write the order to Patricia. To choose, he must click on one word which automatically appears after the last word in the window. We made sure first that children could read all the words.

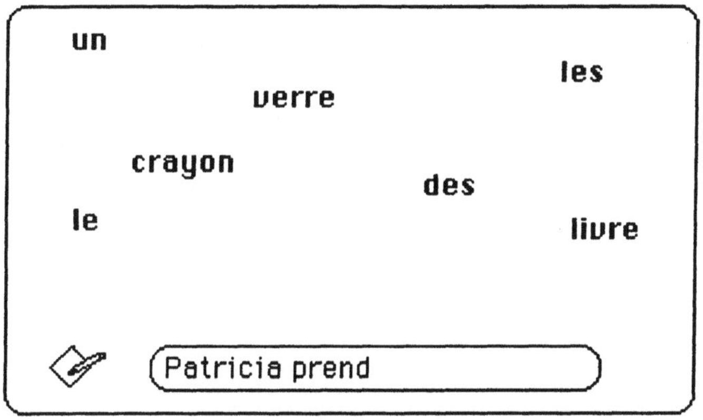

Fig. 4 - The screen at the beginning of the second phase

The system tests on line the subject's production and shows him a corresponding issue. If the child first chooses a noun, or two articles, he immediately sees the signal "no". If he produces a correct sentence, he can modify it by a mouse-click on the "no" button or else he must confirm by a mouse-click on the "yes" button". Note that when a plural article is chosen, the system adds itself an "s" at the end of the noun (cf. Fig. 5).

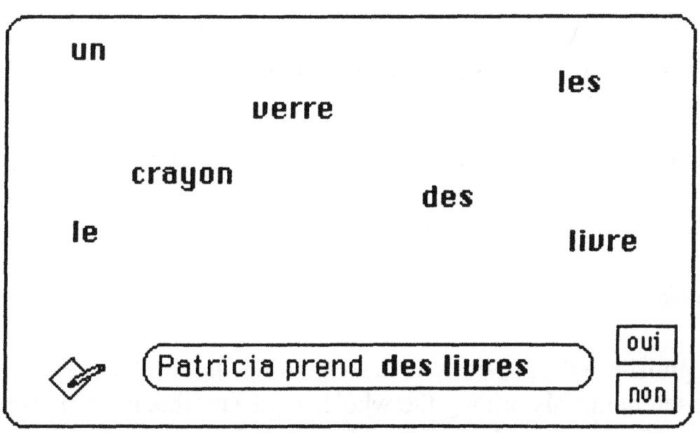

Fig. 5 - The screen when an utterance is written

If the child clicks on the "yes" button, then he sees the corresponding animation. In the initial state, Patricia is motionless and looks at the objects. On the right of the screen, there are, in a cupboard, four identical objects of each three classes, for example four pencils, four glasses, four books, unless the singular definite "the" ("le" or "la" in French) has been chosen. In this case, the screen shows only one object of each class (one pencil, one glass, one book) as shown in Figs. 6 and 7. Patricia then moves and puts in her basket the objects that the child ordered her to pick out. She goes back and places them on the shelves which are on the left part of the screen. In the lower part of the screen is automatically written "Patricia has taken <article> <noun>" ("Patricia a pris <article> <nom>") as shown in Figs. 6 and 7.

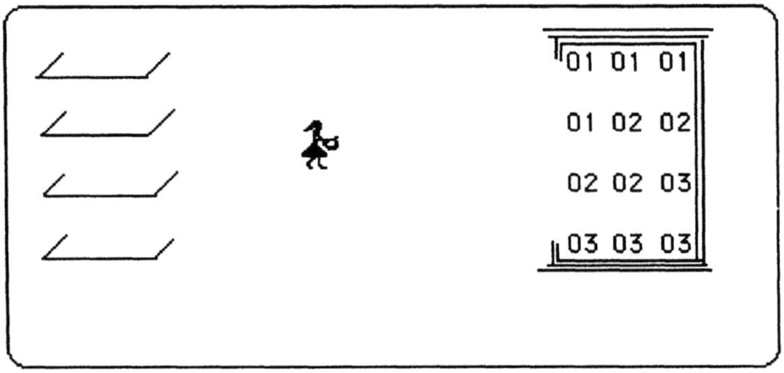

the initial state
of the screen

the initial state
of the screen
when the child
chooses "the, sing."

Fig. 6 & 7 - The screen when Patricia has taken objects

At this time, if the child wants to continue, he only has to click to see the lexicon again or else he can stop.

2.3 Phase of learning

The task is just the opposite of the previous. In the beginning, the child sees Patricia doing an action that it has been chosen randomly among the whole set of possible combinations. He must then write the corresponding sentence which is tested as in the previous exercise.

2.4 First results

We experimented this version of Patricia with the 22 pupils of a first primary classroom in the third month of the school. The computer was in a special room of the school and the children passed individually.

After some short explanations, the child went himself through the three phases, spending as much time as he wished. Each action of the subject, each decision he took, was recorded on an individual protocol card. Figure 8 shows the results of the first production of the subjects in the learning phase.

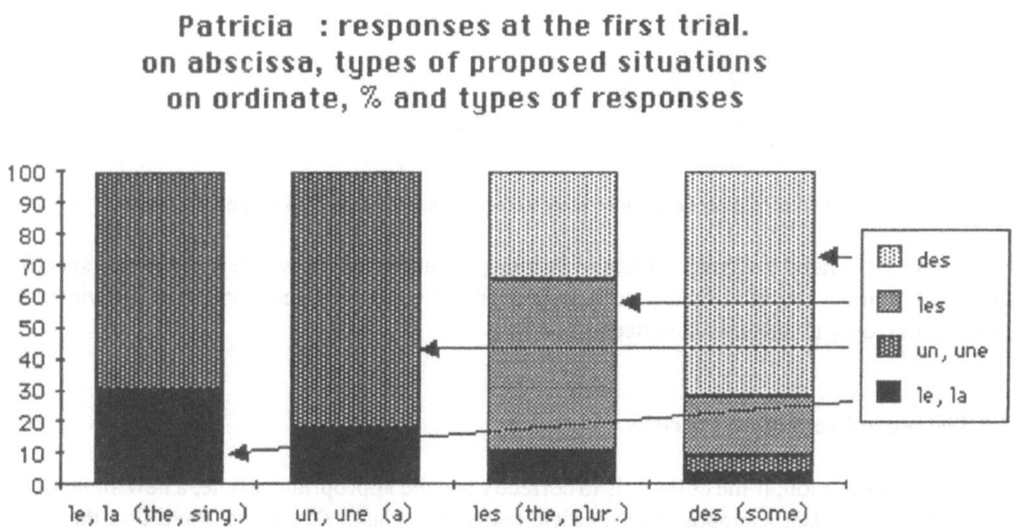

Fig. 8 - The first of the first production of the subjects

On the abscissa are represented the types of proposed situations (feminine and masculine put together). On the ordinate are the rates and types of responses of the subjects.

It can be seen that there is only slight confusion between singular and plural. When the situation requires a plural article, children use the singular in only 10% of the cases, and they never fail when the situation requires the singular. The main problem lies effectively in the differentiation between the definite and the indefinite. When they are confronted with an indefinite situation, the children use a definite article in 18.5% of the cases in plural and 17.7% in singular. The main problem is the use of the definite article: the children use the indefinite in 54.5% of the cases in the plural and 70% in the singular.

Figure 9 shows the number of trials the children need to succeed: the situation that requires the bigger number of trials is the definite singular.

A first rough interpretation in explaining this particular difficulty is that children confuse the definite "the" ("le", in French) with the numeral "one" ("un", in French).

What is more interesting, if our system brought out the difficulty, it was still not able to correctly help the subjects to overcome this difficulty. Actually, it's a classical training system in which the learner is only informed if he succeeds or fails, that corresponds to a behavioristic conception of learning (trials versus errors). In fact, children don't learn in this way.

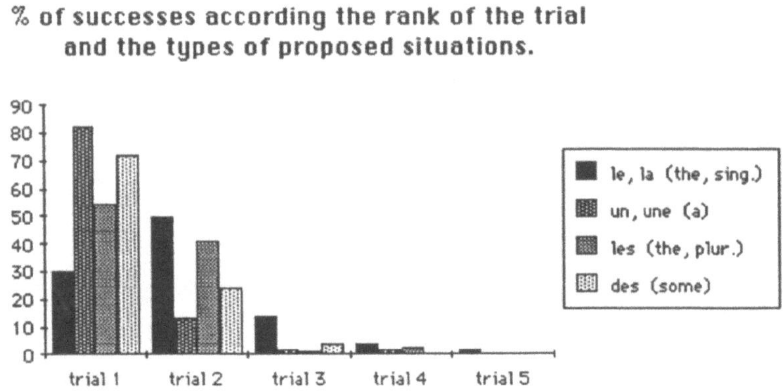

Fig. 9 - Number of trials necessary to succeed according to the types of proposed situations

So, we elaborated a second version of Patricia, the main goal of which is to provide specific information about the kind of difficulties the learners encounter, and moreover, provide this information, only to subjects who need it.

2.5 The second version of Patricia

In this second version, if the child fails to correctly use the appropriate article, a new situation is proposed to him. Let's suppose that Patricia takes "the glass" ("le verre") and that the child answers "a glass" ("un verre"). A new card is then shown as shown in Fig. 10.

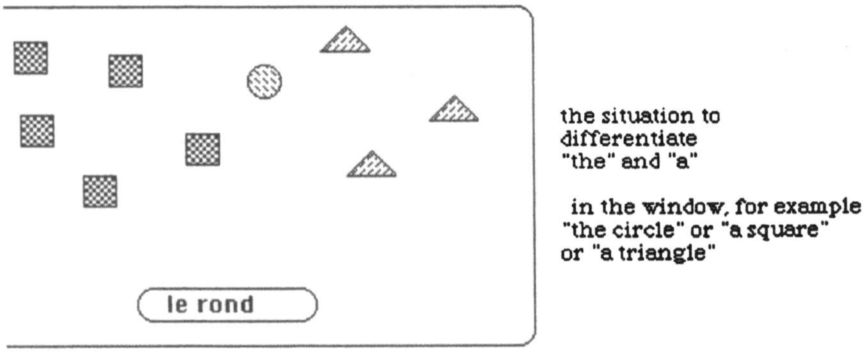

Fig. 10 - The situation to differentiate "the" ("le") and "a" ("un")

In the upper part of the screen, there is a set of objects arranged in subsets, and in the window, a message. The child must click on the corresponding object. In sum, that must conduct him to distinguish "the" and "a" in elaborating a process rule like:

If there is repetition of objects, then I must use "a" ("un")

If there is no repetition, then I must use "the" ("le).

If the child confuses "some" ("des") and "the, plural" ("les"), then he gets this kind of card (see Fig. 11).

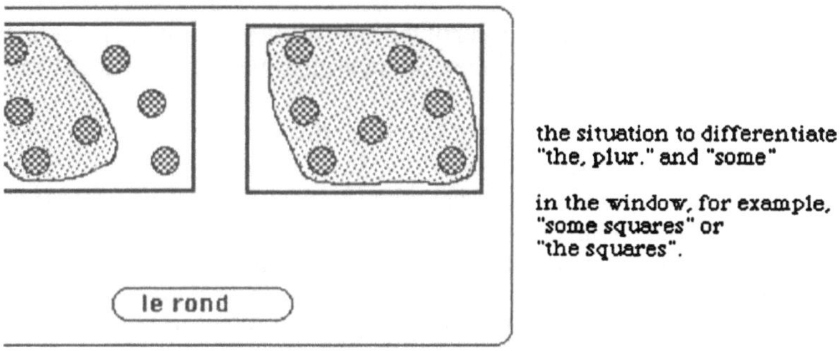

Fig. 11 - The situation to differentiate "the, plur." (les") and "some" ("des")

In the window, he can see for example, the message "some circles" ("des ronds") or "the circles" ("les ronds") and must click on the correct drawing.

The rule he must construct is

If all the objects are picked out, then I must use "the" ("les")

If it remains at least one object, then I must use "some" ("des").

This new version of the tutorial system is now being tested.

3. Conclusion

To summarize, the first version of our system was not really "intelligent" according to the description proposed by Mandl (1988). If it was able to pinpoint the mistakes or the successes, it could not deduce anything about the current knowledge of the subjects. It gave, nevertheless, some precious information about the functioning of the subjects, that is to say it underlined the kind of difficulties they encountered.

The second version is more flexible because the system is able to assess, in the course of learning, the current knowledge of each learner and can propose an adapted situation to help him to improve his knowledge level.

Finally, if we consider the ergonomics of a hypermedia system, I think that three aspects must be taken into account:

(1) the domain in which it applies,
(2) the technical aspects (the way the learner can use the system),
(3) the theoretical aspects (psychological theory which is "put" into the system, representation of the user's reasoning...).

Concerning the first point, that is the domain, the goal of the tutorial system I presented, is of course, closely delimited. It is true that, with respect to the vast domain of the language acquisition, it concerns only a very restricted situation. This way of operating, offers nevertheless the advantage that we can determine the whole set of the possibilities, thus to know at every moment at what stage the subject is at a given moment, then to interact in a suitable way.

About the second point, that is the technical aspects, the most important in our system was that the child could see at the same time, the initial state, the final state and the transformation itself. These constraints are technically rather easy to overcome with an "oriented-object-language" as Hypertalk. Furthermore the possibility of using a mouse permits to avoid the irrelevant tasks. So, the children, even very young, learned very quickly the mouse technique.

If the programming of the drawings and of the animation was quite easy to do, the most tricky question concerned the nature itself of the concrete information we wanted to propose to the subjects.

In fact, this refers directly to third point I evoked, that is the theoretical aspects, which is the most important and the most delicate one.

If we base ourselves on purely perceptual criteria, as the number of objects which are drawn, their size, their colour, and so on, then we don't have really precise decision criteria. Of course, it's necessary that the subject could accurately discriminate and recognize the objects he sees (this was the objective of the first phase of the training). But once these constraints are removed, remains the crucial question: "what criteria can we rely on?". The nature of the information cannot be specified in itself, because the perceptual aspects only constitute insufficient indications.

What really makes the ergonomics of the system is that it can reply, in real time, to the subjects' processes of treatment in a very particular situation. Actually, the most important is clearly determined by the processes which are supposed to be those of the subjects. That means that the system must be modelled on the way we think the subjects function mentally. This is, in sum, a good way to validate our hypotheses.

Literature

1. Anderson, J.R., 1987, Methodology for studying knowledge, Behavioral and Brain Sciences, 10, 467-505.
2. Anzai Y. & Simon H.A., 1979, The theory of learning by doing, Psychological Review, 86, 124-140.
3. George, C., 1883, Apprendre par l'action, Paris, P.U.F.
4. Karmiloff-Smith, A., 1986, From meta-processes to conscious access: Evidence from chidren's metalinguistic and repair data, Cognition, 23, 95-147.
5. Mandl, H., 1988, Introduction, International Journal of Educational Research, 12, 793-798.
6. Toniazzo, M., 1985, Lire pour s'entendre...Mémoire de maîtrise de Psychologie Expérimentale, Université de Provence.

3 Help Tools for Hypermedia and AI in Hypermedia

Hypermedia for Learning Cognitive Instructional Design

J. Lowyck & J. Elen

University Department for Course Development, K.U. Leuven, Belgium

1. Introduction

Within a cognitive view instructional materials help the learner to adapt his cognitive structure to the domain-expert's one [26]. The mapping features of computer programs in general [17, 27, 35], and especially of hypermedia, hypercard and hypertext [26], gained therefore attention of cognitive instructional designers.

In this paper the suitability of hypermedia for learning cognitive instructional design is explored. It is argued that design efforts of authors can be facilitated by a computercoach which incorporates cognitive design principles. It is hypothesized that the repeated use of such a computercoach will diminish the amount of external (computer-initiated) interventions needed by the author. It is further assumed, that coaching an author's decision-making during the developmental process is more effective and efficient than making available an elaborated set of prescriptions.

This contribution starts with a brief discussion of the background and problems of (cognitive) instructional design. An embryonical cognitive instructional design (CID) - model is presented which reflects the theoretical knowledge base of the computercoach. In the second section, differences between domain-experts and domain-novices are outlined in order to identify the information types that should get implemented in the computercoach. A functional description of one of the modules of the coach is also offered. In the last section the possible contributions of hypermedia for various parts of the coach are discussed. In the conclusion the findings are summarized and the problems with the use of hypermedia for learning cognitive instructional design are reviewed.

2. From ID to CID

2.1 Instructional Design (ID)

Instructional design originates from efforts of learning psychologists to make education more effective, e.g. [55]. It was expected that the direct application of behavioristic learning principles would make instruction and education more systematic, controllable and effective [19]. Both the behavioristic origins and the general systems theory strongly influenced the outlook of ID [5, 9]. While in ID the design parameters are selected from a behavioristic framework, the process is structured in line with general systems theory, e.g. [20].

Only recently the possible contributions of cognitive learning theories for the optimization of instructional design has been advocated.

2.2 Cognitive Instructional Design (CID)

Different views on the relation between cognitive sciences and instructional design have been offered. They differ in their approach as to the following issues:

- firstly, each 'prescriptive' discipline, e.g. instructional design needs clarification of questions like [50, 53] : Can descriptive research outcomes be directly translated into prescriptions ? If so, under what conditions and how ?

  Answers on these questions strongly influence the theoretical orientation of prescriptive disciplines, especially when a shift occurs in the descriptive knowledge base of such disciplines. With a changing descriptive knowledge base, the need for underpinning both the selection of the theoretical base and the transition of descriptions into prescriptions is much higher than in a static, unquestionned theoretical environment;
- a second range of issues directly adresses the relation between cognitive psychology and instructional design: Is instructional design, taken its theoretical origins into account, compatible with cognitive psychology ? In other words, can research outcomes from cognitive psychology be integrated in a 'behavioristic' instructional design ?

Toward both issues, different positions are taken by ID researchers. A first position reflects an unambiguous positive view. It is assumed that descriptions can be easily transformed into prescriptions and that traditional cognitive research outcomes can be easily incorporated into instructional design. Integration occurs by adding new parameters to existing ID models, replacing parameters, subsuming parameters, and adding or replacing instruments e.g. metacognition [47], information-processing [29, 59, 60], task analysis [22, 41], practice [44].

A second position questions such a direct transition from description to prescription. Descriptive sciences, like cognitive psychology, aim at solving different problems than prescriptive disciplines, like instructional design. A mere translation of descriptions into prescriptions seems hardly possible, e.g. [12]. Cognitive psychology and instructional design each view learning from a different perspective e.g. [7]. Whereas cognitive theory pursues to describe how learning occurs and to identify the mediating variables, instructional design does not study learning processes but the conditions which influence effective and efficient learning.

Recently a third position has been taken which investigates the consequences of the paradigm-shift in learning theory for instructional design. It is stated that an incorporation of cognitive research outcomes into instructional design is hardly possible due to both the description-prescription problem and the behavioristic nature of instructional design itself [12, 31, 61]. It is argued that the parameters, procedures and process in traditional ID are so deeply influenced by its behavioristic background that an incorporation of cognitive outcomes into ID doesn't make the models cognitive. Not a simple integration but a complete reconceptualization is looked for. This reconceptualization of ID implies (1) the selection of design parameters, (2) the construction of a suitable development process, and (3) the adequate instrumentation of the selected parameters.

2.3 An embryonical CID model

In our research we tried to take into account validated cognitive outcomes to build an embryonic CID model [31]. The premisses of this model and their theoretical underpinnings will be discussed along the following questions:

- What are the essential design parameters?
- Which are the peculiar features of a cognitive design process?

– What are the characteristics of cognitive design procedures?

Before answering these questions, it is necessary to describe the referent system of the model in order to define more precisely its scope.

2.3.1 Referent system

The specific embryonical CID model identifies the design parameters, process and procedures for the design by domain-experts of self-instructional printed materials at the university level. So far, no attention has been paid to other media, delivery systems, or instructional settings.

2.3.2 Design parameters

Two categories of design parameters are distinguished, i. e. student oriented and material oriented parameters. Learning outcomes are hypothesized to be the result of the interaction between these parameters [15].

Cognitive psychology [8, 18, 43, 54, 57] has revealed the following three **student oriented parameters** to be of primary importance for learning:

- cognitive structure before and during the instructional process;
- cognitive processes involved in acquiring new information and integrating this information in the existing cognitive structure;
- metacognitive and regulatory processes, like monitoring, regulating and revising.

Considering these parameters, the learning process itself can be described to be cumulative, active, goal-oriented, and constructive [51, 52].

Our embryonical CID model focusses on printed materials. Therefore, the following *material oriented parameters* are selected:

- structure of the text: the kind of information-elements, their interrelationships and representation in textual format [3, 33, 38, 49];
- elements added to the text in order (1) to help students find their way through the text (textual meta-information); (2) to facilitate study by adding didactical elements (instructional information) and (3) to regulate quality and quantity of learning activities (instructional meta-information) [4, 6, 23, 34, 58];
- format or lay-out of the text which can either have a structuring or a regulatory function [1, 24].

2.3.3 Design process

2.3.3.1 Theoretical background

Traditionally the instructional design process starts with the identification and specification of instructional objectives. This phase is followed by the classification of the selected objectives in order to identify compatible instructional methods [5, 46, 56]. Research on both teacher cognitions and writing processes has clearly showed that even experts do not follow such a linear process [11, 25, 30, 45]. Consequently, the design process prescribed by CID should follow more closely the real cognitions of designers [39]. The following process seems to do so (see Fig. 1).

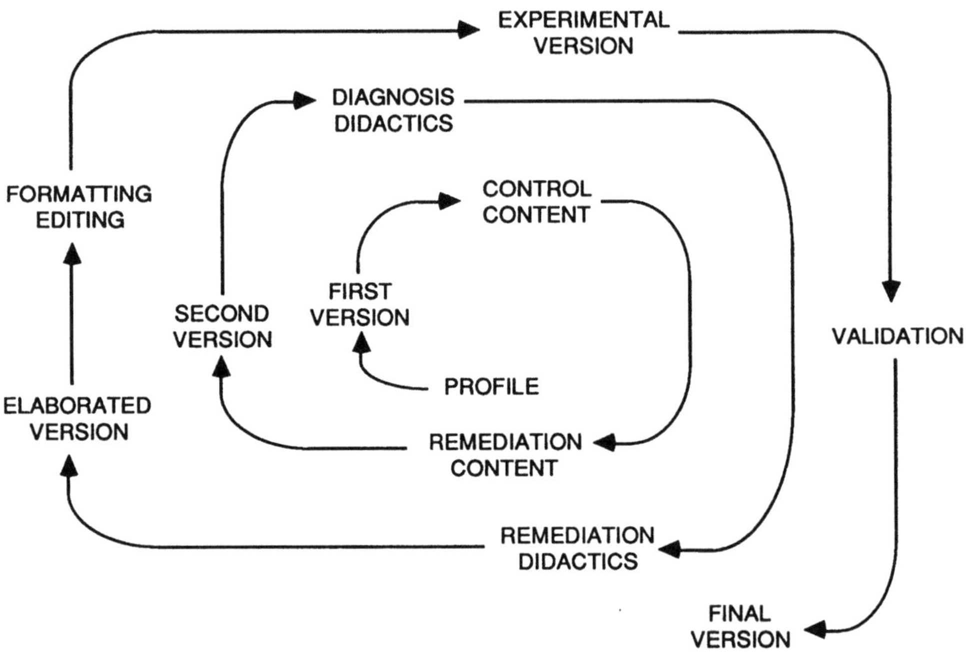

Figure 1

The starting point is not a list of specified objectives, it rather is a *profile* of the instructional material with a description of:

- the purposes and functions of the instructional materials to be designed;
- the main topics to be covered in the materials as well as their interrelations;
- the characteristics of the setting in which the materials will be used (overall curriculum, student characteristics, and practical constraints).

This profile serves as an orientation and reference point toward the work to be done, and especially toward strategic decision-making and continuous quality-control. It is formulated in terms of intended actions, rather than of specific elements of content or operationalized behaviors. Creating this profile, the author explores the possibilities, estimates the value of content elements and generates hypotheses about the most suitable orientations of the material. In some cases, cooperation with colleagues could be of interest. The profile, in other words, describes the problem space of the specific instructional design project [40].

Writing the *first version*, more elaborate decisions about the selection and organisation of the topics are made. One advantage of this approach is that the process builds upon the authors' expertise, instead of forcing them to follow a unfamiliar line of thought [36]. The first version of the material reflects in a concrete manner both the author's aims and his/her conception of the best way to present the content. This version could be compared with the outcomes (terminal and enabling objectives) of a traditional task analysis [21]. Both function as a means to select and specify the aims of the instruction. The difference, however, is that a first version is much more concrete than a formal list of objectives. Moreover, in such a first version the topics are already organized while a list of objectives only reflects isolated elements. Finally, both the content and context boundedness is made explicit.

Next, the text needs control by domain experts to guarantee the quality of the selection, organisation and wording of the material. These comments of domain-experts urge for a *second version*, which is, then, 'didactically' diagnosed.

The *didactical diagnosis* consists of a detailed analysis of content and textual presentation. It aims at the identification of students' problems when integrating the content-elements in their cognitive structure. The didactical diagnosis of the materials leads to the identification of hypothetical cognitive processing problems and their remediation.

The text is revised in view of the facilitation of the student's learning process. Only after this step the *addition of instructional adjunct aids* is considered. Decisions concerning adding aids take both the function of the printed materials (e. g. self-instructional material or handbook material) and student characteristics (learning strategies, level of external regulation needed) into account; for a discussion see [15].

The next step involves the *formatting* and *editing* of the material into an 'experimental version'. Decision making is based on functional and target group considerations. The experimental version is offered to the students for empirical validation. Such a validation is necessary, as most instructional decisions can only be grounded on hypotheses about the characteristics of the target group as a whole and of the individual students. The results of the empirical *validation* are used to design the *final version*.

2.3.3.2 Discussion

It will be clear that the process outlined here is less formal than a traditional ID process. Subject-matter characteristics as well as the cognitions and expertise of the author are taken into account from the first moment on. However, the process is a very systematic one. Although all the different parameters are not considered simultaneously, they are all taken into account by gradually plugging them into the process. Finally, whereas the traditional ID process can be described to be linear, this CID process is cyclical and elaborative.

2.3.4 Design instruments

Design instruments for the implementation of material oriented parameters are diagnostical ones. The instrumentation of the parameter 'structure of text' for example, consists of:

- a strategy to identify main concepts and their interrelations, and
- a set of rules which reveal possible barriers to study the material. In these rules the connections between the material oriented parameter 'structure' and the three student oriented parameters 'cognitive structure', 'cognitive processes' and 'metacognition' are integrated.

As such, the description-prescription problem is not solved, but at least circumvented by adding a diagnostic element to the process.

Similar procedures will be constructed to systemize decision-making about adjunct aids and formatting variables.

3. How cognitive can learning CID be?

As mentioned, it is hypothesized that a computercoach could facilitate the introduction of domain-experts into the field of instructional design. In order to determine the types of information to be incorporated in a computercoach, several characteristics of domain-experts and domain-novices are contrasted. Next, an overview is given of a computercoach for instructional design projects. One of the modules will be described in depth in order to elucidate the argument.

3.1 Domain-experts as authors

Various scholars in the field of CID [15, 26]. have stated the overall goal of instructional materials from a cognitive perspective to be the realization of a greater similarity between the cognitive structure of experts and novices. Instructional materials, within this view, function as a bridge between two states of the cognitive structure of a novice: an initial state and a more expert-like state. Instructional materials should therefore enable the novice to engage in (re-)constructive learning activities.

The cognitive structure of an expert consists of many elements which are highly integrated. Features of the cognitive structure of the expert enables him to: solve problems in a flexible way, automate a number of skills, differentiate easily between main points and details, adequately represent problems to solve, chunk information, easily acquire new domain-knowledge, detect embedded relations, and disregard irrelevant information. The cognitive structure of novices, on the contrary, is not only smaller but also poorly organized or integrated. They consequently show difficulties both to estimate the relevance of information-elements and to distinguish between main points and details. They solve problems step by step, in an inflexible way, and are led by surface-level relationships. Their knowledge holds misconceptions and they experience difficulties to acquire new information.

In sum, there is both a quantitative and qualitative gap between cognitive structures of experts and novices [10, 39].

This assertion leads to the anticipation of a number of problems when domain-experts develop instructional materials. Experts experience problems in explaining the meaning of concepts (for them all is clear and there is no real need to define concepts), in making relations explicit (their cognitive structure is highly integrated and there seems to be no necessity to explicitly link concepts), in anticipating misconceptions (they can't imagine somebody to understand reality in a different way as they do, i.e. to view phenomena in a not domain-bound way), in stressing the relevance or importance of main points (they don't experience problems in differentiating important and less important elements), in sequencing content elements in a way novices can acquire new information [16, 31]. These and other problems should be confronted with the very clear advantages of using domain-experts as instructional developers. Only domain-experts, for example, have a comprehensive and in depth knowledge of a particular field.

3.2 Types of information within a CID coach

From the above it can be derived that authors, though experts within a specific knowledge domain, lack pedagogical/didactical expertise. The question arises what kind of information they need in order to develop printed materials from a cognitive perspective.

Given that authors of printed materials normally do not - as usually students do - lack the perspective of their design endeavours, it seems well suited to offer authors a computercoach which incorporates cognitive design parameters, assists and guides them in their design activities. Essentially, two kinds of information should be integrated in such a coach.

The first type of information is rather technical. On-line technical information is offered in response to questions of the authors. When, for example, the author wants to know how to explain a concept, the coach should be able to answer. The author, however, is not an instructional design specialist, he not only lacks declarative and procedural knowledge but also conditional knowledge about when and why the use of instructional methods and strategies can be useful. He makes errors, shows misconceptions and lacks instructional decision-making skills. Therefore, this second type of information should also be delivered to the author and implemented in the coach.

To summarize, the author, though he may realize to have specific 'technical' problems, also needs external decision-making help. Just giving him on-line help is not sufficient since the author might lack an elaborated and valid framework to decide when and why to look for problems and consecutively for help. In this respect, the author is mostly a didactical novice who, without guidance, wouldn't know how to handle. Therefore, a computercoach should deliver technical information, identify problems and consider various alternatives to solve them compare with the types of information to be included in a 'viable linking science' [50].

3.3 A CID computercoach

At the UDC (University Department for Course Development, University of Leuven) a project has been initiated to build a computercoach for authors who are university domain-experts. It intends to cover the design and development process. The coach, 'ConStruct' (Conceptual Structure), consists of four modules (selection, management, development, and validation). A brief overview of these modules will be given. Next, the development module will be described in greater detail as it covers the development tasks of the author. Each of the modules consists of a number of components (Fig. 2). For a more elaborate description of the coach [32].

3.3.1 Selection module

The selection module has two functions: (1) to explore the need for an instructional program and (2) to select the suitable media and delivery systems to be included in the learning environment.

3.3.2 Management module

The organisation of a development project, financially, administratively as well as logistically is an endeavour that can be facilitated by the automation of a number of tasks. This is the main function of the management module. The module also addresses team management issues.

3.3.3 Development module

The development module is the core of the coach. Using this module, *instructional* materials are designed, developed and produced.

3.3.4 Validation module

The empirical formative evaluation and validation of the materials is an essential step in the design process [42]. This module assists the designer in gathering and analyzing evaluation data and in reporting the results.

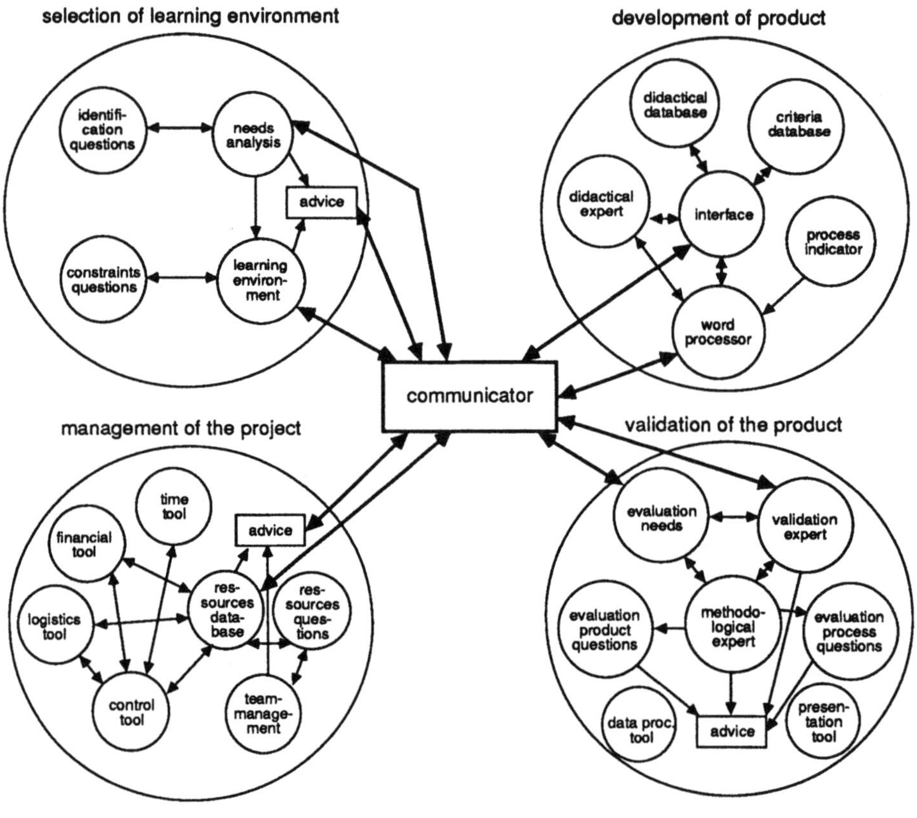

Figure 2 Detailed overview of ConStruct

3.4 The development module

The core of the coach, being the most interesting part in our discussion of CID, is the development module, which consists of a number of specific components.

- Word processor: because ConStruct assists domain-experts in designing printed materials a word processor is a critical tool. ConStruct works with a number of commercial word processing packages (MS-Word, Wordperfect).
- Didactical database: this database contains all kinds of information on how to 'technically' solve problems of authors during their developmental endeavours. By applying information

delivered by the system-user in other modules, this 'technical' information can be adapted to the specific situation of the user. The access to the database, therefore, is regulated by information previously given or asked on-line. The didactical database offers on-line and differentiated help by explaining the function and the effects of various elements (concerning the writing process, the teaching functions, the formatting and the adding of adjunct aids) and by offering implementation procedures. Moreover, it offers guidelines, examples and exercises.

- Criteria database: domain-experts lack the necessary didactical framework to analyze their own material. One way to offer help is to provide criteria as well as procedures on how to use them. These criteria cover both content and instructional issues.
- Didactical expert: an essential premiss of a cognitive instructional design process, is that specific and formal prescriptions are hardly useful for authors lacking a didactical framework and necessary conditional knowledge. Because authors rarely own this framework and knowledge, a diagnostic tool is needed that incorporates this framework and knowledge. A device that analyses on-line the didactical quality of the developed materials and offers adequate remedial advice is requested.

  To enable an automated analysis of instructional materials, the coach needs information such as the main elements of the course and their interrelations. Therefore, a device, which enables the author to create the profile of the instructional material is an integral part of this didactical expert.
- Process indicator: some of the authors might lack essential writing skills, especially the skills to adequately select and organize their knowledge in such a way that it can be understood by novices. A process indicator directs the efforts of less experienced authors. It interactively offers guidelines about the different steps of the writing process, the use of writing procedures and the application of instructional strategies.

4. Possible contributions of hypermedia

In this section, the possible contributions of hypermedia toward the construction of the computercoach, described above, are investigated. First, we summarize the characteristics of hypermedia. Next, the strengths and weaknesses of such an environment for coaching authors are explored.

4.1 Characteristics of hypermedia

Hypermedia offers an environment by means of which a knowledge field can easily be explored. It enables to present segments of information and to link these segments in various ways. All kinds of information can be displayed and linked to each other. Hypermedia, moreover enables navigation, i.e. systematic or random exploration of a knowledge field [2, 26, 28, 48]. The access to the information can be free or constrained depending on the quality of the links between the different information segments. Consequently, the environment created for the user can vary from completely open to fully closed. In the first case decisions to access information are made by the user (learner). In a closed environment, access decisions were made by the designer of the program or, from the user's point of view, access is externally regulated.

4.2 Possible uses of hypermedia

In order to determine the possible uses of hypermedia environments, the four components of the previously described development module are reviewed, by asking the following questions: what use can be made of hypermedia for:

- creating printed instructional materials;
- giving authors on-line help;
- diagnosing printed materials and giving consecutive remedial feedback;
- tutoring the writing process?

4.2.1 Creating printed instructional materials

Hypermedia environments, like hypercard, hypertext or Guid, could be used as word-processor. The advantage would be that in a first move, all chosen topics could be treated separately. By identifying each topic with keywords and by linking the different segments of information with these keywords, the material could be easily restructured. A number of problems arises, however. First, decisions must be made on the structuring principle. Putting cards or information segments into a logical sequence does not guarantee an effective sequencing of instructional material. Second, enabling a student to map his cognitive structure in accordance with that of the expert, implies that the student is enabled to reconstruct meaning. Reconstructing meaning from a text is realized by taking information, co-text and context into account. There is a danger that using hypermedia, glossaries or encyclopedia are developed instead of instructional texts. An instructional text does not only consist of 'factual information' but also comprises textual and instructional meta-information which is used by the learner to construct meaning and to integrate new information in the already existing cognitive structure.

The outlining and restructuring facilities of hypermedia environments as such do not, therefore, solve the problem of creating an instructional text, and may even hamper its solution.

4.2.2 On-line help

With the use of an hypermedia environment, a database can be easily constructed. The database can be ordered in different stacks, each consisting of cards with 'technical' information for the author. For various settings different kinds of help can be given as well as different examples to concretize the information. Exercises can be offered in the same way. Technical information, examples and exercises can be put on a different card, each forming a different segment of information. This information can be accessed by the author by pointing to the appropriate key word. Access to the information can further be regulated by previously given or on-line information concerning the setting within which the instructional material would be used. Consequently, hypermedia environments can be used to build the didactical and criteria database of the computercoach.

4.2.3 Diagnosis and remedial feedback

Domain-experts, it has been discussed, often lack the necessary framework and conditional knowledge to diagnose their own materials from a didactical point of view. A diagnostical instrument should therefore be part of the coach for guiding the decision-making process and urging the author to consult the on-line help. Hypermedia environments are not intelligent 'an sich'. An expert system shell, like NEXPERT, as well as a device to map the content, are needed to perform this diagnosis. The remedial feedback, however, constitutes information which can be delivered by hypermedia environments, while access to this information should be regulated by the outcomes of the diagnosis. This implies that sufficient alternatives and a body of empirical evidence regarding the effects of various methods and strategies can be made available to the author.

4.2.4 Tutoring the process

Tutoring the process implies a need for information about how to proceed in writing instructional materials and a device to measure the kind of information to be displayed interactively. Both aspects could be implemented using hypermedia. Advice can get stored on different cards and access to these cards can be regulated either by the author (in the same way as with on-line help), or the system itself (using information about the stage of the work as previously stated or on-line).

5. Conclusions

Hypermedia environments seem to be attractive. They enable a non-linear presention of information and enlarge the possibilities for discovery during the learning process. Consequently, the components of the cognitive computercoach discussed in this contribution that aim at presenting information to the author could be implemented with an hypermedia environment. However, several caveats should be uttered toward the possibilities to implement more instructional components.

– Even when the cognitive structure of an expert could be represented in a map consisting of nodes and links by applying hypermedia tools, such a map cannot be perceived to be instructional. The cognitive structure of an expert results from a constructive activity. This activity has been led by prior knowledge on the one hand and external regulation (selection and organisation of information by instructors, teachers or authors) on the other. Hence, we are confronted with the tension between the adequate use of non-linear information environments as is the case with experts, and the need for a well structured instruction as is needed by novices. In fact, instructional research reveals the need for structure by novices on the one hand and for openess by experts [13].
– Hypermedia environments generally offer small pieces of information at different levels. The user can easily navigate through the information. Experts within a field will be able to ask themselves the appropriate questions and are able to deliberately look for the information they need in order to solve their problem or find an answer on their questions. Expertise also enables them to integrate the information presented into their cognitive structure. Novices, however, who lack a comprehensive framework of the field cannot effectively interact with a complete non-linear environment because they are unable to ask the appropriate questions. We hypothesize that the interaction of a novice with a hypermedia environment will be characterized by idle navigation and browsing, 'clicking around', getting lost in 'hyper-space' and focussing upon the most attractive animations. Only when some degree of external

regulation (either or not embedded in the computer itself) is added, hypermedia environments might become instructionally useful tools.

- Hypermedia environments lack the intelligence necessary for designing interactive instructional programs. Though it is not a discriminating feature of hypermedia, such environments could be made rather 'intelligent'. This reduces, however, the hypermedia environment to a users-interface [37].
- It seems to us that the applicability of hypermedia within a cognitive view is limited to offering at an appropriate level small pieces of information which are consistent in their own right. When larger pieces of information are given the hypermedia environment is used as an integrated pageturner and audio or videoplayer. When hypermedia would be used instructionally a highly branched version of programmed instruction is offered. This kind of instruction does not stems from a cognitive but from a behavioristic background [14].

Literature

1. Alesandrini, K. L. (1984). Pictures and adult learning. Instructional Science, 13, pp. 63-77.
2. Allred, K. F. (1988). Research, Instructional Design, and New Technology. Journal of Instructional Development, 11, 1, pp. 2-5.
3. Anderson, T. M. & Armbruster, B. B. (1985). Studying strategies and their implications for textbook design. In T. M. Duffy & R. Walker. Designing usable texts (The educational technology series). Orlando/London: Academic Press.
4. Andre, T. (1987). Questions and learning from reading. Questioning exchange, 1, 1, pp. 47-86.
5. Andrews, D. H. & Goodson, L. A. (1980). A Comparative Analysis of Models of Instructional Design. Journal of Instructional Development, 3, 4, pp. 2-16.
6. Ausubel, D. P. (1968). Educational Psychology : A Cognitive View. New York : Holt, Rinehart and Winston.
7. Bonner, J. (1988). Implications of Cognitive Theory for Instructional Design: Revisited. Educational Communications and Technology Journal, 36, 1, pp. 3-14.
8. Calfee, R. (1981). Cognitive Psychology and Educational Practice. Review of Research in Education, 9, pp. 3-73.
9. Case, R. & Bereiter, C. (1984). From Behaviourism to Cognitive Behaviorism to Cognitive Development: Steps in the Evolution of Instructional Design. Instructional Science, 13, pp. 141-158.
10. Chi, M. T. H., Glaser, R. & Rees, E. (1982). Expertise in problem solving. In R. J. Sternberg (Ed.). Advances in the Psychology of Human Intelligence. Hillsdale, NJ: Lawrence Erlbaum.
11. Clark, C. M. & Peterson, P. L. (1986). Teachers' thought processes. In M. C. Wittrock (Ed.). Handbook of Research on Teaching. New York: Macmillan.
12. Clark, R. E. (1989). Current Progress and Future Directions for Research on Instructional Technology. Educational Technology Research and Development, 37, 1, pp. 57-66.
13. Clark, R. E. (1989). When Teaching Kills Learning : Research on Mathemathantics. In H. Mandl, E. De Corte, N. Bennet, & H. F. Friedrich (Eds). Learning and Instruction (Volume 2.2). New York : Pergamon Press, pp. 1-22.
14. Dede, Chr., & Swigger, K. (1988). The Evolution of Instructional Design Principles for Intelligent Computer-Assisted Instruction. Journal of Instructional Development, 11, 1, pp. 15-22.
15. Di Vesta, F. & Rieber, L. P. (1987). Characteristics of Cognitive Engineering: The Next Generation of Instructional Systems. Educational Communications and Technology Journal, 35, 4, pp. 213-230.
16. Elen, J. (1989). A Cognitive Model for the Design of Self-instruction. Paper presented at the third conference of the European Association for Research on Learning and Instruction, Madrid.
17. Fisher, K. M., et al. (1988). Computer-Based Knowledge Representation as a Tool for Students and Teachers. Chico, CA: California State University. Paper presented at the Annual Meeting of the American Educational Research Association, New Orleans.

18. Flavell, J. H. (1979). Metacognition and cognitive monitoring: A new area of cognitive-developmental inquiry. American Psychologist. 34, pp. 906-911.
19. Gagné, R. M. (1965). The Analysis of Instructional Objectives for Instructional Design. In R. Glaser (Ed.). Teaching Machines and Programmed Learning, II Data and Directions. Washington D. C.: National Education Association.
20. Gagné, R. M., & Briggs, L. J. (1979). Principles of Instructional Design (2d ed.). New York : Holt, Rinehart and Winston.
21. Gagné, R. M., Briggs, L. J., & Wager, W. W. (1988). Principles of Instructional Design (3d ed.). New York : Holt, Rinehart and Winston.
22. Gardner, M. K. (1985). Cognitive Approaches to Instructional Task Analysis. Review of Research in Education, 12, pp. 157-195.
23. Hamaker, C. (1986). The effect of adjunct questions on prose learning. Review of Educational Research, 56, pp. 212-243.
24. Hartley, J. (1985). Designing instructional text (2d ed.). London/New York: Kogan Page/Nichols.
25. Hayes, J. R. & Flower, L. (1980). Identifying the organization of the writing process. In: L. W. Gregg & E. Steinberg (Eds). Cognitive processes in writing, Hillsdale, NJ: Lawrence Erlbaum.
26. Jonassen, D. H. (1988). Designing Structured Hypertext and Structuring Access to Hypertext. Educational Technology, 28, 11, pp. 13-16.
27. Kozma, R. B. (1987). The Implications of Cognitive Psychology for Computer-Based Learning Tools. Educational Technology, 27, 11, pp. 20-25.
28. Locatis, C., Letourneau, G., & Banvard, R. (1989). Hypermedia and instruction. ETR&D, 37, 4, pp. 65-77.
29. Low, W. C. (1980-1981). Changes in instructional development: The aftermath of an information processing takeover in psychology. Journal of Instructional Development, 4, pp. 10-18.
30. Lowyck, J. (1980). A process analysis of teaching (report 21). Leuven: Leuven University.
31. Lowyck, J. & Elen, J. (1990). Self-study packages: vantage points for a new instructional design. International Journal of Educational Research, 14, 6, pp. 565-579.
32. Lowyck, J., Elen, J. & Van den Branden, J. (1990). ConStruct: A computercoach for the development of high quality study materials. Paper presented at the Seventh International Conference on Technology for Education, Brussels.
33. Mannes, S. M. & Kintsch, W. (1987). Knowledge Organization and Text Organization. Cognition and Instruction, 4, pp. 91-115.
34. Mayer, R. E., Cook, L. K. & Dyck, J. L. (1984). Techniques that help readers build mental models from scientific texts: definition pretraining and signalling. Journal of Educational Psychology, 76, 6, pp. 1089-1105.
35. McAleese, R. (1988). From Concept Maps to Computer Based Learning: the Experience of NoteCards. Aberdeen: University Teaching Centre, University of Aberdeen. Paper presented at the Annual Meeting of the American Educational Research Association, New Orleans.
36. Merrill, M. D. (1973). Content and Instructional Analysis for Cognitive Transfer Tasks. AVCR, 21, 1, pp. 109-125.
37. Merrill, M. D., Li, Z., & Jones, M. K. (1990). The Second Generation Instructional Design Research Program. Educational Technology, 30, 3, pp. 26-31.
38. Meyer, B. J. F. (1977). The structure of Prose: Effects on Learning and Memory and Implications for Educational Practice. In R. C. Anderson, R. J. Spiro & W. E. Montague (Eds). Schooling and the acquisition of knowledge. Hillsdale, NJ: Lawrence Erlbaum.
39. Nelson, W. A., Magliaro, S. & Sherman, T. M. (1988). The Intellectual Content of Instructional Design. Journal of Instructional Development, 11, 1, p. 29-35.
40. Pirolli, P. L., & Greeno, J. G. (1988). The problem space of instructional design. In J. Psotka, L. D. Massey, & S. A. Mutter (Eds). Intelligent Tutoring Systems. Lessons Learned. Hillsdale, NJ: Lawrence Erlbaum, pp. 181-201.
41. Posner, G. S. (1978). Tools for curriculum research and development: Potential contributions from cognitive science. Curriculum Inquiry, 8, 4, pp. 311-340.
42. Romiszowski, A. (1981). Designing Instructional Systems. London : Kogan Page.
43. Rumelhart, D. E. (1980). Schemata: The building Blocks of Cognition. In R. Spiro, B. Bruce & W. Brewer (Eds). Theoretical Issues in Reading Comprehension. Hillsdale, NJ: Lawrence Erlbaum.
44. Salisbury, D. F., Richards, B. F., & Klein, J. D. (1985). Designing Practice: A Review of Prescriptions and Recommendations from I. D. Theories. Journal of Instructional Development. 8, 4, pp. 9-19.
45. Scardamilia, M. & Bereiter, C. (1986). Research on written composition. In M. C. Wittrock (Ed.). Handbook of Research on Teaching. New York: Macmillan.

46. Schiffman, S. S. (1986). Instructional Systems Design: Five Views of the Field. Journal of Instructional Development. 9, 3, pp. 14-21.
47. Schmitt, M. C. & Newby, T. J. (1986). Metacognition: Relevance to Instructional Design. Journal of Instructional Development, 9, 4, pp. 29-33.
48. Schulmeister, R. (1989). Authoring systems and alternatives. Wheels Europe, 3, p. 3-10.
49. Shimmerlik, S. M. (1978). Organization theory and Memory for Prose: A Review of the Literature. Review of Educational Research, 48, pp. 103-120.
50. Shuell, T. J. (1982). Developing a viable link between scientific psychology and educational practices. Instructional Science, 11, pp. 155-167.
51. Shuell, T. J. (1986). Cognitive conceptions of learning. Review of Educational Research, 56, 4, pp. 411-436.
52. Shuell, T. J. (1988). The role of the student in learning from instruction. Contemporary Educational Psychology, 13, pp. 276-295.
53. Simon, H. A. (1969). Sciences of the Artificial. Cambridge, MA: MIT Press.
54. Simon, H. A. (1979). Information Processing Models of Cognition. Annual Review of Psychology, 30, pp. 363-396.
55. Skinner, B. F. (1954). The science of learning and the art of teaching. Harvard Educational Review, 24, pp. 86-97.
56. Taylor, R. & Doughty, P. L. (1988). Instructional Development Models: Analysis at the Task and Subtask Level. Journal of Instructional Development, 11, 4, pp. 19-28.
57. Thorndyke, P. W. & Hayes-Roth, B. (1979). The use of schemata in the acquisition and transfer of knowledge. Cognitive Psychology, 11, pp. 82-106.
58. Van Hout-Wolters, B. (1986). Markeren van kerngedeelten in studieteksten: Een procesprodukt benadering. Lisse: Swets & Zeitlinger. (Cueing key-elements in texts: a process-product approach)
59. Wildman, T. M. & Burton, J. K. (1981). Integrating Learning Theory with Instructional Design. Journal of Instructional Development, 4, pp. 5-14.
60. Wildman, T. M. (1981). Cognitive Theory and the Design of Instruction. Educational Technology, 21, pp. 14-20.
61. Winn, W. (1989). Toward a rationale and theoretical basis for educational technology. Educational Technology Research and Development, 37, 1, pp. 35-46.

Hypermedia: Influence of Interactive Freedom Degree in Learning Processes

Armando P. Silva

Centro Recursos Multimedia, Instituto Politécnico do Porto, Portugal

Abstract: One of the most promising grounds for teaching within the evolution of new technologies of information and communication is, in our opinion, the existence of documental data bases for hypermedia exploration. Thus, it appears to us justifiable that we begin, since now, to examine what hypermedia technology has of most profitable - **Interactivity**. We believe to be fundamentally important to find out to what extent this interactivity can and may play a relevant role in learning processes. This paper concerns an experiment we have carried out in which a simulation in hypermedia was attained, based on all potentialities of HyperCard, a simulation of a visit to "Palácio da Bolsa" in Oporto which provided information about the consequences of interactive freedom degree in learning.

1. Experimental Study

The aim of this study was to check if different forms of data exploration in hypermedia have diversified effects in information holding. The experiment we have carried out consists of a simulation of a visit to Oporto "Palácio da Bolsa" using a hypermedia informatic program, displayed in computer in two different ways: *exploration of sequential information*, which simulates a guided visit and *exploration of free information*, which simulates a non-guided visit. Whiting exploration of free information three different versions were created: a) *free without plan*; b) *free with plan;* c) *free with interactive plan*.

We have guided the analysis in such a way as to verify whether the form of data exploration (sequential or free) causes differences in the learning process results. In case it does, we will try to analyse the advantages and disadvantages of each of the forms of data exploration, and also to test whether the excess of freedom, in hypermedia exploration — or the excess of help — interferes, in a positive or negative way, with the learning/teaching process.

For this, we have used the HyperCard informatic programme — based upon the new technology Hypermedia — to create a prototype related to two possible ways of visit that, from now on, we will refer to as "*sequential visit*" (simulating the guided visit) and as "*free visit*" (simulating the non-guided visit).

When trying, in our experimental investigation, to simulate these two situations we had as a model two possible real situations:

1. A sequential visit will be conducted by a guide, which normally all follow, with the aim of showing and explaining in a sequential pre-defined form what exists in this palace.

2. As an alternative the situation of a visit when there is no guide to follow but in which, nevertheless we are allowed to explore the different places by ourselves without pre-defined exploration criteria.

In both situations the information is the same either in presentation or in content being different only in the form of exploration.

1.1 Specific aims of the study

1. To investigate whether there are differences in the results of the learning process, namely in the scientific concepts, historical and chronological data, architectonic and pictorial or spatial vision aspects, consequency of the type of data exploration (sequential or free).
2. To try locate where those differences are stronger:
   - 2.1. whether on the global contents (including the general and spatial informative contents).
   - 2.2. whether on the general informative contents (including the direct and indirect informative contents).
     - 2.2.1 whether on the direct informative contents (related to the data on each screen-image, either through the digitized image or through the explanatory text of these same images; pictorial, architectonic and historical data which the users may, initially, think they are going to be questioned about.
     - 2.2.2 whether on the indirect informative contents (related to the data not specifically refered to the user, image or text, but related to data which the users are, initially, supposed to think they are not going to be questioned about.
     - 2.2.3 whether on the location in the hyperspace.
3. To investigate how those differences are displayed.
4. To understand the reason for those differences, raising hypotheses and testing them in a way as to try to conceive a theoretical model capable of justifying the results.

The prototype programme we have created includes four situations of data exploration of the same informative contents, within two big types (sequential and free), just distinguished by the form of data exploration that is allowed, and that we will refer to as: *sequential, free without plan, free with plan and free with interactive plan.*

In the software program in which the form of data exploration is *sequential* the user will have compulsory access to all the available information in the program either when it concerns spaces to visit and details or images or when it concerns written verbal texts.

By pushing the button CONTINUAR, the user will move, successively, from one place to another, and will see all the details in those same places. These places will be emphasized, one by one, by the respective geometric form, there inserted, that will wink quickly during two seconds, after which it will become steady.

This form is now the only compulsory command before continuing the visit, since the command CONTINUAR has become disactivated. By pushing it, the correspondent room detail will appear, obtained through the zoom effect, as well as the respective information. This screen-image contains, in footnote, the necessary indications to continue the visit (in this case, returne to the room the user had left). This detail will then be disactivated and another one shown. This process will be repeated until there is no further details to see in this room. The command CONTINUAR will then appear and it will allow us to move to the next place and so successively till the end of the visit.

In the software program in which the form of data exploration is *free without plan* the user is able to go along several paths, which correspond to several ways branching from the place where he is.

This version allows the user, in correspondence with the existing possibilities in case of a real visit, to go straight ahead, turn left, turn right, turn back (rotating 180º) go up and down the stairs manipulating the commands that comprehend the direction indicator systems.

Through these direction indicators (arrows) the user may also advance or retreat, in case access doors actually exist, from one room to the other through the corridors and he may advance or retreat in the corridor itself.

The command AJUDA will show the screen-image with all the information about the commands existing in all the screen-images and whose command VOLTAR once activated will make the user return to the place where he was when he asked for this help.

The command LUPA, once activated, emphasizes at the same time all the details in that place.

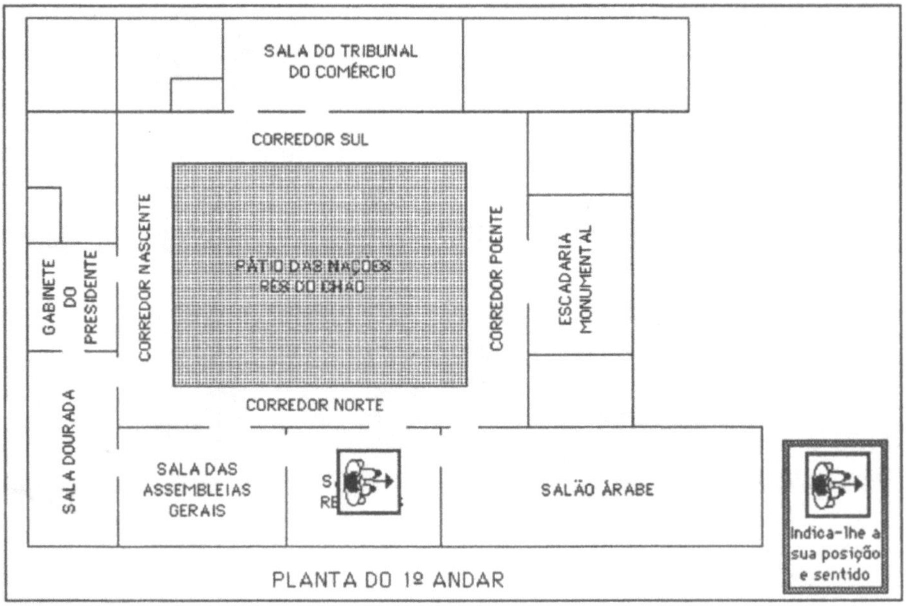

As before the geometric forms there inserted will wink quickly during two seconds, after which they will became constant.

We will have to push the indicated places so that, through the zoom effect, we can see the details as well as the respective information. The return to the respective room will disactivate the

correspondent geometric form indicating, this way, that detail has already been seen. Seeing the details is not, therefore, compulsory since the commands indicating direction keep active, giving the user the freedom of choice.

The command MAIS SALA will show the opposite vision of that same room, reversing the respective observation direction.

In the software program in which the form of exploration is *free with plan* all the characteristics described in the program free without plan are kept on the whole, being added in all places the new command PLANTA that makes way to the screen image where the plant of the Palace is displayed. Once activated this command will show the plant of the "Palácio da Bolsa".

The symbol  whose arrow shows a possible way to take refers to the place where the observer is and his orientation. This is the only existing command that allows, once activated, to come back to the place pointed out by the symbol (to the card in which the bottom "PLANTA" was activated).

These plans also contain all the places to be visited labelled with the respective names, whether on the ground floor or the first floor. They still allow the user to see the relationship between the positions of the various rooms and corridors (spatial relationship); the respective position - North, South, West, East - and their location on the ground floor or the first floor.

In the software program in which the form of exploration is *free with interactive plan* the characteristics described in free with plan are kept on the whole, with a particularity added: all screen images of the plans of the building have commands that allow direct access to all places that can be visited and their respective access ways (rooms corridors and stairs) distinguished by their respective names.

These commands, placed in the area correspondent to each room and corridor and conveniently specified once activated, allow direct access to the place selected in the plan. In case of being selected the existing command placed in the Monumental Stair the program will interact with the user opening a dialogue window through which the user is asked where he wants to place him self: first floor or ground floor.

If the situation described occurs on the ground floor plan, we will face the same situation, the difference being just on the text presented in the interactive window.

Besides the possibilities already shown, this program also allows the user, in all places of visit, and using only the PLANTA command to have access to the building plan in which the spaces work interactively allowing a visit to each of the wanted areas without using the direction operators.

At the end of the visit or when the user considered his visit finished, he was given a questionnaire about it with several questions, some about informative contents (global, general, direct and indirect) and some others about the spatial location of the visited places.

The answers of each student were analysed and assessed with 1 point, in case they were correct and with 0 points, in case they weren't. The absence of an answer was considered as an incorrect answer.

1.2 The main hypothesis

In Hypermedia assisted teaching, the results of learning process depend on the degree of freedom in data exploration and the help to the location in the hyperspace, interactive or not, supplied to the users.

1.3 Population

We would like to emphasize that though the main concern of our experience was not to generalize the results, we have chosen a sample of: a) forty students; b) in the first and second years of the former preparatory school level; c) aged between 11 and 13; d) students from a school in oporto city; e) students who had never been to Oporto "Palácio da Bolsa".

The sample was, aleatorily, divided in four groups (of ten students each), corresponding each one to one of the four experimental situations. Within each group, the order of passage was determined by the order of arrival.

1.4 Results

Group 1 - Sequential (the results obtained in this programme allow us to say that there has been information holding, as far as the following contents are concerned):

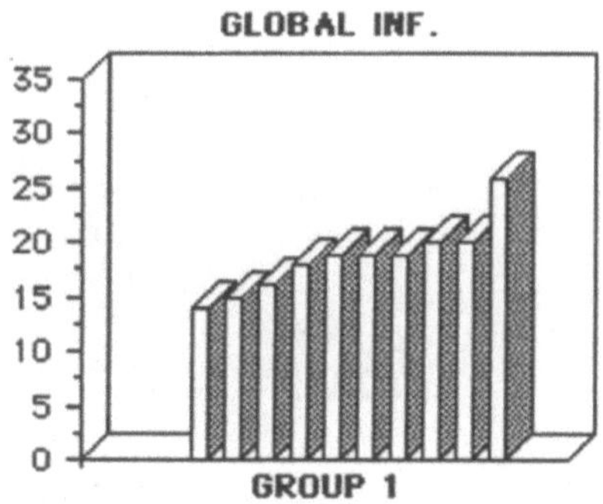

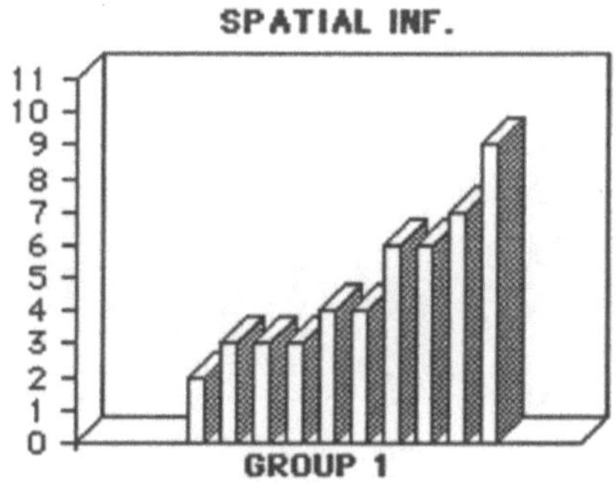

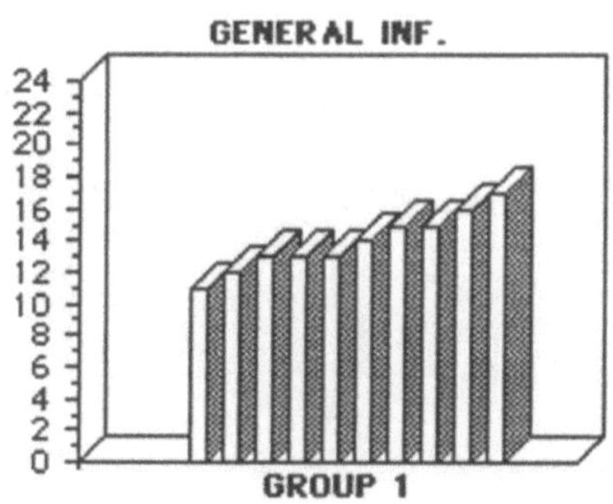

Global Informative — Related to all the information - Average

Spatial Informative — Related to the spatial relationships information, location on the hyperspace - Below Average

General Informative — Including the direct and indirect informative contents - A Little Bit Above Average

Group 2 - Free without plan (the results obtained in this programme allow us to say that there has been information holding, as far as the following contents are concerned):

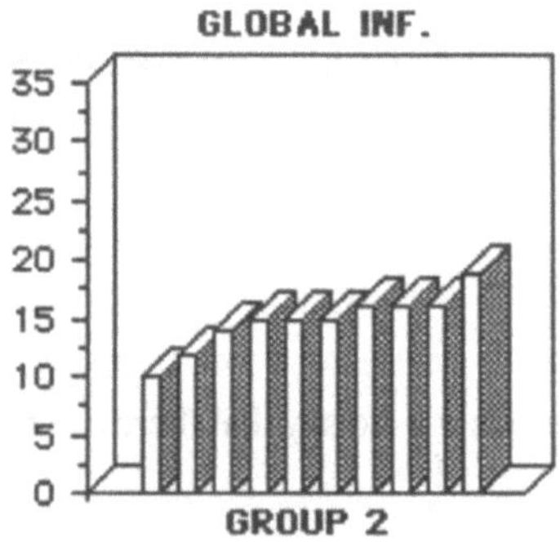

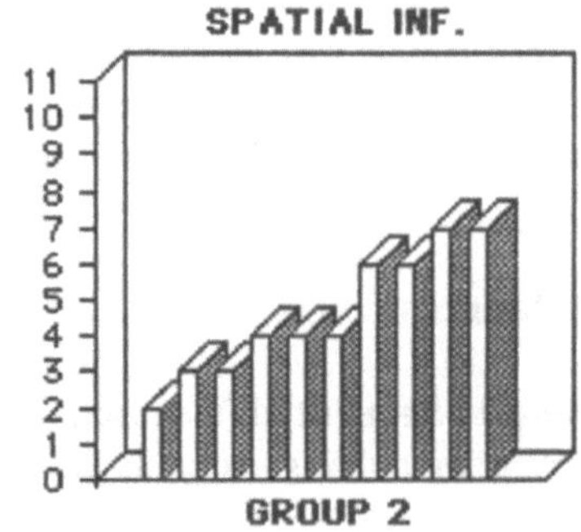

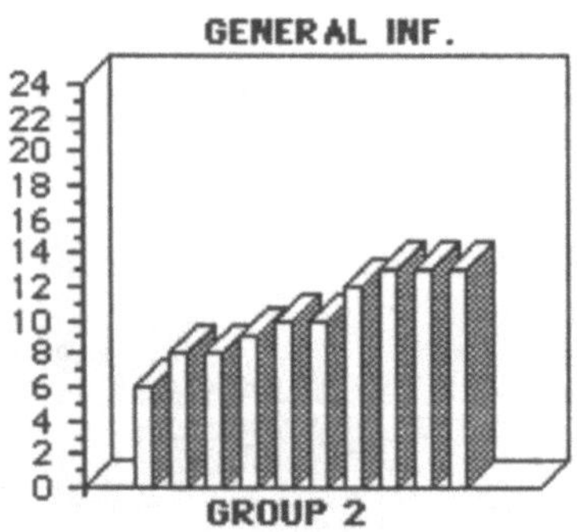

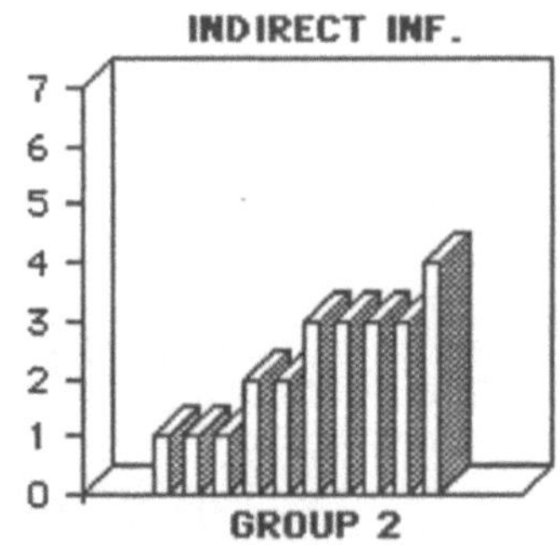

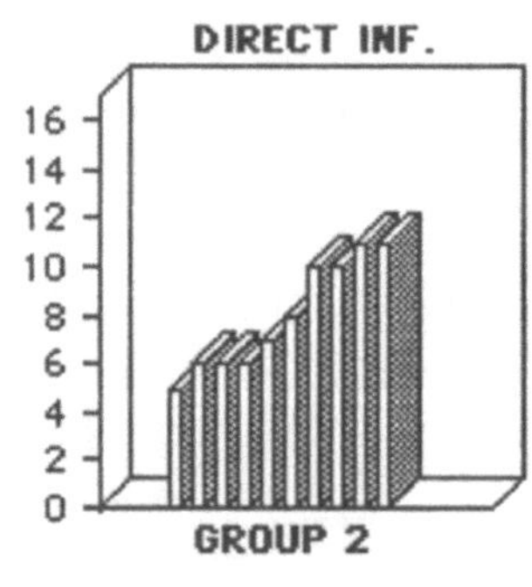

Global Informative — Far Below Average
Spatial Informative — Far Below Average
General Informative — Below Average
Direct Informative — Related to the digitized images information and their explorator text - Average
Indirect Informative — Related to information not explicitly referred to (image or text) - Far Below Average

Group 3 - Free with plan (the results obtained in this programme allow us to say that there has been information holding, as far as the following contents are concerned):

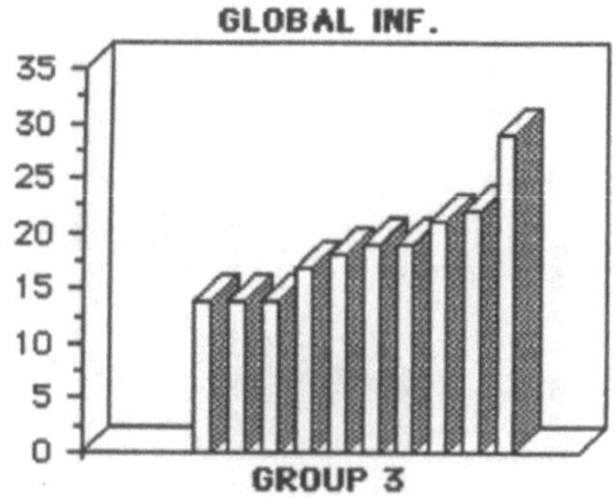

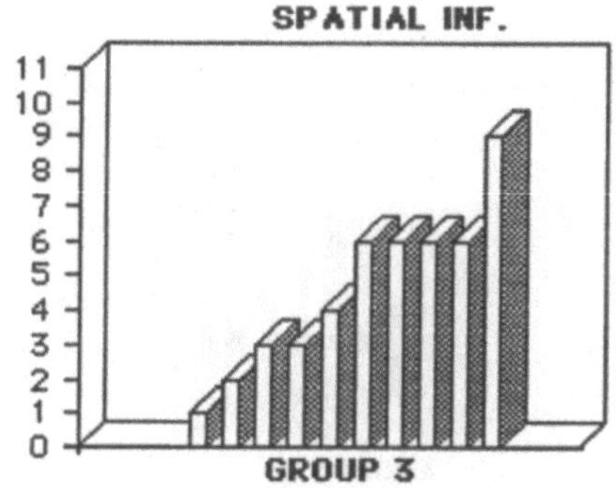

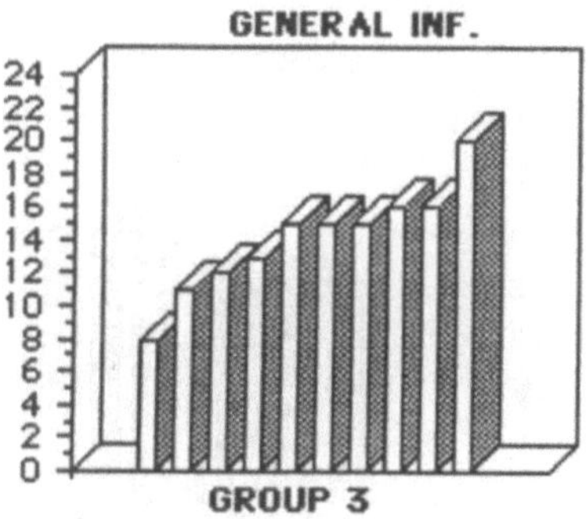

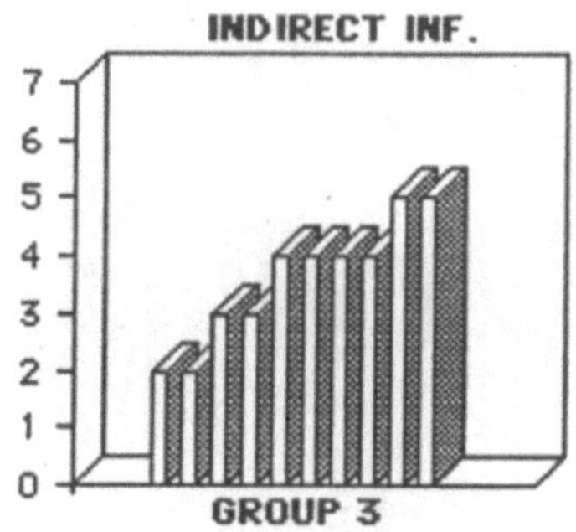

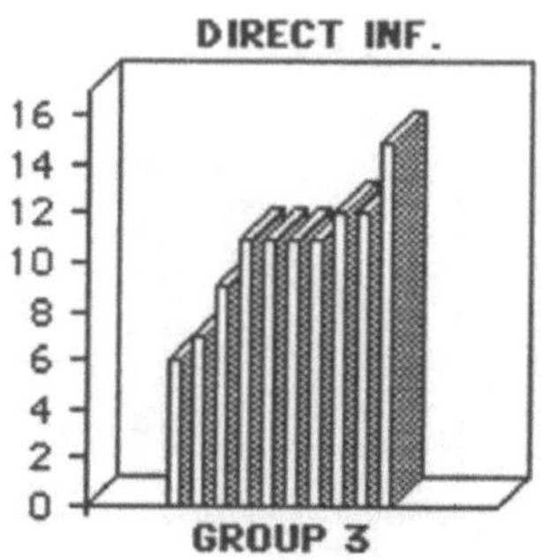

Global Informative — Average
Spatial Informative — Average
General Informative — Above Average
Direct Informative — Above Average
Indirect Informative — Average

Group 4 - Free with interactive plan (the results obtained in this programme allow us to say that there has been information holding, as far as the following contents are concerned):

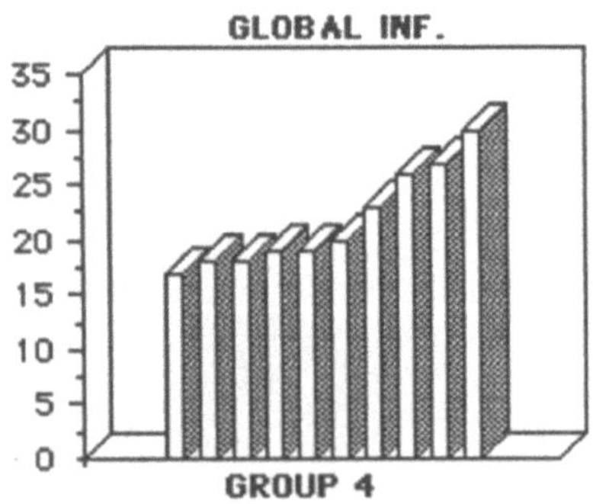

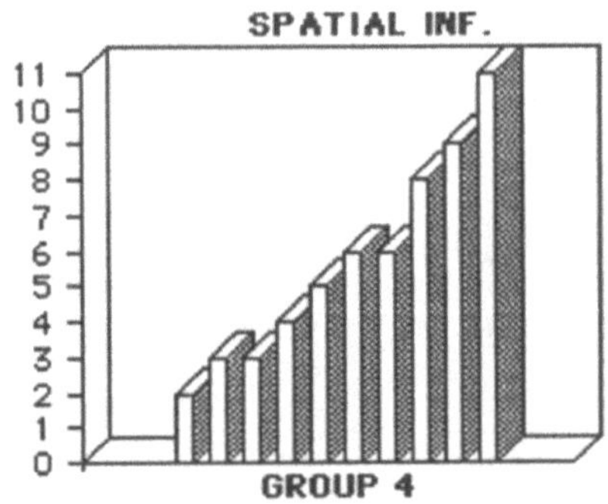

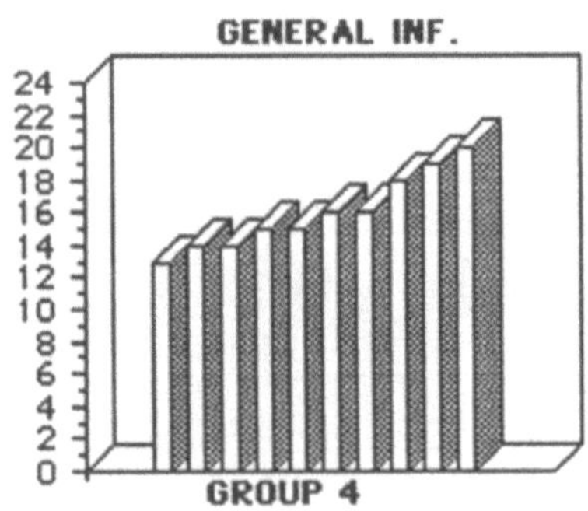

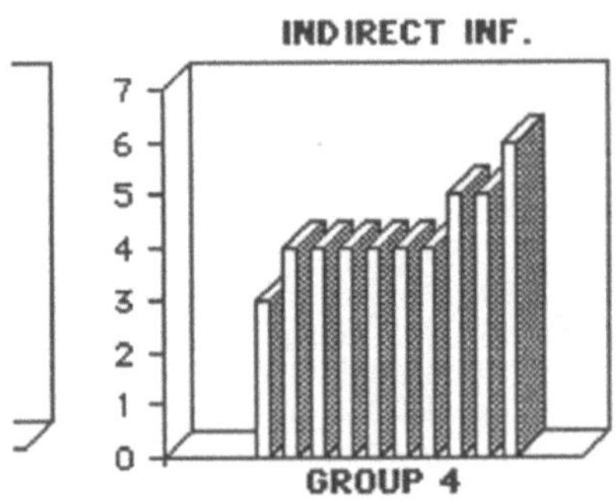

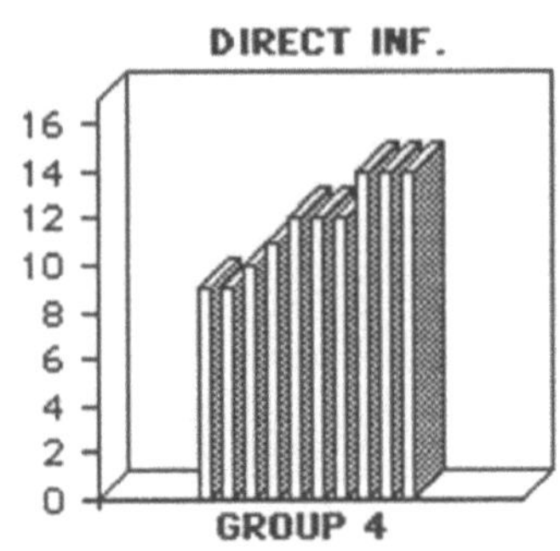

Global Informative — Far Above Average
Spatial Informative — Average
General Informative — Far Above Average
Direct Informative — Far Above Average
Indirect Informative — Above Average

2. Conclusions

1. Concerning the informative contents: Global, General, Direct and Indirect
   - the "free with interactive plan" group always attains the best results,
   - the "free without plan" group always attains the worst results,
   - the "sequential" and "free with plan" groups are always placed between these two.
2. An important detail of this study:
   - the "weakest" students benefit from the "sequential",
   - the "best" students benefit from the "free with plan" and even more from the "free with interactive plan",
   - the "free without plan" is always unfavorable, presenting the lowest levels in the learning process.

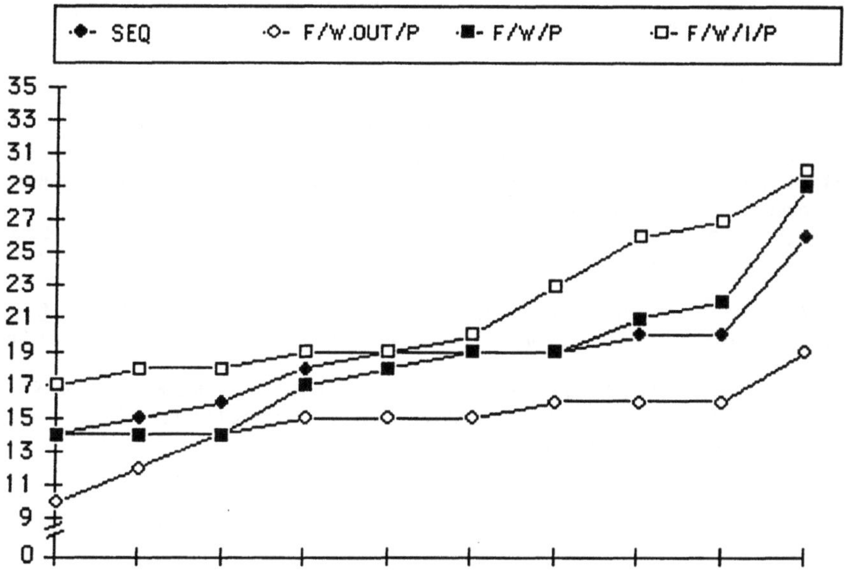

Through the reading of this graph, we see, by comparison, that the "sequential" and "free with plan" cross more or less in the middle, and this suggests that the free with plan programme allows better results for the "best" students while the sequential programme allows better results for the "weakest" students.

3. Final conclusion — The data analysis suggests that the degree of information holding in the learning process, in hypermedia teaching systems, seems to be correlated to the introduction of interactive help to data exploration.

Literature

1. Agret, Leo, (1989), Comme un fil d'ariane. *01 Références*, 3, 78-79.
2. Apple, (1987), HyperCard User's Guide. California: Apple Computer.
3. Apple, (1987), HyperCard Handbook. California: Apple Computer.
4. Apple, (1987), HyperCard Script Language Guide: The Hypertalk Language. California: Apple Computer.
5. Begeman, Michael L. e Conklin Jeff, (1988), The Right Tool For The Job. Byte. October, 255-266.
6. Carr, C., (1988), Hypertext: A new training tool? Educational Technology. 8, 7-11.
7. Chia, J., (1989), Hypertext: Technology, Aplications and Research Issues. Educational Technology. 1, 3-14.
8. Dillon, A., (1989), Designing the Human-Computer Interface to Hypermedia Applications. Paper of the NATO workshop, Rottenburg.
9. Duchastel, P., C., (1989), Discussion: Formal and Informal Learning with Hypermedia. In: D. H. Jonassen, H. Mandl (eds.): Designing Hypermedia For Learning. NATO ASI Series F, Vol. 67. Berlin: Springer-Verlag, 1990.
10. Fiderio, Janet, (1988), A Grand Vision, Hypertext mimics the brain's ability to access information quickly and intuitively by reference. Byte. October, 237-244.
11. Friedler, Yael and Amnon S., (1989), Using the HyperCard Program to Develop a Customized Courseware Generator for School Use. Educational Technology. November, 47-51.
12. Frisse, Mark, (1988), From Text to Hypertext. Byte. October, 247-253.
13. Goodman, D., (1987),The Complete Hypercard Handbook. New York: Bantam Books.
14. Havholm, P.L. e Stewart, L. (1988), Hypertext and Intertextuality at the College of Wooster. Wheels for the Mind, V. 4, Apple Computer: 2, 17-21.
15. Houbart, G., (1988), HyperCard: Un Hommage A Smalltalk. Micro-Systemes. January, 101-108.
16. Jonassen, D., H., (1988), Designing Structured Hypertext and a Structuring Acess to Hypertext. Educational Technology. November,13-16.
17. Karon, P., (1987), What's all the talk about hypertext, anyway? PC Week. 4, 60.
18. Kearsley, Greg, (1988), Anthoring Considerations for Hypertext. Educational Technology. November, 21-24.
19. Kertesz, J., Ayin, B., Jean, S., (1988), HyperCard Mode d'Emploi. SVM Macintosh. 1, 100,110.
20. Malandra, O., (1987), HyperCard, un nouveau concept à votre portée. Apple Contact. October.
21. Mayes, T., (1988), Strathtutor, The development and evaluation of a learning-by-browsing system on the Macintosh. Computer & Education. 12, 221-291.
22. Marchionini, G., (1988), Introduction to Special Issue on Hypermedia. Educational Technology. November, 7.
23. Marchionini, G., (1988), Hypermedia and Learning: Freedom and Chaos. Educational Technology. November, 8-12.
24. MacAleese, R., (1989), Concepts as Hypertext Nodes: the Ability to Learn While Navigating Through Hypertext Nets. In: D. H. Jonassen, H. Mandl (eds.): Designing Hypermedia For Learning. NATO ASI Series F, Vol. 67. Berlin: Springer-Verlag, 1990.
25. Reinhardt, Andrew, (1989), Desktop Manager With HyperText Power. Byte. July, McGraw-Hill, 90-92.
26. Rémy, C. (1988), HyperText ou la documentation intelligente. Micro-Systemes. October, 157.
27. Shafer, Dan, (1988), Hypertalk programming. Hayden Books.
28. Yann, G., (1988), L'Hypertext. Science & Vie Micro. July/August, 49-54.

Hypercard as a Psychological Research Tool — Experimental Studies

Agnès Blaye & Patrick Chambres

Laboratoire de Psychologie Sociale de la Cognition, Université Clermont II, France

1. Introduction

As one of the most widely available hypermedia tool kits - at least in Europe - Hypercard is becoming the prototypical environment for hypermedia courseware and hence for research in education and learning. Our aim is not to debate whether it is a proper prototype or not (for detailed analyses, see for example Jonassen, De Oliveira, this book). The issue to be discussed here deals with the relevance and effectiveness of Hypercard as a psychological research tool. Our research field is concerned with peer facilitation effects in children's individual learning. We will very briefly overview the recent trends of research in this area in order to raise some insufficiently explored issues and see how computer-based learning situations and more specifically Hypercard can help to address them. These considerations will then be illustrated by brief reports of three exploratory experiments. The discussion will finally offer some suggestions for further research in the field of Hypermedia and learning.

2. Social interaction and individual learning

Research which can be categorised under this title has different theoretical backgrounds and focuses of interest. An important theoretical distinction has to be made between, on the one hand, studies dealing with cooperative work in the classroom (see for example Slavin, 1983, 1987, Slavin et al., 1985) and, on the other, research carried out in a more developmental perspective by psychologists. While the first studies put an emphasis on group reward structures and motivational aspects, the second are attempts to analyse the conditions and the mechanisms through which social interaction can promote individual cognitive development.

Since our interest lies precisely in the analysis of the mechanisms at work when peer interaction promotes individual learning in problem solving situations (Blaye, 1988, 1989a, Light & Blaye,1990), we are going to develop a few points on this aspect.

The most influential European research perspective in the field was developed in a Piagetian tradition by Doise and colleagues and has quite clearly demonstrated that "two wrongs can make a right" when solving conservation or perspective-taking problems. The authors have emphasized the role of socio-cognitive conflict as the underlying mechanism of peer facilitation (Doise & Mugny, 1984, Doise & Palmonari (Eds), 1984). Individual progress is considered here as the result of the internalisation of interindividual coordinations which have enabled the resolution of conflicts.

However, when one leaves Piagetian tasks which are mainly judgement tasks to deal with more diverse problem solving situations involving the elaboration and execution of solving procedures, it becomes clear that the explanation of benefits from peer interaction in terms of socio-cognitive conflict is no longer satisfactory. Although conflict may play a role, a plurality of mechanisms have to be considered depending in particular on the nature of the cognitive activity required by the problem and the characteristics of the interactive dynamics between the partners (see for reviews, Blaye, 1989b, Gilly, 1989, Azmitia & Perlmutter, 1989).

Another perspective is offered by the Vygotskian approach which is mainly concerned by social interaction in which one partner knows more than the other. The theoretical schema outlined here is that the more knowledgeable partner will first take charge of the **monitoring** process and gradually let the other take more initiative and control until he/she is capable of autonomous work. This transfer of responsibility is supposed to happen through the internalization process which still remains to be studied in more details.

Although developed to account for progress following from interaction between partners with different levels of knowledge, this approach can be used to highlight critical aspects of interaction between equally knowledgeable partners (by reference to the task at hand). The work of Palincsar and Brown (1984, Brown & Palincsar,1989) on reading comprehension through reciprocal teaching is an illustration of this. Our own work on symetrical peer interaction also suggested that the potential benefit of peer work is mediated by the influence of interaction on the strategies employed by the subjects to **monitor** and **regulate** their solving activities (Blaye, 1989). The Vygotskian perspective seems to be more open and promising than socio-cognitive conflict which has already shown its limits (Monteil & Chambres, in press; Blaye, 1989b). Despite the fact that detailed empirical validation is still rare, one can find in the literature a more and more widely shared assumption according to which peer interaction is a way of enhancing the use of metacognitive activities (e.g. Resnick, 1987; Glaser & Bassok, 1989; Collins et al., 1989) which then results in improved performance. This assumption is based on very general considerations. The ones most frequently refered to are (a) since social interaction requires verbalisation, it must facilitate awareness and reflexion; (b) since interaction permits distributed processing between partners, it makes explicit the different 'cognitive roles' that any problem solver has to play, for instance producer and criticizer, and hence should facilitate the monitoring of the solving activities.

In order to get clearer empirical evidence on these crucial points, our choice, in the exploratory studies reported below was to optimise the opportunity for analysing the influence of peer interaction on monitoring processes by using a problem solving task which involves **advance planning** and thus puts a premium on conscious and explicit monitoring and control.

3. Why use Hypercard as a research tool?

Apart from the classically invoked facility of on-line data collection and recording made possible by computer-based experiments, we chose to use Hypercard - running on Apple Macintosh computers - for two of its main characteristics match our research aims closely.

(a) As emphasized by Duchastel (e.g. this book), Hypercard is a learning environment as opposed to a traditional tutoring system which means in particular, that the learners are free to initiate their own actions.

(b) The non linear presentation of information makes available many different routes for the learner to take. On line recording of the subjects' questions to the database tells which information is judged useful at any particular point of the solving activity and then makes explicit some aspects of the self-monitoring processes. The analysis of the following actions provides indications on the way this information has been processed.

Since our general hypothesis assumed that the efficiency of peer interaction is due to its effects on self monitoring and control strategies, Hypercard offered us a highly suitable environment to further validate this explanation. As its effective use requires self-monitoring of the learning process, it should create an environment which maximises differences between pairs and individuals and thus should help to highlight some aspects of the underlying mechanisms.

As already mentioned, the task proposed to the subjects was a planning task. Effective planning is typically dependant upon a great deal of knowledge regarding the domain in question. It is not always easy to decide whether deficient planning is due to a lack of knowledge or to deficient skills.

Hypercard lends itself particularly well to the creation of an information base in which one can circumscribe most of the knowledge required to develop a plan in the context of the problem solving situation. This was made by using the scenario of an adventure game. The database thus included all the relevant data on the particular microworld (we could assume that the only pieces of knowledge which were not explicit in the data base were shared by all the subjects since it was common sense knowledge such as you need a pilot to move a plane...).

The subjects could have two levels of activity on the piece of software: a/ browsing to get information, and b/ performing moves which implied an automatic updating of the database.

Considering Hypercard as a tool, we had to adapt it to our purposes and had to contain our original enthusiasm for its flexibility by limiting the number of links between pieces of information. Indeed, we needed to be able to **make sense** of the information requests made by the users. What was observed with a first more open and less structured version of the software used in a pre-experiment was that some subjects just navigated around by clicking on any buttons that would work without even reading the information displayed; interestingly this was observed almost exclusively among single users.

4. Social interaction in an Hypercard environment: first data

The following studies have to be considered as first attempts in the direction suggested so far, more experimental work using the same task is currently being carried out.

The first study conducted in collaboration with Paul Light and Richard Joiner (Open University, U.K.) with 11-year-old children, illustrates the overall benefit obtained from peer interaction not only during pair work but more interestingly in the children's individual performance on the post-test. The second study used a small sample of adults who were just as much novices as the children in the task domain and in the use of computers (maybe even more so since some children play video games on their home computer which might have some features in common with our task). A revised version of the software was used which, while being based on the same task structure, allowed for much more refined analysis of information handling strategies. In this case, for practical reasons, no post-test session was possible, but this second study clearly illustrates differences between pair and individual monitoring strategies.

A comparison of results obtained on children and adults solving the same problem in either individual or paired conditions has not yet been done. However a few studies of 'constructive interaction' among adults (e.g. O'Malley *et al.*, 1985, Miyake, 1986) suggest that mechanisms at play could be similar to those involved in children interaction. Noticeably, these authors refer to inter-individual conflict and a distribution of roles ('task-doer' and criticizer) between the partners.

4.1 Study 1

Subjects: All members of two parallel classes, that is 39 children (13 pairs and 13 individuals) were included in this experiment. The pairs were composed of same-sex children, the only restriction being the avoidance of any pairings of children who "did not get on". This was done with the help of the class teacher.

Procedure: The children were taken to a quiet area where the computer was set up. It was controlled by a mouse only, no keyboard being used. None of the children had encountered this type of computer before. The general scheme involved two sessions within one week of either individual or peer work, and an individual post-test for all, one week later. The children were first introduced to the problem via a practice task, lasting about ten minutes, in the course of which the main features of the problem and the interface were introduced. This phase was a tightly scripted tutorial situation very much under the control of the experimenter. Then the main task was presented, and the children were left to work on it with minimal experimenter support for a period of 30 minutes. On the second session, the children were rapidly presented with the introductory task and then had 25 minutes to work on the main task, unless they succeeded before this. On the individual post-test session, the same main task was used but with a different initial state (location of the characters and the transport) so that the subjects could not succeed by directly replicating their previous responses. Twenty minutes was the maximum time allowed on this session.

The task: The task was introduced by bringing the map (Figure 1) up on the screen and giving the subjects a paper copy of the map for reference. Beyond this, they were told only that the game involved a king who lived at Ashlan, and that he had lost his crown which was now at Fruggle. The children were told that they had to give orders to the king's subjects to get the crown and to return with it to the king for a great feast. Where children were working in pairs they were told: "Because there are two of you, and only one mouse, you will have to agree on what you are going to do before you do it." There was no other form of intervention on the part of the experimenter during the session itself to regulate the interaction. They were not informed that they would have an individual session subsequently and no other guidance of the interaction was offered. The level of constraints imposed on the partners to ensure a proper collaborative dynamics between them was then very low.

The characters (i.e. the king and his four subjects: the driver, the guard, the pilot and the captain) were all initially at Ashlan along with a car. Bandits inhabited the mainland and pirates inhabited the sea. The other means of transport were distributed in different places. There were constraints such as "*The bandits will steal the crown on the mainland unless the guard is present*" and "*The pirates will steal the crown from any ship sailing the sea even if the guard is present*" which made certain moves impossible and militated against the otherwise obvious route from Ashlan via Brockley to Fruggle and back. All this information had to be discovered by the subjects by clicking on the buttons of the information screen (Figure 2). There were obviously several ways to reach the goal but there was an optimal strategy which took only 5 moves.

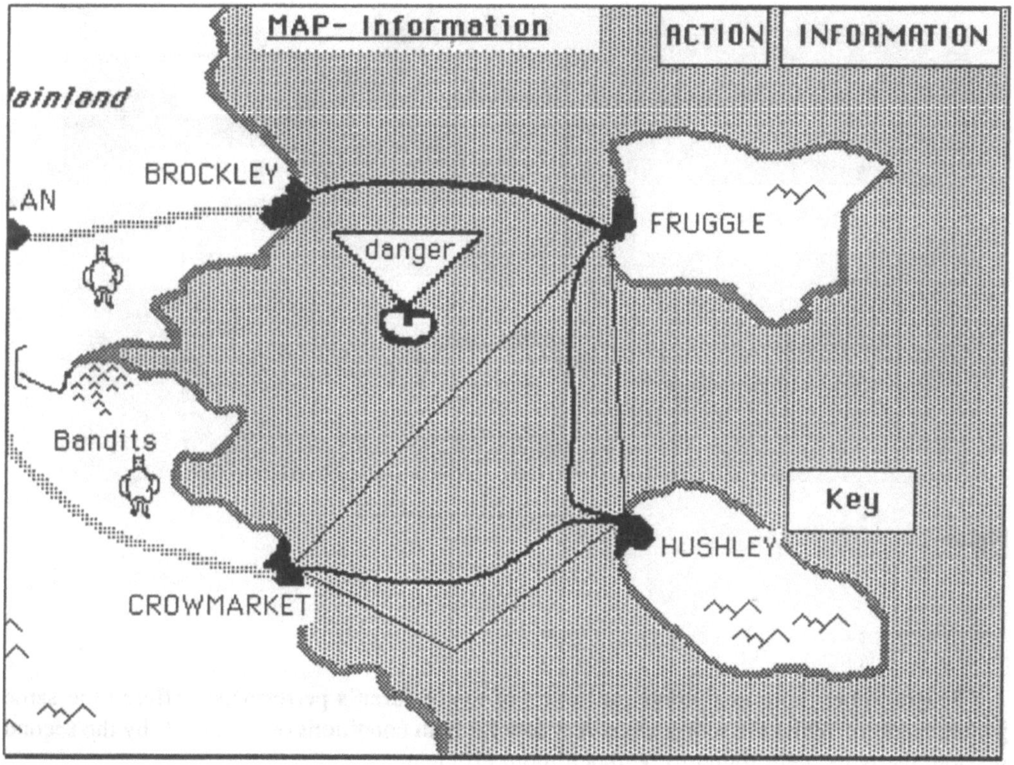

Figure 1.

During the practice task, all the children were familiarised with the need to seek out information in order to decide which actions to perform. During the first session no emphasis was put on completing the task in a minimum number of moves, whereas in the second and third sessions they were encouraged to do so and were also asked to aim for as few error messages as possible (an error message appeared each time an illegal move was attempted).

Results: Complete detailed data and all the results of statistical analysis are developped in Blaye *et al* (in press). In the first session, the proportion of success in achieving the goal within the time limit was nil for the individuals and very low for the pairs (15%). In the second session however only 15% of the individuals succeeded whereas 46% of the pairs did so. On the following individual post-test, the superiority of those children who had **previously** worked in pairs was highly significant. There was an overall high number of moves on this last session which indicates that the children's anticipatory planning, when existent, was not effective. However, on this point again, one could observe a better efficiency of the pairs.

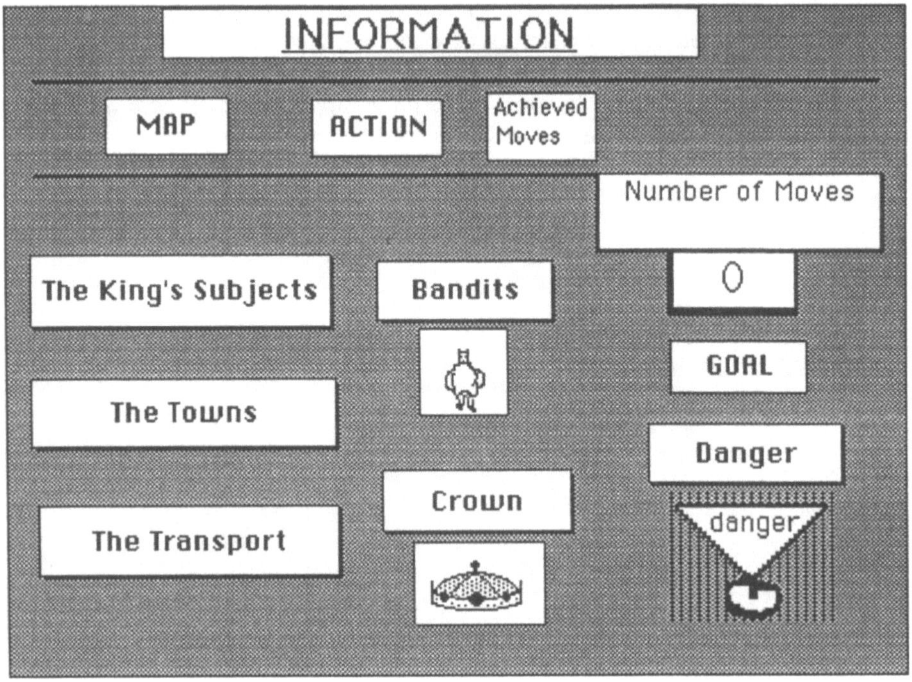

Figure 2.

Several other more qualitative indicators of the children's performance offered the same general pattern: While the scores were very low for both conditions on session 1, by the second session, the pairs were found to be much more efficient.

Another aspect of the subjects' activity concerns the way they deal with the information provided by the system. As we said earlier, the first version of the software did not allow for refined analysis of information handling but it did give us an interesting indicator of the way the error messages were processed. The message that appeared to be the most crucial referred to the pirates' constraint, and informed the subjects that: "*the crown will be stolen by the pirates*" when they attempted to move the crown onto a ship. It is clear that up until the first time they encountered this message most children had failed to see the implications of the fact that the pirates could steal the crown from any ship sailing the sea. When faced with this message, though, significantly more pairs than individuals shifted the focus of their attention straight away to the plane, which was the correct and necessary insight to reach the goal. In order to get further insight into the processes involved, analyses of verbal interaction between the partners are required and are currently being carried out by Light and colleagues (for some details see Blaye et al., in press).

On the whole, indications from the computer trace tend to show that children working in pairs are more effective at handling information provided by the computer. More evidence is provided by the second study with adults.

4.2 Study 2

This pilot experiment was run with 15 adults (5 individuals and 5 pairs) over two sessions, no individual post-test having been possible.

Results: The global comparison between the outcomes of peer and individual work gave very much the same pattern as was obtained with the children, both in terms of overall proportion of success (the superiority of peer interaction was substantial only on the second session) and in terms of more qualitative indicators (Blaye & Light, 1989).

When they thought they had enough information to decide which move to perform, the subjects could describe the required move to the machine by pressing selection buttons and then clicking on a "Go" button to execute the move. In either of the two sessions, there was no significant difference between the mean number of times the "Go" button was pressed by the subjects, be they individuals or pairs. This indicates that the degree of engagement in the task was not lower among individuals than among pairs and thus should prevent oversimplistic interpretation of peer facilitation effects in terms of higher levels of motivation for subjects working in pairs. However, in session 1, the proportion of unsuccessful attempts to perform a move was much higher among the individuals; these failures corresponded to illegal moves with regard to the constraints of the microworld and were thus interrupted by an error message. In session 2, all the pairs achieved all their attempted moves, while, on average, more than one third (38.6%) of the moves made by the individuals were unsuccessful attempts. These important differences in favor of the pairs are clear indications of more efficient information handling on their part.

Information on the subjects' exploration of the database was provided by the number of questions they asked the system, and when they asked them. We distinguished questions which were asked by the subjects **before any attempt to move** the characters, and which reflect the exploration needed to make anticipatory planning possible from those asked **in the course of action,** that is at any time after the first move attempt, which signals an awareness on the part of the subjects of their insufficient exploration of the database before starting to act.

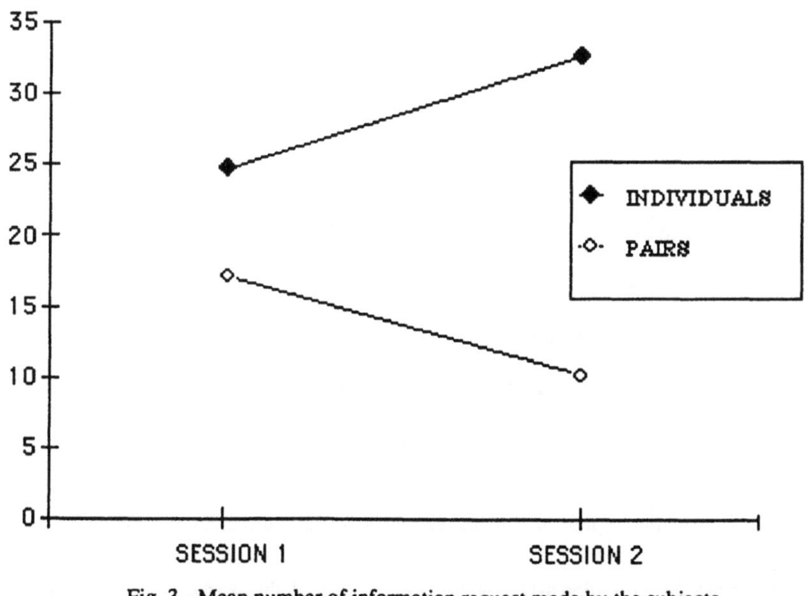

Fig. 3 - Mean number of information request made by the subjects

When considering the overall number of information requests made by the subjects, Figure 3 indicates a tentative interaction between conditions of training and sessions. There was no significant difference between pairs and individuals on session 1. But, on session 2, individuals asked significantly more questions than the pairs since they slightly increased their number of requests compared to session 1 while the pairs asked a lot fewer.

Moreover, in both sessions, subjects working individually produced a significantly higher proportion of redundant[1] questions than the pairs: 31 and 25% - respectively in session 1 and session 2 - for the individuals, and 8 and 0% for the pairs.

Analysis of the distribution of requests to the system before and in the course of action further highlights differences between the two conditions in their monitoring activity.

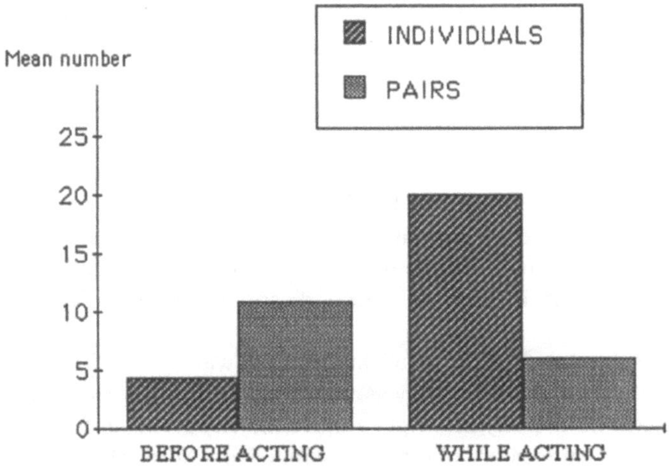

Fig. 4 - Distribution of information requests made by the subjects during session 1.

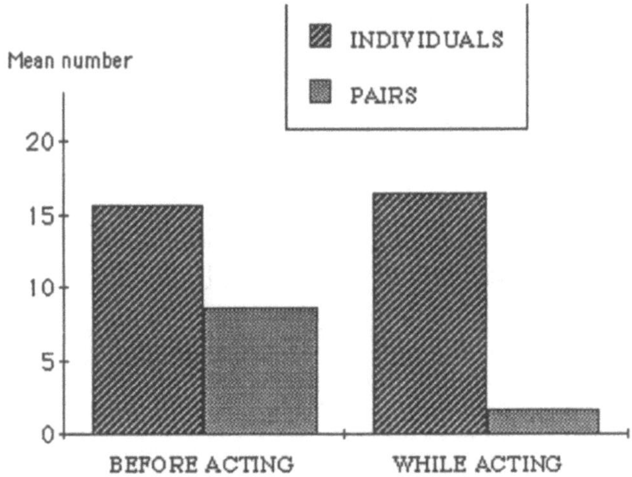

Fig. 5 - Distribution of information requests made by the subjects during session 2.

[1] We call "redundant" question, a question asked by the subjects although they had previously got the information sought in the question and nothing had changed to justify asking it again.

There seems to be a very low level of anticipation among the individuals in session 1, since most of their information requests occurred after the subjects started to move the characters. Among the pairs, however, the majority of questions were asked before the subjects started to act. In the second session the pattern is even clearer: the pairs demonstrated a good mastery of the task by asking almost all of their questions **before** starting to execute their plan while the individuals still asked a lot of questions in the course of execution.

5. From social regulation to computer-based help facilities

The data reported above confirm the idea developed by Miyake and Norman (1979) while studying adults who had to learn how to use a computer text editor: "To ask a question, one must know enough to know what is not known". In other words, one needs to have a proper framework in order to know which questions to ask. It is important to note that this describes the problem that Hypercard browsers have to confront all the time.

Miyake and Norman compared, among other things, the number of questions asked by novice and previously trained learners according to the level of difficulty of the material to be learned (there were two levels: easy and hard). As they expected there was a strong interaction between levels of knowledge of the learners and difficulty of the material. Trained learners asked many more questions on the difficult material while complete novices asked more on the easy one.

In our second study, since the task and the whole microworld were the same in the two sessions, an important decrease of requests was expected. But, while this was the case for the pairs, it is as if the individuals were only becoming aware in the second session of the necessity of getting information in order to devise an efficient plan. In other words, they needed more time than the pairs to build their mental model of what they had to do in the task and then have a framework which enabled them to know what to ask the system, and, in the second session, it is only when they were stuck in the course of their actions that they asked questions.

Knowing which information to request is however only one aspect leading to mastery of the task. Another crucial aspect is the processing of information received by the system (either as a response to questions or as error messages). Is is now well demonstrated that poor problem solvers are also poor information processors (e.g. Chi et al., 1989). Here again data collected in the first study seemed to indicate that pairs were more efficient than individuals at processing information contained in error messages.

Although these exploratory studies did not claim to demonstrate by themselves that peer facilitation was due to the influence of interaction on monitoring strategies they offer a rather clear illustration of this point through several indicators of information handling strategies.

A further step would be taken if what are supposed to be the mechanisms underlying the effectiveness of interaction could be disentangled from the social context which implies the interwoven action of many social and emotional factors. Once artificially isolated, these mechanisms could then be systematically put into play. Although in these studies we focus on an explanation of the underlying mechanisms in terms of an improvement of the monitoring processes, we can not disregard an alternative interpretation according to which in pair-work, there is a sharing between the partners of the cognitive load implied by the task. In particular, the memory load would become lighter since the partner could work as an auxiliary memory.

In the next study, we tried to devise a rudimentary 'Hypercard tutoring system' which offered the subjects external incentives to monitor their browsing and information processing activities (see Duchastel, this book for differences between Hypermedia and intelligent tutoring systems - ITS - and ways to integrate Hypermedia into ITS).

5.1 Study 3

Procedure: There were two training sessions for which the task was the same as in the two previous studies. In the third stage which was an evaluation session common to all the subjects an isomorphic task was used. It involved different characters, means of transport and places and then required new information exploration on the part of the subjects. 30 11-year-old children were randomly **distributed into** three training conditions: a/ a control condition; b/ a 'guided-monitoring' condition c/ an 'auxiliary memory' condition.

The control condition was similar to the individual work condition in the previous studies.

In the 'guided-monitoring' condition, the computer suggested the use of some expert monitoring strategies. Five suggestions had been prepared which had to be read in a particular order, each of them prompted the user to do something specific and then come back to read the next one. The distribution of control between the user and the machine was such that the users could ask for these suggestions whenever they judged it useful but if they did not they were urged to read the suggestions not already read before starting to execute moves. This last constraint was included to prevent the low usage of computer-based help facilities noted in many research reports. As the suggestions were an attempt to test one potential underlying mechanism of peer facilitation, we had to make sure that all the subjects would be influenced by them. In session 2 however, this constraint was removed and subjects were no longer obliged to read any suggestions.

Although presented in the context of a particular problem solving situation, the suggestions were formulated in such a way as to be non specific to this particular task even if it might weaken the effects on the training task itself. This was done in order that any monitoring skills which may have been acquired by the subjects could subsequently be applied in different contexts. Moreover, the data could then be relevant to the metacognitive perspective. The main incentives required of the children were: to make sure that they had understood what was the goal, to read all the information and summarise it, to anticipate the moves following the one to be performed and to process information contained in error messages while bearing in mind the next moves to execute.

In the 'auxiliary memory' condition, the subjects could refer at any stage in their solving process, to a note card on which they could read all the information they had decided to record when they explored the database.

During the familiarisation stage, the subjects of both experimental groups were informed of the functions of the specific buttons: respectively, "advice-buttons" for the 'guided-monitoring' group and "take notes" and "read-notes" buttons for the 'auxiliary memory' group.

Results: Despite the exploratory character of this third study which implied that we could not expect clearcut data, a few tendencies which we will now indicate, could be of great interest for future investigations.

No subject achieved the goal in session 1 and only one in session 2. The proportion of success was also rather low in all three conditions in the post-test which consisted of an isomorphic task: 27, 33, and 40% respectively, in the control, 'auxiliary memory', and 'guided-monitoring' conditions.

In the previous studies, we took as an indicator of advance planning the fact, made necessary by the structure of the task, of taking all the characters or at least the captain on the first move. The proportion of such advance planning was higher among the 'guided-monitoring' subjects than in the two other conditions, although the difference between the two experimental conditions was really striking only in session 2. The frequency of reversed moves[2] which was already taken (Blaye *et al.*, in press) as an indicator of a deficiency in planning was lower among the 'guided' individuals than among the control subjects, the difference being maintained in post-test. The memory group appeared to be at an intermediary level.

When considering the monitoring of the information exploration, the superiority of 'guided' subjects appeared quite clearly: Compared to the two other groups, they asked significantly more questions **before** starting to perform moves. However, unlike the pairs of adults in session 2 of the second study, they still asked as many questions while acting as the subjects in other conditions.

Another point of interest specific to this study was the analysis of the level of use made by the subjects of the facilities offered in the two experimental conditions. In the 'memory' group, we noted an important increase of the amount of information saved on the note card between session 1 and session 2 although the frequency of consultations remains stable. From observing the subjects while they were working, it looks as if in session 1, most subjects "forgot" the function of the "take notes" button. However, it is difficult to decide whether this is the only explanation of this low level of use or if the subjects did not acknowledge the usefulness of having the information displayed in the database recopied in a linear way on the notecard.

While in session 1, they could not begin to perform a move before reading all the suggestions, children in the 'guided-monitoring' condition were not under such an obligation in session 2. It is noteworthy then, that 60% read all the suggestions in session 2, and all the subjects read at least one.

6. Discussion

As already stated, this last study was an exploratory step to judge the validity of some kind of external control implemented by the machine and thus not dependant on a human partner. Obviously the amount of familiarisation with the task and with the kind of help available was insufficient for there to be striking differences. What is interesting then is that despite the lack of inter-condition differences in terms of global performance, subjects trained in the 'guided-monitoring' condition showed some superiority in terms of a greater conformity to the 'expert' strategies. The limited number of subjects on the one hand, and the few tendencies of superiority over the control group on the other, do not allow us to come to any final conclusion on the efficiency of the 'auxiliary memory' condition.

However, the results obtained by researchers analysing the effects of different forms of help associated with the use of word processors (for a recent review, Piolat & Blaye, 1989) are likely to shed some light on our own data in the 'guided-monitoring' condition. Woodruff, Bereiter and Scardamalia (1981) have had to admit the partial failure of their prompting program called procedural facilitation which prompted the subjects to self-questioning and monitoring of their activity of text revision. According to these authors, the facilitating features were too great a disruption to the revising strategies spontaneously used by the writers.

[2] A move is qualified 'reversed move' when it directly negates the preceding one.

In the same field of research, Bryson, Lindsay, Joram and Woodruff (1986) have attempted to constrain the conditions of writing by requiring the subjects to do specific types of revision which characterise expert writers. Here again, the results are on the whole rather disappointing. However while average writers did not take advantage of the constrained conditions, more expert writers did benefit from them. In our own study, the heterogeneity of results in each experimental group suggests that the initial level might also be a crucial factor.

More generally, we agree with Roussey (1989) who stressed the necessity of making sure that the subjects really feel the need to do what they are prompted to do. He demonstrated that effective help can be devised if it is focused on the analysis of the product to achieve - in his study: the text structure - instead of an exclusive focus on procedures.

In the work described here, the necessity of following the suggestions is likely not to have been perceived by the children. Moreover, between sessions 1 and 2, the scores of 'guided' subjects on several qualitative indicators improved which would suggest that extra sessions could demonstrate more clearly the efficiency of our non task-specific messages.

7. Conclusion

Although the preliminary data reported here are not conclusive in themselves, we believe they offer promising perspectives for further research.

First of all, as suggested in the first part of this chapter, Hypercard reveals itself to be a suitable environment for studying peer facilitation effects and mechanisms. As the reader will have noted, the level of analysis we deliberately chose to address here, was the articulation between inter-individual and intra-individual cognitive activities. Obviously, social interaction involves much more than the confrontation of two 'cold cognitions'. In our research team, Monteil's work (in press) insists that studying human behaviour means first to consider the person as a **socially inserted** person and then to conceive explanation systems which take social insertions into account. This implies considering social insertion not as a context likely to modify individual cognitive functioning but as an intrinsic constituent of this functioning. We are currently carrying out studies according a more important place to the social aspects of the situation in which subjects are inserted. For instance, we have recently devised an experiment (Data in the process of being analysed) to investigate the influence of the social position of the partners and of their positional identities on the nature of the interactive dynamics and then on its cognitive effects. The positional identity is mainly characterized by its local and dynamic nature. It involves both social identity which results from social categorisation - e.g. to belong to an expert category - and personal identity which results from social comparison - e.g. to be more expert than a partner - and is elaborated from the characteristics of the situation in which the subjects find themselves.

Coming back to the analysis of cognitive activities while working with Hypercard, we would like to suggest that while Hypercard can be a tool to analyse social interaction, reciprocally social interaction should not be neglected in the attempts to devise intelligent help for hypermedia courseware.

What was shown by our results is that the way in which individuals monitor their exploration of the database is far from being optimal both among children and adults. This supports a more general observation that users are frequently lost in the hyperspace networks.

What is original here is the suggestion that peer interaction can significantly improve the efficacy of this exploration.

We would like to suggest that there could be some advantage in spending more time analysing the mechanisms underlying social interaction facilitation in order to devise intelligent help which would not be exclusively pragmatically grounded as is most of the time the case. Our third study was a preliminary attempt in this direction.

Another important aspect of the usefulness of social interaction in this field of research would be its use as a methodology which can make explicit internal cognitive processes thereby rendering them accessible for analysis. This could then help to collate the information we need to build dynamic models of the learners in order to adapt the intelligent help facilities.

Computer-based help and interaction with a social partner can then be conceived as alternative means of improving the efficiency of learning with hypermedia. Moreover, far from being incompatible alternatives, we would like to suggest that their combination might constitute the optimal situation for the promotion of individual learning.

Literature

1. Azmitia, M., & Perlmutter, M.(1989). Social influences on children's cognition: state of the art and future directions. In H.W. Reese (Ed.) Advances in child development and behavior. New York: Academic Press.
2. Blaye, A. (1988) Confrontation socio-cognitive et résolution de problèmes: A propos du produit de deux ensembles. Unpublished doctoral thesis. University of Provence. France.
3. Blaye, A. (1989) Interactions sociales et constructions cognitives: Présentation critique de la thèse du conflit socio-cognitif. In N. Bednarz & C. Garnier (Dirs.) Construction des savoirs; obstacles et conflits. Ottawa: Agences d' ARC.
4. Blaye, A. (1989) Peer interaction in solving a binary matrix problem: possible mechanisms causing individual progress. To appear in H. Mandl, E. De Corte N. Bennett, & H.P. Friedrich (Eds.) Learning and instruction. European research in an international context. Volume 21. Oxford: Pergamon.
5. Blaye, A., Light, P., Joiner, R., & Sheldon, S. Collaboration as a facilitator of planning and problem solving on a computer-based task.(in press) British Journal of Developmental Psychology.
6. Brown, A.L., & Palincsar, A.S. (1989) Guided cooperative learning and individual knowledge acquisition. In L.B. Resnick (Ed.) Knowing, learning, and instruction, essays in honor of Robert Glaser. Hillsdale, NJ: Lawrence Erlbaum Associates.
7. Bryson, M., Lindsay, P.H., Joram, E., & Woodruff, E. (1986) Augmented word-processing: The influence of task characteristics and mode production on writers' cognitions. Paper presented to the Annual Meeting of the American Educational Research Association, San Francisco, CA, April.
8. Chi, M.T.H., Bassok, M., Lewis; M.W., Reimann, P., & Glaser, R.1989). Self-Explanations: how students study and use examples in learning to solve problems. Cognitive Science, 13, 145-182.
9. Collins, A., Brown, J.S., & Newman, S.E. (1989) Cognitive Apprenticeship: Teaching the crafts of reading, writing and mathematics. In L.B. Resnick (Ed.) Knowing, learning, and instruction, essays in honor of Robert Glaser. Hillsdale, NJ: Lawrence Erlbaum Associates.
10. De Oliveira (1991) chapter in this book.
11. Doise, W., & Mugny, G. (1984) The social development of the intellect. Oxford: Pergamon Press.
12. Doise, W., & Palmonari, A. (Eds.) (1984) Social interaction in individual development. Cambridge: Cambridge University Press.
13. Duchastel, P.C. (1991) Integrating HyperMedia into Intelligent Tutoring. In this book.
14. Gilly, M. (1989) A propos de la théorie du conflit socio-cognitif et des mécanismes psycho-sociaux des constructions: perspectives actuelles et modèles explicatifs. in N. Bednarz & C. Garnier (Eds.) Construction des savoirs: obstacles et conflits. Montréal: Agence d'ARC.
15. Glaser, R., & Bassok, M. (1989). Learning theory and the study of instruction. Annual Review of Psychology, 40, 631-666.
16. Jonassen, D.H. (1991) Adding intelligence to Hypertext with expert systems and adding usability to expert systems with Hypertext. In this book.

17. Light. P. & Blaye, A. (1990) Computer-based learning: The social dimensions. In H. Foot, M. Morgan & R. Shute (Eds.), Children helping children. Chichester: J. Wiley.
18. Monteil, J.M. (in press) Toward a social psychology of cognitive functioning: Theoretical outline and empirical illustrations. In M. Von Cranach, W. Doise, & G. Mugny (Eds.) Social representations and the social bases of knowledge.
19. Monteil, J.M., & Chambres, P. (in press) Eléments pour une exploration de dimensions du conflit sociocognitif: une expérimentation chez l'adulte. Revue Internationale de Psychologie Sociale.
20. Miyake, N. (1986) Constructive interaction and the iterative process of understanding. Cognitive Science, 10, 151-177.
21. Miyake, N., & Norman, D.A.(1979). To ask a question, one must know enough to know what is not known. Journal of Verbal Learning and Verbal Behavior, 18, 357-364.
22. O'Malley, C.E., Draper, S.W., & Riley, M.S. (1985) Constructive interaction: A method for studying human-computer-human interaction. In B. Shackel (Ed.) Human-Computer interaction - Interact'84. Amsterdam: North- Holland.
23. Palincsar, A.S., & Brown, A.L. (1984) Reciprocal teaching of comprehension-fostering and monitoring activities. Cognition and Instruction, 1, 2, 117-175.
24. Piolat, A., & Blaye, A. (1989) Effects of word processing and writing aids on revision processes. Third European Conference for Research on Learning and Instruction, E.A.R.L.I., symposium "Writing and the computer". Madrid, 4-7 September.
25. Resnick, L.B.(1987). Instruction and the cultivation of thinking. In E. De Corte, H. Lodewijks, R. Parmentier, & P. Span (Eds.) Learning and instruction, European research in an international context, Vol. 1. Oxford: Leuven University Press and Pergamon Press. (pp. 415-442).
26. Roussey, J.Y. (1989) Stratégies de révision de texte; évaluation du rôle des connaissances par un paradigme de conformisation. Unpublished doctoral thesis. University of Provence, France.
27. Slavin, R. (1983) Co-operative learning. New York: Longman.
28. Slavin, R. (1987) Developmental and motivational perspectives on co-operative learning: a reconciliation, Child Development, 58, 1161-1167.
29. Slavin, R., Sharan, S., Kagan, S., Hertz-Lazararowitz, R., Webb, C., & Schmuck, R. (1985) Learning to co-operate, co-operating to learn. New York: Plenum.
30. Woodruff, E., Bereiter, C., & Scardamalia, M. (1981) On the road to computer assisted compositions. Journal of Educational Technology Systems, 10, 2, 133-148.

Effects of Prior Knowledge on Learning to Use a Command Device

Anh Nguyen-Xuan

Directeur de Recherche au CNRS - Université de Paris VIII and CNRS, France

1. Introduction

With the blooming of new technologies, people are frequently confronted with complex command devices. A command device possesses some means for inputting and outputting information, and a set of operators for processing information. A videotape recorder, a pocket calculator, a computerized text-editor, or a programming language (and Hypercard can be viewed as a programming language), are examples of command devices.

Any command device possesses a set of elementary operators each of which can be activated by a single command. For example, the simplest pocket calculator possesses only four elementary operators; namely the four arithmetic operations. Hence to obtain the square root of a number, one must activate a sequence of elementary operators. A more sophisticated pocket calculator may possess a square-root key, so that the square root can be obtained by activating a single command, i.e. an elementary operator.

After Shrager and Klahr (1986), I would like to propose that the knowledge the learner must acquire in order to (optimally) use a complex command device can be analyzed into three types of knowledge: syntactic knowledge, semantic knowledge and device model knowledge.

Syntactic knowledge involves the way an elementary operator (i.e. a command) can be activated, and the legal way for organizing a sequence of elementary operators. For example, in a pocket calculator, the command "x" (multiplication) must have two arguments, and the command "square-root" must have only one argument, and there is an order of priority between the four arithmetic operators. Semantic knowledge is knowing what a command, or a sequence of commands, does. That is the knowledge about the result of a particular command, or a particular command sequence. For example, in a pocket calculator that possesses a memory, pressing the key "Recall" results in the displaying of the memory contents. The device model knowledge concerns the device functional architecture and its internal state changes with the activation of a particular command, or a particular command sequence. For example, in some pocket calculators, the two following key stroke sequences produce the same output "10" on the display: {4 + 6 =} and {4 + 6 +}. However, a good device model knowledge must assume that these two sequences do not result in the same internal state.

Shrager and Klahr (op.cit.) found that, although they interact quite strongly, these three types of knowledge are not completely mastered at the same time. The syntactic knowledge is fully acquired before the semantic knowledge, and the acquisition of the device model knowledge is achieved last. A deep understanding of the functioning of the device involves the three types of knowledge, and such an understanding is necessary for an optimal use of the device when new tasks have to be achieved.

How can these three types of knowledge be acquired? I will first argue that: (i) the learning of a command device is necessarily of the learning by doing type (section 2), and (ii) the learning of a command device is prone to analogical transfer (section 3). Then I will discuss the effects of analogical transfer on learning to use a command device (section 4). In this discussion, I will present some results borrowed from my own research and some results from the literature. A brief comment on the implications on training will be presented (section 5).

2. Learning to use a command device cannot be but learning by doing

Three main learning situations can be considered: (i) "learning by observation", or "learning by being taught", is a learning situation in which the student's main cognitive activity is to encode knowledge that is presented to him (her) in a declarative form, or to observe worked out exercises; (ii) "learning by exploration" is a learning situation in which the student is left alone with a device and general instructions such as "try to discover how it works"; (iii) "learning by doing", or "learning by solving problems", is a learning situation in which the student must solve problems using the device.

If a command device is designed to solve only a small set of problems, i.e. to reach a small set of goals, it is easy to teach people how to use it by just describing the command sequences required to solve each of the problems. In other words, the command device can be learned by observation. And the device model knowledge is not necessary for correctly using it.

On the contrary, if the class of tasks that can be potentially accomplished by the device is fairly large, a good instructional material (e.g. a user's manual) must describe completely the syntactic knowledge and the semantics of the elementary operators. However, because the device can solve a large set of problems, it is not possible to describe the semantics of all the possible command sequences. Only a small sample of problem situations and the corresponding optimal command sequences can be described. For the third type of knowledge (the device model), there can be many different device models, and hence different functional architectures. One functional architecture can be chosen and presented to the learner, but all the possible state changes cannot be described, because the set of all these changes is too large.

The device model knowledge being knowledge about the changes of the device internal state during a command sequence, if the set of command sequences that correspond to the set of tasks that the device can accomplish is too large, it is not possible to describe all of them. So the only way for acquiring this knowledge about the device internal state changes is to try to use it. In other words, to acquire the device model knowledge, the learning must be of either two types: by solving problems given by a teacher, or by exploration.

Although, for most devices, it is not possible to describe all the possible sequences of internal state changes of the device, a functional architecture can still be chosen and presented to the learner. However, experimental results (Richard, 1983) suggest that he (she) does not pay attention to either the written descriptions, or the graphical representations, of functional architectures. In a study on learning to use a pocket calculator (Friemel et al., 1983), the calculator was simulated by a computer so that both the display and the memory could be visually accessed. It was found that the beginner subjects did not pay much attention to what was happening to the memory during a sequence of commands they were performing in order to solve a problem. An experimental group that could visually access the memory contents did not learn better than a control group that could not do so. This kind of data suggests that the functional architecture, which is an aspect of the device model knowledge, is not acquired through observation.

There are two differences between the learning by solving problems and the learning by exploration. In the latter situation, first the subject invents small problems he (she) tries to solve and second, the subject's goal is not only to obtain a result, but to test his (her) predictions about the outcome of a command or a command sequence. Exploration thus appears to favor the discovery of the functional property of elementary commands, and the functional property of sequences of commands. Some researchers claim that this learning situation is more favorable to the acquisition of knowledge than the learning by solving problem situation (Shrager, 1987, Sweller, 1988).

Experimental results on learning command device will be presented in section 4. Because there are only a few studies on learning by exploration and learning by predicting the effects of sequences of commands, only the results from experiments based on the learning by solving problems will be discussed with details.

3. The learning to use a command device is prone to analogical transfer

Although a command device can be viewed as belonging to a domain of knowledge, command devices are very frequently tools for reaching goals the meaning of which is independent of the devices. For example, even if a programming language like Fortran can be considered as belonging to the domain of procedural programming languages, building a Fortran program for solving mathematical problems and building a Fortran program for solving problems of search in a data base do not imply the same domain of knowledge. A pocket calculator processes only numbers, and can do only arithmetic operations. But the goal a sequence of calculations is aimed at is defined (and gets its meaning) in a particular domain of knowledge. For example, the sequence of calculations {17-3-4} has different meanings in the two following problems: 1/Ann is 17 years old. She is three years older than Bess, and Bess is 4 years older than Chistopher. How old is Christopher? 2/Albert has played two marble games. In the first trial he gained 3 marbles, in the second trial he gained 4 marbles. He now possesses 17 marbles. How many marbles did Albert possess at the outset?

I have argued above that, in most cases, skill acquisition in command device requires learning by doing. When this learning is monitored by a teacher (or a tutoring system), one of the teacher's tasks is to choose problems to be given to the learner. Two characteristics of the learning of a command device should be pointed out: 1/as just demonstrated, a problem is necessarily defined in a particular knowledge domain which is independent of the device; 2/ for obvious pedagogical reasons, the beginner learner must not be given a problem that belongs to a knowledge domain he (she) is not familiar with. I will call the knowledge domain in which a problem is defined the "source domain". Indeed, most of the time, the problems given to the beginner learner are well known to him (her) in the source domain. That is, these problems are not difficult for the learner: he (she) has a good understanding of the way he (she) can solve it in the source domain. For example, if you want to teach a 10 year old pupil the Logo programming language, you will ask him (her) to write programs for generating drawings, but not to write programs for solving trigonometry problems.

As the learner's semantic knowledge about the command device is limited, the consequence of these two characteristics of the learning of a command device is that the learner is unable to build a representation of the problem in terms of the command device operators. In other words, the learner could have built a problem space, but it is quite probable that this problem space cannot be searched through using the device operators. Two cases may happen: (i) the learner has been given a worked out example, and this example is similar to the problem he (she) has to solve; (ii) there is no available worked out example, but the source domain in which the problem is defined is very familiar to the learner.

In the first case, the learner is prone to use the worked out example as a template for generating the command sequence for solving the problem he (she) is given. This use of prior knowledge is termed "structural analogy", and has been extensively discussed by Anderson & Thompson (1989).

The following is an example of structural analogy extracted from a protocol gathered by a student in my group, Françoise Youssefi (1988), who is conducting a research on analogical transfer in learning PROLOG.

The learner has been given the solution for a problem "find the greater number in a list of two numbers":

```
max([X,Y],X) :- X>=Y.
max([X,Y],Y).
```

The subsequent problem the learner has to solve is "find the largest value in a list of numbers". His solution is:

```
maxlist([X|[Y|Tail]], X) :- max([X,Y],X), maxlist([X|Tail],X).
maxlist([X|[Y|Tail]], Y) :- maxlist([Y|Tail],Y).
```

If no similar worked out example is available, and if the problem to be solved using the device is an easy problem in the source domain, the only way for the beginner learner to understand (i.e. to build a representation of) the problem is to rely on the knowledge of the source domain, hence to think about the problem solution in terms of the means (i.e. the operators) that are available in the source domain.

As an example, let us suppose a 10-year-old child who learns the Logo language. The child is asked to write a Logo program for generating a drawing of an isosceles right-angled triangle. He (she) knows how to produce such a drawing in the familiar domain of hand drawing in which the action of drawing a straight line between two points using a rule and a pencil, the action of drawing a right angle using a pencil and a setsquare, the action of determining two equal segments using compasses, etc., are among the operators one can apply to reach the goal. Let us assume further that the child knows fairly well how to draw an isosceles right-angled triangle with pencil and paper. In this case, he (she) has a precise idea of the different states of the process of drawing. This means that the child has figured out a detailed goal structure. A goal structure is a set of intermediate states that are necessary for reaching the final goal. For example, the following sequence of states belongs to the goal structure for reaching the goal state "an isosceles right-angled triangle": two lines crossing in right angle (drawn by using a setsquare), then two segments crossing in right angle and having the same measure (the equality of the two segments is being determined with compasses)... It is quite likely that the subject will encounter some difficulties if he (she) tries to borrow this goal structure for achieving the drawing of an isosceles right-angled triangle in the Logo world.

Let us examine this case where the learner knows how to solve the problem in the source domain. In such a case, he (she) may have already figured out the process of problem solving, i.e. the successive states together with the relevant operators to transform one state into a subsequent one. I will call this sequence of couples state/operator a "solution-path". It seems then natural that the learner will try to achieve these states when asked to use the command device to do the task. As the building of the goal structure is based on the operators that are available in the source domain, but that do not necessarily exist in the device, three different situations may arise.

The first, and most favorable, situation is where, for each source domain operator involving in the solution-path, one can find an elementary operator in the device that has the same semantic property vis-à-vis all the sub-goals, hence vis-à-vis the final goal. For example, for the assignment in BASIC, typing X=3 and Y=5 is like putting the number 3 in a box called X, and putting the number 5 in a box called Y. The result obtained with BASIC is analogous to the one obtained in the box domain.

Difficulties begin with the second situation: as before, there is some parallelism between some source domain operators and elementary device operators vis-à-vis some sub-goals, but the side-effects may differ. Let us go further into the analogy between the concept of assignment in BASIC and the "put-in-box" concept in the box domain (Burstein, 1988): the action "put object O into box X" produces the result "box X contains object O", and typing "X=3" produces the result "X has the value 3". Now, if you put into the box X a second object, either box X is full and the second object stays on top of the first object, or there is some room left and the second object sinks into box X. But if you type X=3 then X=4, the number 3 disappears.

In the third situation, some elementary operators of the source domain do not have any correspondent in the device. That is, there exists in the source domain an elementary operator to transform, say a state E_i into a state E_{i+1}. But with the device, to generate the state E_{i+1} from a state E_i, a sequence of several elementary commands is needed. For example, in the box domain, one can leave open a set of boxes, then the contents of several boxes can be visually accessed at the same time. Searching for a particular object requires only one action "look at the boxes". In BASIC, there is no single command to answer the question "does a double-entry table T contain an element C, and in which cell?".

In the last two situations, the goal structure imported from the source domain must be modified. An example of this type of problem will be presented in section 4.3.

4. Effects of analogical transfer

In this section, three categories of research results in learning command devices will be presented: the first category deals with learning the functioning of a command device, either by exploration or by predicting the outcomes of an operator sequence; the second category of results concerns the analogical transfer from a programming language to the learning of another programming language; the third category of results involves the analogical transfer of a goal structure from the familiar domain of physical objects into a command device that has the main properties of a procedural programming language.

4.1 Learning by predicting the behavior of the device

Shrager and Klahr (1986) found that learning by exploration (called "instructionless learning") involves making hypotheses about the syntax and the semantics of the elementary operator, and designing "experiments" for testing theses hypotheses. The learner makes predictions about the results of a command sequence; if the outcome is not consistent with his (her) predictions, he (she) modifies his (her) hypotheses and tests them again. For a programmable toy track, adult subjects can discover the syntax and the semantics of the elementary operators in a reasonable amount of time (less than one hour).

Shrager and Klahr recognize that their programmable toy follows a relatively simple model of computation, and the key labels are suggestive of the semantics of the device components. Moreover, it is apparent that in this instructionless learning, the subjects were not prone to build long programs: they limited themselves to discovering the semantics of the various commands, but they did not really try to understand how the commands interact. Therefore, these results do not demonstrate that learning by exploration promotes an optimal use of a command device.

In my laboratory, a research project has been conducted (Friemel et al., 1983) in which two groups of 12-year-old students learnt to use a pocket calculator with a memory. The first group learnt to use the calculator by solving word arithmetic problems. In order to oblige the subjects to optimally use the device (e.g. parallel calculus using the memory), constraints were imposed such as: "you must not type in the same number twice", "you must not write down the intermediate result of a calculus and re-enter it later"... These constraints can be satisfied only if the learner discovers the optimal command sequence. Besides the key for typing in numbers and the keys for the arithmetic operations (MINUS, PLUS...), the keys for processing the memory are:

STO: the number on the Display is copied into the Memory;
RECALL: the number in the Memory is copied into the Display;
SUM: the number on the Display is added to the number stored in the Memory;
EXCHANGE: the number on the Display is copied into the Memory and the number in the Memory is copied into the Display.

An example of problem and an optimal command sequence is presented in Figure 1.

Jean and Paul have each 28 francs. Jean gives to Paul 9 francs. How much money has Jean now? How much money has Paul now? How much money does Paul have more than Jean? Use the calculator to find the answers. You must not enter twice the numbers 28 and 9. You are not allowed to write down any intermediate result.

The optimal command sequence of key strokes is:
/2 / 8 / STO / MINUS / 9 / SUM / = / EXCHANGE / MINUS / RECALL / = /

The result of the key strokes:

2 : "2" is on the Display;
8 : "28" is on the Display;
STO : "28" is copied into the Memory;
MINUS : operator "substraction" is activated;
9 : "9" is on the Display, "28" disappears;
SUM : "9" is added to the content of the Memory, which is now "37";
= : "9" on the Display is replaced by the result of "28-9", i.e. "19": this shows the answer for "how much money has Jean now?";
EXCHANGE : "19" is in the Memory, and "37" on the Display: this shows the answer for "how much money has Paul now?";
MINUS : operator "substraction" is activated;
RECALL : "19" is copied from the Memory into the Display, it replaces "37" on the Display;
= : "19" on the Display is replaced by the result of "37-19", i.e. "18": this shows the answer for "how much money does Paul have more than Jean?"

Fig. 1 - An example of problem with constraints to be solved with a pocket calculator

The second group learnt the command device by predicting the effects of the successive commands in a command sequence. They were given the optimal command sequences for the word arithmetic problems given to the first group, but without the problem contexts. The subjects in this second group had only to predict the changing of the states of the Display and the Memory after each key stroke in a command sequence. This learning situation is in between the learning by observation and the learning by exploration situations.

The comparison of the performance of the two groups on the postests showed that the first group performed better in word arithmetic problems with constraints imposed on the use of the commands, and the second group performed better in the prediction situation.

This result seems trivial, but the lesson we have learned from it is that: the pocket calculator is designed for solving problems, so the best way to learn is to use it to solve problems!

4.2 Analogical transfer from a programming language to the learning of another programming language

Van Someren (1984), among others, found that students who already knew Pascal showed a strong tendency to transfer their knowledge in Pascal when they began to learn PROLOG. As an example, the following program was built by a beginner for the problem "find the smallest value of a list of numbers":

```
min([Head|Tail], Min) :-
    Min is Head, get_least(Tail, Min).
get_least([Head|Tail], Min) :-
    Head< Min, Min is Head, get_least([Head|Tail], Min).
get_least([Head|Tail], Min) :-
    get_least(Tail, Min).
min([], _) :- fail.
get_least([], Min).
```

One of the bugs in the first clause of get_least is "Head< Min, Min is Head". In PROLOG, a variable cannot have two different values in a same clause. So this clause always fails. It seems that the student wanted to reassign to the variable Min a new value in the case where the value of the variable Head is lesser than that of Min. In Pascal, it is quite legal to reassign a new value to a variable within a function. Moreover, the student seems to think that the goals (the predicates) in the body of the clause are commands to be executed in sequence.

In the study mentioned in section 3 (conducted by Françoise Youssefi) on learning PROLOG, we observed that the students who know LISP did not have very much difficulty to understand recursion in PROLOG, but the bugs in their programs showed clearly the interference of their knowledge of LISP. For example, in LISP a function call returns a value, but in PROLOG the notion of "returning a value" is unknown, there is only "instantiation of a variable". The following buggy program is typical from LISP people who are beginners in PROLOG:

The sum of the values of a list of numbers:

```
sumlist([Sum|[]]).
sumlist([Head|Tail]) :- sumlist(Tail, Sum1), Sum is Sum1+Head.
```

This buggy PROLOG program is almost a direct translation from a correct LISP program, as shown in the Figure 2.

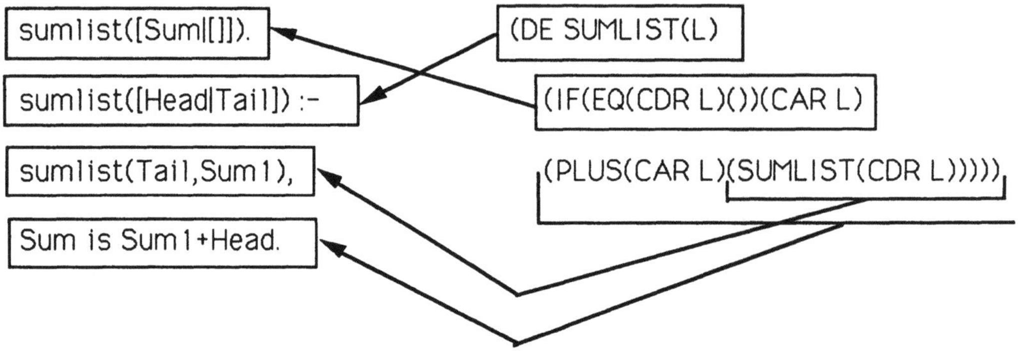

Fig. 2 - Buggy PROLOG program that looks like a translation of a correct LISP function into PROLOG

For his Master's, Eric Cabeira (1989) conducted a research in which he compared the performance of PROLOG beginners who know BASIC and naive beginners. He found that the BASIC beginners had great difficulty to build PROLOG programs for the problems they could very well solve in BASIC, such as sorting, deleting all the occurrences of a given object in a list...These students did not have more difficulty than the naive students with problems they were not used to solve, such as problems about family relationships, or composing a balanced menu...(the classical problems given to beginners in PROLOG). This result suggests that, for BASIC people, it is more difficult to build PROLOG programs for well known problems than to build PROLOG programs for relatively new ones.

4.3 Analogical transfer of a goal structure from the familiar domain of manipulation of physical objects

The experiment that will be described (Nguyen-Xuan & Hoc, 1987) in this section shows with more precise details the same type of result as mentioned above: if the learner has to solve a familiar problem with a command device he (she) does not know well, he (she) is prone to borrow a goal structure that is relevant in the familiar domain, but this goal structure may not be relevant for the device. Thus, somewhat paradoxically, problems that are too familiar to the learner may be more difficult than problems that are less familiar.

The experiment comprises three or four stages, depending on the way the subject will learn a command device. In the first stage, called the "diagnosis stage", we gave 17 to19-year-old male students a problem of sorting objects by their increasing value. The subject was given 11 match boxes marked with different letters, and had to order these boxes and place them along a line. To perform the task, the subject could ask questions of the experimenter about the relative value of any two boxes. The information was given in the form "box X has greater value than box Y". This task is isomorphic to the "weight seriation" task, a very popular task in the circle of Piagetian researchers. We observed that this task was easy for our subjects, and all the 22 subjects used the sorting method called "insertion".

In the second stage, called the "visible device" stage, we asked the subject to command a computer device to carry out the sorting task step by step. The elementary commands available were similar to elementary instructions of a basic-like programming language. The task consisted in sorting 7 letters by their value. The subject could see on the screen a 2 by 7 table, the 7 cells of the first row were filled with seven different letters. The cells of the second row were empty. The subjects were explained that the 14 cells represented the computer's "memories". The row and columns of the double-entry table were numbered (respectively, 1 to 2, and 1 to 7). The goal was to get the second row filled with the letters in a correct order. Figure 3 shows the screen and the available commands. These are:

COMPARE CELL(i,j) AND CELL(k,l) (i,k=1 or 2, and j,l=1,2,3...,7);
COPY CELL(i,j) INTO CELL(k,l);
DELETE CELL(i,j).

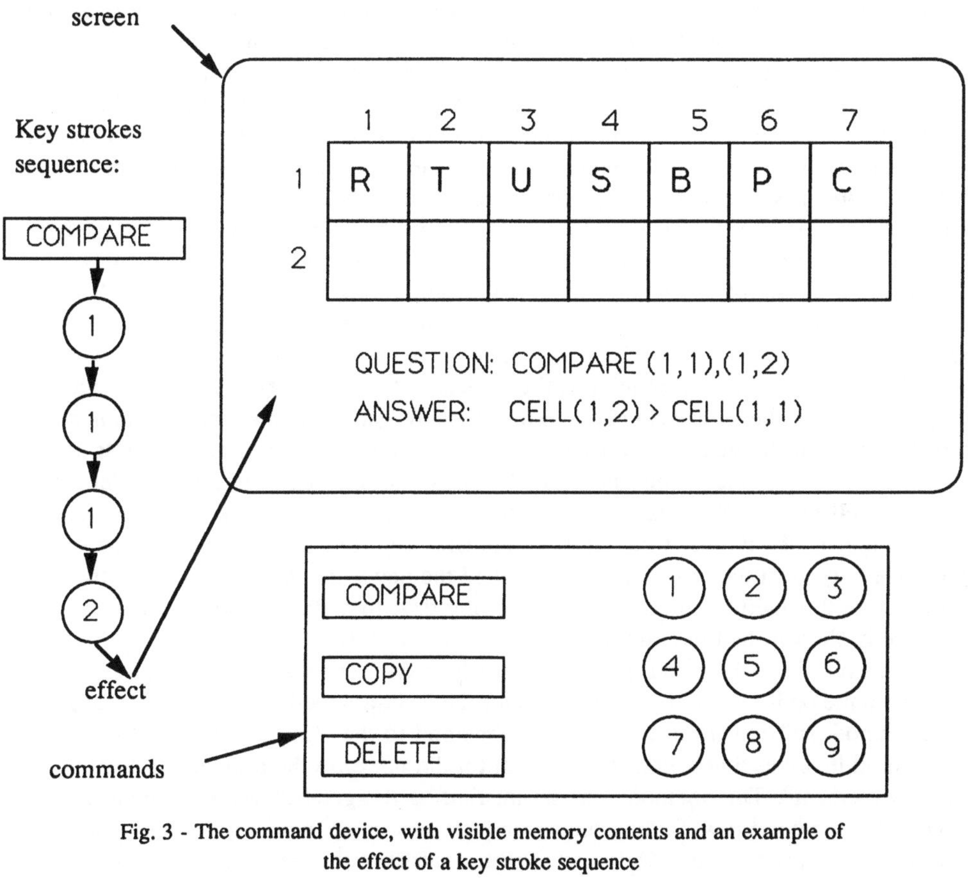

Fig. 3 - The command device, with visible memory contents and an example of the effect of a key stroke sequence

After the subject had completed successfully two successive problems, he went to the third stage.

In the third stage, called the "invisible device" stage, the 2 by 7 double-entry table was still visible, but the letters were no more visible. The subject was told that the only difference between the current situation and the preceding one was that he could no more see what was inside the cells which represented the computer "memories". If the subject solved two successive problems with a procedure (i.e. a command sequence) that was not optimal ("optimality" was defined as involving a minimum mental load), then he was given the fourth stage.

In the fourth stage, the subject had to solve the sorting problem with a device that had the same characteristics as the "invisible device" in the preceding stage. But this time, there were no longer two rows of cells. There was only one row of 7 cells which contained the 7 letters (that were invisible to the subject), and one separate empty cell called T (for "transit"). The subject had to change the location of the letters in the cells of the same row, so as to arrange them in a proper order. The task could be achieved by using the T-cell.

Individual protocol analyses showed that, in the second and the third stages, 21 out of 22 subjects tried very hard to apply the insertion method in the same way as in the box domain. The result I would like to emphasize is the following: half of the subjects did not succeed in finding an optimal procedure for the insertion method. The goal structure of this method can be described as an iterative sub-goal "make a new sub-series" by: 1/finding the relative rank of a new element N in a well sorted sub-series; 2/then inserting N in the sub-series.

The goal structure for finding the relative rank of the new element is the same in the match box world and in the device: the new element must be compared successively to the first, then the second, then the third... element of the sub-series. Its rank in the sub-series is identified when two adjacent elements are found so that one element is greater and the other element is smaller than the new element to be inserted into the sub-series.

But for inserting a new element into a sub-series, the goal structure is not the same between the match box world and the command device. In the box situation, to insert a new box N into the rth place of a line of boxes, the subject can use the box N as an "instrument" to push a whole row of boxes (comprising the boxes from the rth rank to the last of the sub-series) towards the right, so as to make room for the new box N; he can then lay down the box N. This action of inserting a box may be represented by the subject as two elementary actions: "make room", and "place box". In the device situation, to insert a new element into a series, there is no single command to reach the goal "make room". A sequence of commands is needed as shown in figure 4: copy each element from the rth rank one cell to the right, and the first element to be copied one cell to the right must be the rightmost element of the well sorted sub-series.

The subjects who did not find out this command sequence tried to insert the new element in the same way as in the box world: they copied the new element from the first row into the rth cell where this element must be. But by doing this, they deleted the element that was in this cell, this element had the rank (r+1) in the new sub-series.

After many trials (the experiment lasted a whole day for most subjects), 11 subjects (out of 22) found the optimal command sequence for the insertion method; 9 subjects changed their sorting method, shifting from the "insertion" method to the "find the greatest" method. The latter method involves a new goal structure, but it did not raise the problem of "making room for a new element". This method consists in: finding the greatest value, copying it into the first cell of the second row, finding the second greatest value, copying it into the second cell of the second row, and so on... Only two subjects sticked to the insertion method and managed to memorize the cell of the first row where they could find the lost element to copy it into the (r+1)th cell of the second row. But the consequence of this action is the deletion of the element that must be placed into the (r+2)th cell. So it is necessary to memorize in which cell of the first row this lost element must be searched for and copied into the (r+2)th cell of the second row, and so forth... These two subjects had a very good memory: we gave them sorting problems with 11 elements (hence a 2 by 11 double-entry table), they still successfully applied their memory demanding insertion method. We gave up!

The second result I would like to point out is the following. In the fourth stage, the imposed constraint "not to use a second row of cells" was such that the optimal command sequence based on the "find the greatest" method was the only way to obtain a well sorted series. Among the subjects who shifted from the "insertion" method to a "find the greatest" method in the third stage, eight built up command sequences that were not optimal. They were then given the fourth stage. And all but one subject who had been given this fourth stage of the experiment succeeded (within four to ten trials). This result suggests that constraints may be useful when they compel the subject to reach the goal by only the optimal solution path.

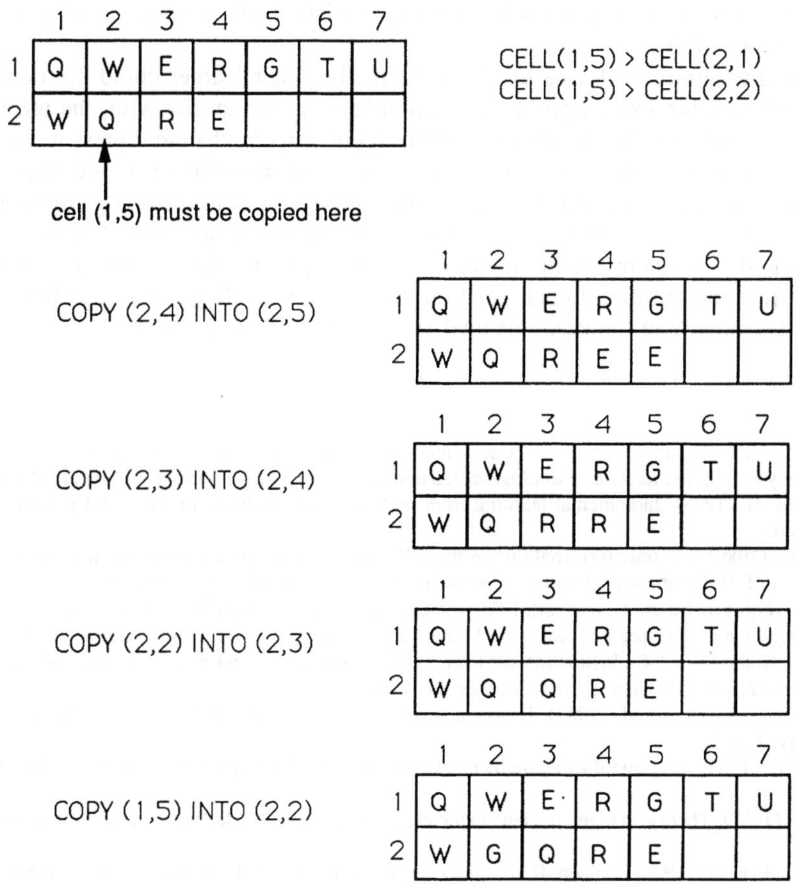

Fig. 4 - Optimal command sequence for inserting a new element: the contents of cell (1,5)

5. Making analogical transfer profitable

The results I have presented suggest that the learning of a command device involves very frequently the use of knowledge from a familiar domain to build a problem representation. The more the problem is well known to the subject in a familiar domain, the greater the tendency to build a precise goal structure on the basis of the operators that are available in this familiar domain. If the goal structure is relevant for the device, the transfer is beneficial. But it may happen that this goal structure is irrelevant for the device.

However, beginners cannot be given problems that are totally new to them, simply because they cannot understand them. That is to say that analogical transfer is inevitable. Note that the use of analogy is a very natural (and cognitively economical) way for understanding new concepts. And it has been shown that teaching new concepts by analogy lead to successful results (Brown, 1989), particularly when the teacher introduces multiple analogy (Burstein, 1988, Spiro et al., 1989).

In learning a command device by doing, as the beginner learner could not do else than borrow a representation from a problem situation he (she) is familiar with, the teacher (or a tutoring system) had better try to make use of this representation than to repress it. The teacher must carefully choose problems so that it is possible to figure out the way the beginners will represent them, i.e. the goal structures they are prone to build. This knowledge of the learner's problem representation helps the teacher to design problem situations in which some constraints may be imposed. These constraints must, on one hand, allow the learner to borrow useful information from the familiar domain, and on the other hand, oblige him (her) to modify the imported goal structure in the case this goal structure is irrelevant for the device.

Literature

1. Anderson, J.R., & Thompson, R. (1989). Use of analogies in production system architecture. In S. Vosniadou & A. Ortony (eds.), *Similarity and analogical reasoning*. New York: Cambridge University Press.
2. Burstein, M. H. (1988). Incremental learning from multiple analogy. In A. Prieditis (Ed.), *Analogica*. London: Pitman.
3. Cabeira, E. (1989). Le transfert analogique dans l'apprentissage du fonctionnement d'un dispositif de commande différé de nature déclarative. Master dissertation, Université de Paris VIII.
4. Friemel, E., Nguyen-Xuan, A., Richard, J.F., Tremezaygues, A., Weil-Barais, A. (1983). Apprendre à utiliser une calculette à mémoire par des élèves de 11 à 13 ans. Rapport de contrat INRP-Université de VIII.
5. Shrager, J., Klahr, D. (1986). Instructionless learning about a complex device: the paradigm and observations. *International Journal of Man-Machine Studies, 25*, 153-189.
6. Nguyen-Xuan, A., Hoc, J.M. (1987). Learning to use a command device. *European Bulletin of Cognitive Psychology, 7*, 5-31.
7. Richard, J.F. (1983). Logique du fonctionnement et logique de l'utilisation. Rapport de Recherche INRIA, N°202.
8. Shrager, J. (1987). Theory change via view application in instructionless learning. *Machine Learning, 2*, 247-276.
9. Spiro, R.J. , Feltovich, P.J., Coulson, R.L., Anderson, D.K. (1989). Multiple analogies for complex concepts: antidote for analogy-induced misconception in advance knowledge acquisition. In S. Vosniadou & A. Ortony (eds.), *Similarity and analogical reasoning*. New York: Cambridge University Press.
10. Sweller, J. (1988). Cognitive load during problem solving: effects on learning. *Cognitive Science*, 12, 257-285.
11. Van Someren, M. (1984). Misconceptions of beginning PROLOG programmers. Department of Experimental Psychology, University of Amsterdam.
12. Youssefi, F. (1988). Categorization of errors due to transfer in learning PROLOG. Working Paper, Université de Paris VIII.

Ergonomics for Hypermedia Courseware

Claude Bastien

Université de Provence, France

Ergonomics for hypermedia courseware, and more generally for all computer assisted systems, must be considered at two levels:

1. a deep level which is global and deals with the architecture and the functionality of the interface between a computer system and a human user;
2. a superficial level, more technical, which is concerned with practical aspects.

In our view the second must be derived from the first. However it seems that the problems in ergonomics have been often directly tackled through the second level. Thus can be explained, in our opinion, that the most of the studies which have been carried out in this field have provided fragmentary, and sometimes conflicting, results.

Let us consider *the first level*, i.e. the deep one.

On the one hand we have a system which has to respect its own requirements (such as memory access paths, knowledge representation, etc.). In addition, since it is a computer system, it cannot work otherwise than by way of logical operations (that means algorithms or predicate calculation, for example). On the other hand, we have a human cognitive system, the architecture of which is uncommonly complicated and remains still unknown for a large part at present, we must admit it. What we know however is that the human cognitive system generally doesn't resort to strong logical reasoning, in processing the situations it has to solve or in learning the knowledge it has to acquire.

So the problem can be seen as follows: how to allow the communication between two sytems that work quite differently?

Two types of solutions have been attempted. The first, since it is the most evident, has consisted of trying to compel the human subject to model his behaviour on the machine's working processes. All things considered, this way obliges the subject to learn the computer's functioning before he can hope to get an aid from the system. Even this aid is not certain - everybody knows systems which run perfectly on the condition that they are used only by their own creator. The second type of solution is the opposite. In this case the purpose lies in adapting the system to the subject's thought processes. But, in our view, an insurmontable difficulty arises on this way. At the present state of our knowledge we are unable to implement anything except processes which are the object of formal logics. Whereas, in all probability, we need to use non-monotonic logics in order to be able to simulate human cognitive processes. Unfortunately such logics are not available on computers, at least at present.

So the previous ways seem to have failed. Doubtless they were too simplistic. It becomes apparent that a successful way would lie in building what can be called an "intelligent interface".

An intelligent interface must be made of three components 1) a representation of the computer system 2) a representation of the user system 3) an interpreter which is the heart of the interface. Of course the representations of the systems are not the systems themselves:

— the representation of the computer system must specify what the system knows and the "format" of this knowledge (that is semantic nets, rules, schemas, ...). Note that, at the level of the interface, there is no need for a representation of how the system works. Under these conditions, representing the computer system is rather easy.

— the second component, that is the representation of the user system, is, of course, more difficult. It depends on the cognitive theory which is supported. For example, from a strongly behaviourist point of view the only need lies in describing the set of stimuli and the corresponding set of issues available. On the other hand, according to Anderson's act theory for example we have to represent the ways by which both declarative and procedural knowledge are accessed. Either in this case it is not necessary to provide a representation of how the user works (that means by analogy, by inference,...).

— the third component, the interpreter, is the most tricky too. Its function is essentially to translate the outputs of one of the two systems into inputs for the other. At its minimum level it consists of a matching process that works on both the representations. At it maximum level it must work as a parser.

Building such an intelligent interface certainly could appear as a too ambitious project. In fact it would be but only if the purpose would be to build an universal interface, capable of working with anyone about any problem. However it is not our aim. I am convinced of the possibility of reaching this goal under the condition that the interface would be concerned with a very strictly limited knowledge domain.

I would like to give an example. We are currently working on a project, the aim of which is a computer aided system. The purpose of this system is to help the operators who have the responsability to watch the reactor on board of an atomic powered submarine. In our research team are engineers from the French navy, researchers in artificial intelligence and cognitive psychologists. The central part of the project lies precisely in building an intelligent interface. We approached the problem from a very restricted point of view. Indeed we have selected only two events one occurs often in a normal driving situation (it is about a demand of increased power); the second constitutes a technical hitch (here a breakdown of a pump). So the domain of the involved knowledge can be clearly delimited. Then it becomes possible to test a model of the cognitive processes used by the operators. (The tests are made on a simulator with experienced operators). On the other hand there is no particular difficulty in determining the knowledge which is relevant in order to elaborate the computer system. When the model and the system will be perfected (we are presently working on them) we expect that we will be able to build the interface itself. In fact, since we have conceived it from the beginning, the other parts have been optimized in order to reach this goal. One could object that a system which is able to provide an help in only two cases is a poor system! We agree with this. But if the system is efficient in these two cases we have a strong hope that it will be easy to improve it. However this improvement will stay limited to the scope of watching a submarine's reactor.

So, in this section, it is emphazised that the ergonomic problems cannot be divorced from the rest. They must be an integral part of the whole system. In fact, if the ergonomic problems are considered after the rest of the system they might prove to be insolvable. Thus what was called the deep level must guide the decisions which must be taken at the superficial level.

However these decisions cannot be *directly* derived from the deep level. The deep level must be used as a frame. There are specific requirements which deal with *the superficial level* and I would try to examine them now.

Regarding the subject, ergonomics is concerned both by his perceptual processes and by the processing load the communication requires. We can consider the problems from three points of view:

— the response modality (i.e. the inputs of the computer system)

— the information displayed (i.e. the outputs of the computer system)

— the control of the subject's navigation (i.e. where the subject is in the system at a given time).

The response modality is certainly the question which creates the least difficulties. Three modalities are usually employed the keyboard, the mouse and, more rarely, the sensitive screens. Because of the well known parallax phenomenon, the sensitive screens (as the electronic pencils) don't allow an exact pointing on limited surfaces. Using keyboard implies more often that the available keys must be clearly located; if not the response system becomes a task in itself. So can be explained the success of the mouse system which is the easiest. In our own experiments we have observed that very young children (they were 5 years old) could learn to move the mouse and to click in only four or five minutes. So it seems there is no problem here.

On the other hand **the display of information** is a real problem which has been the object of a lot of studies. These studies can be classified in three categories depending on wether they deal with the nature, the quality or the amount of information.

The nature of information can be essentially sounds, pictures or text. There is no doubt that the recent progress in new technologies such as video-disks, vocal synthesis, etc., offer new possibilities which are far from being mastered at present. However it seems that all these types of information have been studied separately. Some researchers have studied the text in human-computer interaction (for example Richard et al., 1986, Ben Schneiderman, 1988, Payne, 1987). Others have studied how human subjects investigate pictures (see for example Galitz, 1985, Van Nes, 1986 or Rogers & Oborne, 1987). Finally a few studies have been carried out in order to compare different types of information. Even the good question is not "what is the best type of information in this problem", but "what type of information must be displayed according to the cognitive process that the subject is currently managing". For example we are working on testing the hypothesis that the pictures would be useful in general planning processes (as setting goals for instance), while text would be useful in local monitoring processes (as subgoal achievement for instance).

The quality of the information can be viewed as a problem of classical ergonomics. In fact it concerns in particular the size, the colour and the location of information. In this domain can be directly applied what we know from the great number of studies which have taken place in the field of the perceptual processes.

Finally *the amount of information* is clearly related to the processing load that it implies. So it depends less on the amount of information itself than on the operations the subject has to perform from this information. We shall speak about it in the last section.

The third category of problem, at the superficial level, is **the control of the subject's navigation**. It seems that it is a very important problem, especially in hypermedia courseware. Inded Object-Oriented Languages (as Hypertalk) allow a very great number of possible paths, that is to say "voyages" in almost unlimited number. So the first problem is to be able to situate at every moment where the subject is in the system. It can be solved by keeping the "trace";

the most of the systems at our disposition are capable of doing it. The second problem is that the subject himself needs to know where he/she is and what are the paths available from this point. A classical solution consists of displaying "menus" continuously. But in rather complex systems it becomes necessary to update the menus regularly. Then the main problem is to determine the type of nodes which are displayed (i.e. the nearest specific nodes or the more general?) I have a tendancy to believe that the efficiency of a system often depends on the manner in which this question is managed.

Now I would like to mention two more general questions.

The first one is the **role played by time** in using Hypermedia courseware. As soon as he progresses, the user becomes more and more expert in using the system. So the information which is needed at the beginning can become progressively irrelevant and, in some cases, even can become an handicap. Consider a very simple example. In all the tutorials can be found, at minimum, a signal, the function of which is to tell the subject if he is right or wrong. At the beginning this signal must be displayed during 6 or 8 seconds in order to be correctly understood. After 10 or 15 trials this duration becomes too long and introduces a disturbing break in the subject's activity. It is this kind of problem which has been solved on computers by offering the possibility of using a "short cut keyboard" instead of clicking on a menu. In spite of the fact that the solutions are not at all evident, I am convinced that a good interface is an interface which is capable of evolving according to the degree of mastery exhibited by the user.

The second general question is the following. I believe that there is no absolute rules in ergonomics. In other words I think that ergonomic instructions cannot be deducted from only the objective properties of the situation which is offered. The real problem is about how we think the subject will react to what is offered. So we have to return to the deep level. Let us consider a last illustration.

We have designed a tutorial for learning logical negation by children who were from 6 to 8 years old (Bastien et al., 1990). The problem consists of picking out all the objects which have not some properties. For example, among a set of marbles, we ask the child to select "all the marbles that are not transparent big and blue". Then how can we determine the number and the properties of the marbles that must be displayed? How can we determine the type of information which must be given to the subject when he fails? The answer clearly depends on the hypothesis we have regarding the child's behaviour and regarding the learning process we assume to be the right one. In our view the concept of negation is strongly related to the representation of the objects. In brief the negativity is applied to the features of the object which can be conceived as attributes. So can we observe that the most of the children at this stage produce partial negation (for example for "not big transparent blue" they pick only the opaque marbles. Only the feature "transparency" is taken as an attribute). Then the goal of the tutorial is to induce the child to transform into attributes all the features. This goal is achieved by modifying the question when the child says he/she was finished after producing a partial negation. The new question includes only the properties that are relevant in the remaining material (so in the previous example the question becomes "give me all the marbles that are not big, blue"). From the deep level we have chosen to present the structure of a partial product. This was necessary for testing our hypothesis. From the superficial level we have chosen to present at all 21 elements in order to avoid that the child can use particular strategies based on perceptual pregnancy. From the deep level we have decided to modify the question according to the remaining material. From the superficial level we have decided to present the question on a special card, because the whole sreen was covered with the drawings of the marbles. But now we are not sure that this decision has not induced the child to see the new question as setting on a new problem...

In summary we have commuted continuously between the deep level (symbolic information processing) and the superficial level (perceptual requirements).

Conclusion

In conclusion, all the authors are convinced of the importance of ergonomics in designing tutorials and other computer aided systems. Mandl emphasized this in 1988. More recently Anderson et al. (1990) have written that "we have learned that design of the interface can make or break the effectiveness of the tutor". I agree with them. What I would add was that ergonomic problems are not independant of the whole system. They must be managed from the beginning and from the point of view of all the tools that the subject has at his disposition for processing information. So we have to take into account the subject's processes both at their high level and at their low level, that is to say we have to practice cognitive psychology.

Literature

1. Anderson, J. R., Boyle, C. F., Corbett, A. T. & Lewis, M. W., Cognitive modeling and intelligent tutoring. *Artificial Intelligence* (1990) **42** 7-49
2. Bastien, C., Pelissier, A. & Tete, A., An experiment of learning logical negation by 6- and 7-year-old children. *C. P. C. European Bulletin of Cognitive Psychology* (1990) **10** 45-63.
3. Ben Schneiderman, M., We can design better user interfaces a review of human-computer interaction styles. *Ergonomics* (1988) **0** 1-12.
4. Galitz W. O., *Handbook of screen format design*. North-Holland, New York 1985.
5. Mandl, H., Introduction *International Journal of Educational Research* (1988) **12**, 793-798.
6. Payne, S. J., Complex problem spaces modeling the knowledge needed to use interactive devices in H. J. Bullinger & B. Shackel (Eds) *Human computer interaction*. Elsevier Science Publishers, Amsterdam 1987.
7. Richards, J. N. J., Bez, H. E., Gittins, D. T. & Cooke, R. On methods for interface specification and design *International Journal for Man-Machine Studies* (1986) **24** 545-568.
8. Rogers, Y. & Oborne, D. J., Pictorial communication of abstract verbs in relation to human-computer interaction *British Journal of Psychology* (1987) **78** 99-112.
9. Van Nes, F. L., Space, colour and typography on visual display terminals *Behaviour and Information Technology* (1986) **5** 99-118.

Adding Intelligence to Hypertext with Expert Systems and Adding Usability to Expert Systems with Hypertext

David H. Jonassen

Sherwood Wang, University of Colorado, USA

1. Introduction: System Components

1.1 Hypertext

Hypertext refers to a non-sequential, non-linear method for organizing and displaying text. It was designed to enable the reader to access information from a text in ways that are most meaningful (Nelson, 1981), based upon the assumption that the organization that the reader imposes on a text is more meaningful than that proferred by the author.

The most pervasive characteristic of hypertext is the node, which consists of chunks or fragments of text, graphics, video or other information. The size and modality of a node varies from a single picture or a few words to the size of a large document. Nodes are the basic unit of information storage in a hypertext. Modularizing information enables the user of the information system to determine what chunk of information to access next. Another important characteristic of nodes in many hypertext systems is that they are amendable or modifiable by the user. The user may add to or change the information in a node or create his or her own nodes of information.

The organization of a hypertext, that is, the interrelationships between the nodes, is defined by the links that interconnect the nodes. Links in hypertext systems are typically associative, that is, they define an associative relationship between the node pairs that they connect. The links transport the user through the information space to the nodes that are selected, enabling the user to navigate through the knowledge base. The node structure and the link structure form a network of ideas in the knowledge base, the interrelated and interconnected group or system of ideas.

Hypermedia permits the user to determine the sequence in which to acess information (browsing), to add or amend the information in order to make it more personally meaningful (collaboration), or to build and structure their own knowledge base. Like most information systems, interaction is one of the most important attributes. Hypertext information systems permit more dynamic user control of the information in the knowledge base.

1.2 Expert Systems

Expert systems, an application of artificial intelligence, are intended to capture and make accessible the operational knowledge of an expert. An expert system is an "intelligent computer program that uses knowledge and inferential procedures to solve problems that are difficult enough to require significant human expertise for the solution (Harmon & King, 1985). Expert systems seek to use those procedures and inferences to model the thought processes of an expert practitioner. The expert possesses the knowledge (facts, principles, strategies) that enables him or her to make decisions and solve problems. In order to be useful for building expert system knowledge bases, this knowledge needs to be translated into facts and heuristics.

Most expert systems are logic programming systems (Denning, 1986), where the heuristic knowledge of the expert is converted into logical operations (most often in the form of IF - THEN rules) which are then converted into programming operations. Expert systems are usually built in declarative languages such as Lisp or Prolog or in higher level knowledge engineering shells where the computer translates the rules into computer programs. Shells are either rule-based or object-oriented (frame based).

Most expert systems are rule-based, consisting of hierarchical networks of IF-THEN rules. Rules are fired by searching the conclusions first (backward chaining) or by searching the premises for the co-occurence of certain values (forward chaining). When the search conditions are satisfied, the rule is applied. Applying a rule may access another rule, query the user, or take some action. Rule-based systems are said to reflect procedural knowledge of the expert.

Object-oriented systems store information in frames and slots which contain facts, pointers to other objects, or rules. This combination allows the objects to be interrelated to each other in different ways. In objected-oriented systems, slots may inherit information from other objects rather than creating duplicative objects. The structure of object-oriented expert systems more resembles that of hypertext (discussed above) than rule-based systems. Object-oriented systems contain more declarative knowledge than rule-based systems.

Expert systems are used for solving finite classes of problems, such as troubleshooting, diagnosis and correction (especially in medicine). Most expert systems are also able to explain the reasoning leading to the solution of a problem. Expert systems are able to make decisions as well as experts in various fields, because their structures reflect the manner in which human experts arrange and make inferences from their knowledge (Michaelson, Mickie, & Boulanger, 1985).

2. Adding Usability to Expert System Advisors with Hypertext

2.1 Expert Systems as Intelligent Job Aids

One of the most popular applications of expert systems is an intelligent job aid (Harmon, 1987; Tieman & Markle, 1984). A job aid is any structured information device that an individual consults to help perform some task. Job aids are often used in place of instruction when the task performance is simple enough and non-recurrent. Job aids use linear, algorithmic logic to ensure that the performer is able to complete the task correctly. Expert systems can perform as job aids more effectively than traditional, print, linear job aids because they can represent more complex problems and because they do not use a linear procedure to solve the problem, like most job aids. The reasoning pattern of an expert system is more flexible. Welsh and Wilson (1987) have identified characteristics of expert systems as intelligent job aids:

* They engage the user in a dialogue rather than a sequence of operations.
* They are capable of handling somewhat ambiguous situations (there is a limit to the level of ambiguity that is tolerable).

* They make expert knowledge more available to the task performer.

* They explain choices, decisions, or procedures.

An intelligent job aid can achieve the same results as a traditional job aid with a broader class of problems while engaging the user in thinking about the process.

2.2 IDD Advisor

The IDD Advisor is an on-going project designed to use expert systems as an intelligent job aid for assisting instructional designers, teachers, or course writers to follow the instructional design and development (IDD) process (Jonassen, 1989a). The IDD Advisor is also an intelligent front end to a database containing the components of the instructional sequence being developed, so that as instructional decisions are made, the results of those decisions are stored in a database.

The IDD Advisor is a structured rule-based expert system comprised of several rule sets, the organization of which is illustrated in the context tree in Figure 1. Each node represents a separate rule base which, provides consultation on separate processes in the overall IDD process.

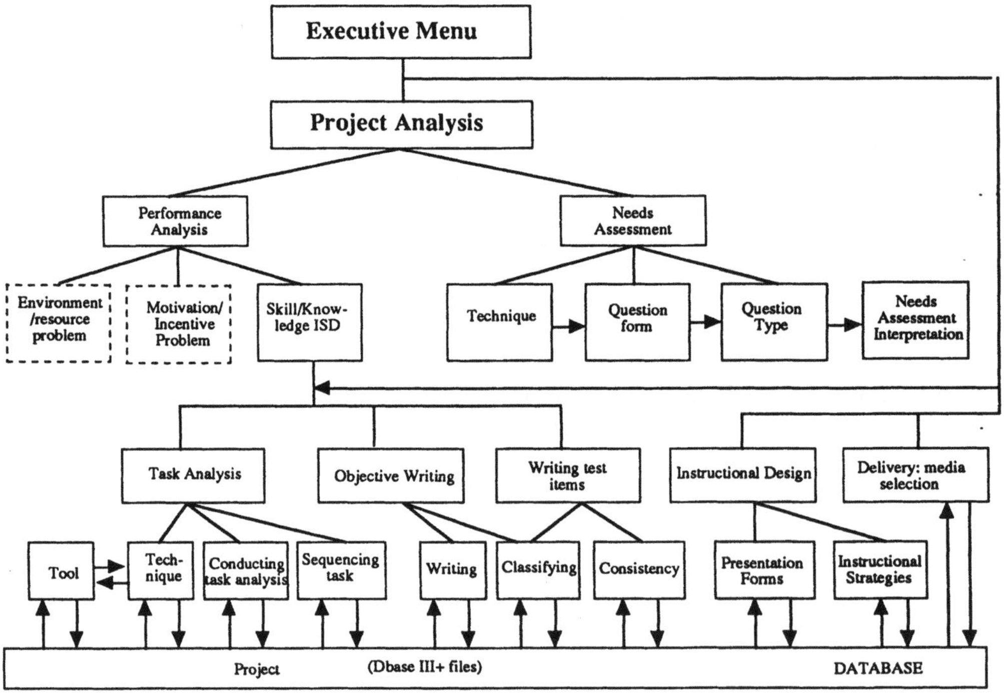

Fig. 1 - Context tree for IDD Advisor

IDD is a useful area for development because of the problem solving nature of the process thast requires numerous informed decisions.

2.3 Problems with Expert Systems

Novices often experience difficulties when consulting expert systems, because of unusable interfaces, lack of familiarity with the functioning of the expert system shell, and lack of mental scripts and schemata for the information being queried or the tasks being represented by the expert system. Poorly designed expert systems interfaces may not be readily usable. Knowledge engineers who produce the expert systems are often more concerned about the content than they are the interface. Second, the novice may not possess adequate declarative knowledge of the subject to be able to make proper decisions or understand the advice that is proferred by the system. When facts about a particular situation are not known by the expert system, it queries the user to gain knowledge. If users do not possess the knowledge necessary for making decisions required by the system, the conclusions will not be valid. For instance, in order to select an appropriate instructional strategy using an expert system advisor, it is necessary to classify the learning outcome. If novice users are not skilled in classifying outcomes, the information that they provide when queried will most likely be incorrect which will invalidate the advice provided by the expert system. Novices need assistance in understanding the problem and making decisions required by the problem. Not all of the information can be encoded in the expert system, especially when it is being used as a job aid. The advice from the expert system will be integrated into the novices knowledge structure only if the novice possesses adequate conceptual knowledge of the process. Therefore, an advisor needs to provide background conceptual information along with the rules that help the novice make decisions. The novice needs declarative knowledge before s/he can understand the procedural knowledge represented in the expert systems.

2.4 Solution: Hypertext Interface and Help System

A solution to the interface and schema-deficiency problems described above is to integrate a hypertext-based user interface and online help system with the expert system. The interface and help system facilitate access to the information and provide the declarative knowledge needed to make decisions and interpret the results of the consultation.

Hypertext-based interfaces and help systems are being developed to support two of the IDD Advisor rule bases, the media selection and instructional tactics rule bases. HyperCard has been used to develop the user interface and the online help system.The user interface presents each decision as a node or screen. For instance, deciding on which learning outcome is represented by the objective (the most important variable in most instructional decision making) requires familiarity with the major types of learning outcomes as specified by Gagne, 1985). Clicking on "More Information" accesses a structured help system which provides a description and examples of various learning outcomes and node sets on each type of learning outcome (see Figure 2), each of which provides a description, examples, practice in classifying, and instructional implications of each type of learning outcome (the antecedent of the rules related to learning outcomes in the knowledge base. So the hypertext help system provides the user with declarative information necessary for making each of the decisions in the knowledge base. After making all of the prerequisite decisions about other variables in the instructional situation (such as instructional event, modality, type of strategy to be used, and so on), HyperCard sends all of the variables and values to the expert system to process. The expert system evaluates its rules with the information provided by the user and sends its recommendations back to HyperCard to display. The recommendations are three or fewer instructional tactics from a list of over 100 (Jonassen, Grabinger, and Harris, 1990).

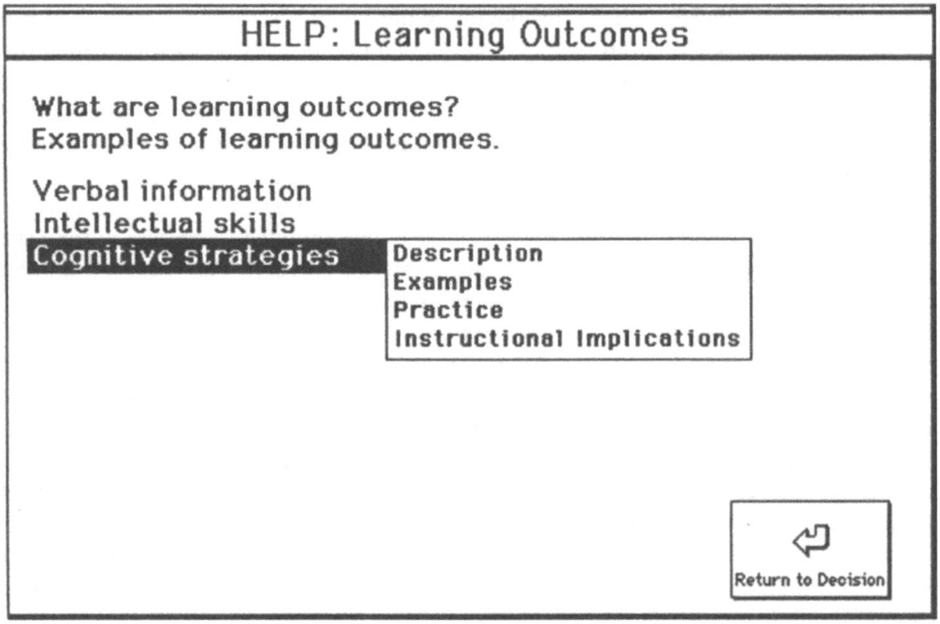

Fig. 2 - Hypertext help system menu

Just as it is improbable that learners are familiar with all of the decision criteria, it is less probable that they are familiar with all of the recommended tactics that may be supplied by the expert system. A help system is being developed that will provide descriptions, examples, instructional implications, and references to information available on each of the recommendations. For instance, if the expert system recommends graphic organizers, by clicking on the term in the solution box, users may access a node set that provides a description, examples, implications, or references on graphic organizers. Help systems represent one of the most common and effective uses of hypertext (Jonassen, 1989b). Hypertext help systems are appearing on many commercial application software packages. Their addition to expert systems can only increase the usability and functionality of expert system advisors.

2.5 Results

Formative evaluation of the system with a limited number of users has indicated that users are willing to use the help system if their knowledge is deficient. However, the advice that is available for novice users of the system is not always adequate. For instance, help screens including examples and limited practice are insufficient to enable novice users to accurately classify learning outcomes. This decision, like most of the others required of the users, is a complex, coordinate concept outcome that requires more instruction. We are exploring options, including the addition of more interactive instructional activities to the help system or the integration of other expert system rule bases. These rule bases will be executed by the help button on the interface screen, in addition to or in lieu of the hypertext help system. For instance, if a user is experiencing difficulty in classifying the learner outcomes, the the expert system will utilize a classification rule base that leads the user through the classification process. The comparative efficacy of hypertext-based vs. expert system-based help systems for supporting expert system utilization needs to be examined. Usability of expert systems is more complicated than navigation issues that concerns hypertext designers.

3. Building an Intelligent Tutor from Hypertext and Expert Systems

3.1 Intelligent Tutoring Systems

Intelligent tutoring systems (ITS) must pass three tests before they are deemed intelligent (Burns & Capps, 1988). First the subject matter content or expertise must be encoded into the system so that the system can access the information, draw inferences or solve problems. Second, the system must be able to assess the learner's acquisition of that knowledge. Third, tutorial strategies must be designed in order to reduce the discrepancy between the expert's knowledge and the learner's knowledge. ITSs consist of an expert model which defines the knowledge domain, a student model which is able to define the student's knowledge at any point during instruction, a tutor which generates appropriate instructional interactions based upon the discrepancy between the expert and the student, and a user interface which enables the learner to interact with the ITS in a meaningful and efficient way. The interface often encompasses an environment, consisting of tools, scenarios, simulations and the like. The most significant dimension of ITS is the ability to model the student's knowledge. Traditional computer-based instruction adapted to specific elements of student performance without integrating them into a model of what the student knows. Modelling the knowledge enables the tutor to more effectively map the expert's knowledge onto the learner's.

3.2 Problem

Intelligent tutors are expensive and complex to develop because of the knowledge engineering and programming requirements, and they are expensive to implement because of the computational requirements. Of all of the intelligent tutoring systems (ITS) reviewed by Wenger (1987) and Polson and Richardson (1988), none run on personal computers, and all have required large development teams to produce tutors on limited topics. If ITS is to impact education, they must be developed for popular PCs using available software. ITS models, procedures, and even (to the extent possible) templates must be built and disseminated before ITS significantly impacts instruction.

3.3 Solution

Jonassen, Grabinger, and Wang (1990) demonstrated different integrations of hypertext and expert systems. In addition to using hypertext as a front-end interface and back-end help system for expert systems (discussed above), expert systems can function as diagnostic tools for accessing information in a hypertext knowledge base, for describing the expert's knowledge base in order to prescribe the most productive learning paths, or as a means for modelling student learning. Hypertext, if properly designed to reduce navigation, integration and synthesis problems (Jonassen & Grabinger, 1990), provides a very usable interface that can supplant most of the need for natural language. Our working hypothesis is that these capabilities replicate most if not all of the functionality of and intelligent tutoring systems (ITS).

3.4 Hypertext/Expert System Tutoring System

The Physics Tutor is a prototype instructional physics information base designed to familiarize students with the basic concepts in rectilinear Newtonian physics. It models the expert's knowledge in the node and link structure of the hypertext and in an expert system. It models the knowledge of the student by analyzing responses to declarative, structural, and procedural knowledge questions. Interactivity is emphasized in the program at several levels. It is a mixed-initiative instructional system (Carbonell, 1970), permitting the learner to query the system for information or structuring student queries in order to model his/her current state of knowledge. The system supports user queries through its browsing capability which is a fundamental compponent of hypertext systems. Browsing in the Physics Tutor is facilitated by a graphical overview (see Figure 3) which allows the user to select information as well as illustrating the structural interrelationships of the ideas and rules in the hypertext knowledge base. There are also two modes of structured browsing in the system.

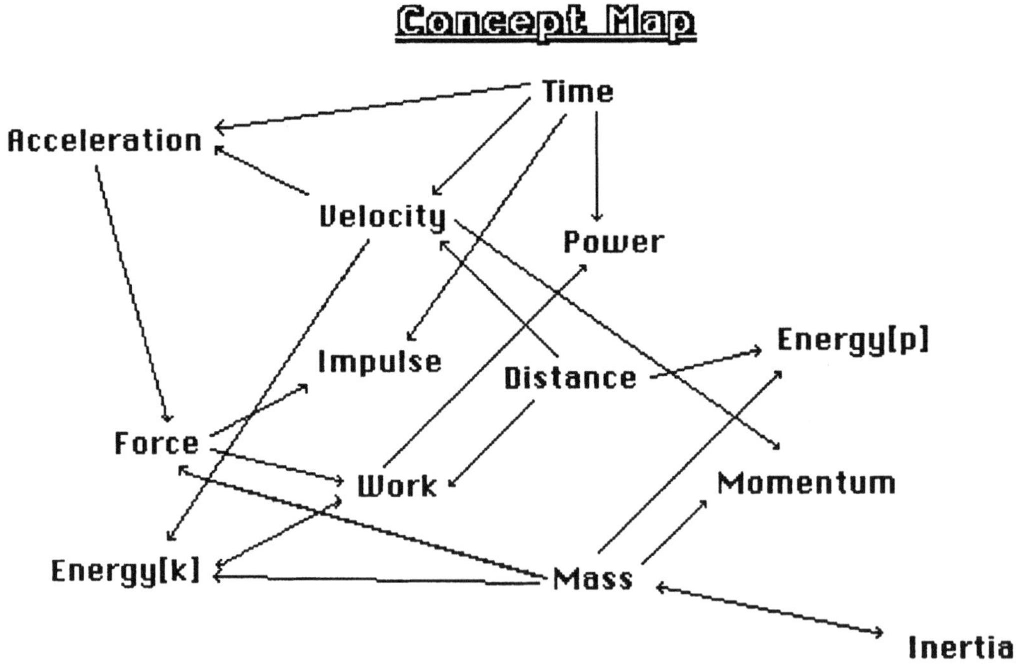

Fig. 3 - Concept map in physics tutor

3.5 Expert Model

Physics was chosen as a subject matter domain because it possesses a highly stable and well-defined semantic structure (Jonassen, 1987). The expert model is defined in terms of a semantic network, the network of concepts and their interrelationships to each other. Structural networks are composed of nodes (schema) and ordered, labelled relationships (links) connecting them (Norman, Gentner & Stevens, 1976). These networks describe what the expert knows, which provides the foundations for the hypertext information model. This is important because hypertext can explicitly model the expert's knowledge structure as well as providing sophisticated instructional transactions that elicit any type of information processing desired (Jonassen, 1989; Jonassen & Mandl, 1990). Several reliable techniques can be used to model the semantic network of the expert onto the hypertext information model (Jonassen, 1990). This semantic network can then be mapped explicitly onto the hypertext, implicitly in terms of the node-link structure and explicitly using a graphical browser (see Figure 3).

Expert system knowledge bases are also used to model the content and prescribe appropriate instructional sequences. A series of expert systems have been developed to provide the expert model in the Physics Tutor. The rule bases begin with each concept as its root and determines the optimal structural paths between the root concept and every other concept. These expert systems provides the metric for defining the relevancy of a property in terms of a given concept (Carbonell, 1970). Carbonell defined relevancy as the distance from one node to another in a semantic network. All intervening nodes between the root and the destination nodes are within the context of that node. The distance (in terms of intervening nodes) provides a "threshold of relevancy." This expert system depicts the most efficient and meaningful interrelationships between the root and every other concept. Simply by clicking on a "Relate" button on the definition node for each concept, the user accesses this structural information. The hypertext queries the user to determine the concept that s/he wishes to relate to the root and then writes that information in a text file to the expert system, which determines the best sequence. By clicking on a "Show Path" button, the learner is shown the optimal path and then presented the concepts in that sequence. So, in addition to modelling the expert, this expert system determines an optimal instructional sequence for the learner. That is, it can function both as an expert model and a tutorial model.

3.6 Student Model

The student model is determined by assessing the learners declarative, structural, and procedural knowledge of the content. Declarative knowledge is the awareness of ideas while procedural knowledge describes the ability of the learner to use or apply that knowledge (Anderson, 1981). Procedural knowledge is associeted with higher order thinking skills, while declarative normally refers to recall of the information. Structural knowledge (sometimes included in the declarative knowledge domain) refers to knowledge of the interrelationships between ideas or nodes in a person's semantic network. Structural knowledge mediates the procedural application of declarative knowledge. The nodes in our semantic network are linked together by various associations. These interconnections enable learners to combine ideas, infer, extrapolate or otherwise reason from them. Learners cannot apply information without knowing the structural interrelatedness between the ideas.

The Physics Tutor assesses declarative, structural and procedural knowledge in building its student model. The declarative knowledge question is a simple multiple choice paraphrasing of the information presented in the node. Structural knowledge is assessed by a question which asks the learner about the degree of relatedness between pairs of concepts in the knowledge base. The procedural knowledge requires the learner to predict the direction and extent of a change in one concept on another. This information is transferred from the hypertext interface into the expert system which evaluates the information in a backward-chaining rule base and concludes that the learner's understanding of the root concept is inadequate, fuzzy or adequate. This information is fed to the tutorial expert system to generate appropriate instructional interactions.

3.7 Tutor

The tutor uses information from the student assessment and from the expert model to generate instructional sequences. At this point, if a student misses a declarative knowledge question, s/he is transported to the hypertext node (card) that contains that information. If the student misses a structural knowledge question, then the expert model expert system is activated, generating an optimal structural path for the learner. This path is then illustrated for the learner. If the learner misses a procedural knowledge question, practice scenarios are provided with standard practice and feedback. The assumptions and sophistication of this part of the tutor needs development.

3.8 Software

The hypertext interface is developed for Macintosh computers in HyperCard. Although it is functionally limited, it remains one of the best prototyping tools available. The expert system shell, Level 5, functions transparently behind the HyperCard stack to organize responses to users' questions regarding relatedness of concepts in the information base. It also navigates the student through a series of nodes to show the relationship between concepts. The expert system will also be used to create a model of the learner's understanding of the relationship between concepts and prescribe sequences of nodes to correct the student model if necessary. System design issues include how to best model different aspects of the expert's knowledge, that is, which aspects of the expert's knowledge structure are more effectively modelled in the expert system or in the hypertext.

4. Conclusion

The Physics Tutor is a prototype to test the potential of integrating hypertext systems and expert systems. It is largely declarative and structural in nature, because it began by studying the assumptions of Carbonell's SCHOLAR. It makes some large-grained assumptions, many of which are arguable. It has been argued that hypertext is a declarative knowledge system, unable to accurately represent procedural knowledge. That remains to be proven, however, our solution is to supplant any limitations by using expert systems. These also need refinement. The expert model needs to integrate more procedural domain knowledge. Most ITSs focus exclusively on procedural knowledge, that is, they are problem solving and simulation based. Increased specificity of the conclusions in the student modelling rule bases is needed. Both of these need to be associated with more context sensitive instructional strategies. The purpose of our prototype is merely to demonstrate functionality, that ITS can be built or at least resembled in hypertext and expert system. Even if a fully functioning ITS fails to result from our work, it may provide models for how to increase the level of intelligence in computer assisted instruction.

Literature

1. Barnard, P., Wilson, M. & McLean, A. (1988). Approximate modelling of cognitive activity with an expert system: A theory-based strategy for developing an interactive design tool. The Computer Journal, 31 (5), 445-456.
2. Carbonell, J. R. (1970). AI in CAI: The artificial intelligence approach to computer-based instruction. International Journal of Man-Machine Studies, 12, 259-282.
3. Denning, P.J. (1986). The science of computing: Expert systems. American Scientist, 74 (1), 1-18.
4. Gagne, R.M. (1985). Conditions of learning, 4th Ed. New York: Holt, Rinehart & Winston.
5. Jonassen, D.H. (1987). Verifying a method for assessing cognitive structure using pattern notes. Journal of Research and Development in Education.
6. Jonassen, D.H. (1989a) IDD advisor: Using expert systems as an intelligent job aid. In Proceedings of the Association for the Development of Computer-based Instructional Systems. Bellingham, WA: ADCIS.
7. Jonassen, D.H. (1989b). Hypertext/Hypermedia. Englewood Cliffs, NJ: Educational Technology Publications.
8. Jonassen, D.H. (1990). Knowledge elicitation tools for semantically structuring hypermedia information bases. In C.Green & R. McAleese (Eds.), Hypertext: Theory into practice, Vol 2. London: Blackwell.
9. Jonassen, D.H. & Grabinger, R.S. (1990). Problems and issues in designing hypermedia for learning. In D. Jonassen & H. Mandl (Eds.), Designing hypermedia for learning. NATO ASI Series F, Vol 67. Berlin: Springer-Verlag.
10. Jonassen, D.H., Grabinger, R.S. & Harris, N.D.C. (1990). Analyzing instructional strategies and tactics. Performance Improvement Quarterly.
11. Jonassen, D.H., Grabinger, R.S., & Wang, S. (1990). IDD Advisor: Merging expert systems and hypertext. Paper presented at the annual convention of the Association for Educational Communications and Technology, Anaheim, CA, February 1, 1990.
12. Jonassen, D.H. & Mandl, H. (Eds.) (1990). Designing hypermedia for learning. NATO ASI Series F, Vol 67. Berlin: Springer-Verlag.
13. Nelson, T. (1981). Literary machines. Swarthmore, PA: The Author.
14. Polson, M.C. & Richardson, J.J. (1988). Foundations of intelligent tutoring systems. Hillsdale, NJ: Lawrence Erlbaum.
15. Wenger, E. (1987). Artificial intelligence and tutoring systems: Computational and cognitive approaches to the communication of knowledge. Los Altos, CA: Morgan Kaufman.
16. Harmon, P. (1987). Intelligent job aids: How AI will change training in the next five years. In G. Kearsley (Ed.), Artificial intelligence & instruction. Reading, MA: Addison Wesley.
17. Harmon, P. & King, D. (1985). Expert systems: Artificial intelligence in business. New York:Wiley.
18. Michaelson, R. A., Mickie, D., & Boulanger, A. (1985). The technology of expert systems. Byte, 10(4), 303-312.
19. Norman, D.A., Gentner, S. & Stevens, A.L. (1976). Comments on learning schemata and memory representation. In D.Klahr (Ed.), Cognition and instruction. Hillsdale, NJ: Lawrence Erlbaum Associates.
20. Tieman, P. & Markle, S. (1984). On getting expertise into an expert system. Performance & Instruction, (11), 25-29.
21. Welsh, & Wilson, B.G. (1987). Journal of Instructional Development.

Integrating HyperMedia into Intelligent Tutoring

Philippe C. Duchastel

LearnTech, Denver, Colorado, USA

1. HyperMedia and Intelligent Tutoring

The merging of hypermedia and intelligent tutoring can occur through two approaches:
— integrating intelligent tutoring into hypermedia;
— integrating hypermedia into intelligent tutoring.

The former involves enhancing a basic hypermedia system with features that provide more structured browsing or tutoring, ranging from the traditional to the AI-based approaches (Barden, 1989; Jonassen, 1990). The second approach is the one explored here. I will be examining some of the possibilities of integrating hypermedia into intelligent tutoring, and some of the problems that are likely to be encountered. I will be using the GEO geographical tutor (Duchastel, 1989) and the OPTICLAB optics workbench (Duchastel et al., 1988) to illustrate some of the views expressed in this discussion.

As information resources, intelligent tutoring systems (ITSs) are quite different from hypermedia systems (HMSs), principally because of the ITS emphasis on representation of knowledge. ITSs are artificial intelligence (AI) systems, whereas HMSs are not. The crucial distinction between them lies in how they treat information.

ITSs structure information into a knowledge base, whereas HMSs keep information unstructured and use it as data. The structured information of ITSs involve semantic relations (see Figure 1) constituting a knowledge web that can be manipulated and interpreted by simple goal-directed rules. The information is thus computationable, which gives it the power ascribed in general terms to AI technology.

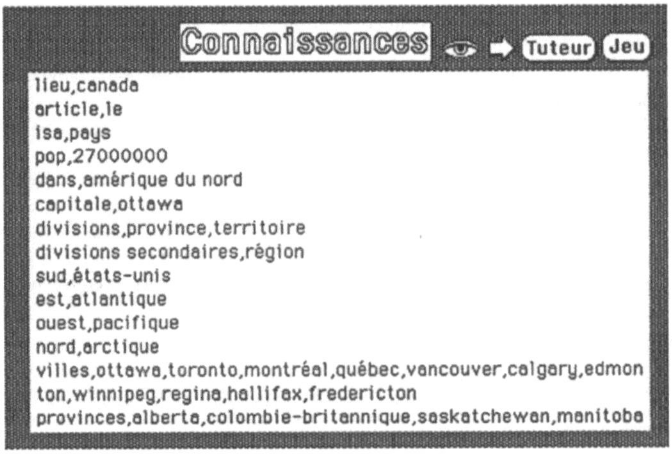

Fig. 1 - Part of the knowledge base of the GEO intelligent tutoring system.

The information contained in HMSs is termed unstructured because it lacks internal semantic meaning (Duchastel, 1986). Even though there are a multitude of connections between information elements within a HMS (that, after all, being the defining characteristic of hypermedia), the connections are merely pointers and generally do not embody semantic relationships (see McAleese, 1990, for a very interesting exception). The rich information contained and displayed in HMSs (see Figure 2), in part because of this very richness, and in part because of the lack of semantic relations, can only be interpreted by very complex rules, which make use of much additional knowledge. What this means essentially is that the interpretation must be performed by a human, and that the information is not computationable, and thus not open to the power of AI technology.

The contrast just presented between ITSs and HMSs deals with their treatment of information either as knowledge (which is computational) or as display data (which is non-computational). This leads to another contrast, this time in terms of pedagogical style. ITSs provide highly adaptive orientation to the learning session. Their computational ability to interpret the student's actions and responses in terms of a knowledge model of the student provides them with this intelligent adaptiveness. It additionally enables them to give the student much more leeway in the interactive instructional transaction, thus allowing greater learner control than traditional CAI while nevertheless keeping track of the unfolding of the learning session. This allows ITSs, at all times, to be ready to intervene in order to orient the session according to the tutorial rules they contain. ITSs are fundamentally teaching systems.

HMSs, on the other hand, are learning systems (Duchastel, 1990): they do not tutor, but they are terrific learning resources. HMSs provide full learner control, and indeed, they rely on the student's intelligence and curiosity to make them educationally useful. Thus, they do not contain any pedagogical expertise (as an ITS does). Their main virtue lies in containing interesting information.

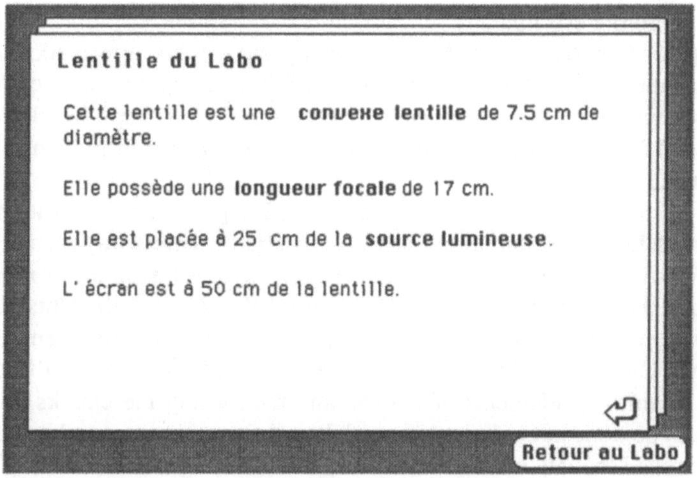

Fig. 2 - Hypertext display from the OPTICLAB prototype

The contrasts just presented lay the foundation for considering the emergence of hybrid systems which can combine the virtues of both ITSs and HMSs. The central component of such hybrid systems will be the student model.

2. Student Modelling for HyperMedia

Student modelling is aimed at deriving and maintaining an explicit picture (a computational representation) of the student's competence in a given domain: what the student knows, does not yet know, and knows incorrectly. To derive this model of the student, a system has to follow the student's interaction with the tasks being undertaken and with the information being presented. The system then derives from this monitoring an interpretation of where the student is situated in relation to the domain knowledge represented in the system. The student model is what an ITS adapts to, it is the basis for all tutoring.

In the hypermedia area, the availability of a student model within an HMS would in principle enable the system to tailor itself to the particular characteristics or interests of the student and to the perceived needs of the moment. This intelligent adaptation of an HMS would not aim to be directive, as an ITS often is, but would instead involve a selective orientation of the information made available or a tailoring of the HMS interface, all with the aim of letting the student make well-informed and wise decisions about where to proceed. One interesting illustration of this (Nielsen, 1990) is the potential for dynamically differentiating between anchors (buttons) in a frame, adjusting their prominence according to estimated relevance to the student, as determined by an examination of the student model.

As indicated above, the process of student modelling involves capturing the flow of interaction during a session, and interpreting that flow for adaptive purposes. In an HMS, a trace of the student's browsing can easily be captured (Macleod, 1990). However, it is the interpretation of this trace that is difficult for a system to perform.

Interpretation involves transforming the student actions into a representation of levels and types of knowledge possessed by the student. A representation of student knowledge, in turn, is overlayed on a formal representation of the knowledge possessed by the system. Some representation of knowledge is therefore essential.

A knowledge base paralleling and characterizing the display information in an HMS is needed. In a local application, this connection between knowledge and the hypermedia display information can be wired-in programmatically; in a more generic system, which would allow for ease of upgrade and for change of knowledge base, the knowledge-information connection must be more explicit and declarative.

Knowledge elements within a knowledge base are fine-grain characterizations of whatever is being represented. Display information in an HMS is often at a much larger grain of description (see Figure 3) in which the elements are themselves composites of many more elementary elements, although the latter are not explicitly represented as distinct elements. Connecting the fine-grain knowledge elements with the large-grain display information elements is therefore not without problems. One possibility is to chunk the hypermedia information into what can be expected to be meaningful elements of interest and then to tag the chunks with knowledge elements. This can be done not only with textual descriptions, but also, and perhaps even more importantly, with the alternate media in an HMS, such as images and sounds (Giardina et al., 1988).

This enhancement would enable an HMS to use the knowledge tags as handles for symbolic manipulation, and in particular for establishing dynamically what information elements are appropriate for tasks which the student is trying to perform. Student tasking is at the core of teaching, and must be considered in the design of a hybrid hypermedia-based intelligent tutoring system (HMITS). As will be seen next, the information technologies that are now emerging in the world of practical application tend to emphasize different views of tutoring, with strong implications for an HMITS.

Fig. 3 - Graphic display from the GEO tutor.

3. Views of Tutoring

Hypermedia is a non-pedagogical technology, one which is open to learning through browsing, but which must count on the student's own intelligence for learning guidance. Didactics, on the other hand, and all technology that support didactics, are essentially goal-directed processes that aim to achieve a result that is focused (a point also made by Nguyen-Xuan, 1990). Enter learning objectives, the essential core of any teaching system.

As I opined elsewhere (Duchastel, 1990), the philosophy behind teaching is essentially at odds with the free access philosophy of hypermedia. Teaching and browsing actually pull the student in opposite directions. It is this conflict (also discussed by Spath, 1990) that I want to further explore here.

An important problem with many teaching systems is their inflexibility in affective terms. Their emphasis is on cognitive adaptation, on providing the student with the proper cognitive elements of knowledge that are needed at a particular time in the learning session. The more a system is geared to individualizing instruction, the more adaptive it can be in these terms.

In contrast, HMSs do not adapt cognitively to the student; this is their weak point. However, they are very strong in learner control, and thus affectively efficient. What we see in the contrast between HMSs and teaching systems is a trade-off along the cognitive-affective dimension. Each type of system emphasizes one pole of the dimension to the detriment of the other.

Adaptation is the essence of what is known as pedagogical knowledge (the tutorial rules of an ITS), which in turn can be characterized mainly as curricular knowledge. Indeed, pedagogical knowledge involves knowing the structure of knowledge, both generic structural knowledge applicable broadly and specific domain knowledge that constitutes the particularities to be taught. Pedagogical knowledge also involves knowing common problems (misconceptions) that can be expected in particular learning situations.

An interesting aside to this is the thought that dealing with misconceptions is necessary either because learning took place erroneously by itself or because the teaching that occurred was itself deficient, probably not making enough use of contrast and analogy teaching strategies.

Applying this curricular knowledge in practice involves constantly adapting to the student's needs through a cycle of testing and remediation/presentation. What this amounts to is keeping the student at the edge of her learning frontier (Goldstein, 1982), that is, beyond what she already knows, but not too far beyond that the knowledge becomes unintelligible. In conceptual terms, the material presented must be new (so as to learnable), but nevertheless fit within a familiar cognitive structure and thus remain meaningful. In affective terms, it must be challenging (so as to be interesting), but also not overly difficult so as to detract from persistence.

Applying curricular knowledge thus becomes a process of tasking the student at the appropriate level. This is what an ITS constantly does (and that all teaching is meant to do). HMSs, though, do not themselves task the student with anything; they merely provide the student with access to information (with browsing capability). An HMITS (HyperMedia Intelligent Tutoring System) would then have as its technical aim to "provoke the student into browsing!"

4. Towards a Student-Centered Didactic Model

Tutoring involves guiding the learner along a certain course, even if that course is open to re-direction along the way; and hypermedia involves making available many different routes for the student to take according to current interest. We are therefore faced with suggesting a course to the student without being too directive about it. This involves a fine act of judgement in order to balance the needs for guidance and for learner freedom of open exploration.

The general thesis underlying this approach is not foreign to ITSs, for their very power at interpreting student needs has permitted them to be flexible in terms of control and actually give the student much more control than is traditionally possible in computer-assisted instructional systems (Duchastel, 1986). So ITSs are powerful and HMSs are alluring. It is this very feature of HMSs that performs the task of keeping the learner involved in exploring what is available for learning. Interest becomes the driving force. The problem for the student is knowing where to go, deciding what path would be the most interesting to pursue.

At the core of hypermedia is the navigation issue. Various aspects of navigation come into play in any HMS: interest pulls in many different directions, while at the same time lack of context (what is described as the homogeneity problem - all text is similar, especially as it is displayed on the small screen of the CRT - Nielsen, 1990) can leave one stranded deep in a section of the information set without an overall view of where one is situated. As a problem, navigation is an instructional issue, in that one way of guiding the learner lies in providing context as and when needed. Indeed, situating the learner in cognitive space is one of the key tasks of an important contemporary theory of instruction, elaboration theory (Reigeluth and Stein, 1983).

Hypermedia destroys spatial context by enabling all information to be juxtaposed in any which way the user wishes (Landow, 1990). This is very beneficial from one point of view: it enables the juxtaposition and highlighting of various points of view, such that an object or event can be analysed from different perspectives (Spiro, 1990). A radio, for instance, can be seen as a set of electronic circuits, as an instrument for listening or for broadcasting, as a design in the modern world, and so on.

Various means of restoring spatial context or of overcoming disorientation, however, can be devised. In addition to the traditional ones such as overview diagrams, these can include large screens for the multi-juxtapositioning of information elements, the use of color to indicate depth of search, or depth bars for the same purpose, along with the possibility of always zooming back out. The student model can also be used to good avail here if the information elements in the system are categorized in some appropriate fashion, in which case an 'orientation agent' could possibly help situate the user or reposition the interaction at an appropriate point.

As can be well realized, the important didactic approach here is a suggestive one. It provides the user with the information of a context nature that will enable quick orientation and re-situating if necessary. The important feature of this soft approach is that decision authority for the evolution of the session is invested in the learner, and not, as is traditionally the case in instruction, with the teacher or author.

5. Conclusions

The design of hypermedia systems involves the design of various fundamental components, such as the information model and the interaction model (Jonassen & Grabinger, 1990). What we see the need for now in seeking to extent the hypermedia paradigm further is the design of yet other components, particularly the student model and a didactic model (Mandl, 1990).

The basic distinction between the ITS world and the HMS world lies in knowledge representation. The design of more intelligent HMSs thus involves structuring knowledge of various kinds: first, knowledge of the student (a student model) that can help interpret student needs; second, knowledge of the inter-relationships between the display elements within the HMS; and third, soft didactic knowledge that can interrelate the two.

It was argued that tutoring involves establishing a workable balance between cognitive and affective needs, a balance that is delicate and extremely important in the conative domain of learning. An HMITS is a hybrid system that must maintain the best of the ITS world and the best of the HMS world, even though each emphasizes a distinct tutorial view. The aim of such a system becomes provocation into browsing.

In the end, the system must basically work together with the student in a symbiotic relationship aimed at fulfilling epistemic needs that keep changing as the interaction evolves. In that basic sense, any computer-based learning system is foremost an interactive environment with its own constraints and possibilities. Our task, then, is very much to both elucidate the grammar of that environment (as Alves de Oliveira & Costa Pereira, 1990, have proposed) and to invent and test new syntactical approaches to the design of that environment (as Nielsen, 1990, is doing). This task is made all the easier as interest grows in hypermedia systems (Jonassen & Mandl, 1990), and in particular in intelligent environments and in their interaction with outside aims such as learning and instruction.

Literature

1. Alves de Oliveira, A. & Costa Pereira, D. (1990) Psychopedagogic aspects of hypermedia courseware. In Jonassen, D. & Mandl, H. (Eds.) The Design of HyperText for Learning. New York: Springer Verlag.
2. Barden, R. (1989) Developing a hypercard-based intelligent training system. ETTI, 26, 361-367.
3. Duchastel, P. Computer Text Access. Computers & Education, 1986, 10, 403-409.
4. Duchastel, P., Imbeau, J. & the STI Group. (1988) On interacting with information: OPTICLAB. International Journal of Educational Research, 12, 811-820.
5. Duchastel, P. Knowledge-based instructional gaming: GEO. Journal of Educational Technology Systems, 1989, 12, 189-203.
6. Duchastel, P. (1990) Formal and Informal Learning with HyperMedia. In D. Jonassen & H. Mandl (Eds.). Designing Hypermedia for Learning. NATO ASI Series F, Vol. 67. Berlin: Springer-Verlag.
7. Giardina, M., Marton, P., Duchastel, P. & Doublait, S. BIOMEC: Modélisation et développement d'un module d'apprentissage intelligent utilisant le vidéodisque interactif. Proceedings of the International Conference on Intelligent Tutoring Systems, Montreal, Canada, 1988, 448-453.
8. Goldstein, I. (1982) The genetic graph: A representation for the evolution of procedural knowledge. In Sleeman, D. & Brown, J. S. Intelligent Tutoring Systems. New York: Academic Press.
9. Jonassen, D. (1990) Adding intelligence to hypertext with expert systems and adding usability to expert systems with hypertext. In this book.
10. Jonassen, D. & Grabinger, S. (1990) Problems and issues in designing hypertext / hypermedia for learning. In Jonassen, D. & Mandl, H. (Eds.). Designing Hypermedia for Learning. NATO ASI Series F, Vol. 67. Berlin: Springer-Verlag.
11. Jonassen, D. & Mandl, H. (1990) (Eds.). Designing Hypermedia for Learning. NATO ASI Series F, Vol. 67. Berlin: Springer-Verlag.
12. Landow, G. (1990) Popular fallacies about hypertext. In D. Jonassen & H. Mandl (Eds.). Designing Hypermedia for Learning. NATO ASI Series F, Vol. 67. Berlin: Springer-Verlag.
13. Macleod, M. (1990) Tools for monitoring and analysing the use of hypermedia courseware. In this book.
14. Mandl, H. (1990) Basic pedagogic-didactic dimensions for evaluation of computer-based systems on open learning. In this book.
15. McAleese, R. (1990) Concepts as hypertext nodes: The ability to learn while navigating through hypertext nets. In D. Jonassen & H. Mandl (Eds.). Designing Hypermedia for Learning. NATO ASI Series F, Vol. 67. Berlin: Springer-Verlag.
16. Nielsen, J. (1990) The art of navigating through hypertext. Communications of the ACM, 33, 296-310.
17. Nguyen-Xuan, A. (1990) Effects of prior knowledge on learning to use a command device. In this book.
18. Reigeluth, C. & Stein, F. (1983) The elaboration theory of instruction. In C. Reigeluth (Ed.) Instructional Design Theories and Models: An Overview of their Current Status. Hillsdale, NJ: Erlbaum.
19. Späth, P. (1990) Design considerations in hypermedia tutorials. In this book.
20. Spiro, R. (1990) Towards a general theory of hypertext: Nonlinear instruction for the development of cognitive flexibility in ill-structured domains. In this book.

4 Ergonomics for Hypermedia

Hypermedia and ITS

Duarte Costa Pereira[1], Armando de Oliveira[2] and José Carlos G. Vaz[3]

[1]Universidade do Porto, [2]Universidade de Aveiro, [3]Projecto Minerva (Universidade do Porto), Portugal

Abstract: ITS research is likely to represent the most important means for optimizing the interface ergonomy of hypermedia, particularly in learning situations and regarding mainly three points. First, the *cognitive model of the user*, which is related to the activity of exploring hypermedia documents. Second, the analysis of the preferences and search strategies of each user as well as the nature and level of the information processed, will lead to hypermedia in which the *user diagnostic module* must itself be intelligent or, in other words, be capable of learning. Finally, the system should be able to determine *preferential paths for learning* in order to direct the student-users.

1. Hypertext/hypermedia problems

For any instructional design (either computer aided or conventional) we consider that the essential characteristics are to be interactive and attractive.

The increasing of the systems interactivity as well as the interface transparency allows for a greater participation of the user in the design of informatic applications, and even for an easier access to the information that microcomputers, in general, can save in large quantities. The appeareance of modern hypertexts makes it easier to reach these goals.

Hypertext is associated to systems where users have access to large quantities of information using flexible and intuitive paths. This is not the way one manipulates traditional databases that, in general, use formal access systems, and force the user to possess a certain prior knowledge about the material saved, as well as about the way to use databases. The modern hypertext concept is based on a computer-supported information environment. This is done through a cross-referenced system, that links discrete elements in a data base, so users can explore the information in any direction. One can name the following kind of hypertext documents (Garrett et al., 1986):

Single author - single reader (ideas organizer),
Single author - many readers (informative or tutorial hypertext),
Many authors - many readers (collaborative hypertext).

A hypertext document extends the text dimensions so one can say that it possesses three significative components:

a) a text database,

b) a semantic network that relates text database components, and

c) tools that allow to create and explore this combination of text and semantic network.

It is also important to note that a hypertext semantic network doesn't fit completely the traditional notion of semantic network. As a matter of fact the nodes can identify themselves with large segments of text or graphics and don't need to correspond to well defined concepts. Nodes and links, vital hypertext elements, can nevertheless be reconstructed in such a way that they form a semantic network (Rada, 1988).

If one considers hypertext as a set of information units that can be linked in several ways, through the computer's electronic support, it is essential to define these information units (the so called nodes), the structure of the relationships between, them and the presentation of that information.

One can get the content of the nodes through filtering (selection of relevant information) and zooming (selection of detail level) strategies that are adequate to document goals.

As to the structure, although in theory all kind of links can be implemented, from non structured hypertext to hypertext with a hierarchical structure (Jonassen, 1989), it is very important to analyze the mechanisms that are based on the expected utilization, in order to choose only the links that optimize that use.

One can point the following questions concerning hypertext design and use:

How to choose where we are?

How to facilitate the access to other documents? What is the most appropriated metaphor?

How to know where one is going?

The most adequate solution depends on how one intends to use the documents. Essentially one can speak of three different types of utilization.

Finding is the most conventional one and it applies when one wants to search information with well defined goals. This is what happens with databases and is nowadays generalizable to all informatic applications.

Navigation is another style of exploring electronic documents mainly based on graphical cues (that are important and easy to implement in any electronic document). This style is different from aleatory exploration, which is another alternative style.

Browsing is a style characterized by the existence of a goal, although not well defined. Mainly it consists on the use of possible associations with the object, in order to choose the next information item.

This last type of exploration can lead to a guided discovery learning situation (McAleese, 1989), with all its accepted advantages, once it preserves motivation and favours the control of learning conditions (Gagné, 1965). Hypertext also allows learner metacognitive control of the learning phenomenon, enhancing it (Ingwersen, 1986).

There are two questions that are frequently mentioned in the literature and are related to the find style: one is the possibility to loose the searching goal; the other one is the increasing difficulty to distinguish the details. To minimize these two problems it is necessary to implement search techniques - the browsing tools. Examples of theses tools are the graphical path structure. These aids should be complemented with searching techniques as well as with the so-called key-words. It is important to associate scanning (covering large areas without depth) and exploring (finding out the extent of the information given) techniques to this search.

It is always necessary to match the document's structure and presentation to the different kinds of expected utilizations. For instance, as to the structure one can not use all the existent associations between the conceptual fields of two information nodes, but should emphasize the most appropriated relationships concerning the used metaphor. In order to achieve this it is necessary to construct a simple network, in which each node must be linked to the three or four nodes that possess stronger associations, instead of being linked to all the others. Therefore the user can follow this pseudo hierarchic structure in a easier way. In this structure a top node can be visualized and the user is also provided with cognitive scaffolding. This last feature is essential for a guided discovery learning strategy. The combinatory explosion (a problem for the computer implementation) can then be avoided, and the phenomenon of getting-lost-in-hyperspace, frequently mentioned in the literature, be also minimized, once scaffolding is essential to support the search (to search with a defined goal).

2. ITS problems

Whatever the confidence we have in A I R&D in latest years, the biggest problem is the transfer and application of this progress to the educational system, either for learning or for training.

In fact, in recent years very interesting AI applications appeared in many fields but unfortunately not many in Education. This applies not only to ITS but to all Computer Aided Instruction.

Another very clear idea that can be drawn from the abstracts is that the help the computer gives in the classroom should be implemented mainly through the teacher rather than directly to the learner.

The problems with ITS may be summarized in 2 points:

The complexity and difficulty of formalizing knowledge about both:

- student modelling and
- didactic system

One first possibility to solve this problem would be to use in ITS R&D multidisciplinary teams integrating people from education, psychology and teacher training.

This solution is not very effective simply because there are no available models either in psychology or education that would adapt readily to the ITS situation.

This is why we decided to promote another strategy not to produce programs to teach something specifically, but instead to build intelligent general helps to the learning process. Unfortunately our first insight into this line of thought seems to indicate that similar problems subsist as we'll refer later.

Roughly any instructional system is essentially based on a 3 point planning:

- the definition of the initial state
- the identification of the goals to be attained (final state)
- the identification and adequacy of the appropriate means to move from the initial state to the final state

The first difficulty which arises in any instructional system (either computer aided or not) is the definition of the initial state. That is, to be able to discover what the learner's knowledge is, directly or not concerned with the didactic module that we are interested in implementing, and what the learning mechanisms that the learner has available are.

Any teacher knows that even in a group that might have been equalized by a knowledge pre-test, the individual performances are very diversified after exposure to the didactic module. Everyone knows that there are students with different curiosity, capacity, and motivation levels for some subjects. This is the subject of study of a branch of applied psychology called vocational orientation. On the other hand Differential Psychology has repeatedly used although with some scientific refutation, the idea of psychological profles and also a less general idea of cognitive styles (Pask).

The truth is that this pragmatic classification was enough to give a reasonable explanation for certain behaviours.

As there is for the time being no universal student model capable of explaining reality (will it ever be possible?) and as it is not operational to consider each individual case, we think that one way out of this difficulty is to try, similarly to what happens in differential psychology, to pragmatically define a limited number of learning profiles capable of explaining the vast majority of cases (not necessarily all!).

For a given didactic module we make the assumption that it is possible to group, in what is essential to attain the goals that are fixed, the interindividual differences in several groups.

Also we should not suppose that all the students have the same level of knowledge even for the pre-requisites for the learning task. So the didactic module must not only allow the user to acquire these pre-requisites, but also the skipping of learning stages for people already possessing the corresponding knowledge.

These two considerations bring into the scene the idea of Hypermedia as one that allows freedom in the choice of the point of departure and in the individual way followed.

3. How can research on ITS help Hypermedia: interactivity and help

As far as interactivity is concerned we may say that this is the best reason for the introduction of the computer in learning and training environments. This is because the computer is the only non-human medium which allows interactivity. The two aspects where this interactivity can play a major role in the instructional process are:

- first, the bidirectional adaptability of the didactic strategy (the two strategies for both tutor and tuttee being maintained in tune, in real time);
- second, the simulation capacity.

We must remember that although the technical interactive capacity of computers is extremely important, it cannot substitute the human interaction in any teaching/learning situation but may and should help the student/teacher relationship, allowing for a better knowledge on the part of the teacher about the cognitive state of the student during the process, not only as to what he/she learns but also as to how he/she learns.

It is precisely in the organization of this kind of help that we think that AI tools may become precious. Thus we think that the intelligent help in any didactic module – not only as a help to the student/learner but above all as a help to the teacher – must always be in the teacher's control (and as we saw above we are not alone in this opinion).

How can we, in practice, implement these ideas?

What we'll do next is to expose how we are working in this implementation.

Our perspective is to try to combine the mutual advantages of Hypermedia and Intelligent tools.

The use of Hypermedia structure allows us to consider that in the initial state the learners do not necessarily havethe same knowledge level or the same strategy for the learning mechanisms. This is because it is possible to build Hypermedia tutorials on a large information basis that will be more or less used by the learners with personal browsing strategies. Hypermedia also allows very easily to get a complete trace of their learning paths. It is evident that any computer program allows that, but the advantage of Hypermedia is that by being defined over a node structure this allows for the creation of exploring profiles regarding the way this structure is used: emphasizing repetitions, jumps and, above all, the creative links used by the student between nodes.

The experimental analysis of the ways really used by the learner, related to the acquisition that they have made, will allow to define the afore mentioned learning profiles.

Once having those first profiles, the problem is to find for each new user what the most adequate strategy is, regarding the didactic objectives imposed.

It is known that in teacher training it is impossible to tell what the best responses to a certain pedagogical situation are, and consequently, the golden rule for a teacher is to analyze this situation vis a vis his/her general teaching knowledge and build, every time, a new answer to the particular situation which is adequate to each student.

A good teacher is someone who learns each time he/she practises his professional activity.

In the same way a good ITS is the one that is not only capable of adapting to each new user, but also to learn with him/her, i.e. capable of changing its own knowledge base in the process of its use.

In order to be able to construct such program the first activity is to construct the information basis of the Hypermedia Tutorial. This is not only the declarative and procedural knowledge about the subject but also, in the special case of Hypermedia information, about the recognized necessary pre-requisites (which will allow students who don't possess them to get them) and also complementary information capable of satisfying the curiosity of the learner (and making the program attractive). In order to define this information as well as the way it is presented and how to control the process (exercises, games, ...) one first attempt must be done based on the experience and intuition of the educationalists.

This program will then be essentially an educational research program: that is, its testing with an experimental group, as large as possible, will eventually permit to define the learning profiles applicable to this module.

The analysis of profiles is in our view the most difficult and critical part of the process, because of the adequacy of these profiles to the sample and the validation of its generalization to the population. This will be fundamental in the elaboration of the working hypothesis that will allow the production of the rules and facts of the knowledge basis for the intelligent help module. So if these hypotheses are correct, the program itself analyzing each new user and comparing his/her behavior to the different profiles (more or less efficient in that learning task), may not only give him a real time help but also help to integrate these new data in order to improve its potential.

What will finally come out will be a help dialogue, not forcing the user into a learning path (this would avoid the program for learning) but suggesting different ways according to the analysis done, comparing the actual behaviour to the one implied by the profiles. These profiles cannot be discarded altogether once adopted but each one of them will be better characterized with the experiment. This is in accordance with the general view that Hypermedia systems should not be viewed principally as teaching tools but rather as learning tools, or even as tools for learning how to learn. The interest of such programs (as in fact hybrids of Hypermedia/ITS) is fundamentally because they are excellent psychopedagogical research tools.

The general idea is to test these programs for consistency of the learning profiles. These learning profiles, as our research has been proving, are more dependent on a situation than on a student model. For example the strategies of exploration of information and acquisition of information vary radically if the experiments are present or absent.

This leads us to conclude that it is not possible to interpret and generalize the learning profiles independently of the learning, and they should only be considered as a help for the teacher who must keep the control of the learning situation and use the information available on the learning profiles to improve this control.

Literature

1. Allinson, L. & Hammond, N. (1989) A Learning Support Environment: The Hitch-Hiker's Guide. In R. McAleese (ed.) Hyperfext Theory into Practice, Oxford: Blackwell Scientific Publications.
2. Charney, D. (1987) Comprehending Non-Linear Text: The Role of Discourse Cues and Reading Strategies, Hypertext 87 Papers.
3. Craik, F. M. I. & Lockhart, R. S. (1972) Levels of Processing: A Framework for Memory, Journal of Verbal Learning and Verbal Behavior, 11, 671 - 684.
4. Duncan, E. (1989) A Faceted Approach to Hypertext?. In R. McAleese, (ed.) Hypertext Theory into Practice, Oxford: Blackwell Scientific Publications.
5. Eysenck, M. K. (1979) Depth, Elaboration and Distinctiveness. In L. S. Cermak and F. I. M. Craik (eds.) Levels of Processing in Human Memory, Hillsdale: Lawrence Erlbaum Associates.
6. Gagné, R. (1965) The Conditions of Learning, New York: Holt Rinehart and Winston.

Intelligent Systems in Education

Alessandro Micarelli[1] and Paolo Balestra[2]

[1]Dipartimento di Informatica e Sistemistica, Università degli Studi di Roma "La Sapienza", Via Salaria, 113, 00198 Roma, Italy
[2]Via Promontori, 50, 00122 Roma, Italy

Abstract: In this paper some implications of the use of artificial intelligence techniques in Education are presented. The peculiar aspects of intelligent tutoring systems are described, pointing out the innovative features of such systems compared with traditional applications. Then, two existing educational systems, developed at the University of Rome "La Sapienza", are presented.

1. Introduction

Several are the tools and technologies that can be conveniently used for helping teachers in their work. Among such tools, we can also count the computers. Their use in education (CAI or Computer Aided Instruction systems) began in the early 1960s. Systems developed to teach with computers have been conceived and realized starting from the behavioural psychology theories [17]. The didactic path was very rigid, based on a "stimulus-response" model, with only a one-way teaching interaction. The system presented some questions and/or problems and evaluated the student answer by a rigid predefined schema. So the behaviour of the system was not adaptable to the various students.

The need of getting over the limits of the traditional CAI led to studies on Cognitive Psychology and Artificial Intelligence, with particular care to the interaction between teacher and student. These researches led to the development of new educational systems, using Artificial Intelligence techniques, called Intelligent Computer Aided Instruction (ICAI) systems or Intelligent Tutoring Systems (ITS).

In this paper some of the implications of the exploitation of Artificial Intelligence in education are presented. In particular, the distinguishing features of Intelligent Tutoring Systems are described and compared with traditional applications.

The paper is organized as follows. In Section 2 the characteristics of ITSs are presented, pointing out the innovative features of such systems compared with traditional applications. In Section 3 and 4 we present two educational systems, developed at the University of Rome "La Sapienza", which use different didactic approaches in the teaching/learning relationship. Finally, in a concluding section, we present a few final remarks.

2. The Intelligent Tutoring Systems

The difference between ITSs and CAI systems is in that in an ITS a student can exploit a two-way dialogue, personalized to his needs, abandoning the stimulus-respose approach in favor of a mixed-initiative dialogue. Furthermore it is possible to build ITSs in such a way as to give students a well defined didactic path (chosen by the system) or to let them free to choose their own path. Between the two possibilities there are some different intermediate strategies that may be adopted.

To build an ITS it is necessary to go from the development of Expert Systems in well limited domains to the realization of teaching and learning systems, dealing with the various problems connected to the knowledge transfer (didactic methodologies and psychological study of a learner behaviour). Actually an ITS is a collection of Expert Systems, suitably designed to interact. First of all an ITS must contain an *expert module* experienced on the subject to be taught. It means that a module is needed able to understand, analyze and solve problems typical of that subject, both if the problem is proposed by the student or by the system itself.

Second, a *tutoring module* is needed experienced on the didactic methodology to use. In fact, it is not sufficient to master very well a subject, to be able to teach it to other people, but it is also essential to know how to teach it: that is, to master a right methodology, taking into account the problems dealing with the learning process, both from a general point of view and from the particular point of view typical of the domain to face.

Third, a module representing the *student model* is needed, that is the knowledge base concerning the learning status of the student as gathered by the system through the dialogue. It is a *qualitative model*, dynamically improved and increased, where the knowledge acquired by the student is explicitly represented. This module allows the system to personalize the teaching dialogue: in fact, the best teaching action is chosen by the tutoring module on the basis of the model of the student presently using the system.

Fourth, an *interaction module* is needed, that plays an important role in determining the effectiveness of the educational system. It must make the system easy to use, provide a pleasant interaction, but, above all, it must allow the student to take the initiative in asking questions, requesting explanations and suggestions, thus realizing a *mixed initiative* dialogue, so that the interaction between the student and the system is easy and constructive [18, 20].

It is very important to have a very high integration among the various modules present in an ITS to make it possible a diagnostic activity on the student behaviour, and a remedial activity, in such a way that the interface module can manage the various tools present in the ITS: pedagogical strategies, possibly linked to external help media, like videodisc, television, etc. That is the student may be directed to see some filmed lessons or he may decide by himself to repeat some lessons or concepts, using such multimedia systems.

As already said, the student model plays a key role in ITSs. Traditional CAI systems used a quantitative model of the student, which was only based on statistical data, concerning the number of correct answers, the number of mistakes, and possibly response times.

Conversely, qualitative models, used in ITS, are designed so that the behaviour of the student could be explained. The knowledge base and the automatic problem solving capabilities of the ITS play an important role because the system compares the student answers to the expert module answers and determines why and how the student reached a certain goal. Qualitative models may be classified in: overlay, bug and simulation models [9, 12].

In an *overlay model* the student knowledge is viewed as a subset of the expert knowledge, and the learning process consists in an enlargement of such subset. Errors are considered as deviations from the correct knowledge.

In a *bug model* the learning status of the student is represented in terms of incorrect knowledge (also called misconceptions) that represent possible student errors (bugs). The student model contains not only correct knowledge, but also incorrect knowledge. The main problem of this approach is the impossibility of foreseeing an exhaustive error set.

A *simulation model* allows the system to foresee the future student answers. Such a model is executable, and can be used to explain the student behaviour.

John Self, in a recent research [16], reviews the actual uses which have been found for student models in existing ITSs. The student model is considered as a 4-tuple <P, C, T, H>, where P describes the procedural knowledge of the student, C the conceptual knowledge, T the individual traits and H the history. The set $K = P \cup C$ describes what the student knows.

Self identified twenty functions of the student model, grouped in six categories:

- corrective functions: the system must eliminate the incorrect knowledge of the student. It needs to find the error, to start a correcting action, to present an example, to draw step by step the wrong chain used by the student to reach his wrong goal, to identify the source of the mistake;
- elaborative functions: the system must intervene when the student knowledge is correct, but incomplete. It has to decide the next action to do, starting from the profile of the student or from a comparison between the student knowledge and the expert knowledge;
- strategic functions: the analysis of the student model may suggest some higher level actions involving methodologies and teaching strategies;
- diagnostic functions: the system may do some diagnostic activities on the student model, if, for example, it needs to identify an inferential chain to find the student conviction;
- predictive functions: the system may also utilize the student model to foresee the future behaviour of the learner (student simulation);
- evaluative functions: the student skills may be evaluated using his history stored in the model.

The interaction between the student and the system to build the knowledge of the student and his model may take place in several different ways:

- using a *Socratic dialogue*: the system asks questions and suggests new situations guiding the student to find where his reasoning is wrong;
- to let the student free to solve his problems without system intervention, unless the student himself asks for some help or some questions;
- using the *learning by doing* technique: the system works actively during the teaching activity and the student is requested of selecting information he thinks relevant to the subject and his choice is compared with the one done by the expert;
- using the *learning while doing* technique: the tutor is hidden in the learning environment, where the student is going to work, and he will give a help if necessary.

Many ITSs have been developed till now on various teaching domains. Here we recall some meaningful examples: GUIDON, developed by Clancey [11], a system to diagnose infections; LMS/PIXIE, developed by Sleeman [19], a system to teach manipulation of algebraic expressions with detection of mistakes; SOPHIE, developed by Brown, Burton and Bell [6], to diagnose failures in electronic circuits, able to value the student capability in finding wrong circuits; PROUST, developed by Johnson and Soloway [14], a system for detection of mistakes of students learning how to program in PASCAL; GEOMETRY TUTOR, developed by Anderson, Boyle and Yost [5], a system to teach elementary geometry.

In the next sections we present two systems, developed at the University of Rome "La Sapienza", which concretely mirror the theoretical guidelines previously mentioned.

3. The System SEDAF

We are involved in a project for the construction of ITSs at the University of Rome "La Sapienza". One of the goals of our project is the development of tools for assisting high school or college students in learning calculus and electrical engineering. The subject domain we have chosen for the first prototype, named SEDAF [4], is the analytical study of mathematical functions.

SEDAF, which has been developed in KEE (Knowledge Engineering Environment) on an Explorer workstation, considers functions defined as the quotient of two polynomials, which are a meaningful subset of the set of continuous functions. It contains all the components of an IES, i.e. a domain expert, a student model, a teaching expert and an interactive component. SEDAF, as most ITSs, is based on *diagnostic modeling*. With this approach, the evolution of the learning status of the student is monitored by posing tasks, evaluating the proposed solutions and possibly diagnosing reasons of mistakes.

The architecture of SEDAF is described in Figure 1. It consists of:

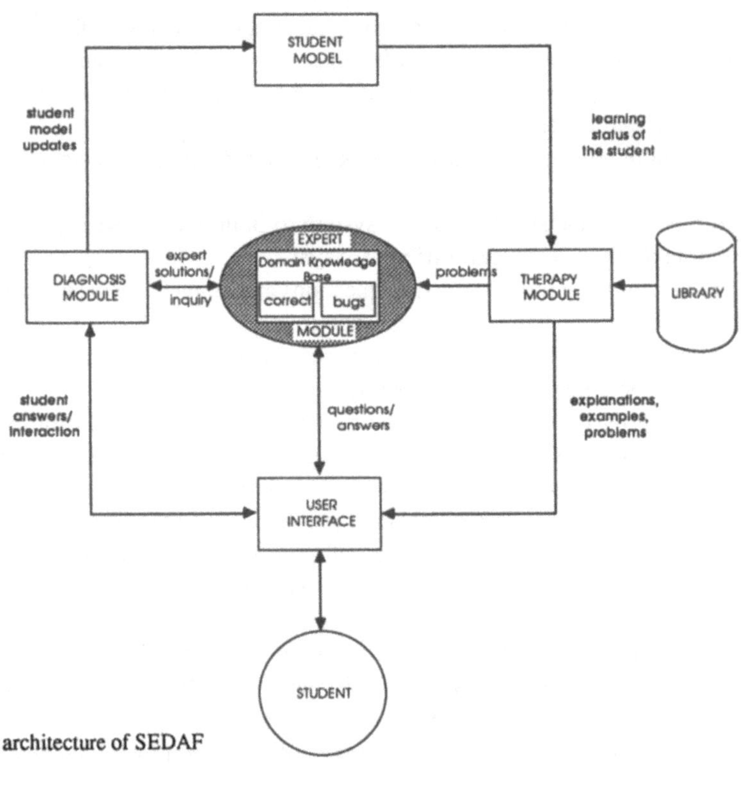

Fig. 1 - The architecture of SEDAF

- an *expert module*, which contains two knowledge bases: the correct knowledge and the misconceptions, and an inference engine, which endows the system with problem solving capabilities;
- a *diagnosis module*, which attempts to find the reasons of the student's errors;
- a *student model*, which contains a description of the learning status of the student;
- a *therapy module*, which proposes the appropriate remedy to a student in order to improve his learning status; it essentially embodies the teaching expertise of the system;
- a *user interface*.

The knowledge base on the subject domain (correct knowledge and misconceptions) has been represented by means of the formalisms provided by KEE: *frames* (called *units*), *production rules*, *methods* and *active values*.

The correct knowledge consists of the notions and concepts relevant to the domain to be taught. Knowledge pertinent to the objects to be dealt with in the analysis of functions is represented declaratively, via a taxonomy of frames. Also the deductive knowledge is represented as a taxonomy: rules are in fact divided into classes, each one relative to a particular phase of the study of a function. An example rule for the class of functions considered by the system is:

IF a point x is a stationary point of the function f(x)
AND the function f(x) is decreasing left of the point x
AND the function f(x) is increasing right of the point x
THEN the point x is a minimum of f(x).

The first condition selects the points generated in the previous phase which are candidates to be minima of the function; the other conditions check if those points are actually minima.

Misconceptions are a sort of a bug catalogue, i. e. a list of common mistakes made by the students. They can be viewed as "perturbations" of the correct knowledge, and are used by the system during the diagnosis phase to identify the reasons for a student error. The following example of misconception would admit among minima also points where the function is undefined:

IF the function f(x) is decreasing left of the point x
AND the function f(x) is increasing right of the point x
THEN the point x is a minimum of f(x).

SEDAF uses also some procedural knowledge, in the form of attached procedures: for instance, a procedural attachment computes the zeroes of the numerator and the denominator of a function, symbolically computes its first and second derivatives, etc.

When starting a teaching session with a student, SEDAF either proposes a function to be analyzed, or waits for a function to be proposed by the student himself. This function is first analyzed by the expert module. Then the system guides the student in the various phases of the study: determination of the function domain, i. e. of the singular points; of the horizontal, vertical and oblique asymptotes; computation of the first derivative, of the maxima, minima, and of the flexes with a horizontal tangent; and finally, computation of the second derivative and of the flexes with an oblique tangent.

During each of the above phases, the system asks questions to the student. The diagnosis module gets the student's response and checks whether it is an admissible solution provided by the expert module. If the response is correct, the system assumes that "it is right for the right reasons" and that the student knows all the facts and rules used in the deduction (inference chain) built by the expert module. The diagnosis module then adds these facts and rules to the student model, possibly removing facts and rules that are contradictory with them.

If the response is incorrect, the diagnosis module starts a reasoning on the entire knowledge base (hence activating also the base of misconceptions), taking the incorrect response as a goal, in order to single out the possible deductions (inferential chains) that have lead to the student solution. The system determines the inferential chain used by the student, possibly through an interaction aiming at discriminating among various allowable inference chains. Such a chain must contain some facts or rules that are incorrect; the diagnosis module points out the reasons for the error and updates the student model (bug model).

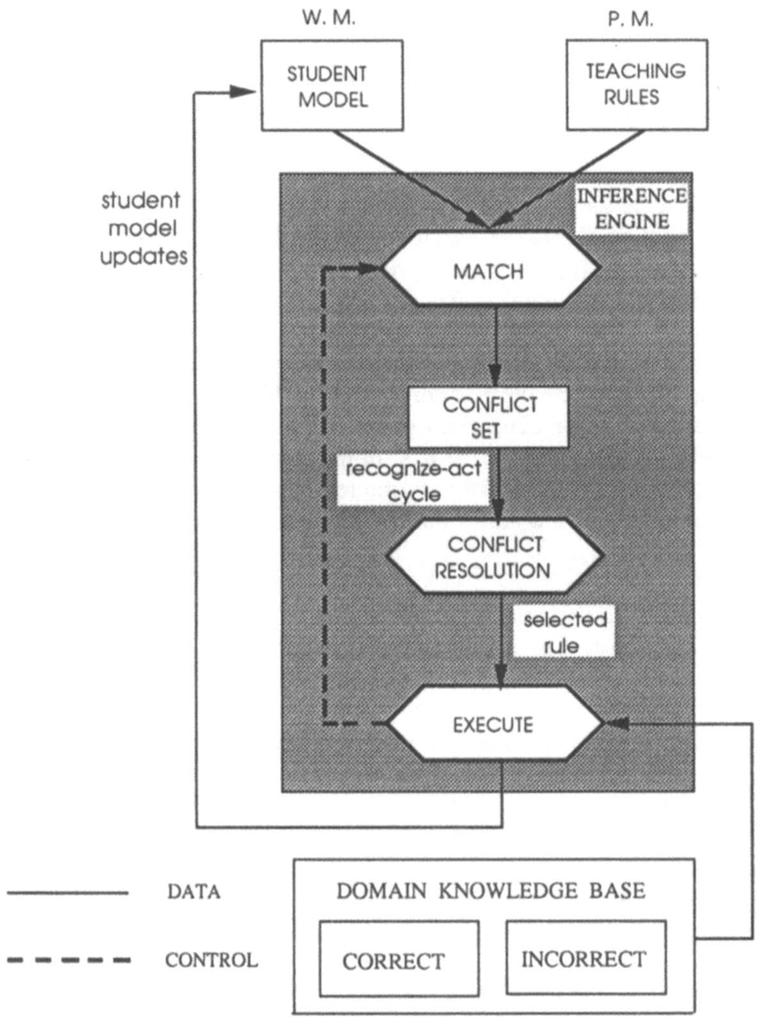

Fig. 2. The architecture of the production system model.

The updated student model is then examined by the therapy module, which attempts to tailor the remedy (the right "therapy") to the needs of the student. It determines the best *teaching action* to perform, taking into consideration the correct and incorrect knowledge present in the student model. The application of the selected teaching action generates explanations and examples, extracted from a predefined library, and proposes a new problem both to the student and to the expert module.

For the realization of the above operations, we have chosen, as an adequate and natural computational model, a production system model equipped with a forward chaining inference mechanism, with the student model as working memory and the teaching rules as production memory (see [7, 10] for a definition of these terms). The application of the teaching rules produces the illustration of concepts dealing with the teaching domain, the illustration of examples, the proposal to the student of new problems to be solved; they are chosen according to particular misconceptions present in the student model. Figure 2 shows the architecture of the production system model.

During the pattern matching phase, all the rules whose conditions are satisfied by the objects existing in the model are searched for. All these instantiations are inserted in the conflict set. Then the conflict resolution phase selects the rule present in the conflict set that, according to given heuristics, is the most suitable one. Successively, the Right-Hand-Side (RHS) of the selected rule is activated, thus generating examples and explanations on the subject domain and the proposal of a new problem both to the student and to the expert module. The student's response to the proposed problem will again activate the diagnosis module which, possibly after an interaction with the student, updates the student model.

Hence, the result of executing the RHS of the selected rule consists of the interaction with the student and the updating of the working memory (student model), even if the last effect is indirect, in so far as it happens via the activation of the diagnosis module. At this point the control (dotted line in Figure 2) passes to the matching phase, and the cycle starts again.

In conclusion, the behaviour of SEDAF consists of the recognize-act cycle of the production system shown in Figure 2 or, from another viewpoint, of the diagnosis-therapy cycle as indicated in Figure 1.

4. The System SAMPLE

SAMPLE [15] is an ITS for teaching high school and college students how to analyze electrical circuits in alternate current in steady condition.

A preliminary analysis of the interviews with teachers and the observation of the students problem solving behaviour have been largely used for the definition of the design specifications of SAMPLE. We noticed that the major difficulty the students have in this domain consists in the acquisition of the "modus operandi", which can be obtained through the individual practice in solving problems. We considered that the most suited teaching strategy was the choice of a less judgmental and a more collaborative relationship in the teaching/learning interaction.

The system helps the student find his way to a solution also by stimulating him in doing reasoning by analogy.

Another distinguishing feature of SAMPLE is its capacity in determining all the possible correct solutions for a given circuit, also if it is proposed by the student.

Also in SAMPLE the knowledge base on the subject domain has been represented by means of the formalisms provided by KEE.

The architecture of SAMPLE is shown in Figure 3. It consists of the following elements:

- An *expert module*, which contains a knowledge base on the domain to be taught and an inference engine, which endows the system with problem-solving capabilities.
- A *student model*, which contains a representation of the learning status of the student.
- A *tutoring module*, consisting of a *control subsystem,* which monitors the interaction with the student, and by a *remedial subsystem*, which attempts to tailor the right remediation to the needs of the student.
- A *bug catalogue*, which is a library of common errors made by the students.
- A *user interface*.

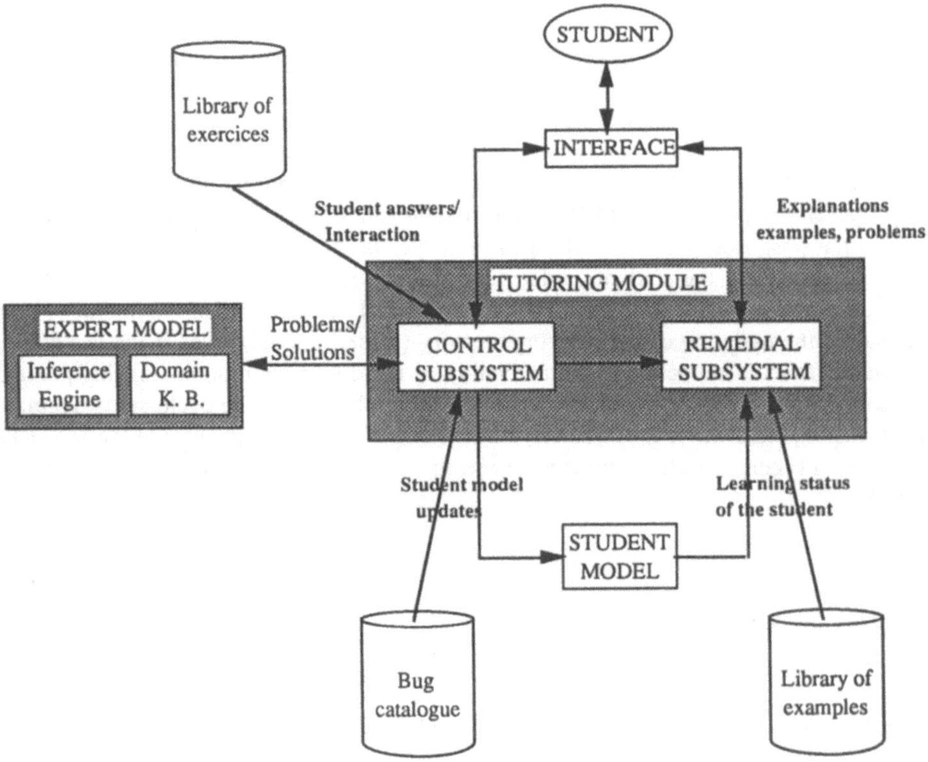

Fig. 3 - The architecture of SAMPLE.

The declarative knowledge pertinent to the topology and the electrical components of the circuit to be analyzed is represented via a hierarchy of units.

The deductive knowledge is represented as a taxonomy of production rules that implements the knowledge relevant to the applicable electrical laws and formulae, such as Ohm law, Kirchhoff laws, equivalent impedance formulae, etc. The system uses the *symbolic method* (electrical quantities represented as complex numbers) in its problem solving activity.

SAMPLE also uses procedural knowledge, essentially in the form of methods and active values. For example, a method determines the values of the module and the phase of the electrical quantities represented as complex numbers.

The expert module of SAMPLE determines the correct solution(s) for the circuit proposed to/by the student during the teaching session using the above mentioned knowledge base and a context mechanism, or *worlds* system[1]. A world is a representation of a set of related facts, i. e. a situation, a belief set, or a hypothetical state of a problem solver. With this facility, users can represent a variety of possible situations (i. e. reasoning over alternative situations using rules), compare them and explore their consequences [13].

As we said before, in SAMPLE the diagnostic tutoring teaching strategy used in SEDAF is abandoned and replaced with a less judgmental and a more collaborative relationship between the student and the system.

At the beginning of a teaching session the system either proposes a circuit to be analyzed or waits for a circuit proposed by the student. At this point the expert module determines the correct solution(s). The system then gives the initiative to the student. The control subsystem monitors the student step by step comparing his resolution process of the exercise with the solution derived by the expert module. At each step, it analyzes the action performed by the student and possibly decides the corresponding teaching actions, in case the student needs to be guided back to the correct path. For example, the formula could be right, but some of the data needed are not yet available, or the formula could be right, but it is unnecessary to solve that subproblem, etc. The control subsystem can send a message to the student or trigger the remedial subsystem. At the same time the student model is updated. During the teaching session, the student is allowed to reason both forwards and backwards, and his reasoning process is presented in the corresponding window.

If the student cannot find the correct next step to the solution, the remedial subsystem tries to stimulate him in doing reasoning by analogy.

Analogy is one of the main reasoning methods in human cognition and is also a powerful computational mechanism. Analogical reasoning serves to solve new problems using past experience acquired in situations similar to the present one. Learning by analogy is composed by two basic phases: the first one consists in recognizing the analogy in the current problem, or the partial analogy, with the knowledge acquired so far. The second phase consists in the recursive process of adaptation of the old solution to the current problem. In many real cases it is possible to find the solution of complex problems only if it is possible to decompose the problem into several subproblems whose solution is already known [8].

These results have been confirmed in the preliminary phase of acquisition of knowledge during the interviews with teachers and by the observation of the student's resolution methodology. In fact teachers begin with the basic circuits, explaining the physical laws that rule the behaviour of the circuit in different situations. Then, they present more complex circuits and teach how to decompose them and how to single out the analogy with basic configurations already studied.

It is important to remark that teachers consider this point as the central goal of the course, because this methodology is general and independent of the domain to be taught. The last step performed by teachers consists in showing and explaining how and why the solution of the basic circuit has to be adopted to obtain the solution of the main problem.

Another useful information obtained from this phase of knowledge acquisition has been the collection and classification of errors (bug catalogue) and the analysis of the cognitive causes of the errors. The right interpretation of these causes is needed to correct the errors.

[1] KEE provides such a mechanism, called *KEEworlds*.

However, the main problems met by students in the resolution process are related to the difficulty in learning how to search for the analogy and the differences between the current exercise and the *configuration clichés*.

The remedial subsystem performs its goal by singling out the situation that brought the student to make the error and searching from the student model data about precedent behaviours of the student in analogous situations. According to this information, the remedial subsystem decides if to give a refresh about the theory, or to ask a simple question about an example that simplify the situation currently under focus. In this way it is possible to give suggestions to students to increase their ability in decomposing a problem into subproblems, and in the search for the analogy.

5. Conclusions

In this paper we have presented some implications of the use of artificial intelligence techniques in the field of Education. In particular, the distinguishing features of a new generation of computer-based educational systems, usually called intelligent tutoring systems, have been pointed out. Such features can be summarized in:

- architectural properties;
- automatic problem solving;
- diagnostic capabilities;
- multimedial interface, friendly, pleasant and flexible.

We have also presented two educational systems, SEDAF and SAMPLE, developed at the University of Rome "La Sapienza". We believe that such systems have interesting characteristics from the points of view previously mentioned.

They both have reached the stage of a research prototype, and they have been tested in experimental settings with school students, who seemed to enjoy the teaching/learning interaction.

We plan a reimplementation of the systems on a Macintosh IIx, to be able to use them more extensively, possibly using also hypermedia techniques.

Acknowledgements

We acknowledge Luidgia Aiello who inspired much of this work.

Literature

1. Aiello, L., and Levi, G.: The Uses of Metaknowledge in AI. Proc. of the 6th European Conference on Artificial Intelligence, North-Holland, pp. 705-720, 1984.
2. Aiello, L., and Micarelli, A.: Knowledge Engineering Environments and Intelligent Tutors. Invited paper in MIPRO-88: 11th Professional-Scientific Meeting, New Generation of Computers Symposia, Rijeka, Yugoslavia, 1988; and in ISCIS III, the Third International Symposium on Computer and Information Sciences, Izmir, Turkey, 1988.

3. Aiello, L., Cialdea, M., and Micarelli, A.: Metalevel Knowledge in Intelligent Educational Systems. Proc. of the First Congress of the Italian Association of Artificial Intelligence AI*IA-89, Trento, Italy, 1989.
4. Aiello, L., and Micarelli, A.: SEDAF: An Intelligent Educational System for Mathematics. Applied Artificial Intelligence - An International Journal, Vol. 4, pp. 15-37 (1990).
5. Anderson, J. R., Boyle, C. F., and Yost, G.: The Geometry Tutor. Proc. of the 1985 International Joint Conference on Artificial Intelligence, Los Angeles, CA, 1985.
6. Brown, J. S., Burton, R. R., and Bell, A. G.: SOPHIE: a sophisticated instructional environment for teaching electronic troubleshooting. BBN Report 2790. Bolt Beranek and Newman, Cambridge, MA, 1974.
7. Brownston, L., Farrel, R., Kant, E., and Martin, N.: Programming Expert Systems in OPS5: An Introduction to Rule-Based Programming. Reading, MA: Addison-Wesley 1985.
8. Carbonell, J. G.: Learning by analogy: formulating and generalizing plans from past experience. In: Machine Learning, An Artificial Intelligence Approach (Michalski, R. S., Carbonell, J. G., and Mitchell, T. M. eds.), Springer-Verlag, 1984, pp. 137-161.
9. Cerri, S. A, and Santangelo, D.: Intelligenza Artificiale e Didattica. Rivista di Informatica, Vol. 18, n. 1, pp. 41-58 (1988).
10. Charniak, E., Riesbeck, C. K., McDermott, D. V., and Meehan, J. R.: Artificial Intelligence Programming. Lawrence Erlbaum Associates, 1987.
11. Clancey, W. J.: GUIDON. Journal of Computer-Based Instruction, Vol. 10, n. 1, pp. 8-14 (1983).
12. Clancey, W. J.: Qualitative Student Models. Annual Review of Computer Science, pp. 381-450 (1986).
13. Filman, R. E.: Reasoning with Worlds and Truth Maintenance in a Knowledge-based Programming Environment. Communications of the ACM, Vol. 31, n. 4, pp. 382-401 (1988).
14. Johnson, L. W., and Soloway, E.: Proust: An Automatic Debugger for Pascal Programs. In: Artificial Intelligence and Instruction, Applications and Methods (Kearsley, G. ed.), Reading, MA: Addison-Wesley, 1987, pp. 49-67.
15. Micarelli, A., Mungo, F., Nucci, F. S., and Aiello, L.: An Intelligent Tutoring System for the Analysis of Electrical Circuits. Proc. of the PEG Conference on Knowledge Based Environments for Teaching and Learning, Rapallo, Italy, 1991.
16. Self, J.: Student models: What use are they? Proc. IFIP Working Conference "AI Tools in Education", Frascati, Italy, 1987.
17. Skinner, B. F.: Teaching machines. Science, Vol. 128, pp. 969-977 (1958).
18. Sleeman, D. H., and Brown, J. S. (eds.): Intelligent Tutoring Systems. New York: Academic Press, 1982.
19. Sleeman, D. H.: PIXIE: A shell for developing intelligent tutoring systems. In: Artificial Intelligence and Education: Learning Environments and Tutoring Systems (Lawler, R. H., and Yazdani, M. eds.), Ablex Publishing, 1987.
20. Wenger, E.: Artificial Intelligence and Tutoring Systems. Morgan Kaufmann, 1987.

Potential Contribution of New Hypermedia Technologies for Man-Machine Communication in Industrial Processes

C. Kolski , P. Millot

Laboratoire d'Automatique Industrielle et Humaine, URA CNRS 1118 - URIAH, Université de Valenciennes, France

1. Introduction

This paper presents the potential contribution of new hypermedia technologies involving man-machine communication in the field of industrial complex processes, for instance production units (electric or nuclear power plants, oil-refineries or iron and steel-works), means of transportation/ transportation networks (airlines, ships, railway...). All of these systems include a centralized control post, or control room in which the human operators perform their control and supervision tasks. These tasks involve a high level of knowledge. This paper presents first the concept of man-machine communication in these systems and secondly a global methodological approach of man-machine system design. The last part is an extended description of a user interface design methodology, outlining potential needs related to new hypermedia technology.

Communication tools are indeed in fast evolution. New programming techniques derived from artificial intelligence have helped designing and creating original communication products. New word processing techniques such as hypertext, or modern technologies offering simultaneous word, graphics and sound processing do indeed increase their efficiency. The evolution of knowledge in the field of interactivity does also involve their ergonomical characteristics. These communication techniques will thus definitely play an increasing part in the field of complex industrial processes.

2. The problem of man-machine communication in automated systems

Until now, automation has been used to make "self-operating" control systems. But the management of trouble-shooting is effected by operators, and this for two main reasons: (i) it is not always possible to modelize all the trouble-shootings, (ii) the solutions for correcting trouble-shootings are generally not analytical, but heuristic. These solutions are issued from a typically human skill acquired though learning or induction.

The human operator has therefore been kept to perform supervision tasks for which decisions can only be made by him. For instance, detection and anticipation of faults, diagnosis or correction of trouble-shooting. In other words, the human supervisor is entrusted with the system's security but only if it is deficient. Beside the fact that human resources, whether cognitive or physiological, are intrinsically limited, it must be pointed out that occasional intervention in the installation implies a non-ergonomical working situation. This situation tends also to reduce the human capacities. Indeed, during the normal functioning of the installation, the human operator is in a state of work underload with two consequences:

- in the short run, a diminishing of his attentiveness and therefore of his fault-detection aptitude,
- in the long run, a degradation of his internal control model of the process and therefore of his aptitude for troubleshooting.

In return, during abnormal or disturbed process operating, the operator is subjected to a work overload, due to a large amount of information to process and action to perform, in order to diagnose and repair the defect.

The research is thus evolving from the initial concept of automatization without the human, to a concept aiming at bringing him back into the automatized system. But the human is presently considered as a "necessary harm" of which it is required to limit the errors. According to this concept, research work has been done to integrate decision aid tools in the process control and supervision systems. Formalizing analytically so as to integrate them into these decision aid tools being difficult, "knowledge-based system" approaches seem attractive, and this particularly for their capacities to explain their reasoning process.

The current tendency consists in integrating in the decision aid tools, the possible taking into account of the process so as to allow early or anticipatory interventions in the case of defect. It is the aim of on-line aid systems which require the definition of methods for representing adequate dynamical knowledge. These methods are based for instance on qualitative models [4, 10], and also on dynamical knowledge and reasoning processing methods [25].

In a parallel direction, the concept of man-machine communication must orientate itself towards a man-system cooperation in which the increasing decisional capacities of the tools must allow to set up a real collaboration between man and machine [19]. In this way, artificial intelligence appears like a tool allowing to providing the man with a "decisional partner". Artificial intelligence appears also like a mean for modelizing normatively the operator's reasoning process during the design of the man-machine cooperation.

However, there are still not enough answers regarding the communication of decision aid systems and operators. There are indeed a number of compatibility problems between the human operator's mental steps and the decision aid tool's reasoning process. Our approach consists then in this workshop, in looking for new solutions in this field, and in considering to which extent the new hypermedia technologies can contribute to the man-machine communication in the industrial complex processes.

In a way to better defining the general problem, the following part presents first the global methodology of man-machine system design. The particular point of industrial imagery designing is then described, and illustrated with some questions facing the potential contribution of the new hypermedia technologies in this field.

3. Methodology of man-machine system design

The methodology includes two sequential steps (Fig. 1):

- A descending conceptual step consisting in the modelization of the man-machine system. It leads to an implementation on the site or to a simulation;
- An ascending step for evaluating the created system according to performance criteria about the process, but also according to specifically human criteria.

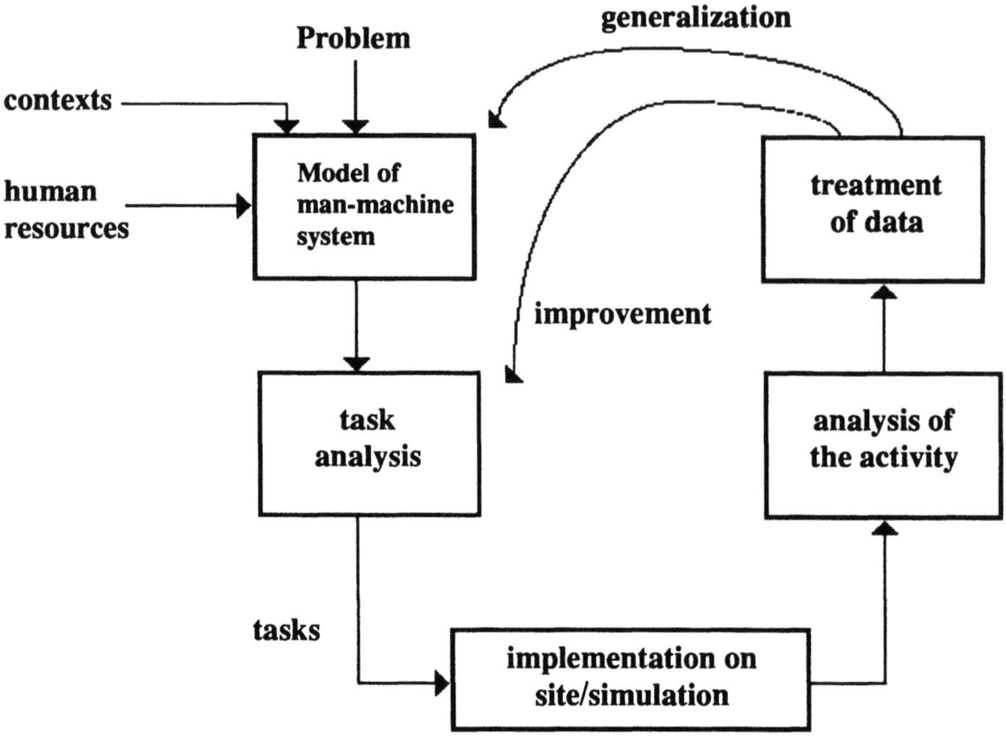

Fig. 1 Methodology of man-machine system design and evaluation

3.1 Descending conceptual step

The man-machine system's model includes a decisional model of the operator, and a model of the process and its control system.

It is necessary to extract the technical constraints from the process to the different contexts of foreseen functioning. If the definition of this model is far from being trivial, it can nevertheless rely on well-tried methods of classical automation.

The operator's decision model is more difficult to define. It necessitates a cooperation with other research disciplines, such as the cognitive sciences. The best thing would be to define a general model of the human reasoning process. This model should be able to explain the individual errors of the operators. In other words, it would include individual parameters of personality, and specific parameters concerning the environment, such as technical, sociological and psychological ones. If searchers do presently begin to identify these parameters, it is still too early to hope to quantify them.

On that account the objectives are less ambitious and tend to define normative models of behaviour for a certain class of operators in specific operational contexts. Given that the tasks of manual control are progressively replaced by decisional cognitive ones, the current research tends to develop cognitive models. For instance, KARL designed by Knaeuper and Rouse [15] is an AI model which includes two knowledge bases with production rules. The first one concerns surface knowledge, and contains the expertise of a class of operators. The second one is related to deeper knowledge, and describes the structure and the functioning of the installation which must be controlled. KARL has been connected to a simulated process. The orders issued of its reasoning process have been compared with those of the operators' whose knowledge has been extracted to build its base. The results have shown that the model allows to predict the average type of behaviour of the operators from the considered class. So, even if this type of approach doesn't help explaining the individual behaviours, it does help designing man-machine system.

Johannsen, Borys et al. [14] and Sundstrom [22] have indeed used this idea and proposed GRADIENT (which is part of an ESPRIT project and aims at designing supervision interfaces). This project is related to a model of man-machine system which includes a model of the process and of the user. The latter encompasses knowledge base of the operator and simulates his cognitive resources. These two models are used to infer the tasks that the so simulated operator must perform, in different contexts of functioning (Fig. 1). For this purpose, the methods of cognitive tasks analysis, which are currently elaborated by the researchers working in the field of cognitive sciences, are very promising [13].

A study of the tasks thus deduced must then help defining the operator's informational needs in order to perform them. This study must also define the type of assistance to provide to the operator. The analysis of the informational needs allows defining the information which will be displayed on the supervision screens. Then, it allows structuring the different displays according to the operational contexts of the process. In parallel, the cognitive tasks analysis bases itself on ergonomical knowledge related to human limits. This process helps defining the proper type of assistance (for decision and/or action) for the considered class of modeled operators. This study builds more or less the schedule of conditions of the decision aid system.

Furthermore, according to the capacities of the decision aid system, it is necessary to define the role of the operator in the supervision loop, the level of automation and the modes of cooperation between the operator and "the intelligent tool":

- One could be a "horizontal" cooperation between the operator and an expert tool whose outputs are directly connected to the process. The principle is to make a dynamical repartition of the tasks using a task repartitor. The latter can be controlled either by the operator or by an optimal command algorithm, this according to a performance criterion of the "man-expert tool-process" system, and under the constraints imposed by the human limits.
- A second one could be a "vertical" cooperation, in which the operator has the responsability of each variable of the process. He can then use the decision aid system if necessary. In extreme situations, the decision aid system can provide him with advice but, in this case, it is necessary to prevent (possible) conflicts when the operator refuses to use the advice. For this purpose, the explanatory capacities of the tool are essential [23]. In non-urgent situations, the decision aid tool can progressively guide the operator during his problem solving process, using for instance tools of intelligent simulation. This solution has a major asset: it helps maintaining and even improving the operator's operative knowledge.

New hypermedia technologies will be most useful in the "vertical" cooperation situation on account of the high level of interactivity between the human and the computer, but also on account of the complexity of the knowledge available. To our knowledge, there are still very few decision aid tools which use the potential offered by the new hypermedia technologies. However we can mention the works by Boy [3] concerning the CID systems (Computer Integrated Documentation). These systems are defined by the author as intelligent aid systems which cooperate with him in order to solve problem. Furthermore, in other fields than industrial processes, it is necessary to mention some promising research which is specific to systems necessitating a complex representation of knowledge, such as biological modeling [21], financial auditing [8], management of knowledge used in a law firm [27], etc.

Finally, when the cooperation modes are chosen, the elements are in place to define the interfaces of "man-expert tool-process" and/or the man-process interfaces. It is also possible to lead to a concrete implementation on site (Fig. 1).

3.2 Ascending step for evaluating the realized system

This second step is vital for assessing the system designed and realized during the previous step. The assessment criteria take into account the performances of the global man-machine system. These performances are expressed for instance in terms of variations between the real production and the objectives of the system. They can also be based on ergonomical criteria, such as the operator's workload, her/his tiredness, etc.

This data is assessed using activity analysis methods. These methods are applied to different operators belonging to the same class, and consist in analysing the man-machine system in predefined contexts (chosen at the previous stage). The inputs/outputs of each operator are also measured and memorized, and his workload, visual strategies (using occulometric methods [1]), displacements, etc., studied.

This analysis must take into account the solicitation level of the operator during his tasks and reflect the trouble he can have performing them, even if his performances are correct. For this purpose, subjective methods, such as questionnaires or approaches using a model, can be used [18, 19]. The set of measures is then analysed and if need be presented to the operators to obtain complementary explanations on their behaviour. The results of this analysis can be either directly used to improve the interfaces (for instance if some information is missing or ill presented) or processed through by data analysis methods aiming at improving or generalizing the initial conceptual model (Fig. 1).

The following paragraph presents a sub-problem included in the man-machine system design: imagery design. This presentation brings out several potential needs related to new hypermedia technologies. We do as a matter of fact think that they can contribute not only to optimizing the imagery design phase, but also to improving man-machine communication in industrial complex processes.

4. User interface design methodology

The operator's needs for performing correctly supervisory tasks depend on the different operation modes of the process. During normal operation it is necessary to present a subset of the variables which need to be monitored. These variables supplied by the supervisory computer must be significant of the safe operation mode and make the occurence of a defect obvious. On the other hand, during abnormal operation, the set of information which must be communicated to the operator is coming both from the supervision computer and from the decision aid system. This information concerns for example alarms, diagnosis, or preventive advice. According to the information available, the first aim of the proposed methodology is to specify the interface which needs to be developed in order to assist the operator in performing the different tasks corresponding to the current operation mode of the process.

The methodology of the interface design can be broken down into five sequential steps (Fig. 2). The first two steps correspond to the ergonomic conceptual stage, which consists in defining the lay out and the content of the set of views that will be developed. Then the following steps deal with the development of the interface and correspond to the ergonomic realization and correction stage. These steps are now described.

Basic questions concerning the potential contribution of hypermedia technology will be associated to each step.

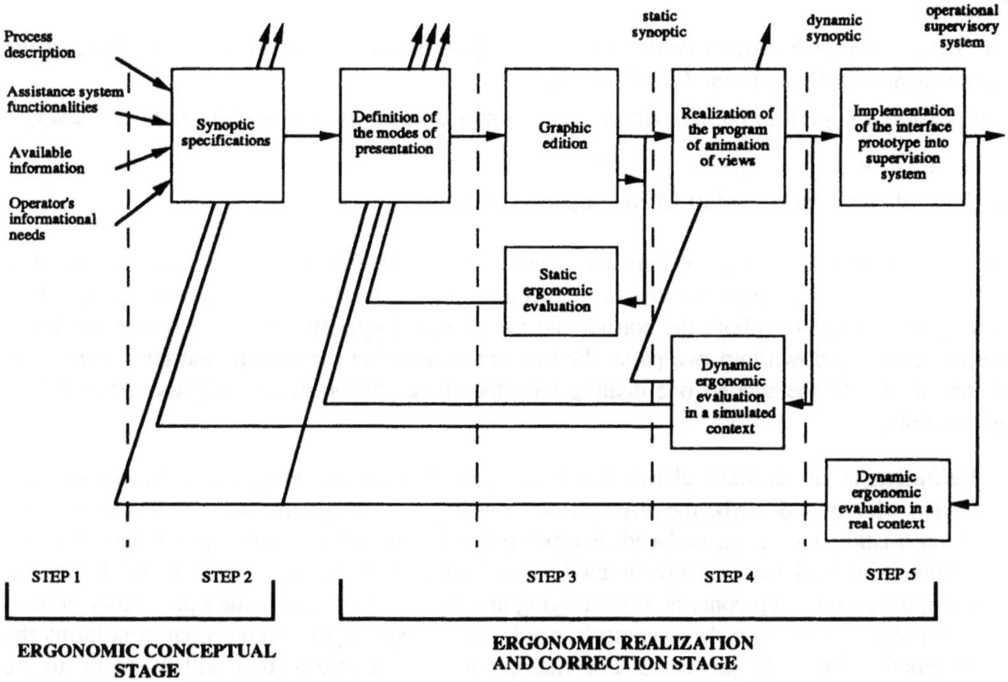

Fig. 2 The different steps of the methodology for designing the interface between an operator and a decision aid system

4.1 First step: preliminary works to become acquainted with the application process

The different tasks performed by the human operator and the constraints associated with their performance depend on the type of process being controlled. Thus, the designer must analyze the operation context in which the supervisory tasks take place, and this to define the operator's informational needs. So the first step of the methodology concerns the study of the process itself, and the analysis of the operator's supervisory tasks (Fig. 2).

The study of the process must allow the interface designer to understand the operation of the different sub-systems constituting it. The operation of some sub-systems is based on complex physical, chemical or thermal mechanisms. So, to allow operators to supervize these sub-systems, it is often necessary to adopt originaly adapted modes of representation. But the designer has to be familiar with the working of the process to develop them.

The second part of the work concerns task analysis. It aims first at recognizing the different variables observed by the operator in order to perform supervisory tasks. To carry out this analysis, it is necessary to study the operator's activities in the control room in order to identify his needs and the different problem solving strategies he can use [6]. This analysis must also emphasize the temporal constraints associated with performing supervisory task. So, the first step, which includes a study of the process and an analysis of the supervisory task constitutes a preliminary work meant to get the interface designer used in the different aspects of the process application, and lead him to defining the functionalities of the interface which needs to be developed.

Questions:

Can hypermedia technologies contribute to making easier the registering and classifying of the tasks which must be performed by the operator?

Is it possible to optimize the description of the process in terms of inter-connected variables?

4.2 Second step: specification of the supervision views

After defining the interface's functionalities, the next step deals with the specifications of the views (Fig. 2). These specifications must take into account the fact that the views which must be developed correspond to both the normal and the abnormal operation modes. We can break this specification step down into two parts; the first one concerning the content and the organization of the views, and the second one dealing with the choice of the modes of presentation of the information:

(i) **Definition of the content of the views:** this part involves the designers of the decision aid system who must describe the different functionalities of the system and establish the amount of information that can be deduced. For example a diagnosis functionality can deduce different hypotheses of faults among a predefined set, and for each of them calculate a credibility factor. Then, the second step consists in identifying among the set of information previously defined that which agrees with the operator's needs, and in specifying under what conditions the information has to be presented. For example a piece of information will be useful to the operator only if a particular fault has been detected. Finally, this second step leads to specifying the organization of the views which ensure the presentation of the set of useful information (identified above) to the operator. This phase is crucial because the specified organization sets the future cooperation between the decision aid system and the human operator. Solving possible conflicts, which can occur if the operator does not agree with the advices provided by the computer, depends on this cooperation. In this case, the system must lead the operator to checking the results corresponding to the different steps of his reasoning process, in order to find the origin of the conflict. A possible solution would be to in analyse in parallel the human and the system's problem solving processes, this would provide the operator with relevant information according to different justification levels, with a view to finding a consensus as quickly as possible [24]. After the organization of the different views has been completed, the designer must then define the different presentation modes which should be adopted for each piece of information displayed on these views.

Questions:

How can hypermedia techniques contribute to facilitate the description and the organization of the synopsis into a network of views?

How can the association of pertinent information with each of these views be made easier?

(ii) Definition of the presentation modes: The definition of the presentation modes of each piece of information must take several ergonomical specifications into account, for instance:

— the organization of the views according to a multi-window structure. This structure is similar for all types of views and each window is allocated to the same type of information so as to speed reading automation;
— ensuring consistency between the chosen presentation modes and the set of other existing supervision views in the control room;
— finally the adoption of symbolic presentation modes in order to facilitate a rapid and non-ambiguous interpretation of the information.

During this phase it seems important to let the operators expose their preferences concerning particular representation modes. Their experience can indeed influence (in a right way) the final result, and their participation can moreover foster their acceptance of the decision aid system in the control room.

Questions:

How to facilitate the association of graphical representation modes with each pertinent piece of information?

More precisely, is it possible to adapt the graphical representation mode of each variable according to the usage context of the latter?

4.3 Third step: graphic edition and static assessment of views

Once the characteristics of the views have been defined, the third step concerns the drawing of these views, generally by means of graphic editors. Editing views leads to a primary set of views, called synopsis. The ergonomic quality of this set must be assessed in order to improve the legibility of the information. So it is necessary to apply a set of ergonomic criteria with respect to the human information acquisition capacities. These criteria concern especially:

— the choice of the representation modes of the information according to its context of use, i.e. bar--graph versus curve, dials versus numeric counters, etc.;
— the choice of the shapes of the different symbols which can be used for displaying the process components in order to enhance the interpretation by the human operator;
— the appropriate size and colour for the information and the contrasts with its environment aiming at insuring a correct legibility and perception;
— the localization of the different items composing each view, and the arrangement of the windows on the screen;
— the maximum number of information the operator can process at a time.

The ergonomic criteria applied are generally expressed in terms of rules in design guidelines. However if a number of rules are general, ones some are specific to a particular industrial area. This is the case for the nuclear area in which specific design norms must be applied. Presently, research works tend to define methodologies or create tools with a view to fostering a better consideration of these criteria for designing the synopsis [9, 16-17, 20].

Questions:

Can the use and the functionalities of the graphical animated control view editors be improved by using hypermedia techniques?

Is it possible to interface a hypermedia data base describing the modes of presentation of each information with an ergonomical knowledge base so as to assess this data?

4.4 Fourth step: realization of a prototype of the interface

After the synopsis has been drawn, a prototype of the interface must be built in order to ensure the development of the program of animation of the views. The assessment of the program requires the process operation simulation. This assessment requires an important work, but it leads to an interface prototype close to the final one. Thus it reduces the work for integrating the interface in the real supervisory system on site which needs generally to stop the production process or which disrupts the production.

Questions:

If a hypermedia approach is possible to represent graphically each variable of the process, can these variables have a dynamical behaviour according to the process state?

Is "the static philosophy" of the hypermedia system not in opposition with such a behaviour?

Are the present material technologies able to ensure an "ergonomically satisfactory" response time for such a system?

4.5 Fifth step: implementation of the interface in the interface in the supervision system

The fifth step concerns the implementation of the interface on line and then its evaluation under real conditions. The importance of this assessment stage can be limited if the fourth step has lead to an achieved prototype. The evaluation aims at enhancing the content of the views (especially the lack of information), and at verifying its agreement with the operator's cognitive activities. For instance, it is important to allow the operator to evolve among the different abstraction levels of the process so as to solve a given problem [11]. Indeed at the higher abstraction level, the operator bases his reasoning process on general concepts related to the goals of the system. At intermediate levels, he considers the physical processes and functions related to each elementary component. Finally, at the lower level, he considers the structure of the installation as the links between the components.

As in the first step of the methodology, there are several complementary methods which can be used to carry out this assessment: cognitive task analysis methods [see 7, 26] or subjective methods (such as questionnaires) which consist in asking the operators various questions about the different characteristics of the interface, and aim at emphasizing eventual difficulties met while performing the tasks. These different methods can be completed by more quantitative ones concerning particularly the measurement of the operator's workload or performance, in order to point out some tasks which induce a high workload, and which therefore justify an improvement of the interface [19]. The choice of a particular method depends on the conditions of its application and particularly on the possible implementation of dedicated sensors in the control room, which can indeed disturb the production when the process is operational. This last step leads to a validated interface or to being sent back to the previous steps for improving the final system (Fig. 2).

Questions:
Can the operator easily and coherently evolve among the different abstraction levels of the process by using hypermedia techniques?
Is it possible to recover easily each pertinent piece of information and to use it with an adequate graphical representation?
To what extent can the manipulations of the operator be facilitated?
Is there a risk for the operator of losing himself in the network of graphical control views?

From the questions formulated until now, we will try to formalize progressively and more precisely some potential needs concerning imagery design and man-machine communication more generally.

5. First reflections about the possible contribution of hypermedias to imagery design in industrial process

This section concerns the possible contribution of hypermedia techniques aimed at designing industrial imagery. In order to meet the requirements of the imagery design, we present our first reflections based on the use of structured objects, and hypermedia and AI techniques. This is mainly related to the computerized checking off and description of tasks, the definition of the different displays, the definition of representation modes, and finally the graphical creation and animation of displays.

5.1 The computerized checking off and description of tasks

In complex processes, defining tasks which the operator must perform should be optimizing a great deal by making a computerized census and description of these tasks. Tasks and their chaining can thus be represented on an tree model, on which the nodes are the tasks themselves, described by structured objects, and branches the "successor" or "predecessor" type relations linking them to one another, as well as the conditions of progression from one task to another [12].

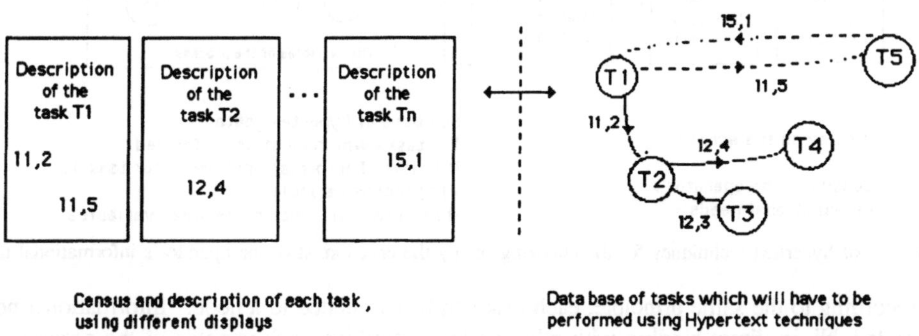

Fig. 3 Counting and describing tasks using a "hypertext" database

Can "hypertext" type techniques make easier the characteristic description of tasks and their chainings, according to the principle presented in Fig. 3, and this in order to help the ergonomist make these computerized census and description?

Thus, a window on the screen, helping the ergonomist to describe a task to be performed, can be in direct correspondence with the nodes and bows of an "hypertext" database. In this exemple, each task Ti (node), can be displayed and described in the window, in direct binding with other tasks, using links called $_{li}$j.

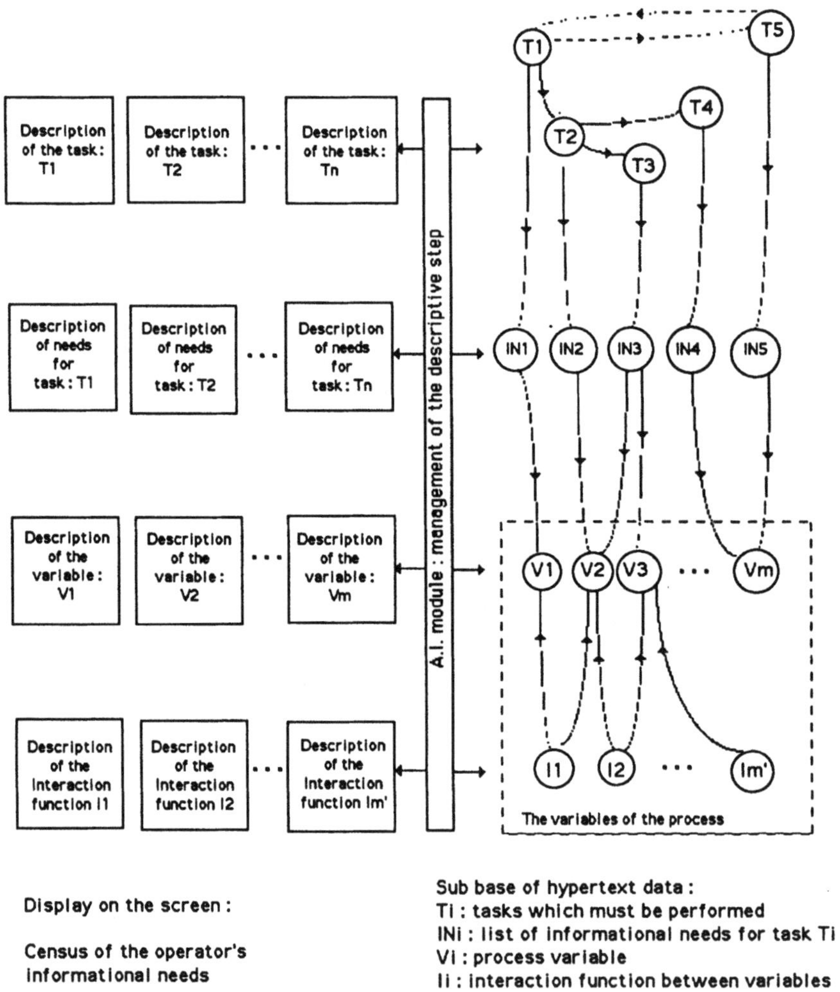

Fig. 4 Use of hypertext techniques for the checking off by the ergonomist of the operator's informational needs

According to the same principle, each task can be associated to a node: "Informational needs list", called $_I$Ni, in direct binding with other nodes, describing each variable of the process (Fig. 4). Furthermore, by associating an AI module, that integrates a base of description coherence rules to the "hypertext" database, it can be possible to improve this descriptive step, by extracting redundance, imprecision or inadequacy.

5.2 View definition

According to the same principle used for the checking off of the operator's needs, can hypermedia techniques facilitate the definition of each view content by taking into account the operator's informational needs already checked off ? For instance, in Fig. 5, "view 1" can be defined by the designer as containing two variables V2 and Vm; in the same way, "view 2" presents one variable V1. This description can be assisted by a AI module managing coherence between the different views.

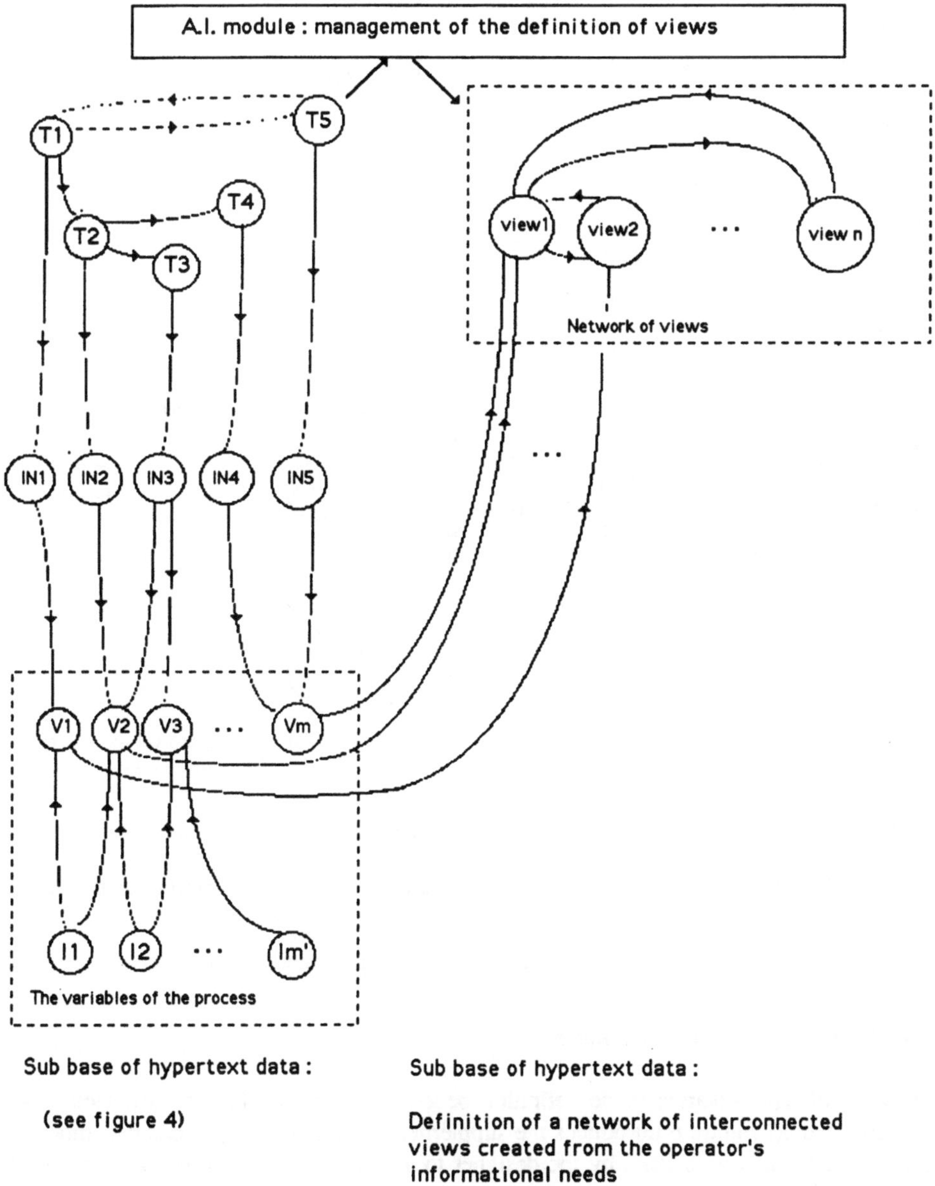

Fig. 5 Definition of views using "hypertext" techniques

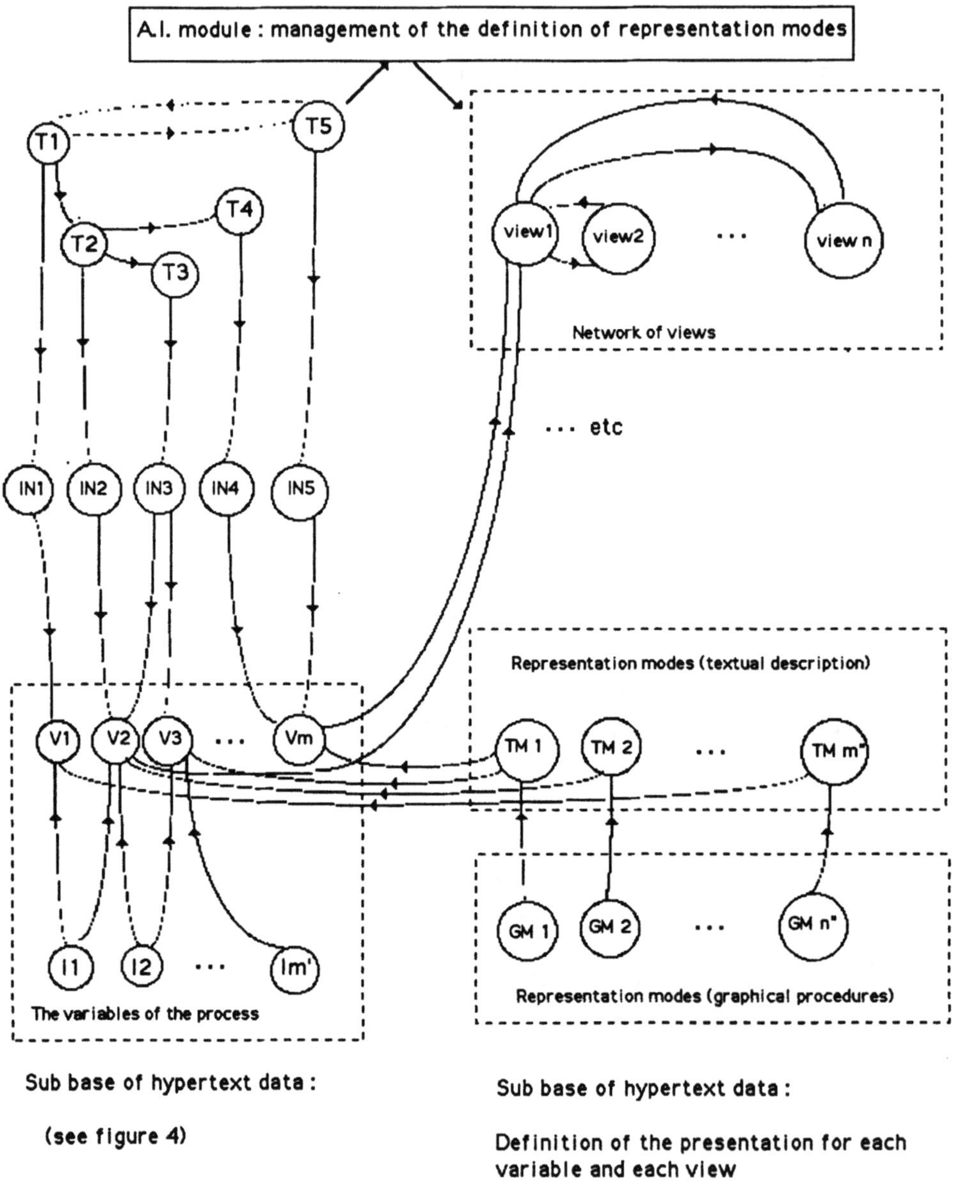

Fig. 6 Definition of the representation modes using "hypertext" techniques

5.3 Definition of representation modes

Can the work of representation mode definition benefit from the facilities of new techniques of information binding? Figure 6 introduces the supplementary notion of representation mode: each variable can be literally associated by the designer to a textual representation mode, called TM_i. For instance, the TM_1 mode correspond to a curve, while the TM_2 one corresponds to a bargraph. Managing this definition phasis can be made easier by the intervention of an AI module.

Two types of ergonomical rule can be taken into account [20]:

* **Type 1:** A first knowledge base created to help the operator while he chooses the representation modes.
  For example: IF *the operator has to visualize a variable tendency*
  THEN *propose a 'curve' type representation.*

* **Type 2:** A second knowledge base assists the operator while he chooses graphical attributes.
  For example: IF *the variable X is in a normal mode*
  THEN *use green color.*

5.4 Graphical creation and animation of displays

As regards to the graphical creation of the views, it would be interresting to associate each representation mode, called $_{T}Mi$ (see Fig. 6) to a graphical representation, called $_{G}Mi$, (they have of course to be constituted with parameters such as colour, height, location on the screen, ...). Furthermore, a AI module can operate the step of graphical display using a third type of ergonomical rules [20]:

* **Type 3:** A third knowledge base proposes - from conclusions of rules type 1 - predifined modes of representation included in data base - from conclusions of rules type 2 - and prints them on the screen.
  For example: IF *mode of representation of type 'curve' is chosen for variable* X
  THEN *print in a window (for eventual selection by the designer) the predefined curve with the parameter 'color' selected for variable X.*

The association of graphical modes of representation with textual ones helps speeding up the phase of prototyping on the one hand, and avoiding the problems of interfacing with a specific software of graphical creation on the other. Finally, each node Vi must be in direct relation with the process and be up dated according to its state. This relation must allow the graphical animation of the different views, and this in real time.

6. Conclusion

This paper has envisaged the contribution of the hypermedia technology in the man-machine communication domain in industrial complex processes. Thus, it appears that each industrial imagery designing step can benefit from the facilities of connected knowledge representation as well as from man-machine interactivity, given by these new techniques.

Given the large amount of ergonomical data and knowledge checked off and used during the different stages, and given the lack of formal ergonomical tools in this field, it seems urgent to study the extent to which new hypermedia techniques can contribute to the representation and exploitation of data and knowledge. At this point, there is one tool used for designing interactive application: ERGOLAB. It is a system which helps creating interactive applications, representing graphically a work station, performing dialogue chaining with the different interfaces, simulating actual work situations, experimenting and assessing with the future users, and the feeding of an illustrated manual for users [2, 5]. This sytem involves an on-line aid based on the "hypertext" GUIDE. The latter helps designing the cognitive activity of interfaces. According to their designers, exploring such new techniques will help giving a new dimension to on-line aid systems.

In brief, after having progressively formalized potential needs in the field of designing user interfaces, it appears that research in the designing domain can be made easier, and this by using these techniques. Conversely, this research could bring into focus some hypermedia limitations and thus play a great part in the improvement of their functionalities, particularly concerning "real-time" use and up dating.

Literature

1. Acier B.: Contribution à la conception et à l'évaluation d'interfaces Homme-Machines par l'analyse du comportement visuel d'un superviseur humain. Thèse de Doctorat, Université de Valenciennes, 1990.
2. Blanquet J., Gauroy P.: La conception d'interfaces: vers une aide intelligente. Actes du congrès de la SELF "Evolutions technologiques et ergonomie", Lyon, 4-6 October 1989.
3. Boy G.: Computer Integrated Documentation: a problem of knowledge acquisition and representation. ESA-ESTEC Workshop: A task oriented approach to human factors engineering. Noordwijk -The Netherland- November 21-23, 1989.
4. Caloud P.: Raisonnement qualitatif: Application à l'aide à la supervision des procédés continus. Thèse de Doctorat - INPG Grenoble, 1988.
5. Crochart K., Damay J., Leprovost J.F., Walfard D.: Méthodologie d'utilisation d'ERGOLAB pour une meilleure implication des futurs utilisateurs dans le développement d'une application informatique. Actes du congrès de la SELF "Evolutions technologiques et ergonomie", Lyon, 4-6 October 1989.
6. De Keyser V.: Temporal decision making in complex environments.International Workshop on New Technology distributed decision making and responsability, Bad-Homburg, May 1988.
7. De Keyser V., Decortis F., Housiaux A., Van Daele A.: Les communications homme-machine dans les systèmes complexes. Rapport politique scientifique FAST n°8, Université de Liège, 1987.
8. De Young L.: Hypertext challenges in the Auditing Domain. Hypertext'89 Proceedings, Pittsburgh, Pennsylvania, November 5-8, 1989.
9. Elzer P., Borchers H.W., Weizang C., Zinser K.: Knowledge-supported generation of control room pictures. IFAC Workshop Artificial Intelligence in real-time control, Clyne Castle, Swansea, UK, September 1988.
10. Feray-Beaumont S.: Modèle qualitatif de comportement pour un système d'aide à la supervision des procédés. Thèse de Doctorat - INPG Grenoble, 1989.
11. Goodstein L.P.: An integrated display set for process operators. Congrès IFAC: Analysis, Design and Evaluation of Man-Machine Systems, Baden-Baden, September 1982.
12. Hessler C.: Use of a task model for the detection of operator errors and for flexible task allocation in flight control. ESA-ESTEC Workshop: A task oriented approach to human factors engineering. Noordwijk, The Netherlan November 21-23, 1989.
13. Hollnagel E.: Performance Improvement trough cognitive task analysis. ESA-ESTEC Workshop: A task oriented approach to human factors engineering. Noordwijk, The Netherlan November 21-23, 1989.
14. Johannsen G., Borys B.B., Fejes L.: Ergonomic Knowledge support in graphical interface design for industrial process operators. Proc. 2nd Symposium on Human Interface, pp 579-584, Tokyo, Society of Instrument and Control Engineers, 1986.
15. Knaeuper A., Rouse W.B.: A rule-based model of human problem solving in dynamic environments. IEEE SMC 15: 6, November /December, 1985.
16. Kolski C.: Contribution à l'ergonomie de conception des Interfaces Graphiques Homme-Machine dans les Procédés Continus: Application au Système Expert SYNOP. Thèse de Doctorat, Université de Valenciennes, 1989.
17. Kolski C., Tendjaoui M., Millot P.: An intelligent Interface Approach, 2nd Int. Conf.. on "Human aspects of Advanced Manuf. and Hybrid Autom." Honolulu, Hawai, USA, August 12-16, 1990.

18. Millot P, Kamoun A.: An implicit method for dynamic allocation between man and computer in supervision posts of automated processes. 3rd IFAC Congress on "Analysis Design and Evaluation of Man Machine Systems". Oulu, Finland, June, 1988.
19. Millot P.: Supervision des procédés automatisés et ergonomie. Editions Hermes, Paris, 1988.
20. Moussa F., Kolski C., Millot P.: Etude de l'intégration d'un outil expert interactif ergonomique dans la démarche de conception d'interface graphique homme-machine. Colloqu, "L'Ordinateur, L'Homme et L'Organisation II", Nivelles, 9-11 Ma 1990.
21. Schnase J.L., Leggett J.J.: Computational Hypertext in Biological Modelling. Hypertext'89 Proceedings, Pittsburgh, Pennsylvania, November 5-8, 1989.
22. Sundstrom G.A.: Modeling information search for design purposes: An example from process control. Proc. 32nd annual meeting of the Human Factors Society (pp 1376-1380), 1988.
23. Taborin V.: Cooperation entre Opérateur et Système d'Aide à la Décision pour la Conduite de Procédés Continus: Application à l'Interface Opérateur Système Expert du Projet ALLIANCE. Thèse de Doctorat, Université de Valenciennes et du Hainaut Cambrésis, 1989.
24. Taborin V., Millot P.: Cooperation between man and decision aid system in supervisory loop of continuous processes, 8 th European Annual Conference on "Human Decision Making and Manual Control", June 1989, Lyngby, Denmark.
25. Tang X.: Contribution à la conception des systèmes à base de connaissances "Temps réel" pour l'aide au contrôle de procédés continus. Thèse de Doctorat, Université de Valenciennes, 1989.
26. Woods D.D., Wise J.A., Hanes L.F.: An Evaluation of Nuclear Power Plant Safety Parameter Display Systems. Proc. Human Factors, Soc. 25th Annual Meeting, 1981, 110-11.
27. Yoder E., Wettach T.C.: Using hypertext in a law firm. Hypertext'89 Proceedings, Pittsburgh, Pennsylvania, November 5-8, 1989.

Index of Authors

NATO ASI Series F

Including Special Programmes on Sensory Systems for Robotic Control (ROB) and on Advanced Educational Technology (AET)

Vol. 22: Software System Design Methods. The Challenge of Advanced Computing Technology. Edited by J. K. Skwirzynski. XIII, 747 pages. 1986.

Vol. 23: Designing Computer-Based Learning Materials. Edited by H. Weinstock and A. Bork. IX, 285 pages. 1986.

Vol. 24: Database Machines. Modern Trends and Applications. Edited by A. K. Sood and A. H. Qureshi. VIII, 570 pages. 1986.

Vol. 25: Pyramidal Systems for Computer Vision. Edited by V. Cantoni and S. Levialdi. VIII, 392 pages. 1986. *(ROB)*

Vol. 26: Modelling and Analysis in Arms Control. Edited by R. Avenhaus, R. K. Huber and J. D. Kettelle. VIII, 488 pages. 1986.

Vol. 27: Computer Aided Optimal Design: Structural and Mechanical Systems. Edited by C. A. Mota Soares. XIII, 1029 pages. 1987.

Vol. 28: Distributed Operating Systems. Theory und Practice. Edited by Y. Paker, J.-P. Banatre and M. Bozyiğit. X, 379 pages. 1987.

Vol. 29: Languages for Sensor-Based Control in Robotics. Edited by U. Rembold and K. Hörmann. IX, 625 pages. 1987. *(ROB)*

Vol. 30: Pattern Recognition Theory and Applications. Edited by P. A. Devijver and J. Kittler. XI, 543 pages. 1987.

Vol. 31: Decision Support Systems: Theory and Application. Edited bv C. W. Holsapple and A. B. Whinston. X, 500 pages. 1987.

Vol. 32: Information Systems: Failure Analysis. Edited by J. A. Wise and A. Debons. XV, 338 pages. 1987.

Vol. 33: Machine Intelligence and Knowledge Engineering for Robotic Applications. Edited by A. K. C. Wong and A. Pugh. XIV, 486 pages. 1987. *(ROB)*

Vol. 34: Modelling, Robustness and Sensitivity Reduction in Control Systems. Edited by R.F. Curtain. IX, 492 pages. 1987.

Vol. 35: Expert Judgment and Expert Systems. Edited by J. L. Mumpower, L. D. Phillips, O. Renn and V. R. R. Uppuluri. VIII, 361 pages. 1987.

Vol. 36: Logic of Programming and Calculi of Discrete Design. Edited by M. Broy. VII, 415 pages. 1987.

Vol. 37: Dynamics of Infinite Dimensional Systems. Edited by S.-N. Chow and J. K. Hale. IX. 514 pages. 1987.

Vol. 38: Flow Control of Congested Networks. Edited by A. R. Odoni, L. Bianco and G. Szegö. XII, 355 pages. 1987.

Vol. 39: Mathematics and Computer Science in Medical Imaging. Edited by M. A. Viergever and A. Todd-Pokropek. VIII, 546 pages. 1988.

Vol. 40: Theoretical Foundations of Computer Graphics and CAD. Edited by R. A. Earnshaw. XX, 1246 pages. 1988.

Vol. 41: Neural Computers. Edited by R. Eckmiller and Ch. v. d. Malsburg. XIII, 566 pages. 1988.

NATO ASI Series F

Including Special Programmes on Sensory Systems for Robotic Control (ROB) and on Advanced Educational Technology (AET)

Vol. 42: Real-Time Object Measurement and Classification. Edited by A. K. Jain. VIII, 407 pages. 1988. *(ROB)*

Vol. 43: Sensors and Sensory Systems for Advanced Robots. Edited by P. Dario. XI, 597 pages. 1988. *(ROB)*

Vol. 44: Signal Processing and Pattern Recognition in Nondestructive Evaluation of Materials. Edited by C. H. Chen. VIII, 344 pages. 1988. *(ROB)*

Vol. 45: Syntactic and Structural Pattern Recognition. Edited by G. Ferraté, T. Pavlidis, A. Sanfeliu and H. Bunke. XVI, 467 pages. 1988. *(ROB)*

Vol. 46: Recent Advances in Speech Understanding and Dialog Systems. Edited by H. Niemann, M. Lang and G. Sagerer. X, 521 pages. 1988.

Vol. 47: Advanced Computing Concepts and Techniques in Control Engineering. Edited by M. J. Denham and A. J. Laub. XI, 518 pages. 1988.

Vol. 48: Mathematical Models for Decision Support. Edited by G. Mitra. IX, 762 pages. 1988.

Vol. 49: Computer Integrated Manufacturing. Edited by I. B. Turksen. VIII, 568 pages. 1988.

Vol. 50: CAD Based Programming for Sensory Robots. Edited by B. Ravani. IX, 565 pages. 1988. *(ROB)*

Vol. 51: Algorithms and Model Formulations in Mathematical Programming. Edited by S. W. Wallace. IX, 190 pages. 1989.

Vol. 52: Sensor Devices and Systems for Robotics. Edited by A. Casals. IX, 362 pages. 1989. *(ROB)*

Vol. 53: Advanced Information Technologies for Industrial Material Flow Systems. Edited by S. Y. Nof and C. L. Moodie. IX, 710 pages. 1989.

Vol. 54: A Reappraisal of the Efficiency of Financial Markets. Edited by R. M. C. Guimarães, B. G. Kingsman and S. J. Taylor. X, 804 pages. 1989.

Vol. 55: Constructive Methods in Computing Science. Edited by M. Broy. VII, 478 pages. 1989.

Vol. 56: Multiple Criteria Decision Making and Risk Analysis Using Microcomputers. Edited by B. Karpak and S. Zionts. VII, 399 pages. 1989.

Vol. 57: Kinematics and Dynamic Issues in Sensor Based Control. Edited by G. E. Taylor. XI, 456 pages. 1990. *(ROB)*

Vol. 58: Highly Redundant Sensing in Robotic Systems. Edited by J. T. Tou and J. G. Balchen. X, 322 pages. 1990. *(ROB)*

Vol. 59: Superconducting Electronics. Edited by H. Weinstock and M. Nisenoff. X, 441 pages. 1989.

Vol. 60: 3D Imaging in Medicine. Algorithms, Systems, Applications. Edited by K. H. Höhne, H. Fuchs and S. M. Pizer. IX, 460 pages. 1990.

Vol. 61: Knowledge, Data and Computer-Assisted Decisions. Edited by M. Schader and W. Gaul. VIII, 421 pages. 1990.

Vol. 62: Supercomputing. Edited by J. S. Kowalik. X, 425 pages. 1990.

Vol. 63: Traditional and Non-Traditional Robotic Sensors. Edited by T. C. Henderson. VIII, 468 pages. 1990. *(ROB)*

NATO ASI Series F

Including Special Programmes on Sensory Systems for Robotic Control (ROB) and on Advanced Educational Technology (AET)

Vol. 64: Sensory Robotics for the Handling of Limp Materials. Edited by P. M. Taylor. IX, 343 pages. 1990. *(ROB)*

Vol. 65: Mapping and Spatial Modelling for Navigation. Edited by L. F. Pau. VIII, 357 pages. 1990. *(ROB)*

Vol. 66: Sensor-Based Robots: Algorithms and Architectures. Edited by C. S. G. Lee. X, 285 pages. 1991. *(ROB)*

Vol. 67: Designing Hypermedia for Learning. Edited by D. H. Jonassen and H. Mandl. XXV, 457 pages. 1990. *(AET)*

Vol. 68: Neurocomputing. Algorithms, Architectures and Applications. Edited by F. Fogelman Soulié and J. Hérault. XI, 455 pages. 1990.

Vol. 69: Real-Time Integration Methods for Mechanical System Simulation. Edited by E. J. Haug and R. C. Deyo. VIII, 352 pages. 1991.

Vol. 70: Numerical Linear Algebra, Digital Signal Processing and Parallel Algorithms. Edited by G. H. Golub and P. Van Dooren. XIII, 729 pages. 1991.

Vol. 71: Expert Systems and Robotics. Edited by T. Jordanides and B.Torby. XII, 744 pages. 1991.

Vol. 72: High-Capacity Local and Metropolitan Area Networks. Architecture and Performance Issues. Edited by G. Pujolle. X, 536 pages. 1991.

Vol. 73: Automation and Systems Issues in Air Traffic Control. Edited by J. A. Wise, V. D. Hopkin and M. L. Smith. XIX, 594 pages. 1991.

Vol. 74: Picture Archiving and Communication Systems (PACS) in Medicine. Edited by H. K. Huang, O. Ratib, A. R. Bakker and G. Witte. XI, 438 pages. 1991.

Vol. 75: Speech Recognition and Understanding. Recent Advances, Trends and Applications. Edited by P. Laface and Renato De Mori. XI, 559 pages. 1991.

Vol. 76: Multimedia Interface Design in Education. Edited by A. D. N. Edwards and S. Holland. XIV, 216 pages. 1992. *(AET)*

Vol. 77: Computer Algorithms for Solving Linear Algebraic Equations. The State of the Art. Edited by E. Spedicato. VIII, 352 pages. 1991.

Vol. 78: Integrating Advanced Technology into Technology Education. Edited by M. Hacker, A. Gordon and M. de Vries. VIII, 185 pages. 1991. *(AET)*

Vol. 79: Logic, Algebra, and Computation. Edited by F. L. Bauer. VII, 485 pages. 1991.

Vol. 80: Intelligent Tutoring Systems for Foreign Language Learning. Edited by M. L. Swartz and M. Yazdani. IX, 347 pages. 1992. *(AET)*

Vol. 81: Cognitive Tools for Learning. Edited by P. A. M. Kommers, D. H. Jonassen and J. T. Mayes. X, 278 pages. 1992. *(AET)*

Vol. 82: Combinatorial Optimization. New Frontiers in Theory and Practice. Edited by M. Akgül, H. W. Hamacher and S. Tüfekçi. XI, 334 pages. 1992.

Vol. 83: Active Perception and Robot Vision. Edited by A. K. Sood and H. Wechsler. IX, 756 pages. 1992.

NATO ASI Series F

Including Special Programmes on Sensory Systems for Robotic Control (ROB) and on Advanced Educational Technology (AET)

Vol. 84: Computer-Based Learning Environments and Problem Solving. Edited by E. De Corte, M. C. Linn, H. Mandl and L. Verschaffel. XVI, 488 pages. 1992. *(AET)*

Vol. 85: Adaptive Learning Environments. Foundations and Frontiers. Edited by M. Jones and P. H. Winne. VIII, 408 pages. 1992. *(AET)*

Vol. 86: Intelligent Learning Environments and Knowledge Acquisition in Physics. Edited by A. Tiberghien and H. Mandl. VIII, 285 pages. 1992. *(AET)*

Vol. 87: Cognitive Modelling and Interactive Environments. Edited by F. L. Engel, D. G. Bouwhuis, T. Bösser and G. d'Ydewalle. IX, 311 pages. 1992. *(AET)*

Vol. 88: Programming and Mathematical Method. Edited by M. Broy. VIII, 428 pages. 1992.

Vol. 89: Mathematical Problem Solving and New Information Technologies. Edited by J. P. Ponte, J. F. Matos, J. M. Matos and D. Fernandes. XV, 346 pages. 1992. *(AET)*

Vol. 90: Collaborative Learning Through Computer Conferencing. Edited by A. R. Kaye. X, 260 pages. 1992. *(AET)*

Vol. 91: New Directions for Intelligent Tutoring Systems. Edited by E. Costa. X, 296 pages. 1992. *(AET)*

Vol. 92: Hypermedia Courseware: Structures of Communication and Intelligent Help. Edited by A. Oliveira. X, 241 pages. 1992 *(AET)*

MIX
Papier aus verantwortungsvollen Quellen
Paper from responsible sources
FSC® C105338

FSC
www.fsc.org

If you have any concerns about our products,
you can contact us on
ProductSafety@springernature.com

In case Publisher is established outside the EU,
the EU authorized representative is:
Springer Nature Customer Service Center GmbH
Europaplatz 3, 69115 Heidelberg, Germany

Printed by Libri Plureos GmbH
in Hamburg, Germany